The Borders of America

The Borders of America

Migration, Control, and Resistance
Across Latin America and the Caribbean

SOLEDAD ÁLVAREZ VELASCO,
NICHOLAS DE GENOVA, GUSTAVO DIAS,
AND EDUARDO DOMENECH, EDITORS

Duke University Press Durham and London 2026

© 2026 DUKE UNIVERSITY PRESS. All rights reserved
Project Editor: Ihsan Taylor
Typeset in Garamond Premier Pro by Westchester Publishing Services

Library of Congress Cataloging-in-Publication Data
Names: Álvarez, Soledad (Álvarez Velasco) editor |
De Genova, Nicholas editor | Dias, Gustavo, [date] editor |
Domenech, Eduardo E. editor
Title: The borders of America : migration, control, and resistance
across Latin America and the Caribbean / Soledad Álvarez Velasco,
Nicholas De Genova, Gustavo Dias, Eduardo Domenech, editors.
Description: Durham : Duke University Press, 2026. |
Includes bibliographical references and index.
Identifiers: LCCN 2025022880 (print)
LCCN 2025022881 (ebook)
ISBN 9781478033066 paperback
ISBN 9781478029625 hardcover
ISBN 9781478061809 ebook
Subjects: LCSH: Border security—America | Refugees—
Government policy | America—Emigration and immigration—
History—21st century | America—Emigration and immigration—
Government policy | America—Boundaries
Classification: LCC JV6350 .B67 2026 (print) | LCC JV6350 (ebook) |
DDC 325.7—dc23/eng/20251113
LC record available at https://lccn.loc.gov/2025022880
LC ebook record available at https://lccn.loc.gov/2025022881

Cover art: Courtesy Adobe Stock / El Media and Anna.

THIS BOOK IS DEDICATED TO
OUR DEAR COLLEAGUE, FRIEND, AND SISTER
VALENTINA GLOCKNER FAGETTI

Valentina passed away suddenly in December 2023. She was not only a contributor to this volume but also an esteemed Mexican anthropologist who dedicated her life to accompanying the everyday struggles of Central American and Mexican migrant children and their families.

We honor and celebrate her intellectual work and her ethical and political commitments, and we are confident that her legacy will continue to inspire and guide new generations of critical migration researchers across the Americas.

Contents

Introduction

THE BORDERS OF (OUR) AMERICA

Soledad Álvarez Velasco, Nicholas De Genova,
Eduardo Domenech, and Gustavo Dias

In dedicating critical scrutiny to the borders of America, we are first confronted with the inherent ambiguity and equivocation surrounding the very notion of "America." As is well known, "America" was originally the name that European colonizers ascribed to the entirety of what they imagined to be "the New World"—what we have since come to understand to be the Western Hemisphere. Since the nineteenth century, however, there has been a profound tension in and across the Americas between the global power and ambitions of the United States as an imperial formation and the (post)colonial provincialization of Latin America and the Caribbean. The veritable usurpation of the very words *America* and *American* as the presumptively exclusive property of US nationalism is perhaps the most perfect manifestation of this historic bifurcation between the wealth, power, prestige, and imperial ambitions of the United States and the derisive relegation of the rest of the hemisphere to its proverbial "backyard." José Martí ([1891] 1979) famously depicted this sociopolitical divide as the difference between the "blond" colossus to the north (referring to the United States) and that other space that he called Nuestra América (Our America). Such a Pan-American, hemispheric perspective that repudiates the familiar and tired legacy of provincializing Latin America and the Caribbean has provided a long-standing counterpoint to the presumptuous imperial conceits of US "Americanism," yet remains agonistic and overdue. This volume—and our inquiry into migration, borders, control, and resistance across the Americas—is therefore posited from the critical standpoint of Nuestra América, Our America: the research showcased here has been produced almost entirely by scholars in and of Latin America.

To speak of *the borders of America*, then, for us requires a single analytical framework that encompasses the United States and Canada along with the Caribbean and the full extent of Latin America. This hemispheric framework entails a critical inquiry into migratory processes and, consequently, also the reaction formations of border enforcement that traverse and encompass the greater global region that is the Americas—North, Central, and South and the Caribbean. Rather than a merely cumulative composite of diverse depictions of migration, control, and resistance across this variegated and expansive world region, however, we insist on the recognition of heterogeneous migratory movements and transnational corridors of human mobility that crisscross the Americas in multiple directions and that increasingly incorporate human mobilities that span the globe. Adopting such a hemispheric perspective on the processes of migration and border control in the Americas is not meant to minimize or disregard the central and defining significance of the United States border with Mexico, which has long been a premier space of encounter and mobility between the so-called developed countries and the vast so-called periphery of underdeveloped countries, and which has therefore been a truly iconic site of migrant struggles and border policing for more than a century. The US-Mexico border remains a crucial flashpoint for interrogating struggles over human mobility on a global/postcolonial scale—perhaps now more than ever, as migrations from across the globe increasingly converge in the Americas and inexorably seek routes over land toward the United States. Indeed, with the diversification of migratory movements across the Americas over recent decades, it is more evident now than ever before that the ostensible line partitioning the United States and Latin America is not reducible to a mere international boundary between the richest nation-state in the history of humankind and its poorer neighbor to the south. Instead, in the third decade of the twenty-first century, the US-Mexico border must be apprehended as a space of convergence for countless multifarious confrontations and transits, an ever-multiplying array of postcolonial human mobilities and the infrastructures facilitating them that extend throughout the Americas and beyond. Simultaneously, as the US border, immigration, and asylum regime has become pronouncedly more restrictive and draconian over recent years, and as the US-Mexico border zone has become ever more violent and perilous, Canada has likewise increasingly emerged as a destination of choice. Migrant and refugee mobilities across the Americas at times have notably converted the United States into a global space of migratory "transit" from which to move onward into Canada, or have circumvented the United States altogether in favor of migration directly to Canada (Landolt and Goldring, this volume, ch. 1).

Amid the proliferation of new and unforeseen migratory routes and platforms across the Americas, there has thus been a concomitant diversification of migrant itineraries and destinations. As with many other areas of the world, Latin America and the Caribbean constitute a global region increasingly distinguished by numerous countries that are at once "sending," "receiving," and "transit" countries. Indeed, rather than a self-contained insular geographical region, within which migratory movements might be presumed to merely amplify and intensify *intra*regional dynamics of human mobility that thus appear to reinscribe Latin America and the Caribbean as a discrete world area, the Americas have become newly articulated through human mobilities with a diverse array of other areas of the globe. From Afghanistan to Zimbabwe, from Senegal and Nigeria to Ukraine, from Syria to China, from Sudan to Iraq, from Somalia to Pakistan, from the Congo to Bangladesh, intercontinental migrant and refugee movements increasingly arrive in destinations across Latin America and the Caribbean. Amid intermittent periods of temporary, sometimes indefinite waiting and ongoing or renewed mobility, migrants and refugees move through multiple countries and transgress numerous borders (Álvarez Velasco 2020; this volume, ch. 6). Consequently, while we focus our collective inquiry in this volume primarily on bordering and migration across the Americas, this hemispheric orientation exceeds the conventions and customary constraints of research in Latin American "area studies," because we foreground the constitutive interrelations of Latin America and the Caribbean with the United States and Canada and, furthermore, because we highlight the repercussions of global migratory movements that are profoundly reconfiguring the Americas as a whole. This volume therefore showcases the dynamics of migration, control, and resistance across Latin America and the Caribbean to illuminate the existence and ongoing consolidation and entrenchment on a hemispheric scale of a *heterogenous trans-American border regime*.

A Border Regime

Building on the insights of related work in critical migration and border studies, we deploy the concept of the *border regime* to signal an epistemological, conceptual, and methodological approach that conceives of borders not merely as physical demarcations between state territories and jurisdictions but rather as expansive uneven and heterogeneous spaces of constant encounter, exchange, dispute, tension, conflict, and contestation (Casas-Cortés et al. 2015; Mezzadra and Neilson 2013; Hess 2017; Hess and Kasparek 2017; Tazzioli 2014, 2015; Tsianos and Karakayali 2010). For some readers, the term *regime* may connote an integrated and comprehensive grid of unified sovereign power and may even imply an asphyxiatingly absolute or total form of domination, as in colloquial uses of the term to describe more or less dictatorial forms of state power. Here, however, we are deploying *regime* to signal precisely the opposite. Whereas other words, such as *assemblage*, might reasonably approximate what we aim to conceptualize, the enduring association of *regime* with state-sponsored violence supplies a critically important reminder and allows us to underscore that the variegated regime that we identify and describe in this volume nevertheless remains inextricable from the indisputable structural and infrastructural violence of borders and the commonplace and casual brutality of border enforcement. Adapting the concept from regime analysis in critical international relations scholarship, Vassilis Tsianos and Serhat Karakayali (2010) elaborate an understanding of *border regime* that emphasizes a multiplicity of actors engaged in a plurality of unstable sociopolitical relations, antagonisms, conflicts, and negotiations over norms, rules, and decision-making procedures, never reducible to any governmental or even intergovernmental process of sheer regulation. The analytical purchase of the concept of border or migration regime, therefore, is that it "rejects the primacy of control . . . in favor of the primacy of the practices of migration" and thereby "provides a framework wherein aspects of the autonomy of migration can be articulated" (375) and aims "to understand regulations of migration as effects, as condensations of social actions instead of taking regulations functionalistically for granted. . . . A multiplicity of political agents is supposed to deal with social processes, where the regulation capacities of nation states have failed" (376). As a mode of governmentality that exceeds any single sovereign power, this conception of the border regime highlights how, against all the brutal asymmetries of power that migrants and refugees confront, the subjective autonomy of migration nevertheless daily throws the government of human mobility and border control into question, instigating "the transformation of mobility into politics" (378).

An emphasis on the conflictual character of a border regime, unevenly constituted by rival contenders for sovereignty or prerogative, highlights how borders must be recognized as thoroughly political spaces. Rather than a unified, homogeneous, monolithic notion, here the concept of regime signals complexity and contradiction. From this perspective, as Sandro Mezzadra and Brett Neilson (2013) argue, we are challenged to analyze the border regime as a heterogeneous assemblage of institutions, logistics, practices, discourses, and procedures that is configured in correspondence with the incessant production and circulation of capital (19–20). It is likewise always articulated to the subordination of labor, and to the role of the state and the law in the mediation of the capital-labor relation (De Genova 2016). A border regime thus entails a constellation of efforts to domesticate and regulate human life and mobility by subjecting people on the move across state borders to various operations of power and, commonly, multiple formations of violence. Thus bordered and branded as "migrants," "asylum seekers," "refugees," and so forth, these mobile subjects may be alternately or simultaneously depicted as "victims" or "threats." As "victims," they may be subjected to the operations of humanitarian governance and rendered objects of "protection." As "threats," they are predictably subjected to more or less violent forms of policing, securitarian surveillance, and punishment. In both instances, they are subjected to the multifarious machinations of border "control." However, control here is never simply a matter of "exclusion"; instead, "filtering, selecting, and channeling migratory movements—rather than simply excluding migrants and asylum seekers—seems to be the aim of contemporary border and migration regimes" (Mezzadra and Neilson 2013, 165). Pervasively subordinated to the operations of the law and various forms of law enforcement—whether illegalized or governed within the constrictions and conditionalities of immigration or asylum law—the capacity for labor embodied in these mobile subjects comes to be disciplined and rendered as eminently exploitable and ultimately disposable, and finally susceptible to deportation, in a process of subordinate (illegalized) inclusion (De Genova 2002, 2005, 2010a).

Despite the customarily one-sided association of borders with control, human mobility—in all its discrepant manifestations as the subjective projects of "migrants" and "refugees," inevitably diverse in nationality, race, gender, age, and social class but all seeking to cross borders in order to remake their lives—is a co-constitutive element of any border regime. Affirming the autonomy-of-migration thesis (Moulier-Boutang [1998] 2006; see also De Genova 2010b, 2016, 2017; Mezzadra 2011; Hess 2017; Papadopolous and Tsianos 2013; Papadopoulos, Stephenson, and Tsianos 2008), we understand migration as the active autonomous social force at the very center of the complex, heterogeneous border enforcement projects that respond to and aim to control and govern such unruly mobilities. "We should see movement before capital—but not independent from it—and mobility before control—but not disconnected from it" (Martignoni and Papadopoulos 2014, 38). Thus, the border regime is both actual (already existing) and nevertheless always contingent: as yet incomplete, unresolved, and riddled with contradictions and conflicts, which themselves arise as the effect of the struggles of migrants and refugees to appropriate mobility and realize their diverse migratory projects.

Responding in sometimes discrepant and divergent ways to the subjective force and autonomy of transnational migration and refugee movements, a convulsive constellation of multifarious bordering practices emerges that both produce and enforce borders but also must repeatedly revise and reassemble them. These bordering practices and the borders that they produce (and reproduce) are the work of multiple state powers, but also a variety of non-state actors (such as migrant smuggling operations, international and local humanitarian organizations, drug cartels, religious charities, criminal syndicates, migrant solidarity movements, paramilitary militias, and insurgent guerilla movements), which likewise contend to varying extents for sovereign power and aspire to produce and intervene in the governance of these transnational spaces of human mobility. The ever uneven and unequal relations among these numerous contenders for sovereignty, which *together* constitute a heterogeneous border *regime*, may at times be fractious or even hostile and yet also entail significant degrees of complicity, harmonization, cooperation, and coordination. In all cases, nevertheless, they respond to the primacy of human mobility and migrants' and refugees' exercise of their elementary freedom of movement (De Genova 2010a).

The Trans-American Border Regime

Indisputably, the United States has played a preponderant role in the creation and consolidation of the border regime across the Americas. As we have already suggested, the consolidation of this hemispheric border regime must also be apprehended in relation to the complex geopolitical and geo-economic processes that articulate the countries of the Americas, and the United States above all, in relation to the rest of the world. In this regard, while we focus in this volume on migratory movements and border formations across the hemisphere, mainly during the two first decades of the twenty-first century, these are never separable from the multifarious ways US imperial power on a global scale has long sought to consolidate the full extent of the Western Hemisphere as its exclusive "sphere of influence," and thus to reinstate virtual borders around the Americas as a greater whole in relation to its global geopolitical and geo-economic rivals and competitors (see De Genova et al., this volume, ch. 12). Borders, after all, serve multiple purposes in the political partitioning of the geographies of the capitalist world economy, purposes not exclusively restricted to regulating the transnational mobility of people. Yet, in their mediation of the unequal exchange of value, not least the potential value to be realized from the human labor power embodied in migrants who traverse them, borders have become inseparable from state power's service to capital in the global-scale subordination of labor (De Genova 2016; Mezzadra and Neilson 2013). That is to say, borders have become inextricably involved in the work of modulating and governing human mobilities.

Alongside measures implemented to extend US borders inward through unprecedented forms of "interior" immigration policing, the United States has *externalized* its southern border through various deployments of its economic, political, and military power and influence. In a prolonged campaign to outsource border policing, the United States has increasingly come to rely on junior-partner states (so-called "third countries"), subcontracted to serve as de facto US border guards across the Americas. These junior partners violently intercept and interdict migratory mobilities long before they ever reach US territory, and not uncommonly develop and deploy detention and deportation powers to receive, immobilize, contain, decelerate, sometimes block, and even reverse the momentum of migrants' and refugees' autonomous movements. The heterogenous trans-American border regime that we examine in this book owes much to the concerted efforts of the United States to materially and practically transpose the US-Mexico border and its enforcement across an ever greater expanse of the American hemisphere.

Far from being a monolithic or homogeneous process, the United States' efforts at "remote control" have operated unevenly and heterogeneously across the hemisphere: the intensity and form of those efforts vary according to the geographic proximity of the "third countries" and their respective histories of shared migration and security cooperation with the United States (Winters and Mora Izaguirre 2019; see also De Genova et al., this volume, ch. 12). As demonstrated by several of our contributors (Velasco Ortiz; Basok and Rojas Wiesner; and Núñez Chaim, Varela Huerta, and Glockner Fagetti, this volume, chs. 2–4), the United States' externalized border control has thus been more intense and violent in Mexico than elsewhere. This "hard" version of the externalization of the US border has materialized in reinforced restrictive visa schemes targeting "unwanted" migrants, militarized borders, criminalizing policies, and coordinated programs and practices of detention and expulsion that have made the full extent of the Mexican territory an extremely dangerous extended border zone (Vogt 2017; Varela Huerta and McLean 2021). This "hard" version of border externalization has likewise been extended to Central American countries, particularly Honduras, El Salvador, and Guatemala (Miller 2019). For instance, during the first Trump administration, the United States introduced the cynical contrivance whereby the same Central American countries from which most asylum seekers arriving at the US-Mexico border had fled would be designated "safe third countries" for the purpose of deporting asylum seekers who had fled violence or persecution in neighboring Central American countries.[1] Hence, the plan was that Guatemalans and Salvadorans would be dumped in Honduras, while Hondurans and Salvadorans would similarly be dumped in Guatemala, and so forth. Thus, the United States imposed on its junior partners in the region to accept and detain the asylum seekers who could not otherwise be refouled to neighboring states, from which they often claimed to be fleeing for their lives; but they would thereafter be deported from the United States and indefinitely imprisoned in other countries disingenuously labeled as "safe" but repudiated as unsafe by many of their own ostensible citizens. The second Trump administration has gone further, deporting migrants to various "third countries," including Panama and Costa Rica (and, prospectively, Guatemala, Ecuador, and even Libya and Rwanda), and most infamously, deporting others to El Salvador to be imprisoned indefinitely as "criminals"—with no formal charges, incriminating evidence, or any semblance of due process of law—in that country's notorious maximum-security so-called Terrorism Confinement Center (De Genova 2025).

In countries located farther south of the United States, "soft" modes of migration control have been implemented. These are modes of externalized control that are less explicit, less policed, and more rooted in the production of knowledge and the management of data, working through formats such as mobility policy frameworks and technical innovations for harmonizing the government of migration and asylum (Hess 2010, 97–98). According to the hegemonic narratives regarding "safe, orderly, and regular" migration, examples of such soft forms of US remote control border governance include anti-(migrant) smuggling and antitrafficking campaigns; restrictive visa schemes targeting select "Global South" nationalities whose presence in the United States is massive yet purportedly "unwanted" or who are branded as a potential "national security risk"; and programs for training immigration and border agents in partner countries and providing technical assistance for their border control operations (Hess 2010; Mansur 2015). Examples include Costa Rica, Panama, and Colombia (Winters and Mora Izaguirre 2019; Gómez Johnson and González Gil 2022), and Ecuador (Álvarez Velasco 2024). These dynamics are also examined in this book in chapters that analyze the Colombian-Panama borderlands (Ordóñez and Echeverri Zuluaga, this volume, ch. 5) and migration policies in Ecuador (Álvarez Velasco, this volume, ch. 6).

The externalized trans-American border regime, extending across multiple state territories and jurisdictions, is an uneven and contradictory assemblage of disparate and sometimes competing sovereignties. These state powers' respective investments in their own projects of border making and border control coexist and sometimes collude with an eclectic array of nonstate competitors for what is seldom exclusively the state's monopoly on violence or, indeed, on the government of mobility—an array including not only "smugglers" (*coyotes, enganchadores, guías*), drug cartels and other organized crime syndicates, local gangs, paramilitaries, and insurgent guerrillas but also a diversity of humanitarian border actors. Thus, the heterogenous border regime that the contributors to this book depict through various empirically grounded and descriptively rich inquiries emerges not as a simple apparatus for smooth and efficient migration governance and control imposed and operated unilaterally by the United States but as a transnational formation of migration governmentality, replete with competing and contradictory imperatives, impulses, and interests, rife with discord and conflict, and permanently bedeviled by open-ended and unresolved border struggles. And, again, these discrepant and often convulsive gambits for border control never cease to be reaction formations responding to the primacy and incorrigibility of the autonomy of human mobility and migrant and refugee resistances that supply the inextricable and irrepressible ghost in the machine (De Genova 2009, 2010b).

Ungovernable Subjects on the Move

The current configuration of the trans-American border regime as a heterogeneous and contradictory composite of tactics and technologies of bordering would be truly inexplicable without training our critical focus on the unruly social force that is migration. Human mobilities have shaped the Americas from the outset, and intercontinental and transregional migrations have been in ample evidence since at least the colonial era. Whereas the United States alone hosts roughly one-fifth of the global migrant population (nearly 46 million people), Canada hosts another 8.3 million migrants, and the countries of Latin America and the Caribbean together host another 11 million migrants (IOM 2022). Those numerical differentials will come as no surprise to anyone and merely confirm what is well known: that the United States, long the wealthiest country in the world and the nation-state with a singularly outsized political, economic, cultural, and military influence in other countries across the globe, has likewise long been a premier destination for migrants. Historically, Latin American and Caribbean countries, long marginalized in the world economy by the (post)colonial heritage of perpetuated impoverishment and inordinate inequalities, have primarily been places from which migrants and refugees have departed, either deserting social conditions that have been deemed inadequate to support a decent life or fleeing from violence and oppression.

In spite of the securitization of migration and the externalization of the US border across the region, Latin American and Caribbean migrants and refugees have not ceased to move northward. This is why the region is crisscrossed with multiple land, sea, river, and air routes of migration, intensifying and dramatically expanding those pathways used during much of the twentieth century by multiple generations of migrants to reach the United States. In the face of the continuous illegalization of migration to the United States from other parts of the Western Hemisphere (De Genova 2004, 2005), these movements have inevitably been compelled to increasingly depend on smuggling networks (*coyoterismo*) (Achilli and Kyle 2023; Dias et al. 2020; Sánchez 2017). Although Mexicans have long been the predominant migrant group in the United States, far outnumbering newcomers from every other country in the world, they have been joined since the 1970s by ever larger and more visible migratory flows from Central and South America and the Caribbean (Budiman 2020).

Nevertheless, what is also increasingly evident is that Latin America and the Caribbean today constitute a region in which migrant and refugee mobilities have proliferated, with movement in all directions and lasting social repercussions across the hemisphere. Although it has become increasingly significant, so-called South–South migration within the region is in fact a well-worn and long-standing practice. Some notable historical cases include the migrations of Nicaraguans to Costa Rica; Haitians to the Dominican Republic; and various movements within South America, such as Bolivians migrating to Argentina, Brazil, or Chile; Peruvians migrating to Chile or Ecuador; Ecuadorians migrating to Chile, Argentina, or Colombia; and Brazilians migrating to Paraguay. Due to its decades-long and ongoing internal political conflicts, Colombia has the second-largest number globally of internally displaced persons (an estimated 3.5 million people) and is the country of origin of one of the highest numbers of refugees internationally, with substantial numbers residing in Ecuador, Canada, and Chile (UNHCR 2020), while also more recently becoming the single largest host country for millions of Venezuelan refugees and migrants. So-called transit migration—with the ultimate aim of arriving in the United States—has also increasingly made its mark across the hemisphere: since the early 1980s, migrants from across the Americas as well as from Asia and Africa have sought to appropriate mobility toward the United States through the migratory corridors of Latin America and the Caribbean, but have found themselves stalled or stranded en route for greater or lesser periods of time in various stopover countries, with increasing numbers settling long-term and forming increasingly visible, enduring communities (Álvarez Velasco 2020; Miranda 2021; Méndez Barquero 2021; Winters and Reiffen 2019; Boatcă and Santos 2023). Given the high proportion of refugees among these mobile subjects, states across the region have consequently also been challenged in new ways to institute processes for adjudicating asylum (Clavijo 2018; Gómez Martín 2022; Ortega Velázquez 2022; París Pombo 2022; see also Velasco Ortiz; Álvarez Velasco; Clavijo; and Moulin, all this volume, chs. 2, 6, 9, and 10). Meanwhile, some South American countries, including Ecuador, Chile, Argentina, and Brazil, have emerged on the global map of asylum seeking as new destinations (Álvarez Velasco 2020; Winters and Mora Izaguirre 2019; Espiro 2021).

This book focuses on the first two decades of the twenty-first century, the period when the trans-American border regime was consolidated even as its entrenchment assured that it has simultaneously grown ever more heterogeneous and convulsive. These contradictions and convulsions arise to a great extent because this regime's mandate has been to govern what are ultimately ungovernable mobilities, which have only continued to multiply and diversify. Irregularized mobilities across the numerous borders of Our America—originating in Latin American and Caribbean countries and heading not only north but also south, or not only from but also to the Caribbean—have proliferated without historic precedent. Among the by now best-known mass movements are the Salvadoran, Honduran, Guatemalan, and Nicaraguan migrations through Mexico to reach the United States, often assuming the remarkable form of self-organized migrant caravans (Gandini, Prieto, and Lozano Ascencio 2020; Álvarez Velasco and De Genova 2023; Varela Huerta and McLean 2021; Velasco Ortiz and Hernández López 2021; see also Velasco Ortiz; and Núñez Chaim, Varela Huerta, and Glockner Fagetti, this volume, chs. 2 and 4). From the Caribbean, well-established large-scale migrations, particularly from Cuba, Haiti, and the Dominican Republic, have shown themselves to be increasingly oriented not only toward the United States but also southward (Correa 2020; Miranda 2021; Trabalón 2019, 2020; see also Quinteros, Ramos, and Dufraix-Tapia; Clavijo; and Moulin, this volume, chs. 7, 9, and 10). Moreover, the massive exodus of several million Venezuelans in all directions has profoundly unsettled conventional assumptions regarding migratory dynamics across the hemisphere (Ordóñez and Echeverri Zuluaga; Quinteros, Ramos, and Dufraix-Tapia; Clavijo;

Moulin, this volume, chs. 5, 7, 9, and 10). While the majority of Venezuelan migrants have moved to neighboring Colombia, and some have been able to relocate to the United States or Canada, many others have settled in Ecuador, Peru, Chile, Argentina, Brazil, Mexico, or one of the Caribbean island countries. Having been a pole of attraction for intraregional migrations from the late 1970s until the 1990s, Venezuela's multifaceted political, economic, and social collapse has rendered it one the world's top countries of origin of migrants and refugees, and has indisputably emerged as the leading source of migration across the Western Hemisphere (Herrera and Cabezas 2019). These Venezuelan mobilities, moreover, have only continued to become more complex and diversified over time in terms of class, race, gender, and age (Gandini, Lozano Ascencio, and Prieto 2019). The contributors to this volume not only provide detailed empirical research on these contemporary intraregional and transcontinental mobilities across the borders of Our America, but also critically analyze and interpret them in light of a paradoxical geopolitical scenario whereby an ostensible "openness" characterizing many Latin American and Caribbean legal regimes of immigration has ambiguously and problematically coexisted with an overall "punitive turn" (Domenech 2017). This co-constitution of the conditions of possibility for human mobilities that are partly facilitated while also increasingly irregularized (or outright illegalized) is one of the premier distinguishing features of the heterogenous trans-American border regime.

Mobility/Control

During the first decade of the twenty-first century, Latin America experienced its so-called Pink Tide. Beginning with Venezuela (1998), Brazil (2003), Argentina (2003), Bolivia (2006), Ecuador (2006), and Uruguay (2008), among others, electoral victories brought to power ostensibly leftist or left-of-center governments promoting social democratic reforms and, to varying degrees, an explicit repudiation of neoliberalism. Among other reforms—in some cases, including altogether new constitutions—these governments often adopted relatively "progressive" legal frameworks around migration that appeared to constitutionally recognize "the right to migrate" and "the right to refuge" (Domenech 2017). Even before the rise of these left-populist and social democratic governments, however, following the demise of long-standing Latin American dictatorships and the return of democratic elections, states had already instituted various intraregional agreements facilitating cross-border mobility and residence (Domenech 2008; Romano 2009; Stang 2009).[2] In 1984, delegates from ten Latin American countries signed the nonbinding Cartagena Declaration on Refugees, which proposed a much more extensive legal definition of "refugee," paving the way toward more inclusive national legal frameworks. Thus, the region has long been associated with a semblance of comparative "openness" in the legal regulation of migration and refugee movements.

As the contributors to this volume demonstrate, one consequence of these early-twenty-first century reforms in South America was the relative facilitation of travel from African, Asian, and Caribbean countries, particularly Cuba, the Dominican Republic, and Haiti. In the aftermath of the 2010 earthquake in Haiti, mobility and settlement in South America were further facilitated with the granting of humanitarian visas in some countries, such as Ecuador and Brazil (Dias et al. 2020; Domenech and Dias 2020; Miranda 2021; Trabalón 2018). With relatively liberal visa programs, Ecuador and Brazil thus emerged as gateways to the Americas. Some migrants arrived in those countries with the intention of staying. For many others, however, these openings converted the countries into platforms for onward movement toward the United States through the established but rapidly expanding migratory corridor that begins in the Andean region and traverses Central America and Mexico (Álvarez Velasco 2019, 2020). Still others moved southward, attracted by impressions of Chile, Argentina, and Brazil as promising migratory destinations (Canales 2018; Espiro 2019; Tapia and Liberona 2018; Vammen 2019; Zubrzycki 2018; Espiro 2021), many of them crossing Peru or Bolivia to reach those countries (Berganza 2017; Ceja 2015; Pacecca, Liguori, and Carril 2016; Vásquez, Busse, and Izaguirre 2015). In almost all of these examples, these new, protracted mobility projects were confronted with the challenge of circumventing multiple borders and prevailing against the enforcement authorities of multiple states.

Faced with the rising numbers of ungovernable subjects on the move, particularly from Venezuela, Central America, and the Caribbean but also increasingly from Africa and Asia, governments across the region hardened various migratory policies during and since the first decade of the twenty-first century, complementing the apparent openness and liberalizing reforms of the Pink Tide with a concomitant reaction formation, including renewed visa requirements and travel restrictions according to selective criteria. In the following chapters, our contributors demonstrate clearly that regional border control mechanisms were repeatedly hardened, even in direct contradiction of the ostensibly "progressive" new constitutions and immigration laws. Examining evidence from Mexico, Panama, Colombia, Ecuador, Peru, Chile, Brazil, and Argentina, respectively, contributors to this book demonstrate how the region's liberalizing pretensions around migration have commonly not been realized in practice or, in other instances, when purportedly put into practice, have been interpreted and implemented by street-level bureaucrats and law enforcement agents in ways diametrically opposed to the putative spirit of the law. Thus, the purportedly "progressive" legal frameworks have tended to be dead letters for the actual migrants struggling to remake their lives within those jurisdictional domains.

The real effect of increasingly restrictive Latin American and Caribbean visa programs, moreover, has not been to halt intraregional and transcontinental mobilities but to divert and decelerate them, often containing and confining them to ever more violent routes, putting migrants at risk of predation, mutilation, and death. The iconic example of this phenomenon is the recent intensification of northward migratory crossings of the Darién Gap, the rugged jungle passage at Panama's southern border with Colombia: as a direct effect of the reimposition of visa restrictions, this deadly land crossing connecting South and Central America has turned into a space of global transit where migrants and refugees must navigate a treacherous terrain at the mercy of *coyotes*, gang members, guerrillas, and corrupt border police, all seeking to profit from the precarity of these human mobilities (Ordóñez and Echeverri Zuluaga, this volume, ch. 5; see also Amnesty International 2000). The Darién Gap has thus become yet another cruel and unforgiving extension of the violent migratory corridor of externalized border control through Mexico and across Central America.

The more punitive dimension of these enforcement policies has also manifested in summary rejections of select categories of travelers on arrival at land borders and in airports, as has been the case for Cuban or African migrants when landing in Ecuador (see Álvarez Velasco, this volume, ch. 6); for Haitians and Dominicans when arriving in Chile (Rojas Pedemonte et al. 2015; Tijoux and Córdova Rivera 2015); and for Haitians, Dominicans, and certain other "sensitive nationalities" when reaching Argentina (Domenech 2017; Trabalón 2018, 2020; see also Domenech, this volume, ch. 8), to note only some of the better-documented examples. As this research suggests, Caribbean, Venezuelan, and African migrants have frequently encountered social hostility and discriminatory treatment by state authorities, driven by racism and racial nativism. Selective rejections at borders and the selective reimposition of visa requirements, furthermore, serve as a reminder of how selectivity and racism have provided the historical foundation of immigration law and border enforcement policies since the colonial era (see Santos; and De Genova et al., this volume, chs. 11 and 12), and verify the enduring and systemic workings of state racism and racialized criminalization.

Alongside the multiplication of obstacles and modes for rejecting select categories of migrants outright, the immigration regimes of various states have also enacted programs of migrant "regularization," which are also always selective and inherently operate to revise the terms and conditions of the "legalization" of some in return for the renewed or refortified illegalization of others (Álvarez Velasco 2020; Berganza 2017; Domenech and Dias 2020; Dufraix-Tapia, Ramos Rodríguez, and Quinteros 2020; Trabalón 2018). Thus, these sorts of "regularization" procedures are intrinsically entangled with the multiplication of migrant "illegality," deportability, and exploitability (De Genova 2002, 2010a). Similarly, limitations on refugee recognition and the persistent erosion of the right to asylum (Gómez Martín and Malo 2019; Mountz 2020) have exacerbated the confinement of asylum seekers to conditions of legal limbo (Menjívar 2014), subjecting them to protracted waiting (Jacobsen, Karlsen, and Khosravi 2021) while they are effectively trapped in nation-state territories and indefinitely subject to eventual rejection and prospective illegalization. This was the case of Haitian migrants stuck between Ecuador and Colombia in 2016 (Constante 2016), of Venezuelan migrants trapped at Ecuador's borders with Peru and Colombia in 2019 (Rivadeneyra 2019), and of African and Haitian migrants contained in Tapachula, at the Mexico-Guatemala border (Miranda 2023). The cases of Mexico's northern and southern borders are iconic in this regard: those borderlands have turned into open-air detention camps for migrants where protracted waiting and uncertainty serve to convert the interruption and deceleration of their mobilities into spaces of degradation and peril for migrants' lives and well-being (De Genova 2022; Miranda 2023; París Pombo, Buenrostro Mercado, and Pérez Duperou 2017; see also Velasco Ortiz; Basok and Rojas Wiesner; and Núñez Chaim, Varela Huerta, and Glockner Fagetti, all this volume, chs. 2–4).

Deportations, though comparatively low in number, have also been selectively deployed (Domenech 2017; this volume, ch. 8), enhancing the precarity of all who remain susceptible to such punitive repercussions (De Genova 2002, 2010b). Examples include the deportations of Cubans from Ecuador (Correa 2020; see also Álvarez Velasco, this volume, ch. 6), Venezuelans from Colombia (*Infobae* 2022), and Haitians and Venezuelans from Chile (France 24 2021). Meanwhile, the number of border police across the hemisphere has doubled, and on numerous occasions, particularly since 2016, various states have deployed their military forces to bolster border and immigration enforcement in the name of upholding public order and enforcing the "orderly control of [migratory] flows" (IOM 2015). Thus, the Latin American and Caribbean region has turned into an increasingly hostile space for migrants and refugees. The state violence and racism of the border regime, enmeshed with social hostility and racial nativism and the unrelenting generalized deterioration of living conditions across the hemisphere, have converged.

Against the violence of the border regime, however, migrants and refugees persist in the pursuit of realizing their mobility projects. Reducible neither to passive subjects satisfying the demands of capital for "orderly" (regulated, tractable, docile) labor-power, nor to helpless "victims" trafficked by smugglers, migrants and refugees exude their own heterogeneous subjectivities and embody an autonomous social force on the move, defying the sociopolitical regimes that perpetuate the oppressive conditions from which they flee as well as those that seek to obstruct their freedom of movement with barricaded borders and detention and deportation dragnets. Perhaps the best evidence is the caravans that have emerged as collective formations of self-organization, self-protection, and mutual aid, and that have become increasingly politicized (see Núñez Chaim, Varela Huerta, and Glockner Fagetti, this volume, ch. 4). Moreover, migrants' mobile ethics of care and their politics of solidarity are enacted, however tenuously, by strategically pooling resources (sometimes sharing food, housing, living costs, and migratory knowledge); caring for one another through illness, injury, and debility; caring for one another's children; and protecting one another during police raids, border crossings, encounters with corrupt officials, or predatory smugglers or when confronted with racism and anti-immigrant hostility. Such practices of solidarity en route marks a radical contrast with the organized hostility, violent control, and callous negligence of state powers toward migrants and refugees in transit. These forms of everyday solidarity and care among migrants (sometimes also enacted by local residents in support of migrants) serve to affirm a diminutive politics of life that rejects and refuses the larger necropolitics of the border regime (Varela Huerta 2017).

Either actively deserting or violently expelled from various unviable social, political, and economic conditions, the unruly subjectivities of migrant and refugee mobilities have further consolidated the migratory corridors that traverse the Americas, such as those connecting Mexico and the United States (París Pombo and Montes 2020); Central America and Mexico (Alba Villalever and Schütze 2021; Varela Huerta and McLean 2021); the Caribbean, South America, and Central America (Miranda 2021); the Caribbean and the Southern Cone (Trabalón 2021); and the Andean region and destinations northward, southward, and into the Caribbean (Álvarez Velasco 2020, 2022; Álvarez Velasco, Pedone, and Miranda 2021). Within these corridors, irregularized mobilities are subjected to diverse forms of control exerted not only by state agents but also by paramilitaries, guerrillas, gang members, smugglers, and others who operate within dense entanglements of legal and illegal economic and social practices to either facilitate or obstruct migratory projects (Van Schendel and Abraham 2005). Such practices are embedded in border economies, which manifest an important facet of the larger complex of informalized Latin American and Caribbean economies that employ more than half of the region's population (ECLAC 2022). In fact, those informalized economies are not "marginal" but rather must be recognized as a central and constitutive element of "actually existing" neoliberalism (Gago 2017). While the mobilities of migrants and refugees abide by their own autonomous subjective logics, they nonetheless remain thoroughly ensnared by the violence of border enforcement and the power of immigration law, as well as embedded in the contradictory textures of social life. The trans-American border regime, therefore, entails not only a top-down logic of the control presumed to be the exclusive domain of states exercising their sovereign power, but also the multifarious logics of both people on the move aspiring to cross borders and the heterogeneous spectrum of others who seek to sustain their own endeavors and enterprises through the informalized economic and political logics of engaging with the autonomy and subjectivity of migration.

The Trans-American Border Regime in the Postpandemic Era

The beginning of the third decade of the twenty-first century is indelibly distinguished by the unforeseen advent of a world historical landmark: the COVID-19 pandemic. With the declaration of a global public health emergency in March 2020, unprecedented control measures were taken across the world to immobilize populations and close borders in the name of containing the spread of the virus. These exceptional measures severely exacerbated an anti-immigrant climate that was already directly impacting the lives of irregularized migrants and refugees (De Genova 2022).

The Americas were no exception. The findings of the transnational, trilingual, digital collaborative research project COVID-19 and (Im)Mobilities Across the Americas provide evidence of six intertwined dynamics that took shape during the peak of the pandemic:[3] (1) border closures in all Latin American and Caribbean countries, the militarization of borders, and increased internal policing; (2) the suspension or limitation of the right to refuge; (3) limitations on regularization processes; (4) the immobilization and confinement of migrants to border zones and indefinite waiting in migrant camps and zones of abandonment; (5) forced mobilities via deportation, including, as some of the most prominent examples, deportations from the United States to Mexico, Central America, and the Caribbean; deportations of Haitians and Venezuelans from Chile; deportations of Venezuelans from Colombia and Brazil; deportations of Bolivians and Paraguayans from Brazil; and (6) the adoption or expansion of anti-immigrant legal architectures in the United States, Chile, Ecuador, Brazil, and Peru. All these measures confirm that during the first two years of the pandemic (2020–22), a de facto state of exception in migration matters was enacted, intensifying an anti-immigrant and racist turn directed against asylum seekers and irregularized migrants across the region (Inmovilidad Americas 2024). Several of our contributors analyze how border policies were transformed during the COVID-19 pandemic in ways that directly impacted migrants' lives in various border zones (see Velasco Ortiz; Núñez Chaim, Varela Huerta, and Glocker Fagetti; Ordóñez and Echeverri Zuluaga; Quinteros, Ramos, and Dufraix-Tapia; and Moulin, this volume, chs. 2, 4, 5, 7, and 10).

As the risks posed by COVID-19 decreased considerably across the globe, many of those border control measures nonetheless remained in effect. Undoubtedly, the most iconic was Title 42, an obscure 1944 statute imposed by the United States under the first Trump administration to prohibit entry of asylum seekers on public health grounds, which remained in force until May 2023, directly affecting the border-crossing prospects of hundreds of thousands of migrants and refugees at the Mexico-US border (Torres et al. 2022).[4] The enduring postpandemic crisis has pressed migrants and refugees to redouble their efforts to pursue irregularized means to transit to the United States or onward from there to Canada or, in other instances, has served to divert these mobilities toward the Southern Cone countries of South America. By the end of October 2021, for instance, a total of 1.7 million migrants coming from more than 160 countries were detained at the US-Mexico border (Sullivan and Jordan 2021); that figure reached 2.4 million by October 2022 (Melhado 2022). Though much lower in numbers, analogous dynamics were simultaneously at play to the south. In Chile, quickly emerging as the preferred South American destination for migrants, approximately 17,000 migrants were documented to have crossed its northern border in 2020, but that figure had tripled to 56,000 by the end of 2021 (Plataforma R4V 2022). Although most of those migrants were Venezuelans, others came from Haiti, the Dominican Republic, Cuba, Colombia, Bolivia, and Peru (INE 2022).

Predictably, we have witnessed numerous state powers across the trans-American border regime refortify their efforts at control. Under the reflexive justification of containing "illegal" migration and combating smuggling networks, Latin American and Caribbean nation-states have resorted to newly restrictive immigration policies and enhanced border controls. For example, in the immediate aftermath of the pandemic, Mexico and Guatemala reimposed travel visa requirements to deter Venezuelan, Ecuadorian, and Brazilian migrations heading to the United States (CNN 2022), and Costa Rica did the same to slow down the arrival of Venezuelans (Murillo 2022), while Mexico, Chile, and Panama accelerated deportations (MMC 2022). These restrictions on air travel have predictably provoked a rise in migration over land, instigating several "crises" at multiple borders, including at both Mexico's southern and its northern borders; the land borders between Peru and Chile, Ecuador and Colombia, and Honduras and Guatemala; and in the complex and hyperperilous Darién Gap between Panama and Colombia (MMC 2022). Migrants and refugees have consequently found themselves increasingly "stuck" in "transit," indefinitely stranded in these border zones in makeshift self-organized camps, as state repression has intensified, alongside heavily fortified border crossings that inevitably drive migrants into more perilous crossings and force them to navigate more remote or treacherous geographies, escalating the risk of death. Between 2014 and 2022, thousands of migrants disappeared or died across the Americas, with roughly half of the documented deaths recorded for the period 2020–22 alone (IOM 2022; see also De Genova 2021; De León 2015). While these tactics of border control generally do not reverse or halt migratory mobilities, they do nonetheless obstruct and decelerate them, multiplying the impediments and risks that migrants and refugees must circumvent in their efforts to prevail against borders converted into prolonged and lethal obstacle courses (De Genova 2013).

The chapters of this book contribute to understanding the history of our present. By providing empirical evidence and analysis from several critical sites of border struggles across the Americas, the authors of the following chapters demonstrate that the reinforcement of borders across the region during the initial COVID-19 shutdown and during the pandemic's protracted aftermath can be adequately comprehended only in light of the more extended consolidation of the heterogenous trans-American border regime that has arisen as a reaction formation in the face of the multiplication of diverse migrant mobilities.

Contributions to this Book

The contributions to this volume scrutinize an array of critical nodes in the larger heterogenous and uneven configuration that we have here designated to be the trans-American border regime. The chapters arise from historical and ethnographic work located in diverse nation-state bordering contexts and local realities. They also have been produced by a diverse group of researchers working in numerous disciplines and interdisciplinary fields of inquiry. While the diverse scholarly orientations of the authors inevitably shape their respective approaches and emphases, all nonetheless adopt a migrant-centered approach, starting from the perspective of the movements and trajectories of migration to advance the larger analysis of multidimensional and multiscalar border zone spaces of conflict and negotiation constituted by the ever-shifting constellation of opposed forces that is the border regime. Thus, even the chapters that focus on the legal and political regimes governing migration and borders in a single nation-state provide evidence of how an ethnographic approach to border regime analysis can unsettle and repudiate the sort of methodological nationalism that for decades has hampered the study of migration. Across these chapters' respective contributions, then, we begin to discern a composite of the borders of Our America.

The intellectual work and research of the contributors to this volume are politically positioned as diverse expressions of a collective project of activist scholarship dedicated to approaching migration from the standpoint of a radical critique of the enduring legacies of colonialism, racism, patriarchy, capitalism, and the global regime of border control. Their multidisciplinary perspectives contribute to an interdisciplinary dialogue showcasing how Latin America and the Caribbean have become a pivotal spatial conjuncture within a violent global system for governing migrant and refugee mobilities that largely originate in formerly colonized, impoverished, and conflict-ridden countries, and the ways in which the autonomy and subjectivity of migration supply the motive force behind an unceasing proliferation of postcolonial border struggles.

This book proceeds from the understanding that migrants are historical subjects whose mobility is "a political act in itself" (Mitropoulos 2007; see also De Genova 2010b; Hess 2017; Mezzadra 2011; New Keywords Collective 2016; Papadopoulos, Stephenson, and Tsianos 2008) that consequently has spatial (and potentially world-making) effects. It is this autonomous mobility that regimes of border control pursue and seek to domesticate under the neoliberal regime of "migration management." As a contribution to the wider literature on the autonomy of migration, this volume thus intervenes in a transnational dialogue with critical migration and border studies. Much of the critical literature, however, has focused on the analysis of migration and borders in the so-called Global North—investigating primarily the European, Australian, and North American contexts. *The Borders of America* instead foregrounds migratory dynamics and the tactics of bordering in Latin America and the Caribbean.

This book arises in a moment of renewed intellectual ferment in this field of study. From deeply historicized and postcolonial perspectives, Latin American and Caribbean migration scholarship has been striving to understand the new configurations of migration across the region, the collapse of former legal systems governing migration and refugee movements, and the multiple spatial, economic, and political transformations triggered by the incessant human mobilities that shape the hemisphere. The various chapters address specific nation-state legal and political contexts while underscoring their relations with regional and global processes.

This volume has been conceived to showcase research produced almost entirely by scholars originating from the region, nearly all of whom continue to be professionally based in academic institutions in the region. Their work is presented here in English translation with the deliberate intention of generating and expanding this transnational and transdisciplinary dialogue. The book therefore also seeks to initiate a wider dialogue with the emerging critical literature in Latin America and the Caribbean, published largely in languages other than English, that has historicized and problematized the developments of immigration policies and practices of border control, as well as foregrounding migrant struggles and resistances, over the past two decades in the region (Cordero, Mezzadra, and Varela Huerta 2019; Domenech, Herrera, and Rivera Sánchez 2022; Feldmann et al. 2022; Feldmann, Bada, and Schütze 2019; Herrera and Gómez Martín 2022). As the contributions to this book show, an ample body of scholarship is arising from the region and being published in Spanish, Portuguese, and other languages, devoted to critically analyzing transformations in national and regional migration policies. Indeed, some of the most significant research and analysis in this body of scholarship has often been generated by many of our contributors to this volume. In 2020, notably, the Brazilian sociological journal *Sociologias* published a special issue, "*Sociologia e fronteiras: A produção da ilegalidade migrante na América Latina e no Caribe*" (Sociology and borders: The production of migrant illegality in Latin America and the Caribbean), coedited by Gustavo Dias and Eduardo Domenech (2020), which sought to reflect critically on the production of migratory "illegality" at various Latin American and Caribbean borders. This volume builds on those insights for an English-speaking readership and includes chapters by some of the researchers who contributed to that project.

Given the brutal effects of "cannibal capitalism," to use Nancy Fraser's (2022) memorable phrase, the recent intensification of irregularized migrant movements by land and maritime routes is likely only to increase. In response, an exacerbation of anti-immigrant policies and overt border violence involving a consequently inevitable rise of disappearances and deaths will proliferate in tandem. This is a grim scenario, indeed, but one in which migrant struggles must be recognized alongside the escalation of countless other audacious social movements across the Americas and the globe as manifestations and modalities of resistance that repudiate the merciless patterns of colonial and postcolonial dispossession and capital accumulation that have prevailed for the past five hundred years across the hemisphere. In the face of the urgent certainty that ever

CANADA

UNITED STATES

ATLANTIC OCEAN

MEXICO

CUBA

BELIZE

JAMAICA

DOMINICAN REPUBLIC

HONDURAS

HAITI

NICARAGUA

GUATEMALA

EL SALVADOR

PANAMA

COSTA RICA

VENEZUELA

GUYANA

SURINAME

FRENCH GUYANA

COLOMBIA

ECUADOR

PACIFIC OCEAN

PERU

BRAZIL

BOLIVIA

PARAGUAY

CHILE

URUGUAY

ARGENTINA

0   600   1,200 mi
0 1,000   2,000 km

more migrants and refugees will brave the violent and often deadly migratory corridors of the Americas, critical research and activist scholarship are more vital than ever.

Millions of migrants and refugees—adults, youth, children, and families—unceasingly mobilize themselves to defy borders in the effort to remake their lives. They thereby also remake Our America. In so doing, these human mobilities compel us to comprehend that the irrepressible character of migration, and thus its intrinsic tendencies toward ungovernability, implicitly asserts a radical challenge to statist systems of sovereignty and rule. Over the past century and a half, state powers have ever increasingly reacted to the primacy of human mobilities by resorting to exclusionary tactics of border violence, accompanied by subtle but durable forms of subordinate inclusion through the illegalization or highly conditional accommodation of impoverished labor migrants or refugees. By exercising their elementary freedom of movement, migrants and refugees nonetheless constantly struggle to appropriate mobility and space in order to remake life and enact alternative possible futures. Today, more than ever, theirs is a struggle that is reshaping Our America.

NOTES

1. Asylum cooperative agreements (ACAs), also known as "safe third country" agreements, were initiated unilaterally by executive fiat by the first Trump administration in July 2018, beginning with Guatemala. After Trump threatened to ban Guatemalans with valid US visas and to tax migrant remittances, Guatemala complied. In the following weeks, El Salvador and Honduras signed similar agreements.

2. Among the most noteworthy regional integration agreements adopted since 1990 to facilitate intraregional mobility are the Andean Community of Nations (CAN), the Southern Common Market (MERCOSUR), the Community of Latin American and Caribbean States (CELAC), and the Union of South American Nations (UNASUR). The Agreement on Residence for Nationals of the States Party to MERCOSUR and Associated States provided a tool for accessing legal residence in South America. Similarly, El Salvador, Guatemala, Honduras, and Nicaragua signed the Central America–4 Free Mobility Agreement (CA-4) in 2006.

3. COVID-19 and (Im)Mobilities Across the Americas was a transnational, trilingual (English, Spanish, and Portuguese), collective digital research project initiated by Soledad Álvarez Velasco and developed collaboratively during the first two years of the pandemic. When the public health crisis was declared, forty-five migration scholars from nineteen countries in North, Central, and South America and the Caribbean

MAP 1.1. The borders of the Americas borderlands, national and transnational spaces studied in this book. Map produced by Gabriel Moss.

came together online to inquire into the situations of thousands of migrants and asylum seekers across the hemisphere, focusing on: (1) migration and border measures adopted by states, (2) risks faced by migrant populations, and (3) social responses by migrants or by solidarity movements supporting migrant struggles. Based on this research, a digital archive was created which accounted for the changing tensions between mobility and control during the pandemic from a hemispheric perspective. The authors of this introduction and some of the contributors to this volume took part in this project. See https://www.inmovilidadamericas.org.

4. Title 42 of the US Code is a public health provision. It gives the surgeon general the authority to prohibit noncitizens from entering the United States from a country where the surgeon general determines there is a danger of communicable disease being introduced into the United States. This practice can be implemented for as long as deemed "necessary for such purpose." Someone expelled under Title 42 cannot apply for asylum.

REFERENCES

Achilli, Luigi, and David Kyle. 2023. *Global Human Smuggling Buying Freedom in a Retreating World*. 3rd edition. Baltimore, MD: Johns Hopkins University Press.

Alba Villalever, Ximena, and Stephanie Schütze. 2021. "Trayectorias migratorias y violencia organizada en el corredor Centroamérica-México-Estados Unidos." *Periplos: Revista de Investigación sobre Migraciones* 5 (1): 82–108.

Álvarez Velasco, Soledad. 2019. "Ecuador-México-US: La producción de una zona de tránsito entre políticas de control y la autonomía de la migración." In *América Latina en movimiento: Migraciones, límites a la movilidad y sus desbordamientos*, edited by Blanca Cordero, Sandro Mezzadra, and Amarela Varela Huerta, 63–97. Mexico City: Universidad Autónoma de la Ciudad de México; Madrid: Traficantes de sueños.

Álvarez Velasco, Soledad. 2020. "From Ecuador to Elsewhere: The (Re)configuration of a Transit Country." *Migration and Society* 3 (1): 34–49.

Álvarez Velasco, Soledad. 2021. "Mobility, Control, and the Pandemic Across the Americas: First Findings of a Transnational Collective Project." *Journal of Latin American Geography* 20 (1): 11–48.

Álvarez Velasco, Soledad. 2022. "En búsqueda de un lugar: Tránsitos irregularizados por las Américas." In *Movilidades, control fronterizo y luchas migrantes*, edited by María Guadalupe, Liliana Rivera Sánchez, Gioconda Herrera Mosquera, and Eduardo Enrique Domenech. Buenos Aires: Consejo Latinoamericano de Ciencias Sociales (CLACSO); Mexico City: Siglo XXI.

Álvarez Velasco, Soledad. 2024. "Between 'Trochas,' Orphanages, Mourning, and Migrant Mobilities: The Repressive and Productive Double Effect of the U.S. 'Soft' Remote Control in Ecuador." *Geopolitics*, 1–27.

Álvarez Velasco, Soledad, and Nicholas De Genova. 2023. "'A Mass Exodus in Rebellion'—The Migrant Caravans: A View from the Eyes of Honduran Journalist Inmer Gerardo Chévez." *Studies in Social Justice* 17 (1): 28–47.

Álvarez Velasco, Soledad, Claudia Pedone, and Bruno Miranda. 2021. "Movilidades, control y disputa espacial: La formación y transformación de corredores migratorios en las Américas." *Periplos: Revista de Investigación sobre Migraciones* 5 (1): 4–27.

Amnesty International. 2000. "Colombia: Amnesty International's Position on Plan Colombia." https://www.amnesty.org/en/documents/amr23/049/2000/en/.

Berganza, Isabel. 2017. "Los flujos migratorios mixtos en tránsito por Perú: Un desafío para el Estado." In *Migración haitiana hacia el sur andino*, edited by Nicolás Rojas Pedemonte and José Koechlin, 41–65. Pueblo Libre, Lima: Universidad Antonio Ruiz de Montoya.

Boatcă, Manuela, and Fabio Santos. 2023. "Of Rags and Riches in the Caribbean: Creolizing Migration Studies." *Journal of Immigrant and Refugee Studies* 21 (2): 132–45.

Budiman, Abby. 2020. "Key Findings About U.S. Immigrants." Pew Research Center. August 20. https://www.pewresearch.org/short-reads/2020/08/20/key-findings-about-u-s-immigrants.

Canales, Alejandro. 2018. "Nueva era de las migraciones en Chile: De la diferenciación migratoria a la desigualdad social." In *Migrações Sul-Sul*, edited by Rosana Baeninger, 37–53. Campinas: UNICAMP.

Casas-Cortés, Maribel, Sebastian Cobarrubias, Nicholas De Genova, Glenda Garelli, Giorgio Grappi, Charles Heller, Sabine Hess, Bernd Kasparek, Sandro Mezzadra, Brett Neilson, Irene Peano, Lorenzo Pezzani, John Pickles, Federico Rahola, Lisa Riedner, Stephan Scheel, and Martina Tazzioli 2015. "New Keywords: Migration and Borders." Special section, *Cultural Studies* 29 (1): 55–87.

Ceja, Iréri. 2015. "Migraciones haitianas en la región andina." *Andina Migrante* 19:2–13.

Clavijo, Janneth. 2018. "El proceso de elegibilidad en Argentina: Rituales y ambivalencias en el reconocimiento de los refugiados." *REMHU: Revista Interdisciplinar da Mobilidade Humana* 26:171–88.

CNN. 2022. "Los países de Latinoamérica que necesitan visado para ingresar a México." August 19. https://cnnespanol.cnn.com/2022/08/19/visa-brasil-mexico-paises-latinoamerica-que-requieren-visado-orix/.

Constante, Soraya. 2016. "El puente que no pueden cruzar los haitianos." *El País*, August 7.https://elpais.com/internacional/2016/08/06/america/1470506130_621443.html.

Cordero, Blanca, Sandro Mezzadra, and Amarela Varela Huerta. 2019. *América Latina en movimiento: Migraciones, límites a la movilidad y sus desbordamientos*. Mexico City: Universidad Autónoma de la Ciudad de México; Madrid: Traficantes de sueños.

Correa, Ahmed. 2020. "Deportación, tránsito y refugio: El caso de los cubanos de El Arbolito en Ecuador." *Periplos: Revista de Investigación sobre Migraciones* 3 (2): 52–88.

De Genova, Nicholas. 2002. "Migrant 'Illegality' and Deportability in Everyday Life." *Annual Review of Anthropology* 31 (1): 419–47.

De Genova, Nicholas. 2004. "The Legal Production of Mexican/Migrant 'Illegality.'" *Latino Studies* 2 (1): 160–85.

De Genova, Nicholas. 2005. *Working the Boundaries: Race, Space, and "Illegality" in Mexican Chicago*. Durham, NC: Duke University Press.

De Genova, Nicholas. 2009. "Conflicts of Mobility and the Mobility of Conflict: Rightlessness, Presence, Subjectivity, Freedom." *Subjectivity* 29:445–66.

De Genova, Nicholas. 2010a. "The Deportation Regime: Sovereignty, Space, and the Freedom of Movement." In *The Deportation Regime: Sovereignty, Space, and the Freedom of Movement*, edited by Nicholas De Genova and Nathalie Peutz, 33–65. Durham, NC: Duke University Press.

De Genova, Nicholas. 2010b. "The Queer Politics of Migration: Reflections on 'Illegality' and Incorrigibility." *Studies in Social Justice* 4 (2): 101–26.

De Genova, Nicholas. 2013. "Spectacles of Migrant 'Illegality': The Scene of Exclusion, the Obscene of Inclusion." *Ethnic and Racial Studies* 36 (7): 1180–98.

De Genova, Nicholas. 2016. "The 'Crisis' of the European Border Regime: Towards a Marxist Theory of Borders." *International Socialism*, no. 150, 33–56. http://isj.org.uk/the-crisis-of-the-european-border-regime-towards-a-marxist-theory-of-borders/.

De Genova, Nicholas, ed. 2017. *The Borders of "Europe": Autonomy of Migration, Tactics of Bordering*. Durham, NC: Duke University Press.

De Genova, Nicholas. 2021. "Anonymous Brown Bodies: The Productive Power of the Deadly U.S.-Mexico Border." In *Migration and Mortality: Social Death, Dispossession, and Survival in the Americas*, edited by Jamie Longazel and Miranda Cady Hallett, 83–100. Philadelphia: Temple University Press.

De Genova, Nicholas. 2022. "Viral Borders: Migration, Deceleration, and the Re-Bordering of Mobility During the COVID-19 Pandemic." *Communication, Culture, and Critique*, 15 (2): 139–56.

De Genova, Nicholas. 2025. "From Border War to Civil War: The Despotism of the Border and Full-Spectrum Authoritarianism." *Citizenship Studies* (May 15): 1–24. https://doi.org/10.1080/13621025.2025.2506383.

De León, Jason. 2015. *The Land of Open Graves: Living and Dying on the Migrant Trail*. Berkeley: University of California Press.

Dias, Gustavo, and Eduardo Domenech. 2020. "Sociologia e fronteiras: A produção da ilegalidade migrante na América Latina e no Caribe." *Sociologias* 22 (55): 24–38.

Dias, Gustavo, João Carlos Jarochinski Silva, and Sidney Silva. 2020. "Travelers of the Caribbean: Positioning Brasília in Haitian Migration Routes Through Latin America. *VIBRANT: Virtual Brazilian Anthropology* 17:1–19.

Domenech, Eduardo. 2008. "La ciudadanización de la política migratoria en la región sudamericana: Vicisitudes de la agenda global." In *Las migraciones en América Latina: Políticas, culturas y estrategias*, 53–72. Buenos Aires: Consejo Latinoamericano de Ciencias Sociales (CLACSO), Catálogos.

Domenech, Eduardo. 2017. "Las políticas de migración en Sudamérica: Elementos para el análisis crítico del control migratorio y fronterizo." *Terceiro Milênio: Revista Crítica de Sociologia e Política* 8 (1): 19–48.

Domenech, Eduardo, and Gustavo Dias. 2020. "Regimes de fronteira e 'ilegalidade' migrante na América Latina e Caribe." *Sociologias* 22 (55): 40–73.

Domenech, Eduardo, Gioconda Herrera, and Liliana Rivera Sánchez, eds. 2022. *Movilidades, control fronterizo y luchas migrantes*. Buenos Aires: Consejo Latinoamericano de Ciencias Sociales (CLACSO); México City: Siglo XXI.

Dufraix-Tapia, Roberto, Romina Ramos Rodríguez, and Daniel Quinteros. 2020. "'Ordenar la casa': securitización y producción de irregularidad en el norte de Chile." *Sociologias* 22 (55): 172–96.

ECLAC (Economic Commission for Latin America and the Caribbean). 2022. "Las tasas de pobreza en América Latina se mantienen en 2022 por encima de los niveles prepandemia, alerta la CEPAL." CEPAL. November 24. https://www.cepal.org /es/comunicados/tasas-pobreza-america-latina-se-mantienen-2022-encima-niveles -prepandemia-alerta-la.

Espiro, M. Luz. 2019. "Labor Pathways of Migrants Between Africa and Latin America: The Case of Senegalese in Argentina." *REMHU: Revista Interdisciplinar da Mobilidade Humana* 27:81–98.

Espiro, M. Luz. 2021. Prácticas comerciales entre migrantes africanos wolofs en Argentina: Aportes para el análisis. *Estudios de Asia y África* 56 (1): 95–123.

Feldmann, Andreas, Xóchitl Bada, Jorge Durand, and Stephanie Schütze, eds. 2022. *The Routledge History of Modern Latin American Migration*. New York: Routledge.

Feldmann, Andreas, Xóchitl Bada, and Stephanie Schütze, eds. 2019. *New Migration Patterns in the Americas: Challenges for the 21st Century*. Cham, Switzerland: Palgrave Macmillan.

France 24. 2021. "Chile expulsa a 55 venezolanos en un nuevo proceso de deportaciones." April 25. https://www.france24.com/es/minuto-a-minuto/20210425-chile-expulsa-a -55-venezolanos-en-un-nuevo-proceso-de-deportaciones

Fraser, Nancy. 2022. *Cannibal Capitalism: How Our System Is Devouring Democracy, Care, and the Planet and What We Can Do About It*. London: Verso Books.

Gago, Verónica. 2017. *Neoliberalism from Below: Popular Pragmatics and Baroque Economies*. Durham, NC: Duke University Press.

Gandini, Luciana, Fernando Lozano Ascencio, and Victoria Prieto, 2019. *Crisis y migración de población venezolana: Entre la desprotección y la seguridad jurídica en Latinoamérica*. Mexico City: Universidad Nacional Autónoma de México.

Gandini, Luciana, Victoria Prieto, and Fernando Lozano Ascencio. 2020. "Nuevas movilidades en América Latina: La migración venezolana en contextos de crisis y las respuestas en la región." *Cuadernos Geográficos* 59 (3): 103–21.

Gómez Johnson, Cristina, and Adriana González Gil. 2022. "Violent Contexts and 'Crisis' in Mexico–Central America and Colombia-Venezuela Cross-Border Dynamics, 2010–2020." In *Crises and Migration: Critical Perspectives from Latin America*, edited by Enrique Coraza de los Santos and Luis Alfredo Arriola Vega, 177–200. Cham, Switzerland: Springer.

Gómez Martín, Carmen. 2022. "El sistema de protección internacional de los refugiados en entredicho: Escenarios y manifestaciones de su debilitamiento en el contexto latinoamericano." In *Movilidades, control fronterizo y luchas migrantes*, edited by Eduardo Domenech, Gioconda Herrera, and Liliana Rivera Sánchez, 239–64. Buenos Aires: Consejo Latinoamericano de Ciencias Sociales (CLACSO); Mexico City: Siglo XXI.

Gómez Martín, Carmen, and Gabriela Malo. 2019. "Un recorrido por la literatura sobre refugio y desplazamiento forzado en América Latina y el Caribe: Abordajes principales y nuevos ejes críticos de estudio." *Periplos: Revista de Investigación sobre Migraciones* 3 (2).

Herrera, Gioconda, and Gabriela Cabezas. 2019. "Ecuador: De la recepción a la disuasión; Políticas frente a la población venezolana y experiencia migratoria 2015–2018."
In *Crisis y migración de la población venezolana: Entre la desprotección y la seguridad
jurídica en Latinoamérica*, edited by Luciana Gandini, Fernando Lozano Ascencio,
and Victoria Prieto, 125–55. Mexico City: Universidad Nacional Autónoma de
México.

Herrera, Gioconda, and Carmen Gómez Martín, eds. 2022. *Migration in South America:
IMISCOE Regional Reader*. Cham, Switzerland: Springer.

Hess, Sabine. 2010. "'We Are Facilitating States!': An Ethnographic Analysis of the
ICMPD." In *The Politics of International Migration Management*, edited by Martin
Geiger and Antoine Pécoud, 97–117. Basingstoke, UK: Palgrave.

Hess, Sabine. 2017. "Border Crossing as Act of Resistance: The Autonomy of Migration
as Theoretical Intervention into Border Studies." In *Resistance: Subjects, Representations, Contexts*, edited by Martin Butler, Paul Mecheril, and Lea Brenningmeyer,
87–100. Bielefeld, Germany: Transcript Verlag.

Hess, Sabine, and Bernd Kasparek. 2017. "Under Control?; or, Border (as) Conflict:
Reflections on the European Border Regime." *Social Inclusion* 5 (3): 58–68.

Inmovilidad Americas. 2024. "(In)movilidad en las Americas." https://www
.inmovilidadamericas.org/.

INE (Instituto Nacional de Estadísticas). 2022. "Población extranjera residente en Chile
llegó a 1.482.390 personas en 2021, un 1,5% más que en 2020." October 12. https://www
.ine.cl/prensa/detalle-prensa/2022/10/12/población-extranjera-residente-en-chile
-llegó-a-1.482.390-personas-en-2021-un-1-5-más-que-en-2020.

Infobae. 2022. "Más de 4.000 venezolanos que vivían en Bogotá han sido expulsados o
deportados: cuál es la razón." October 7. https://www.infobae.com/america/colombia
/2022/10/07/mas-de-4000-venezolanos-que-vivian-en-bogota-han-sido-expulsados-o
-deportados-cual-es-la-razon/.

IOM (International Organization for Migration). 2015. "Facilitation of Safe, Regular, and
Orderly Migration." Global Compact Thematic Paper. https://www.iom.int/sites/g
/files/tmzbdl486/files/our_work/ODG/GCM/IOM-Thematic-Paper-Facilitation-of
-Safe-Orderly-and-Regular-Migration.pdf.

IOM (International Organization for Migration). 2022. "Financial Report for the Year
Ended 31 December 2021." https://governingbodies.iom.int/system/files/en/council
/113/c-113-3-financial-report-2021.pdf.

Jacobsen, Christine M., Marry-Anne Karlsen, and Shahram Khosravi, eds. 2021. *Waiting
and the Temporalities of Irregular Migration*. London: Routledge.

Mansur Dias, Guilherme. 2015. "Notas sobre as negociações da 'Convenção do Crime'
e dos Protocolos Adicionais sobre Tráfico de Pessoas e Contrabando de Migrantes."
REMHU: Revista Interdisciplinar da Mobilidade Humana 23, 215–34.

Martí, José. (1891) 1979. "Nuestra América." In *Tres documentos de nuestra América*,
169–78. Havana: Casa de las Américas.

Martignoni, Martina, and Dimitris Papadopoulos. 2014. "Genealogies of Autonomous
Mobility." In *Routledge Handbook of Global Citizenship Studies*, edited by Engin Isin
and Peter Nyers, 38–48. London: Routledge.

Melhado, William. 2022. "Border Patrol Reports 2.4 Million Migrant Arrests at South-west Border This Year, the Most Ever." *Texas Tribune* (Austin), October 22. https://www.texastribune.org/2022/10/22/border-patrol-migrant-encounters/.

Méndez Barquero, Juan C. 2021. "Los flujos extrarregionales en tránsito por Centroamérica: Una revisión de literatura y miradas futuras para comprender un complejo fenómeno migratorio." *REMHU: Revista Interdisciplinar da Mobilidade Humana* 29:189–208.

Menjívar, Cecilia. 2014. "Immigration Law Beyond Borders: Externalizing and Internalizing Border Controls in an Era of Securitization." *Annual Review of Law and Social Science* 10:353–69.

Mezzadra, Sandro. 2011. "The Gaze of Autonomy: Capitalism, Migration, and Social Struggles." In *The Contested Politics of Mobility: Borderzones and Irregularity*, edited by Vicki Squire, 121–42. London: Routledge.

Mezzadra, Sandro, and Brett Neilson. 2013. *Border as Method; or, The Multiplication of Labor*. Durham, NC: Duke University Press.

Miller, Todd. 2019. *Empire of Borders: The Expansion of the US Border Around the World*. London: Verso Books.

Miranda, Bruno. 2021. "Movilidades haitianas en el corredor Brasil-México: Efectos del control migratorio y de la securitización fronteriza." *Periplos: Revista de Investigación sobre Migraciones* 5 (1): 108–30.

Miranda, Bruno. 2023. "Migración africana en situación de espera: Nuevo alcance y dimensión de la contención migratoria en México." *Revista Pueblos y fronteras digital* 18:1–30.

Mitropoulos, Angela. 2007. "Autonomy, Recognition, Movement." In *Constituent Imagination: Militant Investigations, Collective Theorization*, edited by Stevphen Shukaitis, David Graeber, and Erika Biddle, 127–36. Oakland, CA: AK Press.

MMC (Mixed Migration Centre). 2022. "Quarterly Mixed Migration Update: Latin America and the Caribbean." July. https://mixedmigration.org/wp-content/uploads/2022/07/QMMU_Q2_2022_LAC.pdf.

Moulier-Boutang, Yann. (1998) 2006. *De la esclavitud al trabajo asalariado*. Madrid: Akal.

Mountz, Alison. 2020. *The Death of Asylum: Hidden Geographies of the Enforcement Archipelago*. Minneapolis: University of Minnesota Press.

Murillo, Álvaro. 2022. "Costa Rica Imposes Visa Requirements for Venezuelans as Migration Surges." February 17. https://www.reuters.com/world/americas/costa-rica-imposes-visa-requirements-venezuelans-migration-surges-2022-02-17/.

New Keywords Collective. 2016. "Europe/Crisis: New Keywords of 'the Crisis' in and of 'Europe,'" edited by Nicholas De Genova and Martina Tazzioli. *Near Futures Online* 1:1–16. http://nearfuturesonline.org/europecrisis-new-keywords-of-crisis-in-and-of-europe/.

Ortega Velázquez, Elisa. 2022. *El asilo como derecho en disputa en México: La raza y la clase como dispositivos de exclusión*. Mexico City: Universidad Nacional Autónoma de México.

Pacecca, María Inés, Gabriela Liguori, and Camila Carril. 2016. "La migración dominicana en Argentina. Trayectorias en el nuevo siglo (2000–2015)." Buenos Aires: International Organization for Migration

Papadopoulos, Dimitris, and Vassilis Tsianos, 2013. "After Citizenship: Autonomy of Migration, Organisational Ontology, and Mobile Commons." *Citizenship Studies* 17 (2): 178–96.

Papadopoulos, Dimitris, Niam Stephenson, and Vassilis Tsianos. 2008. *Escape Routes: Control and Subversion in the 21st Century*. London: Pluto Press.

París Pombo, Dolores. 2022. "Externalización de las fronteras y bloqueo de los solicitantes de asilo en el norte de México." *REMHU: Revista Interdisciplinar da Mobilidade Humana* 30:101–16.

París Pombo, Dolores, Diana Buenrostro Mercado, and Gabriel Pérez Duperou. 2017. "Trapped at the Border: The Difficult Integration of Veterans, Families, and Christians in Tijuana." In *Deportation and Return in a Border-Restricted World: Experiences in Mexico, El Salvador, Guatemala, and Honduras*, edited by Bryan Roberts, Cecilia Menjívar, and Nestor P. Rodriguez, 131–48. Cham, Switzerland, Springer.

París Pombo, Dolores, and Verónica Montes. 2020. "Visibilidad como estrategia de movilidad: El éxodo Centroamericano en México (2018–19)." *EntreDiversidades: Revista de ciencias sociales y humanidades* 7 (1): 9–36.

Plataforma R4V (Inter-Agency Coordination Platform for Refugees and Migrants from Venezuela). 2022. "Key Figures." https://www.r4v.info/en.

Rivadeneyra, Dánae. 2019. "Los migrantes venezolanos atrapados en el limbo peruano-ecuatoriano." *RFI*, November 14. https://www.rfi.fr/es/americas/20191114-los-migrantes-venezolanos-atrapados-en-el-limbo-peruano-ecuatoriano.

Rojas Pedemonte, Nicolás, Nassila Amode, and Jorge Vásquez Rencoret. 2015. "Racismo y matrices de 'inclusión' de la migración haitiana en Chile: Elementos conceptuales y contextuales para la discusión." *Polis: Revista Latinoamericana* 42: 217–45.

Romano, Silvina. 2009. "Integración económica, desarrollo y migraciones en el MERCOSUR: Una aproximación crítica." In *Migración y política: El Estado interrogado; Procesos actuales en Argentina y Sudamérica*, edited by Eduardo Domenech, 257–99. Córdoba: Universidad Nacional de Córdoba.

Sánchez, Gabriella. 2017. "Critical Perspectives on Clandestine Migration Facilitation: An Overview of Migrant Smuggling Research." *Journal on Migration and Human Security* 5 (1): 9–27.

Stang, Fernanda. 2009. "El dispositivo jurídico migratorio en la Comunidad Andina de Naciones." In *Migración y política: El Estado interrogado*, edited by Eduardo Domenech, 301–53. Córdoba: Universidad Nacional de Córdoba.

Sullivan, Eileen, and Miriam Jordan. 2021. "Illegal Border Crossings, Driven by Pandemic and Natural Disasters, Soar to Record High." *New York Times*, October 22. https://www.nytimes.com/2021/10/22/us/politics/border-crossings-immigration-record-high.html.

Tapia, Marcela, and Nanette Liberona, eds. 2018. *El afán de cruzar las fronteras: Enfoques transdisciplinarios sobre migraciones y movilidad en Sudamérica y Chile*. Santiago: RIL Editores.

Tazzioli, Martina. 2014. *Spaces of Governmentality: Autonomous Migration and the Arab Uprisings*. London: Rowman and Littlefield.

Tazzioli, Martina. 2015. "The Desultory Politics of Mobility and the Humanitarian-Military Border in the Mediterranean: Mare Nostrum Beyond the Sea." *REMHU: Revista Interdisciplinar da Mobilidade Humana* 23 (44): 61–82.

Tijoux, María Emilia, and María Gabriela Córdova Rivera. 2015. "Racismo en Chile: Colonialismo, nacionalismo, capitalismo." *Polis: Revista Latinoamericana* 14 (42): 7–13.

Torres, Rebecca María, Valentina Glockner Fagetti, Nohora Niño-Vega, Gabriela García-Figueroa, Caroline Faria, Alicia Danze, Emanuela Borzacchiello, and Jeremy Slack. 2022. "Lockdown and the List: Mexican Refugees, Asylum Denial, and the Feminist Geopolitics of *Esperar* (Waiting/Hoping). *Environment and Planning C: Politics and Space* 41 (8): 1503–20.

Trabalón, Carina. 2018. "Política de visado y regulación de las fronteras: Un análisis desde la movilidad de haitianos en Sudamérica." *Polis: Revista Latinoamericana* 51:163–86.

Trabalón, Carina. 2019. "Estrategias de movilidad, visados y fronteras: Trayectorias de haitianos y haitianas hacia la Argentina." *Estudios fronterizos* 20:1–23.

Trabalón, Carina. 2020. "Violencia estatal, control fronterizo y racialización: Experiencias de haitianos y haitianas en aeropuertos de Argentina." *Historia y sociedad* 39:155–83.

Trabalón, Carina. 2021. "Racialización del control y nuevas migraciones: Procesos de ilegalización durante la última década en la Argentina." *Periplos: Revista de Investigación sobre Migraciones* 5 (1): 207–34.

Tsianos, Vassilis, and Serhat Karakayali. 2010. "Transnational Migration and the Emergence of the European Border Regime: An Ethnographic Analysis." *European Journal of Social Theory* 13 (3): 373–87.

UNHCR (Office of the United Nations High Commissioner for Refugees). 2020. *Global Report 2020*. https://www.unhcr.org/flagship-reports/globalreport/.

Vammen, Ida M. 2019. "New Contested Borderlands: Senegalese Migrants en Route to Argentina." *Comparative Migration Studies* 7 (1): 1–17.

Van Schendel, Willem, and Itty Abraham, eds. 2005. *Illicit Flows and Criminal Things: States, Borders, and the Other Side of Globalization*. Bloomington: Indiana University Press.

Varela Huerta, Amarela. 2017. "Las masacres de migrantes en San Fernando y Cadereyta: dos ejemplos de gubernamentalidad necropolítica." *Íconos: Revista de Ciencias Sociales* 58:131–49.

Varela Huerta, Amarela, and Lisa McLean. 2021. "From Vulnerable Victims to Insurgent Caravaneros: The Genesis and Consolidation of a New Form of Migrant Self-Defence in America." In *Migration and the Contested Politics of Justice*, edited by Giorgio Grappi, 184–99. London: Routledge.

Vásquez, Tania, Erika Busse, and Lorena Izaguirre. 2015. *Migración de población haitiana a Perú y su tránsito hacia Brasil desde el año 2010*. Lima: Instituto de Estudios Peruanos.

Velasco Ortiz, Laura, and Rafael A. Hernández López. 2021. "Salir de las sombras: La visibilidad organizada de las caravanas de migrantes centroamericanas." In *Caravanas migrantes y desplazamientos colectivos en la frontera México–Estados Unidos*, edited by Camilo Contreras Delgado, María Dolores París Pombo, and Laura Velasco Ortiz, 103–29. Tijuana: El Colegio de la Frontera Norte.

Vogt, Wendy. 2017. "The Arterial Border: Negotiating Economies of Risk and Violence in Mexico's Security Regime." *International Journal of Migration and Border Studies* 3 (2–3): 192–204.

Winters, Nanneke, and Cynthia Mora Izaguirre. 2019. "Es cosa suya: Entanglements of Border Externalization and African Transit Migration in Northern Costa Rica." *Comparative Migration Studies* 7 (27): 1–20.

Winters, Nanneke, and Franziska Reiffen. 2019. "Haciendo-lugar vía huellas y apegos: Las personas migrantes africanas y sus experiencias de movilidad, inmovilidad e inserción local en América Latina." *REMHU: Revista Interdisciplinar da Mobilidade Humana* 27:11–33.

Zubrzycki, Bernarda. 2018. "Unauthorized Migration and Regularization Processes in Argentina: The Senegalese Case." *Revista del CESLA: International Latin American Studies Review* 22:367–82.

1

Latin American Refugeeships in Canada and the Hemispheric Border Regime

Patricia Landolt and Luin Goldring

This chapter examines the politics of Latin American refugeeship in Canada as a distinct element of the hemispheric border regime. More precisely, we explore the material and discursive formation of three country-specific narratives of Latin American refugeeship in Canada: Chileans as educated political activists fleeing targeted persecution, Salvadorans as victims of civil war, and Mexicans as "bogus" refugees simply seeking work. We show how state policy responses to different refugee crises, media coverage, the dialogue between state and nonstate actors, and the actions of migrants themselves inform the assessment and categorization of Latin Americans in relation to refugeeship. In each case, the assessment of refugee deservingness leads to different collective experiences of migration and bordering, with significant long-term effects on settlement and incorporation. Our analysis of the three cases captures how differential inclusion for Latin Americans is produced through the politics of refugeeship and how that politics changes over time in an iterative fashion, contributing to the dynamic hemispheric border regime.

The politics of refugeeship operates as a multiscalar and multiactor assemblage that classifies people and their mobilities into recognizable and manageable categories (Baker and McGuirk 2017; Villegas et al. 2021). The classification of migration as refugee migration or a humanitarian crisis deserving of asylum or protection is contested and dynamic. It involves tensions around the geography and modality of selection (where, by whom, and at what point in a migrant and legal status trajectory), with consequences for rights and entitlements (Reynolds and Hyndman 2021; Landolt and Goldring 2016). The actors in this classification struggle can include national, regional, and municipal governments; the media; international organizations and agreements; migrant rights organizations, advocating for the safe passage and stable resettlement of refugees; antimigrant organizations, patrolling borders and nationhood (Elcioglu 2020); and migrants themselves.

Our tracing of three instances of refugee migration from Latin America to Canada over five decades reveals the contentious and iterative nature of the politics of refugeeship, and its relationship to differential inclusion. In Canada, the contemporary state management of refugeeship has two modalities of assessment: "resettled refugees," whose deservingness has been determined *before* their arrival, and "refugee claimants," or asylum seekers, who are assessed once they are in Canada. These modalities have different socio-legal histories and patterns of inclusion and layering within the hemispheric border regime. They contribute to the classificatory struggles that produce the differential inclusion of hierarchically organized populations that are sorted and managed based on interlocking facets of oppression (Casas-Cortés et al. 2015). Each modality sets refugees on distinct legal status trajectories and grants different rights and entitlements before and after arrival.

Chileans, Salvadorans, and Mexicans have traversed the politics of refugeeship differently. Each group has shown variations in terms of the balance between refugee resettlement and in-land asylum, and this variation, in turn, has shaped each group's experience of securitization, time with and forms of precarious legal status and deportability, illegalization, and resulting *work of status*[1] (Goldring 2022; Goldring et al. 2024b), and access to social entitlements. At the same time, the political battles over refugee deservingness sparked by each instance have extended beyond the actual case to impact the broader political and policy landscape. As we show in the following sections, the classification struggles that emerge in the context of refugee crises have long-term effects on the politics of refugeeship, while producing the differential inclusion of hierarchically organized Latin American populations (Casas-Cortés et al. 2015; Basok et al. 2022).

The Place of Refugeeship in Migration Management Policy

In Canada, the federal government has always played a key role in organizing the classification, selection, settlement, and deportation of noncitizens. It has used a mix of immigration and labor market policies, as well as national security priorities and measures to balance the structural tension between permanent immigration for population growth and nation-state building, on one hand, and temporary migration to meet employer demands for flexible labor, on the other (Sharma 2006; Pratt 2005; Landolt 2017; Goldring and Landolt 2012).[2] Never orderly, this management process always precipitates the need for adjustments and "fixes" (Goldring and Landolt 2021). The state has also responded to geopolitics, national lobbying, and powerful civil society advocacy to address humanitarian crises, thereby creating mechanisms for the managed selection and resettlement of refugee populations.

State policy responses to humanitarian crises echo the broader logic of selection, settlement, and removal through deportation. According to this logic, the state has been less responsive to calls for the regularization of illegalized people who live, work, and study in Canada (Khandor et al. 2004; Migrant Rights Network 2021; Goldring and Landolt 2021). Since 1967, permanent immigration (legislated in 1976) has been organized based on education, official language ability, and family ties. In the 1970s, immigration policy was explicitly linked to citizenship and residence rights and entitlements through settlement services. The federal government partnered with provincial governments and civil society in the resettlement of immigrants and refugees, funding and designing programs delivered by nonprofit or language- or ethno-specific community agencies. The federal government also developed a national administrative plan that set the scope of and eligibility criteria for access to settlement services, focusing on permanent residents and those with refugee status. Refugee claimants were added to the settlement infrastructure in the late 1980s. Temporary migrant workers entering Canada under the Non-Immigration Employment Authorization Program (NIEAP) framework were and remain ineligible for settlement services.

First set into law by the Immigration Act of 1976, Canada's humanitarian migration framework established two forms of refugee recognition. Both evolved through court battles and procedural adjustments, and both prioritize immigration officials' discretion in assessing applicants' credibility, suitability, and deservingness (Dauvergne 2009). Canadian refugeeship as refugee resettlement was formalized in the 1976 Immigration Act. The act recognizes refugees as a distinct class of immigrants, institutionalizes the government's role in selecting refugees living abroad, and allows Canadian citizens to privately sponsor refugees. Refugeeship as in-land asylum was formalized in 1985 when the Supreme Court ruled that anyone in Canada could make a refugee claim.[3] The framework also provides for extemporaneous initiatives designed to admit people not otherwise eligible under the United Nations High Commissioner for Refugees (UNHCR) definition of "convention refugee" for emergency purposes and through special programs.[4]

The humanitarian migration framework overlaps with and pushes up against other mechanisms and logics for permanent and temporary selection and settlement. It too necessitates ad hoc fixes and continual tinkering to recapture the autonomous activities of noncitizens, migrants, and other "unruly subjects." Two mechanisms allow illegalized and authorized temporary migrants to apply for permanent residence on humanitarian grounds (other mechanisms offer precarious legality rather than secure status; see Basok and Rojas Wiesner 2018). These mechanisms essentially act as "fixes" to the systemic production of precarious legal status (Goldring, Berinstein, and Bernhard 2009; Landolt and Goldring 2016).[5] One fix is the in-land refugee claim (RC); the other is the application for permanent residence based on humanitarian and compassionate (H&C) grounds. These two highly discretionary processes permit the status adjustment of people without a work permit or authorization to reside (McDonald 2009) and are open to all migrants. The RC is explicitly defined as part of the humanitarian migration framework, and H&C is framed as an exception, a compassionate way to regularize nonstatus residents (Khandor et al. 2004; Delisle and Nakache 2022). In practice, the RC and H&C mechanisms overlap since there is no time limit on how long an individual can reside in Canada before submitting either application. The unspecified time window for submission opens the door to late refugee claims (LRCs) and to overlaps between LRCs and H&Cs (Goldring and Landolt 2022).

As we go on to show, the politics of these distinct forms of refugeeship contributes to differential inclusion. Refugeeship based on resettlement typically provides greater discursive legitimacy than refugeeship based on claiming asylum. Resettled refugees have earlier access to public services and citizenship than refugee claimants; H&C applicants have the most fragile protection from deportability and thinnest access to services. This fragility reflects the fact that spending time and resources navigating a precarious legal status trajectory has cumulative negative impacts on livelihood and well-being (Goldring et al. 2024b).

Latin American Migration and the Politics of Refugeeship

Latin American migrations to Canada have been characterized as "waves" generated by economic insecurity (Ecuador and Peru in the early 1970s), political violence (Argentina, Chile, and Uruguay in the mid-1970s), and civil war and economic insecurity (El Salvador and other Central American countries from the 1980s) (Mata 2022; Basok et al. 2022). In 2021, a tiny share of the immigrant population in Canada reported birth in Mexico or Central and South America (6 percent), compared to 3 percent born in North America (mainly the United States), 5 percent in the Caribbean, 24 percent in Europe, 10 percent Africa, 52 percent Asia, and 1 percent in Oceania (Statistics Canada 2022). The 2021 census found Latin American immigrants were relatively recent arrivals: at that time, 21 percent of all Latin Americans in Canada had arrived in the previous five years (2016–21), whereas only 9 percent had arrived before 1980. This trend was not mirrored in the total immigrant population: 15 percent of immigrants to Canada had arrived recently, compared to 18 percent before 1980. Moreover, Latin American immigrants were twice as likely as the total immigrant population to be nonpermanent residents (21 percent and 11 percent, respectively) (Statistics Canada 2022).

Between 1980 and 2001, close to one-third of Latin Americans (31 percent) granted permanent residence were granted asylum prior to their arrival in Canada or via the in-land refugee determination system (Landolt, Goldring, and Bernhard 2011). The majority of Chilean refugees arriving in the 1970s did so as resettled refugees. Many Salvadorans fleeing civil war in the 1980s also arrived as resettled refugees with a relatively straightforward path to permanent residence and citizenship. However, a significant proportion of Salvadorans made an in-land asylum claim at a border crossing, which meant that acquiring permanent residence and secure status for them took longer and constituted a process filled with doubt and fear. In contrast, for much of this period, many Mexicans came and went as low-wage *temporary* agricultural workers and were not counted as residents, as part of any wave, or as permanent residents (Basok et al. 2022). In the early 2000s, it became harder to identify clear-cut migrant cohorts or waves, or clear groups of refugees: Mexicans, Colombians, and then Venezuelans from diverse class backgrounds sought asylum at the border, airports, or in-land, sometimes years after settling in Canada, and also arrived through other categories (Lujan 2021; Villegas 2020b; Basok et al. 2022).

Over time, the entry of people from different Latin American countries into Canada shaped immigration management policy, including the development of a classification system determining who is a legitimate refugee. Different Latin

American migration flows have been classified outside the scope of refugee protection, or their recognition as refugees has been slow, partial, and suspect. The assessment and classification of refugee deservingness is connected to the changing scope, territorialization, and governance of securitization, and the management of a bimodal refugee determination system (resettled versus in-land asylum seekers) and its overlap with precarious legal status "fixes." The changing politics of refugeeship contribute to differential inclusion within and across national origin groups.

The Chilean Movement

The Chilean refugee movement was triggered by a coup d'état that overthrew the democratically elected socialist government of Salvador Allende in September 1973. The military junta was targeted and vicious in its violence against supporters of Allende's socialist project. The military swept the country, tracking down and detaining men and women who had been leaders and supporters of the Popular Unity government. People were rounded up, jailed, tortured, and executed or sent to makeshift concentration camps. In the immediate aftermath of the coup, thousands fled Chile, often without a clear plan of escape and with an uncertain destination. They piled into embassies in Santiago, made their way to Argentina, Peru, Panama, and Mexico and eventually resettled across Europe, North America, or elsewhere. An estimated 200,000 people fled Chile in the 1970s (Landolt 1993).

The Canadian government's response to the Chilean refugee crisis changed dramatically over a period of just three months, from September to November 1973. The Liberal government's early response was callously negligible. In September, the government recognized Chile's military junta and approved $5 million in credit for the new administration. Canada's ambassador to Chile reported that targeted political persecution was minimal, that the situation was largely under control, and the military junta had no intention of staying in power. In early November, fact-finding delegations were dispatched to Santiago and to Panama and Honduras, where Chileans were awaiting processing for resettlement. The processing of asylum seekers was painfully slow and included an assessment of personal suitability and security screening. Yet on November 30, Prime Minister Pierre Trudeau announced the establishment of a special refugee program—the Special Program Chile—to quickly process hundreds of people at risk and transport them to Canada for permanent resettlement (Peddie 2013; Diab 2015; Hanff 1979; Landolt 2023).

The government's policy reversal was a direct result of grassroots collaboration and mobilization by organizations with very different political trajectories (North

2023; Simalchik 1993). One set of organizations included unions, political parties, student groups, and faith-based organizations committed to transnational solidarity with Third World movements for national self-determination. They had formed the Committee in Solidarity with Democratic Chile (CSDC) in support of Allende and "Chile's socialist spring." At its peak, the CSDC had fifteen chapters across Canada that hosted teach-ins and organized exchanges with a variety of Chilean organizations. A second set included national faith-based organizations and local church affiliates that had years of experience partnering with the federal government to support refugee resettlement. These local groups had offered resettlement support when the federal government organized the rapid exit of 30,000 Hungarians fleeing Soviet reoccupation in 1956, when 11,200 Prague Spring refugees arrived in 1968, and when 6,000 Ugandan Asian refugees arrived in 1972 (Schwinghamer and Raska 2020). In spite of their different foci and experiences, the organizations had a common response to the government's inaction and its ideologically motivated double standard on Chilean asylum seekers.

The grassroots Chile movement disrupted the state's assessment of Chilean refugees as undeserving and eroded the narrative of Chileans as "Marxist riff-raff" and security threats. The movement capitalized on the government's early inaction in order to generate public criticism, attract media coverage, and start an intense lobbying campaign. Backed by the UNHCR call for a global response to the crisis, local grassroots activism escalated into a nationwide, multisectoral movement that pushed the government to create the Special Movement Chile to process asylum seekers on relaxed criteria vis-à-vis the UN's refugee definition. The movement continued to pressure the government to ensure that processing times were faster. Movement members offered to accompany Canadian officials to the region to help with translation and selection. In Canada, they welcomed Chileans and aided in their resettlement.

By 1978, just over 7,000 Chilean refugees were resettled in Canada, and a steady flow continued through the 1980s and early 1990s. While security checks and state surveillance continued for years, the Chilean pathway to permanent residence and citizenship was comparatively expeditious. The grassroots support and lobbying efforts ensured that the vast majority of Chileans who resettled in Canada in the 1970s entered the country as intact two- and one-parent families with children. In that pre-internet era, the organized welcome made it easier for Chileans to find one another and reconnect with friends, family, and political allies in resettlement cities and across the country. Canada slowly became home to a vibrant Chilean exile community (Magocsi 1999).

The narrative and legal status trajectory forged through grassroots organizing made the Chilean settlement process—access to housing, work, and social support—predictable. This is not to diminish the profound trauma families carried with them, but it certainly put Chileans on a distinct path to incorporation as compared to Salvadorans and Mexicans.

The Chilean refugee crisis consolidated civil society—specifically a multisectoral, national network of locally rooted individuals and organizations—as a distinct actor in immigration and refugee policy. Local communities that supported refugee resettlement based on shared faith or ethnicity shifted to a more ecumenical and humanist stance on refugee selection and resettlement. The relationship between development, human rights, and global refugee flows came into clearer focus for many organizations. New, multisectoral, faith-based organizations were consolidated, including the Interchurch Committee on Human Rights in Latin America (ICCHRLA) and the Interchurch Committee on Refugees (ICCR). The ICCHRLA served as a starting point for transnational solidarity and acted as a watchdog on human rights in Latin America (Landolt and Goldring 2010). The ICCR brought together a cohort of refugee rights lawyers who challenged government immigration policies in the courts for years to come.

The Chilean refugee crisis and the political battle leading to the creation of the Special Movement Chile contributed to legal reforms in Canada's immigration and refugee laws. Until the 1978 Immigration Act, asylum procedures, including selection and admission, evolved without legislation or the creation of a specific regulatory framework. The act provided a legal framework for the refugee determination process for those applying for asylum in Canada and abroad. Convention refugees became an admissible class in their own right. At the time, three designated classes were established for the Indo-Chinese, self-exile persons (primarily Eastern Europeans), and political prisoners and oppressed persons. The third designated class was a direct consequence of the Chilean refugee crisis and was later applied to Salvadoran political prisoners, among others (Bissett 1987, 59). The government also had the discretion to designate, from time to time, other classes of persons in refugee-like situations to be admitted and resettled on the same basis as convention refugees.

Salvadorans as Victims of Civil War

In the 1980s, civil war and economic collapse forcibly displaced over a million people from El Salvador (Hamilton et al. 1988). The Salvadoran flight from violence was characterized by protracted displacement and transcontinental legal status precarity. While many Salvadoran refugees fled to safety through established regional and US-bound migration networks, others sheltered in refugee camps in Honduras and in a reception center in San Salvador (Montes 1989; Zolberg, Suhrke, and Aguayo 1989). Salvadoran migration routes to Canada developed slowly. Many Salvadorans traveled directly from El Salvador to Canada as convention refugees. Still others moved first to Costa Rica and Mexico, where the UNHCR facilitated their relocation. As conditions in the region worsened and new migration networks developed, they also made their way to Canada (Basok 1993). The vast majority of displaced traveled overland to the United States, lived and worked there for some time, and then applied for asylum in Canada. Regardless of their trajectory, 80 percent of those who applied were granted asylum in Canada (Dirks 1995). Approximately 38,000 Salvadorans came to Canada during this period, making them the largest group of Latin American migrants arriving in that era (Dirks 1995).

The state response to the Salvadoran refugee crisis contrasted with the position of the United States and with Canada's response to the Chilean refugee crisis. The Canadian government used the policy levers of the Immigration Act of 1976 to enable the accelerated entry of Salvadorans from Central America *and* from the United States to Canada for permanent resettlement. It recognized El Salvador's civil war as a refugee-producing situation and used the category of "designated class of political prisoners and oppressed persons" to facilitate asylum for those who did not qualify under the UN refugee convention definition (Basok and Simmons 1993). In 1981, the government created several emergency programs for the entry of high-risk Salvadoran refugees, including political prisoners and people living in refugee camps in Honduras. It also enacted a moratorium on the deportation of Salvadoran students and visitors and, in 1982, extended the moratorium to include Salvadorans facing deportation from the United States (Dirks 1995). The government steadily increased its quota for government-sponsored Latin American refugees to accommodate more Central Americans.

Transnational grassroots organizations in Canada and international nongovernmental organizations (NGOs) were integral in shaping the Canadian state response to the Salvadoran refugee crisis (Garcia 2006b; Landolt and Goldring 2010). Transnational organizations applied the political lessons and social movement strategies of the Chilean movement to their analysis and lobby work on El Salvador. Their calls for a proactive and independent response to the refugee crisis linked US Cold War geopolitics with the social inequalities that led to the civil war and the ensuing refugee crisis. They capitalized on their established rapport with the federal government to influence immigration and foreign policy. The ICCR criticized the federal government for having insufficient consulates and visa officers to ensure Salvadorans could apply for asylum. The Canadian

Council of Churches visited Honduras and provided firsthand accounts of the conditions in the refugee camps there (Adelman 1983). Amnesty International encouraged the Canadian government to consider Canada an accessible and logical country of first asylum. Ultimately, civil society pushed a reluctant Canadian government to articulate a policy position on the civil war and the refugee crisis that was independent of the US stance in the region and vis-à-vis US immigration and deportation policy (Ferris 1987; Kowalchuk 1999). Canadian advocacy groups, including the Canadian Council for Refugees (CCR), established in 1978, were instrumental in shaping Canadian foreign policy and weakening restrictive refugee legislation (Garcia 2006b).

The Salvadoran refugee crisis tested the integrity and purpose of Canada's new in-land refugee determination system. State policies established in the early 1980s, which started from the assumption that Salvadorans were legitimate refugees fleeing violence, faced a new challenge in 1986 when the US government's passage of the Immigration Reform and Control Act (IRCA) motivated thousands of Central Americans living undocumented in the United States to make their way to the Canadian border and claim refugee status.[6] The asylum framework established by the 1976 Immigration Act and operationalized via the Immigration and Refugee Board (IRB) was ill-equipped to handle the growing volume of claims. A huge processing backlog quickly developed, and the political climate turned, raising doubts about the validity of Salvadorans as genuine refugees. A new, much broader set of anxieties emerged about Canada's border integrity (Hier and Greenberg 2002; Macklin 2011).

In February 1987, the Canadian government imposed new restrictions to discourage overland migration, particularly affecting Salvadorans. It canceled the "B-1 list" of eighteen countries deemed genuine refugee-producing states, whose nationals, including Salvadorans, were automatically allowed to work and receive social services pending asylum decisions. Transit visa requirements for Salvadorans were implemented to prevent asylum petitions during brief stays, often resulting in visa denials for potential claimants. Special programs for Salvadorans with relatives in Canada were modified to require processing abroad. Those entering Canada via the United States and claiming refugee status had to remain in the United States until their hearings, often scheduled months later. Concurrently, the government introduced reforms to the in-land refugee claims process. The IRB was created, and expedited hearings and a simplified claims process were introduced. Soon thereafter, a series of legislated changes systematized and then stepped up security screenings and set eligibility criteria—including exclusion clauses for serious criminals, limited appeal rights, and added detention provisions for rejected claimants (Dubois 2014).

The increasing securitization of the immigration system and parallel thinning of the refugee determination process generated new types of refugee rights activism. A cadre of refugee rights lawyers and advocates shifted their attention from country-specific solidarity to a broad focus on migrant and refugee rights. This shift eroded the existing link between transnational political solidarity and refugee rights. Given the design of the new refugee determination system, advocacy required case-by-case support for claimants navigating the asylum system, even as activists continued to demand recognition for the rights of all people to migrate and seek protection. The CCR became increasingly important for refugee advocacy and participation, as indicated by the 1997–2001 tenure as director of a Salvadoran lawyer who had arrived as a refugee. The 2011 formation of the Canadian Association of Refugee Lawyers also reflected the trend toward broader advocacy around the fundamental rights of people fleeing violence.

Shifts in conceptions and discourses of deservingness continued to inform struggles over refugee legitimacy. With Chileans, the lobbying and activism had required flipping the narrative of "Marxist riffraff" to claim the deservingness and suitability of refugees. However, in the Salvadoran case, the media made the link between civil war and the refugee crisis. The place of Salvadorans in the Cold War context was ambiguous, and newspapers called on their readership to show compassion. In the early eighties, Salvadorans were depicted as a helpless, homogenous group of peasants fleeing violence (Dubois 2014). In the late eighties, as autonomous movement via the United States—the flight from violence—triggered border securitization, refugee rights groups articulated a narrative of deservingness that linked UN frameworks for human rights and refugee rights with the unmanaged and at times chaotic movement of individuals seeking safety. However, racism, xenophobia, and a neurotic obsession with border integrity made and continue to make this narrative shift difficult to sustain.

The Salvadoran case illustrates transformations in both hemispheric and national border regimes. In the process of responding to the Salvadoran refugee crisis, Canadian state and nonstate actors assumed a new presence in regional politics and on the global stage. Refugee policy became a mechanism for the Canadian government to distinguish itself politically from the United States and assert a distinct role in the region (Garcia 2006b), reflecting a counternarrative of the civil war and the ensuing migration crisis as a flight from violence. However, this independence eroded with the autonomous arrival of Salvadorans (and others) at the Canadian border. The state moved toward a legislated framework for securitizing the border and criminalizing free movement that was part of an emergent North American reterritorialization (see the following section). Bordering and rebordering shifted. State and nonstate actors engaged in struggles over the national border regime, and the hemispheric (and global) regimes used securitization, particularly after the events of September 11, 2001, to focus on refugee determination as the identification of "legitimate" refugees versus "bogus" asylum seekers or security threats.

Mexican Mixed Migration and "Bogus" Refugees

Mexican refugeeship presents a striking contrast to that of Chileans and Salvadorans. Mexicans have never been considered candidates for refugee resettlement despite widespread and escalating violence and the enormous death toll associated with the War on Drugs, cartel wars, and rise of the narcostate (Schmidt 2020; Amnesty International 2024). Instead, the Canadian modality of Mexican refugeeship is to process them entirely as in-land refugee claimants or H&C applicants. Their refugeeship emerged in the context of Mexico's incorporation into the new North American trade and security zone, which was initially formalized through the North American Free Trade Agreement (NAFTA) and has been consolidated through subsequent governance-, securitization-, and migration-related agreements and policies (Young 2018; Reynolds and Hyndman 2021; Atak, Hudson, and Nakache 2018; Hellerstein 2023).

Mexican migration to Canada began in the mid-1960s and has been diverse in modalities of entry and permanence or temporariness. In the 1960s, Mexicans entered Canada as permanent residents, selected based on education and training, or through the Seasonal Agricultural Worker Program (SAWP). Since then, SAWP workers have outnumbered immigrants (Villegas 2020b, 10). International students joined this process; some returned to Mexico while others became permanent residents (Van Haren and Masferrer 2024; Mueller 2005; Reitz and Jasso 2021; Basok et al. 2022). The number of refugee claims was not a cause of public concern in the late 1980s.

This pattern began to change in the late 1980s and 1990s when violence in Mexico began to rise and expand geographically due to US and Mexican programs associated with the War on Drugs, and Mexican refugeeship in Canada gained visibility through rising refugee claims.[7] At the same time, the United States was becoming increasingly expensive and dangerous to reach, and more unwelcoming for Mexicans and others who became subject to the discursive and material effects of "crimmigration" (Stumpf 2006). In 1996, 917 Mexicans applied for asylum (CIC 2006). In 2000, 1,300 Mexicans applied for asylum in Canada. The number grew to 4,948 in 2006, 8,069 in 2008, and 9,296 in 2009. However, Mexicans' lack of credibility as legitimate refugees was evident in acceptance rates. In the 2000s, the acceptance rate for Mexican refugee claims was low and in constant decline. The number of accepted versus rejected claimants was 322 versus 547 in 2000, 931 versus 1,693 in 2006, and 516 versus 3,382 in 2009 (UNHCR 2001).

The sharp rise in Mexican asylum applications in Canada took place in the context of the development of what Samuel Schmidt (2020) refers to as "authorized crime." This concept captures the constitutive role of the state in what could be seen as distinct "organized" crime and underscores that the narcostate is implicated in the violence that affects everyday citizens and continues with impunity. This violence takes many forms, including abductions for ransom, killings, torture, and disappearances. Disappearances include peasants, children of politicians, municipal authorities, migrants, journalists, human rights defenders, and others. Meanwhile, militarization has increased, along with femicide and the deaths of migrants and others (Martinez 2014; Vogt 2015; Espinal-Enríquez and Larralde 2015; Amnesty International 2024; Human Rights Watch 2023; Badillo Pérez 2024).

The Canadian state has refused to acknowledge systemic violence; the inability and unwillingness of local, regional, or national authorities in Mexico to protect its citizens; and rampant insecurity. Instead, its response to Mexican asylum claims has involved successive deterrence measures combined with limited and controlled acceptance of claimants. It is part of a coordinated hemispheric shift in state migration management that prioritizes securitization and criminalization. Julie Young (2018) proposes the concept of the *Mexico-Canada border* to capture a series of processes organized by Canadian (and Mexican and US) state policies to police Mexico's borders in response to the rising number of refugee claims. These processes began with NAFTA, implemented in 1994, which set off a bordering process that "reconfigured understanding of North America as a political, economic and cultural space" (37). The treaty reregulated trade and created a single North American security zone; in this context, Canadian policies also established a *direct* link between Canadian (national) bordering and Mexico.

The Mexico-Canada border represents a border regime that operates both within and separately from NAFTA. After September 11, 2001, securitization and migration management became particularly entwined, in part because NAFTA failed to address the systemic causes of mobility from Mexico. In response to rising refugee claims in Canada, the Safe Third Country Agreement (STCA), implemented in 2004, required Mexicans (and others) to apply for asylum in the first of the three "safe" NAFTA countries they reached. Mexico was implicitly and explicitly constructed as a safe country in the unitary North American region and Mexico-Canada border regime. Mexicans could apply for asylum only if they reached Canada without first going through the United States, and Canada's immigration and bordering policy was firmly tied to US security concerns and conditions in Mexico.

As Mexican claimants found their way to Canada, the narrative of "illegality" and "criminality" linked to Mexican migrants in the United Stated spread northward and was indiscriminately applied to refugee claimants in Canada (Gilbert 2013, 829). The Canadian state and mainstream media consistently rejected the notion of Mexicans as refugees in need of protection or even as migrants with the right to apply for asylum. During Stephen Harper's Conservative government (2006–15), the discursive figure of the queue-jumping and bogus refugee was recurrent (Reynolds and Hyndman 2021; Villegas 2020a, 2020b). The negative discourse compounded suspicion and increased scrutiny of Mexican claimants (Villegas 2020b) and contributed to their higher rejection rates and ongoing deportability, while they joined the gallery of "most wanted" for seeking asylum on suspicious grounds.[8]

Canada imposed a visa requirement in 2009 to deter Mexican asylum claimants. It remained in place until 2016, a year after the Conservatives lost power. The visa requirement decreased travel to Canada and deterred refugee claims. After rising to 9,296 in 2009, the number of Mexican claims dropped to 1,299 in 2010, after the visa rule was put in place. It remained under 100 in 2013 and 2014 and was just over that (121) in 2015. It climbed slowly to 821 in 2016, the year the visa was lifted, and reached 1,000 the following year. The number of claims continued to rise, reaching 5,950 in 2019 before dropping slightly during the pandemic (5,954 in 2020), then climbing steeply to 18,655 in 2022 (UNHCR 2001). As a result, encounters between Mexican visitors (and others, including international students) and Canadian border officials became and continue to be fraught, as Mexicans perform deservingness to convince officials that they are not potential claimants (Villegas 2020b).

The visa requirement's deterrent effect was not uniform, because of Mexico's preexisting "mixed" migration. The suppression of claims was accompanied by increased entry through other pathways. The visa did not affect the arrival of seasonal agricultural workers, whose numbers increased. It likely complicated travel for international students, NAFTA visa professionals, and immigrants entering Canada through the point system. Nonetheless, Mexicans continued to arrive through these pathways in rising numbers, and the overall number of Mexicans in Canada grew while the visa was in place (Van Haren and Masferrer 2024). This highlights the fact that Mexican refugeeship developed alongside other categories of entry, which undoubtedly compounded suspicion of Mexican claimants. The perception was that if Mexicans could migrate to Canada as workers, immigrants, and students, why should they seek and deserve humanitarian protection?

The Canadian state continued to implement policies to control refugee claims, including those of Mexicans. In 2013, Canada added Mexico to the official list of more than forty designated countries of origin (DCOS). These countries were deemed "safe" and did "not normally produce refugees and respect[ed] human rights and offer[ed] state protection" (IRCC 2013). This designation expedited the processing of refugee claims and provided a bureaucratic rationale for denying protection to "suspicious" or "bogus" claimants from state-designated "safe" countries. The policy was reversed in 2019 after courts found the policy to be inconsistent with the Charter of Rights and Freedoms (IRCC 2019). The DCO status limited access to work permits, appeals, and interim health care, and compounded the deterrent effect of the visa requirement.

In a move echoing the Conservative government's visa response (2009–16), the current Liberal government recently imposed a new visa for Mexicans, effective February 29, 2024. Most Mexicans now need a visitor visa or an electronic travel authorization (eTA) to enter Canada. The new rules make it somewhat easier for those who have held a Canadian visitor visa in the past ten years or who currently hold a US nonimmigrant visa to get a visa (IRCC 2024a). It may be more difficult for newer migrants with less education and fewer networks in Canada to enter as visitors. In any case, the new visa signals the continuation of efforts to deter Mexican claimants attempting to cross the Mexico-Canada border and offers more tools to select "desirable" entrants.

Civil society organizing around Mexican refugeeship differed from the Chilean and Salvadoran cases in terms of actors, institutions, and focus. The fact that Mexican migration has a long-standing history of diverse modalities of entry may be part of the reason for a lack of refugee-focused civil society organizing in Canada or transnationally. More generally, over time, the actors and organizations involved in Chilean and Salvadoran advocacy and support changed as people became active in other arenas, including unions, housing cooperatives, and municipal politics. In the late 1990s, changes in state funding contributed to transformations in the landscape of refugee-related faith-based and human rights organizations and in the settlement sector. Migrant rights activists and social service providers focused on supporting Mexicans in Canada as they navigated the asylum process and their imminent illegalization. This strategic civil society response continues and is not limited to Mexicans; it reflects grassroots, largely urban responses to the systemic production of precarious legal status transitions for *all* migrants who enter Canada without permanent residence (Goldring and Landolt 2022; Goldring et al. 2024b; Migrant Rights Network 2024).

In this context, and with the hegemony of negative discourse against refugee claimants, civil society organizing specifically around Mexican refugeeship has been limited. Important mobilization has focused on education and solidarity regarding human rights violations in Mexico and is typically organized by academics and NGOs such as Amnesty International. Examples include the 2012 "No More Blood" tour of Mexican human rights defenders and a 2015 panel commemorating the 2014 killing of forty-two students in Ayotzinapa (CERLAC 2015).[9] These events included meetings with media and Canadian officials focusing on educating Canadians and improving the situation in Mexico rather than linking it to advocacy for Mexican refugeeship.

State management of Mexican refugeeship has included restricting the entry of Mexicans at the border through visa requirements, rejecting asylum claimants in Canada, and managing the presence of Mexicans in the country through H&C applications.[10] Once they have been rejected as refugees or after a visa has expired, Mexican asylum seekers can apply for permanent residence on H&C grounds. The H&C is the only official mechanism whereby nonstatus migrants, including denied asylum seekers, can apply for permanent residence. In the past, people could make a refugee claim and then, if denied, make an H&C application, and if that was denied, apply again for asylum (Goldring and Landolt 2022). Under amendments to IRPA, that is no longer possible (Atak, Hudson, and Nakache 2018). Both the refugee claim and H&C rest on the discretionary power of adjudicators and on their interpretations of guidelines designed to inform their decision-making process. H&Cs offer the state flexibility and the discretion to "fix" problems, but the process is opaque, and it is difficult to determine acceptance rates (Delisle and Nakache 2022; Alhmidi 2021; Migrant Rights Network 2021). Unlike a refugee claim, the application does not grant access to any social entitlements or a work permit and leaves migrants subject to deportation while the application is in process.

Mexican refugeeship epitomizes the tension identified by Azar Masoumi (2019) between liberal states' notions and policies of humanitarian protection, on one hand, and bureaucratic efforts to control and manage asylum seekers (and other "irregular" migrants) on the other. In the Mexican case, this tension is further complicated by the presence of Mexicans who are not asylum seekers, which may help to explain public and government discourse against suspected "bogus" refugees. The "mixed" migration of Mexicans contributes to the refusal to recognize their refugeeship. In this context, Mexican precarious and differential inclusion is produced at multiple levels, not just locally and nationally but also hemispherically through the Mexico-Canada border and associated trade and securitization agreements and changing visa regimes, and as part of the global refugee regime that criminalizes and tries to erase spontaneous movement (Reynolds and Hyndman 2021; Young 2018; Macklin 2011).

Assembling Latin American Refugeeships and Differential Inclusion

We have presented three overlapping assemblages of refugeeship that vary in terms of reasons for exit, patterns of movement, and modality of border crossing; Canadian policy responses, including selection, processing, and securitization practices; involvement of civil society actors; and the discursive constructions of deservingness negotiated through political contention in relation to protection. They present successive but somewhat overlapping temporalities and differ in the way each has been entangled in Canada's geopolitical priorities. They also demonstrate how the in-land refugee claim process, originally intended to expand access to protection, becomes part of the trigger for exclusionary adjudication (Masoumi 2019) and Canada's enmeshment in a North American militarization and securitization project that also generates overlapping bordering regimes (Young 2018).

Chileans were fleeing persecution and dictatorship; Canadian and Chilean civil society organizations lobbied the Canadian government and were able to shift its initial suspicion of "leftist" exiles, reframing them as deserving protection as resettled refugees. Cold War securitization took the form of processing delays in Chile and individual security checks that often extended for years, even after families had settled in Canada (Aguirre 2014). Salvadorans fleeing civil war experienced a mixed modality of refugeeship that combined refugee resettlement in the region and asylum claims at the US-Canada border. Salvadoran refugee resettlement echoed the political lessons of the Chilean movement. Transnational political solidarity and refugee rights organizations came together to support Salvadorans' struggle for self-determination at home and the right of people to seek asylum abroad. The shift to asylum seeking in Salvadoran refugeeship reflected changes in US immigration policy that pushed Salvadorans northward, and in Canadian refugee policy that allowed asylum claims to be made in Canada. Yet Canada's ambivalent response to autonomous arrivals led to the implementation of bordering restrictions as part of a wider strategy to control claims and migrant autonomy. Salvadorans' mixed modality of entry slowly eroded the deservingness assessment and introduced the specter of the "bogus refugee."

In contrast, Mexican refugeeship has been characterized by negative public discourse, the absence of sustained civil society advocacy, and a complete failure by the state to recognize Mexico as refugee-producing and Mexicans as deserving of protection as refugees. And it takes place in the context of mixed migration that includes Mexicans entering in other categories. As a result, Mexican refugeeship occurs only through in-land asylum claims and H&Cs. Individuals gather information online prior to leaving Mexico, through coincidental encounters online and on the street, or through a small number of nonprofit organizations that work with nonstatus migrants and claimants (Goldring et al. 2024a). Service providers are often the main point of contact between Mexican claimants and civil society actors. At the same time, efforts to claim refuge and subsequent applications for H&C reflect migrants' agency, creativity, and endurance in the face of state-imposed barriers, poor working conditions, and deportability (Goldring and Landolt 2022; Villegas 2020b).

The assessment of refugeeship deservingness determines access to permanent residence and citizenship. In contrast to Chileans in the 1970s and Salvadorans in the 1980s, Mexicans seeking humanitarian protection have consistently been refused the material and discursive recognition of refugeeship by the state and the public. As a result, the majority of Mexicans who enter Canada and make an asylum or H&C application endure a complex legal status trajectory riddled with uncertainty and an inability to plan (Villegas 2014). Their stalled settlement process leads to indefinite periods of precarious work and deportability, with no access to public education, health care, and other services, except via negotiated access and debordering by frontline service providers. These precarious legal status trajectories significantly impact well-being and experiences of recognition, membership, and community, producing differential inclusion.

Over time, Latin American refugeeship has shaped and been shaped by the formation of Canada's refugee determination system. In the process of responding to the Chilean and then Salvadoran refugee crises, Canadian state and nonstate actors began to play a new role in regional and global politics. Refugee policy became a mechanism for the Canadian government to distinguish itself politically from the United States and assert itself in the region (Garcia 2006b; Landolt 2007). Chilean refugeeship in Canada offered a counternarrative that flipped the initial description of leftists who did not deserve protection to one of refugees fleeing persecution as political exiles deserving protection in the wake of the coup against Allende, understood as the undemocratic imposition of a military junta. Salvadoran refugeeship offered a counternarrative of the civil war, with the migration crisis understood as a flight from political violence. However, this view eroded with the autonomous arrival of Salvadorans (and others) at the Canadian border, combined with the emerging processes of rebordering and reregulating through NAFTA and additional securitization, particularly in the wake of September 11, 2001. The Canadian state moved toward a legislated framework for securitizing the border and criminalizing the free movement of human beings.

Mexican refugeeship has been trapped within a framework of securitization and criminalization. The weight of North American securitization and the "Mexico-Canada border," together with the absence of a consistent and widespread counternarrative, leaves them cast as "bogus" claimants who are clogging up and undermining the integrity of the refugee determination system with false claims. At the same time, civil society continues efforts—in the form of legal battles and efforts to create counternarratives—to protect the legal category of asylum and access to it, despite national and global efforts to erase refugees, particularly refugee claimants (Macklin 2011; Reynolds and Hyndman 2021; Macklin 2004). This advocacy is linked to wider mobilizing for migrant rights.

The past two-and-a-half decades have also witnessed transformations in civil society advocacy regarding refugees. This period included the rise (and dissolution) of Latin American and Canadian civil society organizing on behalf of refugees from specific countries and the emergence of migrant rights organizations that advocate for a wide range of precarious-status migrants. Key organizations in Toronto, Montreal, and Vancouver are advocating for status for all in the face of a growing recognition that precarious legal status trajectories and illegalization are possible across all entrance categories (Rivas-Sánchez 2024; Goldring et al. 2024b; Migrant Rights Network 2024). These organizations have shifted their strategies to bring together former agricultural workers, international students, caregivers, and others, regardless of country of origin. Meanwhile, legal advocates are contesting changes to the Safe Third Country Agreement and the closing of land borders. And migrants continue to find ways to escape violence, whether it is recognized as producing refugees or not.

Over the past decade, geopolitics and global preferences for managing migration through resettlement rather than by accepting refugee claims from "irregular" migrants have also transformed Canada's humanitarian policy. The government's recent closure of the entire southern border as part of the latest legal struggle surrounding the STCA (Tasker 2023) brought into sharper relief Canada's efforts to seal porous borders and fill loopholes. Canadian discourse has focused on the presumably uncontentious deservingness of refugees from Afghanistan, Syria, and now Ukraine. While providing relatively small-scale and controlled resettlement for Colombians and Venezuelans (IRCC 2024b), Canada supports initiatives to keep the great majority of migrants from Latin America (understood as potential asylum claimants) *in* Latin America (IRCC 2023).

Conclusion

Our analysis of these three cases of Latin American refugeeship in Canada shows how the Canadian border regime has been assembled dynamically, by multiple actors and institutions engaged in a range of contentious bordering practices, within, at, and beyond the national borders. Classification struggles between the Canadian state, transnational and national instances of civil society, and migrants have produced changing configurations of who is included, where, how, and when. This has taken place in the context of changing discourses of deservingness and suspicion. In the 1970s, the protection of groups of fairly clear-cut "worthy refugees" through *resettlement* changed to a mixed and somewhat contested mode of protection that included ongoing resettlement and the resettlement of people in emergency situations, as well as mechanisms for granting asylum to people making refugee *claims* in Canada or at the border. The distinction between resettlement and seeking asylum has significant implications. Resettled refugees arrive as permanent residents, while refugee claimants undergo a temporally indefinite and discretionary adjudication process that may result in illegalization. The H&C offers a potential and discretionary "fix," but the outcome is also uncertain. Thus, refugeeship is merged with humanitarian concerns in and outside Canada, and humanitarian mechanisms are used to selectively admit people into the status of permanent residence on H&C grounds.

The history of these three cases demonstrates the importance of contention between the Canadian state and transnational and national civil society and of changes in the dynamics of mobility from Latin America. Chilean refugeeship was shaped by a strong civil society that mobilized local and transnational networks to influence the state toward the recognition and inclusion of a specified group. In the case of Salvadorans during the civil war, there was also a strong civil society able to build on an earlier social infrastructure of transnational advocacy to support the formation of new social networks that could facilitate the movement of refugee-seeking Salvadorans to Canada. However, Salvadorans' changing mobilities toward in-land asylum and the *Singh* decision, which ensured every migrant had a legal right to make an asylum application, created a backlog and a sharpened neurosis about border integrity. This eroded the deservingness narrative previously associated with Salvadoran refugeeship. In the Mexican case, many things have changed: the landscape of civil society, the Canadian state's approach to migration management, and Canada's relationship to continental and hemispheric border politics. One tragic result of these changes is that in-land asylum claims and the H&C process have become the only avenues for the protection of Mexicans fleeing violence; another is that the demand to be seen as rights-bearing subjects always operates in a context of suspicion.

Our analysis reveals the complexity and layering of the Canadian border regime, and the ways it has become entangled with other border regimes, particularly the North American, Mexico-Canada, and hemispheric border regimes. These juridically, geographically, and temporally distinct but overlapping regimes situated Canada as a player in a hemispheric and transnational human rights and humanitarian bordering process starting in the early 1970s that included refugee resettlement from Chile, El Salvador, and other countries in the hemisphere. The extraterritorial dimension of Canada's humanitarian bordering added an in-land dimension in the mid-1980s. The geographic orientation, actors and institutions, and modality of refugeeship changed when Canadian humanitarian protection appeared to expand with the possibility of making a refugee claim in Canada. This opening was accompanied by the expansion of inland bordering through the establishment of the refugee determination bureaucracy, which ensured discretionary state control of the selection of humanitarian cases, and the development of the H&C as a "fix" for illegalization that has also become part of the protection system.

Canada's humanitarian bordering was multiplying, consistent with broader trends in the multiplication of borders. Latin American refugee protection in Canada was decentered as protection was reoriented through a shift in refugee resettlement from other continents. At the same time, Latin American refugeeship continued to be restricted through refugee claims, changing visa requirements, and securitization and biometrics; variable and unpredictable treatment by the refugee system; subsequent uncertain (in)humanitarian incorporation through the back door "fix" of H&Cs; and deportability.

The contraction of Latin American refugeeship evident in the Mexican case must be understood in relation to Canada's changing and layered bordering in the North American and hemispheric context. NAFTA set the stage for a security perimeter between the "three amigos" and ensured that Canada's migration control policies would operate in a manner consistent with the construction of a shared political and economic zone. The realities of Mexico's state-authorized violence could not be recognized within this framework, which contributed to policies that created the space of the Canada-Mexico border as a border regime nested within yet also overlapping the North American border regime.

The evolving history of Latin American refugeeships in Canada thus demonstrates temporally distinct phases, from refugee resettlement through refugee claims making. The most recent example of Mexican refugeeship is not unique but part of broader hemispheric and global shifts in the control of human mobility. In this context, the governance of "irregular" and spontaneous migration will continue to involve efforts to manage people escaping violence and insecurity in ways that go unrecognized through humanitarian frameworks.

NOTES

The authors appreciate comments from Soledad Álvarez Velasco and Nicholas De Genova on an earlier draft of this chapter.

1. The "work of status" refers to the unpaid work that migrants with forms of precarious status devote to trying to obtain secure status. This work may vary by setting; normally it involves time, resources, information gathering, filling out applications (that may or may not result in secure status), gathering supporting documents, and performing deservingness or eligibility. See Chauvin and Garcés-Mascareñas 2014; Villegas 2020b.

2. Canada's history as a British and French settler colony with ongoing Commonwealth ties has also framed immigration policies. This is evident in the persistence of racialized logics of empire in which temporary migration is consistently racialized as nonwhite (Sharma 2006).

3. The 1985 decision in *Singh v. Minister of Employment and Immigration* established the right of all persons in Canada to make a refugee claim; the Immigration and Refugee Board (IRB) was established in 1989. Scholars note that the refugee determination system was not ready for the number of claims (Garcia 2006a). Subsequent tensions between humanitarian priorities and a bureaucratic agenda, they argue, established the pattern of classification struggles and bordering through in-land refugee determination (Masoumi 2019), a discretionary process that produces acceptance rates that vary by adjudicator (Rehaag 2012).

4. A convention refugee is an individual who meets the criteria outlined in the 1951 United Nations Convention Relating to the Status of Refugees. A convention refugee is defined as a person who has a well-founded fear of being persecuted due to reasons of race, religion, nationality, membership in a particular social group, or political opinion; is outside their country of nationality; and is unable or unwilling to avail themselves of the protection of that country. An asylum seeker is an individual seeking international protection whose refugee status has not yet been determined.

5. The government has expanded ad hoc avenues for temporary and nonstatus migrants to access permanent residence, but these are numerically insignificant and outside the scope of this chapter (Goldring and Landolt 2021).

6. There are several reasons for this response to IRCA: First, many Salvadorans did not qualify for the act's regularization scheme, because of their more recent arrival or lack of qualified employment. Second, Salvadorans and other Central Americans faced an exclusionary asylum system in the United States, evident in extremely low recognition rates (Hamilton et al. 1988). Third, unlike most undocumented Mexicans in the United States, a growing number of Salvadorans had personal networks as well as connections to the "migration infrastructure" that acted as an overground railroad taking Salvadorans to Canada (Bezelberger 2011).

7. Violence and insecurity in Mexico began to expand during the Reagan-era War on Drugs, which effectively relocated drug production and distribution away from the Andean region to Mexico, where President Felipe Calderón's (2006–12) drug war escalated cartel competition and violence (Rosen and Zepeda Martínez 2015).

8. This category included Roma from the Czech Republic, who were included under the visa requirement imposed on Mexicans in 2009, and "spontaneous" arrivals by sea (Hier and Greenberg 2002).

9. The No More Blood tour was organized by six universities and Amnesty International (CERLAC 2015).

10. Detention and deportation are also part of the toolbox for managing presence through removal. On deportations, see Van Haren and Masferrer 2024.

REFERENCES

Adelman, Howard. 1983. "Refugees in Central America." *Refuge: Canada's Journal on Refugees* 3 (2): 1–23.

Aguirre, Carmen. 2014. *Something Fierce: Memoirs of a Revolutionary Daughter*. Toronto: Vintage Canada.

Alhmidi, Maan. 2021. "Canada Refusing More Immigration on Humanitarian, Compassionate Grounds: Data." *Global News* (Vancouver), July 14. https://globalnews.ca/news /8026341/canada-immigration-humanitarian-compassionate-undocumented-migrants/.

Amnesty International. 2024. "Mexico: Rushing Headfirst into an Abyss of Human Rights?: Amnesty International Submission to the 45th Session of the UPR Working Group." https://www.amnesty.org/en/documents/amr41/6992/2023/en/.

Atak, Idil, Graham Hudson, and Delphine Nakache. 2018. "The Securitisation of Canada's Refugee System: Reviewing the Unintended Consequences of the 2012 Reform." *Refugee Survey Quarterly* 37 (1): 1–24.

Badillo Pérez, Oscar. 2024. "Violence in Mexico: Organized or Authorized Crime?" *Revista CISAN* 121:7–9.

Baker, Tom, and Pauline McGuirk. 2017. "Assemblage Thinking as Methodology: Commitments and Practices for Critical Policy Research." *Territory, Politics, Governance* 5 (4): 425–42.

Basok, Tanya. 1993. *Keeping Heads Above Water: Salvadorean Refugees in Costa Rica*. Montreal: McGill-Queen's University Press.

Basok, Tanya, Luin Goldring, Patricia Landolt, Fernando Mata, and Paloma E. Villegas. 2022. "Latin American Migration to Canada: Understanding Socially Differentiated Inclusions." In *The Routledge History of Modern Latin American Migration*, edited by Andreas E. Feldmann, Xóchitl Bada, Jorge Durand, and Stephanie Schütze, 261–74. New York: Routledge.

Basok, Tanya, and Martha Rojas Wiesner. 2018. "Precarious Legality: Regularizing Central American Migrants in Mexico." *Ethnic and Racial Studies* 41 (7): 1274–93.

Basok, Tanya, and Alan Simmons. 1993. "A Review of the Politics of Canadian Refugee Selection." In *The International Refugee Crisis: British and Canadian Responses*, edited by Vaughan Robinson, 171–88. Hampshire, UK: Macmillan.

Bissett, Joseph. 1987. "Canada's Refugee Determination System and the Effect of U.S. Immigration Law." In *In Defense of the Alien*, vol. 10, edited by Lydio F. Tomasi, 57–64. New York: Center for Migration Studies.

Bezelberger, Gavin R. 2011. "Off the Beaten Track, on the Overground Railroad: Central American Refugees and the Organizations That Helped Them." *Legacy* 11 (1): 17–34. https://opensiuc.lib.siu.edu/cgi/viewcontent.cgi?article=1009&context=legacy.

Casas-Cortés, Maribel, Sebastian Cobarrubias, Nicholas De Genova, Glenda Garelli, Giorgio Grappi, Charles Heller, Sabine Hess, Bernd Kasparek, Sandro Mezzadra, Brett Neilson, Irene Peano, Lorenzo Pezzani, John Pickles, Federico Rahola, Lisa Riedner, Stephan Scheel, and Martina Tazzioli. 2015. "New Keywords: Migration and Borders." Special issue, *Cultural Studies* 29 (1): 55–87.

CERLAC (Centre for Research on Latin America and the Caribbean). 2015. "Education and Mobilization in Contested Mexico: Situating Ayotzinapa." March 18. Uploaded to YouTube, March 28, 2025, by LeftStreamed. https://www.youtube.com/playlist?list=PLhiXBRrj94PeiRyBRo9s4XSSTrfUgssK2.

Chauvin, Sébastien, and Blanca Garcés-Mascareñas. 2014. "Becoming Less Illegal: Deservingness Frames and Undocumented Migrant Incorporation." *Sociology Compass* 8:422–32.

CIC (Citizenship and Immigration Canada). 2006. "2005 Facts and Figures—Immigration Overview: Permanent and Temporary Residents." Ottawa.

Dauvergne, Catherine. 2009. *Making People Illegal: What Globalization Means for Migration and Law*. New York: Cambridge University Press.

Delisle, Anthony, and Delphine Nakache. 2022. "Humanitarian and Compassionate Applications: A Critical Look at Canadian Decision-Makers' Assessment of Claims from 'Vulnerable' Applicants." *Laws* 11 (3): 40. https://doi.org/10.3390/laws11030040.

Diab, Suha. 2015. "Fear and (In)Security: The Canadian Government's Response to the Chilean Refugees." *Refuge: Canada's Journal on Refugees* 31 (2): 51–61.

Dirks, Gerald E. 1995. *Controversy and Complexity: Canadian Immigration Policy During the 1980s*. Montreal: McGill-Queen's University Press.

Dubois, Danielle Jacqueline. 2014. "Representing Refugees: Canadian Newspapers' Portrayals of Refugees of El Salvador's Civil War, 1980–1992." Master's thesis, University of Manitoba.

Elcioglu, Emine Fidan. 2020. *Divided by the Wall: Progressive and Conservative Immigration Politics at the US-Mexico Border*. Oakland: University of California Press.

Espinal-Enríquez, Jesús, and Hernán Larralde. 2015. "Analysis of México's Narco-War Network (2007–2011)." *PLOS ONE* 10 (5): e0126503. https://doi.org/10.1371/journal.pone.0126503.

Ferris, Elizabeth. 1987. *The Central American Refugees*. New York: Praeger Press.

Garcia, Maria Cristina. 2006a. "Canada: A Northern Refuge for Central Americans." *Migration Information Source*, April 1. https://www.migrationpolicy.org/article/canada-northern-refuge-central-americans.

Garcia, Maria Cristina. 2006b. *Seeking Refuge: Central American Migration to Mexico, the United States, and Canada*. Berkeley: University of California Press.

Gilbert, Liette. 2013. "The Discursive Production of a Mexican Refugee Crisis in Canadian Media and Policy." *Journal of Ethnic and Migration Studies* 39 (5): 827–43.

Goldring, Luin. 2022. "Precarious Legal Status Trajectories as Method, and the Work of Legal Status." *Citizenship Studies* 26 (4–5): 460–70.

Goldring, Luin, Carolina Berinstein, and Judith K. Bernhard. 2009. "Institutionalizing Precarious Migratory Status in Canada." *Citizenship Studies* 13 (3): 239–65.

Goldring, Luin, and Patricia Landolt. 2012. "The Impact of Precarious Legal Status on Immigrants' Economic Outcomes." IRPP: Institute for Research in Public Policy. October 23. https://on-irpp.org/3qRuSUJ.

Goldring, Luin, and Patricia Landolt. 2021. "Status for All: Pathways to Permanent Residency in Canada Need to Include Every Migrant." *The Conversation*, April. https://theconversation.com/status-for-all-pathways-to-permanent-residency-in-canada-need-to-include-every-migrant-157855.

Goldring, Luin, and Patricia Landolt. 2022. "From Illegalised Migrant Toward Permanent Resident: Assembling Precarious Legal Status Trajectories and Differential Inclusion in Canada." *Journal of Ethnic and Migration Studies* 48 (1): 33–52. https://doi.org/10.1080/1369183X.2020.1866978.

Goldring, Luin, Patricia Landolt, Jana Borras, Nira Elgueta, Sara Hormozinejad, and Sarah Marshall. 2024a. "Multiple Jeopardy: Impacts of the COVID-19 Pandemic on Non-Status Families and Workers in the GTA." Citizenship and Employment Precarity (York University, Toronto). https://cep.info.yorku.ca/fcj-cep-covid-19-project.

Goldring, Luin, Patricia Landolt, Marie-Pier Joly, and Salina Abji. 2024b. "Hidden in Plain Sight: Precarious Legal Status Trajectories and Their Long-Term Consequences." Citizenship and Employment Precarity (York University, Toronto). https://cep.info.yorku.ca/files/2024/05/CEP-Hidden-in-Plain-Sight_12022024.pdf?x24645.

Hamilton, Nora, J. Frieden, L. Fuller, and M. Pastor. 1988. *Crisis in Central America: Regional Dynamics and U.S. Policy in the 1980s*. Boulder, CO: Westview Press.

Hanff, George. 1979. "Decision Making Under Pressure: A Study of the Admittance of Chilean Refugees by Canada." North/South Institute.

Hellerstein, Erica. 2023. "When Your Body Becomes the Border." *Coda*, June 7. https://www.codastory.com/authoritarian-tech/us-immigration-surveillance/.

Hier, Sean P., and Joshua Greenberg. 2002. "Constructing a Discursive Crisis: Risk, Problematization, and Illegal Chinese in Canada." *Ethnic and Racial Studies* 25 (3): 490–513.

Human Rights Watch. 2023. "Mexico. Events of 2022." https://www.hrw.org/world-report/2023/country-chapters/mexico.

IRCC (Immigration Refugees and Citizenship Canada). 2013. "Archived—Backgrounder—Designated Countries of Origin." Government of Canada. https://www.canada.ca/en/immigration-refugees-citizenship/news/archives/backgrounders-2012/designated-countries-origin-2.html.

IRCC (Immigration Refugees and Citizenship Canada). 2019. "Canada Ends the Designated Country of Origin Practice." Government of Canada. May. https://www.canada.ca/en/immigration-refugees-citizenship/news/2019/05/canada-ends-the-designated-country-of-origin-practice.html.

IRCC (Immigration, Refugees and Citizenship Canada). 2023. "Details on Transfer Payment Programs. Actual Spending of $5 Million or More." Government of Canada. https://www.canada.ca/en/immigration-refugees-citizenship/corporate/publications-manuals/departmental-performance-reports/2023/details-transfer-payment-programs.html.

IRCC (Immigration Refugees and Citizenship Canada). 2024a. "Changes to Electronic Travel Authorization (eTA) and Visitor Visa Requirements for Mexican Citizens." Government of Canada. https://www.canada.ca/en/immigration-refugees-citizenship/campaigns/eta-work-visa-mexico.html#eligible.

IRCC (Immigration Refugees and Citizenship Canada). 2024b. "Temporary Public Policy to Facilitate Issuance of Permanent Resident Visas to Certain Colombian, Haitian, and Venezuelan Nationals with Family in Canada." Government of Canada. https://www.canada.ca/en/immigration-refugees-citizenship/corporate/publications-manuals/operational-bulletins-manuals/service-delivery/temporary-pr-visa-colombian-haitian-venezuelan-family.html.

Khandor, Erika, Jean McDonald, Peter Nyers, and Cynthia Wright. 2004. "The Regularization of Non-Status Immigrants in Canada, 1960–2004: Past Policies, Current Perspectives, Active Campaigns." Status Campaign, Access Alliance. https://accessalliance.ca/wp-content/uploads/2018/06/Regularization-of-Non-Status.pdf.

Kowalchuk, Lisa. 1999. "Salvadorans." Edited by R. P. Magocsi. *Encyclopaedia of Canada's Peoples*. Toronto: University of Toronto Press.

Landolt, Patricia. 1993. "Chilean Immigration to Canada, 1973–1990s." Report. Toronto: York University.

Landolt, Patricia. 2007. "The Institutional Landscapes of Salvadoran Refugee Migration: Transnational and Local Views from Los Angeles and Toronto." In *Organizing the Transnational: Labour, Politics, and Social Change*, edited by Luin Goldring and Sailaja V. Krishnamurti, 191–205. Vancouver: University of British Columbia Press.

Landolt, Patricia. 2017. "Immigration, Precarious Noncitizenship, and the Changing Landscape of Work." In *Immigration and the Future of Canadian Society*, edited by Robert Brym, 66–82. Oakville, Ontario: Rock's Mills Press.

Landolt, Patricia. 2023. "Role of Contexts and Political Culture in Political Incorporation: A Case Study of Chilean Migration to Toronto." In *Selected Topics in Migration Studies*, edited by Frank D. Bean and Susan K. Brown, 103–11. Cham, Switzerland: Springer. https://doi.org/10.1007/978-3-031-19631-7_16.

Landolt, Patricia, and Luin Goldring. 2010. "Political Cultures and Transnational Social Fields: Chilean, Colombian, and Canadian Activists in Toronto." *Global Networks* 10 (4): 443–66.

Landolt, Patricia, and Luin Goldring. 2016. "Assembling Noncitizenship Through the Work of Conditionality." *Citizenship Studies* 19 (8): 853–69.

Landolt, Patricia, Luin Goldring, and Judith Bernhard. 2011. "Agenda Setting and Immigrant Politics: The Case of Latin Americans in Toronto." *American Behavioral Scientist* 55 (9): 1235–66.

Lujan, Omar. 2021. "The 'Other' Mexicans: Transnational Citizenship and Mexican Middle Class Migration in Toronto, Canada." PhD diss., Toronto Metropolitan University (formerly Ryerson University). https://rshare.library.torontomu.ca/articles/thesis/The_Other_Mexicans_Transnational_Citizenship_And_Mexican_Middle_Class_Migration_In_Toronto_Canada/14660442.

Macklin, Audrey. 2004. "Disappearing Refugees: Reflections on the Canada-US Safe Third Country Agreement." *Columbia Human Rights Law Review* 36:365.

Macklin, Audrey. 2011. "Using Law to Make Refugees Disappear." Centre for Refugee Studies, York University. Posted to YouTube, September 21, by refugeesearch. http://www.youtube.com/watch?v=8YqE0NuUE08.

Magocsi, Paul Robert. 1999. "Chile." *Encyclopaedia of Canada's Peoples*. Toronto: University of Toronto Press.

Martinez, Hepzibah Munoz. 2014. "Criminal Violence and Social Control." *NACLA Report on the Americas* 47 (1): 35–36.

Masoumi, Azar. 2019. "The Paradox of Refugee Protection in Canada: Law and Bureaucratic Politics of Efficiency." PhD diss., York University. https://yorkspace.library.yorku.ca/xmlui/handle/10315/37351.

Mata, Fernando. 2022. "The Immigrant Waves from Latin America to Canada: A Look at Immigration and Census Statistics." Paper presented at Women, Gender, and Intersectionality in the Lusophone World conference, June 29 to July 2, Ponta Delgada, Azores, Portugal. https://www.researchgate.net/publication/356793900_The_Immigrant_Waves_from_Latin_America_to_Canada_A_Look_at_Immigration_and_Census_Statistics.

McDonald, Jean. 2009. "Migrant Illegality, Nation-Building, and the Politics of Regularization in Canada." *Refuge* 26:65.

Migrant Rights Network. 2021. "Canada Rejected Double the Number of Humanitarian Applications for Immigration in 2020." https://migrantrights.ca/hc202rejections/.

Migrant Rights Network. 2024. "Send a Message: Don't Back Down on Regularization for All!" https://migrantrights.ca/take-action/email/.

Montes, Segundo. 1989. *Refugiados y Repatriados en El Salvador y Honduras*. San Salvador: Universidad Centroamericano Editores.

Mueller, Richard E. 2005. "Mexican Immigrants and Temporary Residents in Canada: Current Knowledge and Future Research." *Migraciones Internacionales* 3 (1): 32–56.

North, Liisa, ed. 2023. *Canada-Chile Solidarity, 1973–1990: Testimonies of Civil Society Action*. Toronto: Novalis.

Peddie, Francis. 2013. "Shaming an Unwilling Host: The Chilean Solidarity Movement, Fall 1973." *Left History: An Interdisciplinary Journal of Historical Inquiry and Debate* 17 (2).

Pratt, Anna. 2005. *Securing Borders: Detention and Deportation in Canada*. Vancouver: University of British Columbia Press.

Rehaag, Sean. 2012. "Judicial Review of Refugee Determinations: The Luck of the Draw?" *Queen's Law Journal* 38 (1): 1–58.

Reitz, Jeffrey G., and Melissa H. Jasso. 2021. "Mexican Migration to Canada: Trends and Prospects." In *Migration and Borders in North America: Views from the Twenty-First Century*, edited by Kiran Banerjee and Craig Damian Smith. Montreal: McGill-Queen's University Press.

Reynolds, Johanna, and Jennifer Hyndman. 2021. "Shifting Grounds of Asylum in Canadian Public Discourse and Policy." In *Refugee States: Critical Refugee Studies*, edited by Vinh Nguyen and Thy Phu. Toronto: University of Toronto Press. https://utorontopress.com/ca/refugee-states-3.

Rivas-Sánchez, Eloy. 2024. "Unruly Political Uprisings: Migrant Justice Activism in Canada and the United States." In *Migration Governance in North America*, edited by Kiran Banerjee and Craig Damian Smith. Montreal: McGill-Queen's University Press.

Rosen, Jonathan Daniel, and Roberto Zepeda Martínez. 2015. "La Guerra Contra El Narcotráfico en México: Una Guerra Perdida." *Revista Reflexiones*, no. 1, 153–68.

Schmidt, Samuel. 2020. *Crimen Autorizado: La Estrecha Relación Entre El Estado y El Crimen*. Mexico City: Random House (Kindle edition).

Schwinghamer, Steven, and Jan Raska. 2020. *Pier 21: A History*. Ottawa: University of Ottawa Press.

Sharma, Nandita. 2006. *Home Economics: Nationalism and the Making of "Migrant Workers" in Canada*. Toronto: University of Toronto Press.

Simalchik, Joan G. 1993. "Part of the Awakening: Canadian Churches and Chilean Refugees, 1970–1979." Masters thesis, University of Toronto.

Statistics Canada. 2022. "2021 Census: Immigrant Status and Period of Immigration by Place of Birth and Citizenship—Canada, Provinces and Territories, and Census Metropolitan Areas with Parts." Census of Canada. Table: 98-10-0302-01. https://www150 .statcan.gc.ca/t1/tbl1/en/tv.action?pid=9810030201.

Stumpf, Juliet. 2006. "The Crimmigration Crisis: Immigrants, Crime, and Sovereign Power." *American University Law Review* 56: 367–419.

Tasker, John Paul. 2023. "Supreme Court Upholds Agreement That Lets Canada Send Refugees Back to U.S." *CBC News*, June 16. https://www.cbc.ca/news/politics/supreme -court-ruling-safe-third-country-agreement-1.6878870.

UNHCR (United Nations High Commissioner for Refugees). 2001. "Data Finder, Asylum Seekers 2001–2004." *UNHCR*. https://www.unhcr.org/refugee-statistics /download/?url=VtjdE1.

Van Haren, Ian, and Claudia Masferrer. 2024. "Visitor Visa Policy Changes and Mexico-Canada Migration." *Journal of Immigrant and Refugee Studies* 22 (1): 22–36.

Villegas, Paloma E. 2014. "'I Can't Even Buy a Bed Because I Don't Know If I'll Have to Leave Tomorrow': Temporal Orientations Among Mexican Precarious Status Migrants in Toronto." *Citizenship Studies* 18 (3–4): 277–91.

Villegas, Paloma E. 2020a. "Flexible and Assembled Bordering Practices for Mexicans Travelling to Canada." *International Migration* 58 (5): 69–86. https://doi.org/10.1111 /imig.12688.

Villegas, Paloma E. 2020b. *North of El Norte: Illegalized Mexican Migrants in Canada*. Vancouver: University of British Columbia Press.

Villegas, Paloma E., Patricia Landolt, Ranu Basu, Victoria Freeman, Joseph Hermer, and Bojana Videkanic. 2021. "Contesting Settler-Colonial Accounts: Temporality, Migration, and Place-Making in Scarborough, Ontario." *Studies in Social Justice* 14 (2): 321–51.

Vogt, Wendy. 2015. "The War on Drugs Is a War on Migrants: Central Americans Navigate the Perilous Journey North." *Landscapes of Violence* 3 (1): article 2.

Young, Julie E. E. 2018. "The Mexico-Canada Border: Extraterritorial Border Control and the Production of 'Economic Refugees.'" *International Journal of Migration and Border Studies* 4 (1–2): 35–50.

Zolberg, Aristide R., Astri Suhrke, and Sergio Aguayo. 1989. *Escape from Violence: Conflict and the Refugee Crisis in the Developing World*. New York: Oxford University Press.

2

Mobility Control Regime and Clandestine Practices in the US-Mexico Border

Laura Velasco Ortiz

This chapter builds on the perspective of the global regime of mobility control (Papadopoulos, Stephenson, and Tsianos 2008; Glick Schiller 2021; Shamir 2005; Mezzadra and Neilson 2013; Domenech and Dias 2020) and on critical views of the relationship between the state and illegal but socially legitimate practices (Heyman and Smart 1999; Abraham and van Schendel 2005) to analyze all the practices of clandestine mobility that take place in the margins of legality. Josiah Heyman and Alan Smart (1999) argue that the social sciences possess more robust theoretical and methodological tools than the legal field for observing and analyzing the complexities of state formation. They emphasize that this insight is essential for understanding the mobility practices that arise in everyday life and exist at the margins of legality. Indeed, approaching and understanding mobility practices from the perspective of border control regimes allows us to go beyond the idea of a totalizing and cohesive state (Rumford 2012).

The main argument of this chapter is that borders are places where surveillance and mobility control become crucial for the sovereignty of nation-states, which, however, are also places of clandestine practices as expressions of bordering processes. The term *clandestine practices* refers to strategies and tactics employed to elude surveillance, along with mobility controls resorted to not only by labor migrants and asylum seekers but also by border residents. The fragmented view of such mobilities is partly the outcome of categories traditionally used in migration studies. The study of border mobility cannot exclude displacements that respond to drug and human smuggling; cross-border mobility is an opportunity, a resource for survival, and an expression of spatial creativity. Moreover, analytical fragmentation impedes understanding practices of transit and border crossing supported through moral and social legitimacy, practices that are indifferent to or go against the legal framework of the state (Velasco Ortiz 2016).

The first part of this chapter is a theoretical discussion based on two elements of the human mobility regime: border control and clandestine practices. Paying attention to everyday mobility practices, particularly those whose practitioners seek to escape from the power of the state, provides the social sciences with a critical vantage point of the state's logic from which to study the phenomenon of mobility control. While border control has historically been a state prerogative, clandestine border crossing is the opposing force of the borderwork process (Rumford 2012). The second part of the chapter analyzes the clandestine practices of four sorts of mobilities in the Mexico-US region: commuters, long-distance migrants, asylum seekers, and drug smugglers. The argument is that the mobility regime at this border region involves, at the same time, invisibility and illegality, in apparently detached cross-border practices. The chapter concludes with main findings.

Human Mobility Regime, Border Control, and Clandestine Practices

Mobility regime is a frequently used term in the migration and border studies literature. Nevertheless, it is commonly used with a vague meaning or taken for granted. Only sometimes are "everyday practices in crossing the border" conceptualized as part of such a mobility regime. In order to build a straightforward conceptual approach, this section considers two contradictory bordering processes (Rumford 2012): border control and clandestine practices.

The border regime control approach reflects a recurring critique of the state-centered nature of migration policies. Ronen Shamir (2005) defines a *mobility regime* as an epistemological, technical, and institutional expression of global economic policies. These three dimensions are essential contributions to this conceptual definition, in that they focus attention on the construction of migrants as a universal danger, not as a functional anomaly but intrinsic to the spatial dialectic of globalization. From this viewpoint, the border's mission is to preserve inequalities through the novel, analytically suspicious mechanism that comes from a complex interaction between natives and migrants.

Drawing on Shamir's definition, Nina Glick Schiller (2021) analyzes institutional practices of border control and conceives of a mobility regime as a network of states, institutions, officials, and individual actors that connect and manage populations on the move inside and beyond specific states. Concurring with the Foucauldian notion of the regime, Glick Schiller and Noel Salazar (2012) point out: "The term 'regime' calls attention to the role of individual States and changing international regulatory and surveillance administrations that affect individual mobility. At the same time, this term reflects a notion of governmentality and hegemony with constant struggles to understand, query, embody, celebrate and transform categories of similarity, difference, belonging, and strangeness" (7).

Regarding mobility, governmentality entails a consensus about who can move and in what direction. It is an order that citizens and noncitizens accept. Documents, walls, gatekeepers, and international agreements to contain South–North mobility are parts of this global social order (Torpey 2000; Horton 2020). The institutional perspective on mobility control has documented the increase of surveillance and deterring infrastructure, not only in border zones but also within countries and vast continental regions. Eduardo Domenech and Gustavo Dias (2020) argue that the current border conflicts in Latin America have arisen from international and regional border control policies.

Sandro Mezzadra and Brett Neilson (2013) go further and define a border control regime as a complex and heterogeneous assembly of institutions, logistics, *practices*, and procedures to domesticate the life and labor of mobile subjects under the continuous production and circulation of capital. In an innovative view, they include militarism, humanitarianism, and pastoral practices, distancing their definition from Shamir's assumption that the human rights narrative opposes mobility regimes. Migrants' bordering practices are essential to Mezzadra's work (2012), which criticizes the approaches to studying migration that incorporate categories imposed by the state. Instead, he proposes using perspectives and categories of the migrants themselves, concentrating on their ability to re-create and resist forces that control mobility.

As an alternative theoretical approach, the from-below, migrants' and asylum seekers' perspective considers border regimes as a result, in part, of mobility practices. That is to say, the everyday practices of mobility and the border are constitutive elements of such a regime and appear as a reaction or resistance. For Dimitris Papadopoulos, Niamh Stephenson, and Vassilis Tsianos (2008), "the concept of regime allows us to investigate the relation between the actions of migrants and those of control agents without invoking a simplistic relation between subjects (cast as agents of control) and objects (understood as migrants or individuals who assist migrants) of migration" (164).

Migrants and asylum seekers are subject to the mobility regime and, at the same time, agents who construct it. This chapter puts forward clandestine mobility, particularly border crossing, as an empirical expression of ordinary people's borderwork (Rumford 2012). As Chris Rumford (2012) underscores, the role ordinary people play in the construction of borders is underrepresented in border literature. In his view, a *multiperspectival* study of borders can avoid privileging the state's point of view. Borders serve not only the state but also ordinary people. While bordering is a process built by various actors, including the state, *borderwork* refers to the practices of ordinary people through which borders are produced. As Rumford (2012) explains:

> The importance of borderwork is that it causes us to rethink the issue of who is responsible for making, dismantling, and shifting borders rather than relying upon the assumption that this is exclusively the business of the State. It also introduces us to a world of bordering which is not governed by consensus: here, there is no guarantee that the borders constructed by border workers will be recognized by everyone. (897)

The contribution of Rumford (2012) and colleagues (Cooper and Tinning 2021) sheds light on the analysis of some border practices, such as those that involve crossing without documents or seeking asylum, which necessarily confronts the role the state plays in controlling cross-border mobilities. The notion of clandestinity comprises all types of border mobilities that seek to escape surveillance, not only by the state but also from criminal or even humanitarian agents. David Spener (2009) has proposed an empirical concept of clandestinity and defines it as surreptitious mobility strategies used to overcome a lack of documents or permission to cross the border. In a comprehensive vision of borderwork, clandestine border crossing includes practices such as using tourist visas or borrowed documents to work in the United States. It also considers the activities of smugglers and drug-dealing employees. Historically, the construction of transborder mobility as illegal has turned long-standing everyday spatial practices into clandestine, criminal ones (Ngai 2004; De Genova 2002). In this chapter, the term *clandestine* takes an ambiguous meaning, as a rebellion against control by state authorities and as a possibility to escape, through invisibility or disobedience, from state surveillance and from other actors who control the territory; it is a radical perspective that defies the postliberal logic of capitalism. Clandestine mobility practices take place in what Papadopoulos, Stephenson, and Tsianos (2008) call a "'third space': the negotiation level between and across segments of interwoven political and economic transnational processes, which are no longer simply intergovernmental but emerge with the instauration of the regime" (164).

Papadopoulos and colleagues (2008, 202) have produced an autonomous migration perspective against the liberal view of agency. In what sense can human mobility be conceptualized as autonomous? The authors (203) use the term *autonomous migration perspective* to refer to the creative force of human beings within the structure. An autonomous perspective implies a sensibility to reread the history of human mobility as facing social control, not just performing as an adaptive labor force or being victimized human beings (203). Nicholas De Genova (2017, 30) points out that "even if borders are deployed to facilitate cross-border mobility (as in the recruitment of 'legal' migrants), migrants remain autonomous subjects, with their aspirations, needs, and desires, which necessarily exceed any regime of immigration and citizenship." As Mezzadra and Neilson (2013) emphasize, migration autonomy may be seen as a form of resistance and struggle against the regime. In this regard, the literature on the mobility regime closely parallels the discussion of illegal practices as part of the state's interstices, ambiguities, and tensions that give rise to struggle and conflict (see Heyman and Smart 1999; Abraham and van Schendel 2005).

The perspective outlined above concurs with frameworks developed in state anthropology (Das and Poole 2004). According to these scholars, individuals establish highly complex relationships with the state, through its agents and institutions, because of its inability to fully govern its population. In its margins and interstices, there is room for the agency of individuals to escape control, as through mobility. Heyman and Smart (1999) offered a way to understand clandestine practices as moral practices that deny legality, in which risky means of action to avoid surveillance and achieve specific objectives are justified by group consensus. With this thesis, Itty Abraham and Willem van Schendel (2005, 31) have distinguished what is illegal from what is illicit: whereas the former assumes the state's political legitimacy, the latter is based on the social legitimacy of a particular community. Cross-border practices are a theoretical and methodological approach to studying the inequality and hierarchization of transnational mobility and the constitution of the border space. Mezzadra and Neilson (2013) state that the border is not only an object of study but also an epistemic standpoint regarding ongoing globalization processes.

The US-Mexico Border and the Mobility Control Regime

The September 11 attacks were the inflection point to militarize the US-Mexico border under a national security policy. The current mobility control regime at the US-Mexico border dates back to the 1990s when border control became a priority for migration policy and when the legal framework for criminalizing the migrant population was produced (D. Martínez, Heyman, and Slack 2020). Ever since, on one hand, the Mexican border has been virtually pushed inside the US due to deportations of Mexican residents (Coleman 2007), while, on the other, US internal migration tensions have moved toward Mexican and Central American borders (Heyman 2012; Rojas and Winton 2018).

As Sarah Horton (2020) suggests, at least three national security bureaucratic inscription mechanisms are relevant to understanding migration policies: (1) criminalization through the legal construction of migrants as undesirable and illegal subjects based on a tight regulatory fabric at federal and local levels, and on a robust anti-immigrant narrative; (2) militarization of the system for the detention and expulsion of migrants, residents, and asylum seekers; and (3) the strengthening of border and surveillance infrastructure, as well as via regional third-country agreements that set up migration dams to contain people who, clandestinely or visibly, head toward the north of the continent.

Militarization appears to be a key aspect of this regime, linked closely to the war industry and security policy. This connection is evident in the increased budgets allocated for infrastructure, technology, and personnel dedicated to surveillance, detection, and expulsion.[1] As Timothy Dunn (2021) points out, however, the gradual militarization of the border has not caused a decrease in clandestine crossings. Detention statistics support that conclusion: Whereas in 2010, there were 447,731 detention events, in 2021, the number grew threefold to 1,659,206 (table 2.1). A plausible explanation for this contradictory fact is put forward by De Genova (2013), who talks about the border as a spectacle, referring to the performative dimension of the border control regime. The spectacle of militarization has become a daily experience for the inhabitants of the Mexican side of the border and for border crossers.

Nevertheless, militarization is not just a spectacle; for border crossers, it has had practical consequences, such as increasing the risk of transit and preventing settlement through criminalization and deportation. Dangerous effects

TABLE 2.1. Detentions Registered by the US Border Patrol at the US-Mexico Border, 2010–2021, by Nationality

Country	Encounters per fiscal year											
	2010	2011	2012	2013	2014	2015	2016	2017	2018	2019	2020	2021
Brazil	601	284	183	274	543	1,267	3,118	2,621	1,504	17,893	6,946	56,735
Colombia	307	217	185	365	233	282	302	196	192	401	295	5,838
Cuba	84	66	40	73	98	106	78	147	74	11,645	9,822	38,139
Ecuador	1,571	1,064	2,226	3,958	4,748	2,556	2,713	1,429	1,495	13,131	11,861	96,092
El Salvador	13,123	10,368	21,903	36,957	66,419	43,392	71,848	49,760	31,369	89,811	16,484	95,930
Guatemala	16,831	17,582	34,453	54,143	80,473	56,691	74,601	65,871	115,722	264,168	47,270	279,033
Haiti	89	36	3	2	2	2	3	57	12	2,046	4,395	45,532
Honduras	12,231	11,270	30,349	46,448	90,968	33,445	52,952	47,260	76,513	253,795	40,191	308,931
India	1,049	2,414	495	949	1,425	2,484	3,480	2,943	8,997	7,675	1,092	2,555
Mexico	396,819	280,580	262,341	265,409	226,771	186,017	190,760	127,938	152,257	166,458	253,118	608,037
Nicaragua	760	520	876	1,389	1,809	1,015	1,298	1,057	3,282	13,309	2,123	49,841
Romania	384	575	901	598	838	396	2,006	433	250	289	266	4,029
Russia	11	16	12	18	12	14	11	8	13	21	24	509
Turkey	15	5	8	24	43	37	72	35	52	57	67	1,366
Venezuela	35	28	28	34	15	23	40	73	62	2,202	1,227	47,752
Other	3,821	2,552	2,870	3,756	4,974	3,606	5,588	4,088	4,785	8,607	5,570	18,889
Total	447,731	327,577	356,873	414,397	479,371	331,333	408,870	303,916	396,579	851,508	400,651	1,659,208

Source: Author's elaboration based on information from US Customs and Border Protection (2020 and 2022).

Note: Only detentions by the US Border Patrol under Title 8 and Title 42 (2020 and 2021) are considered. Returns of inadmissible by the Office of Field Operations are not included. The fiscal year runs from October 1 of the prior year to September 30 of the current one.

are palpable in the conditions of clandestine journeys, which open the door to human smuggling. The smuggling system is part of the mobility regime, working to restrict the autonomy of migrants or asylum seekers. According to a US Customs and Border Protection report (CBP 2001, 2020b), the hiring of smugglers (*polleros*) grew between 80 and 95 percent among undocumented migrants over the previous decade. The recent surge in migrant kidnappings and deaths indicates the positive relationship between increased clandestinity and higher costs and risks. It is no surprise that in 2018, migrant caravans emerged as a way for migrants to protect themselves and decrease mobility costs (Velasco Ortiz and Hernández 2021; Varela Huerta and McLean 2019). After 2001, costs grew depending on the route and border location chosen for the crossing (CBP 2001). For Central Americans, costs have reached US$12,000 per migrant due to the Mexican government's expansion of control at the southern border.

Another adverse effect of the militarization of the border and the criminalization of migrants has taken place in settlement processes in the family separations triggered by the removal of people with longtime residence in the United States, a result of the reclassification of administrative offenses as criminal under changes in the law made in the 1990s and activated a decade later. Rafael Alarcón Acosta and William Becerra's (2012) findings regarding deportees hosted in the largest shelter in Tijuana have demonstrated that 63 percent were deported after being detained for traffic violations and routine police inspections. In 2012, a third of the people detained had been living in the United States for 8.5 years on average, and many of them were 1.5-generation migrants, meaning that they arrived in the United States as children or teenagers (Velasco Ortiz and Coubès 2013; Albicker and Velasco Ortiz 2016; Alarcón Acosta and Becerra 2012).

In conjunction with the criminalizing legal structure, the militarization of the border has not been limited to undocumented migration. It encroached on the international protection system through legislative changes, which, according to various analysts, have undermined the asylum and refugee system, creating entrapment spaces in third countries (Mountz 2020). The Mexico-US border is an example of such consequences for the asylum system; as Didier Fassin (2005) points out, since the nineties, migration policies have considered asylum seekers illegal migrants. The changes in the nationality of arrested individuals in this border region reflect the asylum system's debacle and the regionalization of migratory conflicts, as Domenech and Dias (2020) documented in Latin America. Table 2.1 shows the drop in the flow of Mexican migrants as compared with Central American and Caribbean migrants between 2010 and 2021. For their part, in 2010, countries such as Venezuela, Nicaragua, Ecuador, and Brazil had comparatively little participation, but eleven years later, the numbers from these countries increased to tens of thousands.

The number of migrants and national composition in table 2.1 reflect a turn in border externalization policies with effects on the Mexico-US border, third country for asylum seeker policies, and migrant health policies under COVID-19. Haitian and Central American migration to the Mexico-US border have faced restrictive policies in the past decade. In 2016, after the cancelation of Temporary Protected Status (TPS), about five thousand Haitians arrived in Tijuana from Brazil and Chile, looking for international protection. They opted for the small advantages offered by the family reunification program and humanitarian parole, including being allowed to remain for three years in the United States (Alarcón Acosta and Ortiz Esquivel 2017). In this case, both countries' migration authorities coordinated to manage asylum requests at the northern Mexican border, supported by some shelters in Tijuana. According to the US Department of Homeland Security, only 537 requests were approved for Haitians in 2014, which amounted to only 2 percent of the total number of applicants (Mossaad 2016).

The most crucial policy to externalize migration and asylum requests appeared in 2019. To face the Central American migrant caravans, the Migrant Protection Protocol (MPP; also known as Remain in Mexico) came into force for the first time in the history of these countries. Under this program, Mexico became a third country where asylum seekers were to apply for international protection. They would register on waiting lists (metering), cross the border to appear in courts, and gather papers to attest for credible fear. Between 2019 and 2021, CBP returned 71,000 asylum seekers to Mexico to continue their MPP processes in border cities. As a result, only 1 percent of seekers were granted asylum, and 50 percent were deported (TRAC Immigration 2021).

The fear of COVID-19 contagion led to tightening the border for residents, labor migrants, and asylum seekers. On one hand, the border checkpoints were closed to nonessential visa holders; on the other, in 2019, Title 42, the US Public Health Service Act, was activated to allow the expedited deportation of nearly half a million people to date, mainly Central Americans. Juan Del Monte Madrigal (2021) points out that in 2021, 63 percent of deportations were because of this regulation; for Mexican detainees, the figure was 92 percent (CBP 2022). Del Monte Madrigal (2021) notes that the construction of migrants as sources of infection is not new. Early in the twentieth century, under the Bracero Program, the protocol for entering the United States included the fumigation of workers with DDT, a chemical banned in the United States in 1962 (Sulbarán Lovera 2021). In the pandemic era, the body is a site for mobility regulation and control and is made a mobile border through control technology (Shachar and Mahmood 2021).

At the opposite pole from repression and expulsions, a compassion policy has emerged as a mark of the moral economy of the contemporary biopolitics of migration (Fassin 2005). There is selective humanitarianism in asylum seekers' policies, as Janneth Clavijo, Andrés Pereira, and Lourdes Basualdo (2019) found in studying the categorization of migration policies, differentiating them from humanitarian care in Argentina. According to Fassin (2005), asylum seekers' illegalization has occurred since the nineties.

Humanitarian efforts at the Mexico-US border are complex and involve various actors, with the most significant components being migrant shelters and, more recently, legal-aid organizations. The geography of migrant hospitality influences the routes taken by individuals traveling, either openly or clandestinely, from the southern to the northern border. The US-Mexico border concentrates the highest number of shelters for asylum seekers and migrants in the country. Since 2008, Tijuana has seen a surge in the number of shelters, which have expanded across Mexico since 2015. Large-scale deportations to Mexico, particularly from 2008 onward, have led to the establishment of more shelters, primarily to assist families separated during these deportation processes. According to the latest reviewed data, 86 percent of shelters were created after 2008, providing support as an alternative to these separations. By 2016, the influx of Haitian, Central American, and Mexican asylum seekers prompted significant changes in shelter regulations to address the long wait for asylum seekers' families in border cities (Coubès, Velasco Ortiz, and Contreras 2021) as a result of third-country policies.

Cross-Border Mobilities and Clandestine Practices

The Mexican border is home to 7,869,264 people, most of them concentrated in large cities such as Tijuana, Ciudad Juárez, and Matamoros, neighbors of San Diego, El Paso, and Brownsville, respectively. For this population, border-crossing cards are an everyday topic in conversations with family, friends, and colleagues. Border cards are part of the state eligibility criterion and an indicator of border stratification due to the class selectivity of access (Das and Pool 2004, 9). Early in the twenty-first century, only about 50 percent of border inhabitants had visas (Velasco Ortiz and Contreras 2011).

Transborder interaction intensity arises from formal crossings at the ports of entry, which in 2018 reached 192,903,250—the highest annual number recorded during the 2011–20 period. During 2020, the pandemic effect lowered the number to 106,581,725 crossings, but it seemed to recover in 2021, with 125,846,669 crossings (Bureau of Information Statistics 2022).

These big numbers include crossings with improper documents to work as part of clandestine commuter practices. Another type of clandestine cross-border mobility involves crossing without documents through various areas regardless of whether they have walls, such as deserts or riverbeds; this includes climbing over fences or wading through rivers to evade formal control measures. These practices create a spectrum of interactions that include both legal and illegal mobility activities. This spectrum covers a range of issues: family ties, consumption, work, trade, drug trafficking, human smuggling, deportations, and asylum processes.

Inhabitants, either residents or people in transit, adopt transborder mobility practices that do not necessarily abide by the logic of state legality. It is possible to observe border crossings without documents, with false documents, with a visa but no work permit, and even drug smuggling across the border, as means justified by local meanings and practices to survive as well as borderwork, all of which contributes to the production of the border itself.

Unauthorized mobility, either as an organized political action or through clandestine everyday practices, challenges the legitimacy of the state's authority and borders. Transborder mobility is a source of inequality. Heyman (2012, quoting Pallito and Heyman 2008) distinguishes the privileged from the unprivileged in the function of their rights, speed, and risk in mobility. The present study adds to our understanding of the clandestine condition. Violence marks these clandestine practices as an external force imposed on the individuals and as a legitimate means to survive.

As Veena Das and Deborah Poole (2004, 10) have observed, the power of the state is related not only to its territory but also to the bodies found in it. Clandestine practices involve the human body as it goes invisible in vehicles, through the jungle, or on isolated roads—performative simulation, repeating historical know-how, or national identity appearance. A great deal of the mobility regime is the vitality of trafficking networks, which has turned into a mediated clandestinity that threatens the migrants' individual and collective agency. Feasible strategies produce constant vulnerability by subjecting the migrants to kidnapping, smuggling, detention, and deportation (Ruiz 2001; Velasco Ortiz 2016). In short, their invisibility exposes them to the violence of people and drug smuggling, due to state violence, by placing them in liminal legality (Menjívar 2006) and depriving them of their right to protection in transit. Nevertheless, at the same time, that invisibility prevents them from being stopped; in the dialectic between movement and impediments to movement, the boundaries can be observed (see Parker 2020).

In a previous work (Velasco Ortiz 2016), I proposed three types of trans-border mobility strategies that involve specific clandestine practices: long-distance labor mobility without documents, commuter mobility for work, and mobility through the smuggling of drugs and people. In this chapter, a fourth mobility strategy combines visibility and invisibility with group displacements or caravans to cross various borders. It is listed in the metering system to seek asylum under MPP. All these modalities can be seen as the ideal type proposed by Parker (2020, 41). They have in common, explicitly or implicitly, the intention to confront or even destroy state borders.[2]

Crossing the Border as a Labor Commuter with a Tourist Visa

A form of mobility associated with border life is commuting work, which means daily travel from some Mexican border city to the US locality and back. Sergio Chávez (2016) and I (2016) have found that some commuting workers use tourist visas; hence, they are classified as border-crossing card violators (BCCVS). In 2005, BCCVs amounted to between 250,000 and 500,000 individuals, adding to the 4–5.5 million overstayers who extended their authorized stay in the country after legally entering the United States under migration inspection (Pew Research Center 2006). In 2005, 45 percent of unauthorized migration entered with inspected documents, both BCCV and overstayers. There is limited data on the labor use of border-crossing cards. However, given the overwhelming traffic at the border, "if even a minuscule share of these individuals overstayed, they would contribute significantly to the unauthorized population" (Pew Research Center 2006).

Labor commuting has been affected by changes in the border control regime. In 1967, the largest number of labor commuters crossed from Ciudad Juárez, representing 10 percent of the city's employed population. This significant figure highlights the essential role of cross-border mobility in the local economy (Dillman 1970, 493); in addition, the commuters' lives became more difficult after 1993 with Operation Blockade implemented in this city to dissuade undocumented crossings. Alegría (2002) documented that this segment accounted for 8 percent of the economically active population at the border in 2002. By 2020, commuters from Tijuana were about 4 percent of the city's employed population, most of whom were born in the United States (INEGI 2020). Qualitative studies on this topic (Chávez 2016; Orraca 2015; Velasco Ortiz and Contreras 2011; Velasco Ortiz 2016) highlight the negative impacts of heightened border control measures. These include extensive inspections at ports of entry and the implementation of facial recognition technology, which has made daily commuting more challenging for workers. The clandestine practices of visa labor commuters are based on simulation and performance. Elsewhere (Velasco Ortiz 2016, 274–75), I have distinguished two courses of action in the crossing: (a) avoiding repeated interactions with the same migration officer by changing lanes constantly to prevent being recognized as frequent crossers, and (b) pretending to be a consumer, changing one's appearance (dyed light-colored hair, wearing American brands) and having some stories ready for the interrogators—what Chávez (2011, 1331) calls the "masking [of] U.S. occupational identity," which leads to noticeable social creativity so as not to be discovered. It is a negotiation and an everyday struggle for crossers who resort to border-crossing cards. Heyman (2004) underscores the difficulty of these daily negotiations since inspectors are knowledgeable, owing to their cultural background: 74 percent are Chicano, 89 percent grew up in border cities, and 59 percent work in the town where they were born.

Border asymmetry emerges in the labor conditions of this stratum of commuters. According to Orraca (2015), in 2010, commuting workers made US$7.36 per hour, almost US$6 less on average (US$13.03) than workers of Mexican origin who live on the US side of the border. These are the terms of inequality in the border region. Facial recognition surveillance technology makes daily crossings increasingly difficult for this cohort of workers. When the border closed for crossings with nonessential visas due to the pandemic, they temporarily had to resort to other forms of survival.

Crossing the Border Without Documents:
Labor Workers and Asylum Seekers

Over the past two decades, the human consequences of displacements due to violence and climate catastrophes have caught the attention of activists and human rights advocates. A complex and multiactor intervention field has emerged around compassion policies (Fassin 2005; Agnew 2020; Clavijo, Pereira, and Basualdo 2019). Xóchitl Bada and S. Schutz (2019) distinguish military, political, and social violence as the push factors of contemporary migration in Latin America. The Mexico-US border may be seen as a precarious space of unequal mobility due to the accumulation of risky experiences and suffering of those who travel from faraway geographies through the dam system built to contain and surveil migration flows on the Latin American border corridors (Hess 2012, 145). Despite being the most surveilled, the US-Mexico border is the most dangerous in the continent, with 8,609 migrant deaths recorded between 1998 and 2021 (CBP 2020a; IOM

2022), and with the border accounting for 61 percent of the 5,969 disappearances recorded across the continent between 2014 and 2021 (IOM 2021).

Over the past decade, three changes have taken place in migration behavior and affected the mobilities of border cities. These changes have involved national origin, migration motives, and migration dynamics. National origin has become ever more diverse over the past decade: Central Americans, Haitians, and other nationalities added to the significant proportion of Mexican migrants. Labor-related reasons give rise to the search for international protection by asylum seekers due to violence or climate disasters. Finally, traveling in families and organized groups appears as a relevant phenomenon.

The COVID-19 pandemic changed the context of mobility at the border for two reasons: the closing of the border for residents for two years; and mass deportations under Title 42, which enabled sending any migrant who crossed the border without documents back to Mexico on the grounds of health risks. Table 2.1 shows that despite the decreasing presence of Mexicans in comparison with Central Americans up to 2019, during 2020–21, under pandemic expulsion policies, there was an upturn in the number of Mexicans detained to more than half a million, close to the number of mass deportations during the Barak Obama administration. Most deportations in 2020–21 occurred under Title 42, a health policy applied to migration. This section of the chapter presents two types of undocumented mobility strategies analyzed for their clandestine practices: Mexican labor mobility and Central American and Haitian asylum seekers.[3]

Undocumented Mexican Labor Mobility

The Mexican-origin population has had demographic and political relevance ever since the border was redefined in the twenty-first century. In 2017, there were 4.9 million undocumented Mexicans in the United States (López, Passel, and Cohen 2021). Despite the fact that the number of undocumented Mexican individuals had decreased by 50 percent by 2019 (EMIF 2003–2012, in Velasco Ortiz and Coubès 2013; DHS 2020),[4] my colleagues and I noticed a significant increase in the number of Mexicans staying in shelters along the US-Mexico border. In a recent study, we confirmed that this rise was linked to their displacement due to violence. By 2021, Mexicans made up the majority of shelter residents in the cities of Tijuana and Matamoros (Coubès, Velasco Ortiz, and Contreras 2021; Velasco Ortiz et al. 2025). The 50 percent decrease may be balanced by the importance that documented migration has gained under guest worker programs (H2A and H2B), another face of the mobility control regime. In general terms of labor, undocumented migrants had two strategies, which could be combined: travel with family or community networks or with a smuggler.

Since the 1990s, the second enforcement strategy, which involves the militarization of border control, has been utilized more frequently. Increasing physical and technical infrastructure and policing staff displaced migration toward the most dangerous, inhospitable places in the border region. The result was an increase in deaths, disappearances, and kidnappings of migrants in places where organized crime contested the state's territorial control. In this way, migrants were left at the mercy of these criminal networks (Slack and Whiteford 2011). The smuggler (*coyote*) system that worked during the 1980s and early nineties experienced a dramatic change to the detriment of migrant safety. John Agnew (2020, 67) and Polly Pallister-Wilkins (2017, 87) agree that humanitarian borderwork comprises other forms of security in border practices, such as a safe life and well-being for people on the move.

The current control regime has prompted Mexicans and other people seeking international protection to resort to clandestinity mediated by the smuggling industry, increasing its income and power to define border-crossing routes (Guillén 2022). The community or local *coyotes* began to work for human-trafficking networks as decentralized businesses with differentiated functions, including recruiter, gatherer, and crosser (*enganchador*, *juntador*, and *cruzador*) (Velasco Ortiz 2016). According to a 2001 Department of Homeland Security report (CBP 2001), undocumented detention boosted the hiring of *coyotes* by between 80 and 95 percent. The economic costs for migrants and families increased from US$1,000 to US$6,000 between 2000 and 2018 (EMIF, Módulo Sur, 2000–2018, quoted in DHS 2020, 56). In 2019, DHS (2020, 56) found, the cost depended on migrant nationality, the distance of the journey, and border locality. Commonly, payments were made by moving drugs or requiring relatives in the place of origin to pay off the debt (Slack and Whiteford 2011; Velasco Ortiz 2016).

Asylum Seekers' Mobility

As of the beginning of the twenty-first century, the externalization of border control by the United States extended toward Mexico's southern border and into Central America. Regional cooperation programs contributed to migration control from Central and Latin America and from outside the continent (Basok et al. 2015; París Pombo 2017; Guillén 2022). Basok and colleagues (2015) have pointed out that Mexico became a vast continental border zone with its various transit routes and complex mobilities; it is now considered a vertical border (Rigoni 2007; Varela Huerta 2019; Domenech and Dias 2020). Between 2016 and 2019, Mexican cities at the border with the United States received an extraordinary flow of international asylum seekers. With their national origins (Haiti, Honduras, El Salvador, and Guatemala) and collective mobility patterns (groups and caravans), these displacements were unusual on the Mexico-US border. For five decades, this border region has been a transit zone and space for the gradual settlement of Mexican people looking for employment or deported from the United States. The collective arrival pattern of foreigners started at western border cities—for example, Tijuana and Mexicali—though it expanded to other cities such as Ciudad Juárez, Piedras Negras, Reynosa, and later Matamoros (París Pombo 2017; Velasco Ortiz and Peña 2021). Data on detentions (CBP 2020b) show displacements toward the center and east of the Mexican border and the myriad of crossing points increasingly farther away from large cities. As displayed in table 2.1, the foreign population is more numerous and diverse in the deportation flows. Suppose it is contrasted with the approximate number of people in the various caravans between 2018 and 2019 who did not reach 50,000. In that case, it is plain to see that Central American and Caribbean flows are still largely clandestine.

Caravans have brought visibility to migrant advocacy and highlighted the right to free mobility. They represent a shift toward greater autonomy and agency for migrants. But mobility does not always effectively protect migrants during their journey, particularly when they are seeking international protection. US military tactics aimed at confronting caravans and carrying out mass deportations often discourage collective movement. As a result, migrants are forced into the shadows and must rely on clandestine methods. (C. Martínez, 2019). In the late 1980s, Jorge Bustamante (1989) showed how traveling long distances heightened migration risks, as it exposed migrants to the surveillance of Mexican migration authorities. In Guillén's (2022) opinion, the contention was aimed at visible mobility in groups, forcing the majority to travel with smugglers. As smugglers' businesses increased profits, so did migrants' risks. After 2001, Olivia Ruiz (2001) documented the main risks in Central American migration trajectories by the end of the 1990s: theft, extortion, rapes, and physical harm that may be mortal, not only by private individuals but government authorities, plus accidents commonly associated with the journey on the train called "*la Bestia*" (the Beast). According to Varela Huerta and McLean (2019), these risks grew exponentially after the increase in surveillance at Mexico's southern border, criminal gangs strengthening, and state agents' corruption. As pointed out before, border surveillance, migrants' clandestinity, and vulnerability are emergent relationships in the current mobility regime (Spener 2009; Slack and Whiteford 2011; Velasco Ortiz 2016).

Research carried out in 2019 and 2020 (Velasco Ortiz and Peña 2021) with residents from Haiti and Central America in Tijuana and Ciudad Juárez since 2015 showed different risk trajectories depending on the distance and precariousness of the migration corridors. For Haitians, such corridors of precariousness and violence included the Dominican Republic, with stays of years in Brazil or Chile to later follow an international route over Ecuador, Peru, Panama, Central America, and Mexico. They were moving in small groups, organized based on friendship and common background, using smugglers by stages and stretches. For instance, Tapón del Darién, a dangerous jungle between Panama and Colombia, is almost impossible to cross without a guide or *coyote*. The journey takes months, with death, rape, theft, and detention impending at every step. At the gates of Mexico, with humanitarian visas, they carried on with their journey toward the US border by land or air. In Tijuana, they faced changes in the international protection policy. Few managed to cross under a protection modality; later, others applied for MPP, but most had to undergo metering, which meant being on long lists and waiting in some Mexican border city to ask for US international protection. Since the wait could last months or years, an unknown number of people decided to jump the walls in groups or with guides, or else with false documents through the ports of entry to surrender themselves to authorities and speed up their asylum request.

Central American migration, closer in distance than from Haiti, bears a historical mark linked to civil war, whereas at present, to gang violence (París Pombo 2018). According to Coubès, Velasco Ortiz, and Contreras (2021), Central American flows are distinctive for their familial pattern. In this way, risks and clandestine practices are different as they reflect the presence of women and children. There are two well-documented clandestine options for Central Americans (Velasco Ortiz 2022): traveling with *coyotes* over various stretches, which are agreed on in their hometowns with the promise of payment on arrival or with a debt at the place of origin; otherwise, the migrants travel hidden in transports, on foot, and on a freight train (*la Bestia*). The Instituto Nacional de Migración (National Institute of Migration) provides information on en route detentions for 2022: 16,740 detainees from outside Mexico were arrested while traveling on foot or in vehicles in caravans, on buses or motorbikes, in trailer cabins, or in fake ambulances (Segob 2022).[5] Death statistics show that most land accidents involve migrants traveling over the US-Mexico route. The concept of "accident," however, has a strong connotation of a series of random events. The way the migrants are transported, hidden, and stacked, in collusion with governmental authorities involved in smuggling, does not match with the idea of an accident but with the outcome of the global migration control regime.

Another sort of transborder mobility may be found in the employment of thousands of people in drug and human smuggling. The trafficking of drugs and people has played a symbolic role in justifying border controls (Andreas 2009). Viridiana Ríos (2008) has estimated that the drug industry employed 468,000 people in Mexico—as many as Pemex, the country's largest company. The Mexico–United States region is strategic for this industry; according to field findings and reports from the Department of Homeland Security (CBP 2017), likely thousands of workers have been hired in drug distribution networks and have infiltrated people-smuggling networks in recent decades (Velasco Ortiz 2016; Slack and Whiteford 2011). In 2011, the border region maintained its importance as a place where *coyotes* recruited their customers, as 60 percent of the migrants hired one at the border (Segob et al. 2013). In 2021, the US-Mexico border was one of the three most important routes for the human-trafficking industry on the continent (Badillo 2021).

With enhanced border infrastructure, authorized border residents became engaged with drug cartels as smugglers. In previous research (Velasco Ortiz 2016), I have distinguished two social strata in the population that engages in this sort of mobility: those with a tourist visa or residence or citizenship status, who cross through checkpoints; and those generally without the necessary documents, who cross by jumping the wall or traversing hills, desert, or river. In the authorized stratum, we find homemakers who constantly cross to shop and make family visits. There are also cases of students and professionals with residence or citizenship who went unnoticed by drug enforcement authorities for some time. All the interviewed students, professionals, and "homemakers" were recruited to carry drugs in cars or on their bodies, often driving cars "loaded" with hidden people (Velasco Ortiz and Contreras 2011; Velasco Ortiz 2016).

The strategies are similar to those used by commuting BCCV, as they try to simulate the reasons for crossing, such as a family visit or consumption. At the same time, they carry or drive a drug shipment or someone hidden in the vehicle. Although the context of clandestine practices distinguishes them, as in this case, it follows not only an individual or family logic but the one of the *cartel*, as employees. Cases of crossers of drugs and people show that individuals engaged in drug trafficking consider it a legitimate activity, and cross-border mobility is part of the nature of their jobs. Crossing drugs or people is a job offering disproportionately higher earnings than most wage work in Mexico. I have documented that violence is part of the regime that regulates these job posts; employees exercise violence, but they also experience it at the same time (Velasco

Ortiz 2016). Death, imprisonment, extortion, or kidnapping are all parts of the machinery of violence with which drug and people smugglers operate; Jeremy Slack and Scott Whiteford (2011) call it poststructural violence when subordinates exert it on one another.

Matamoros has been one of the most important crossing points for Central American migrants since the 1980s because it is on the shortest route from the south of Mexico. Spener (2009) has observed that as the migrant flow moved toward the eastern border, drug cartels resorted to kidnapping migrants and were responsible for the deaths of dozens of Central American migrants.

The cases of individuals involved in people smuggling across the mountains or the desert show a decentralized and fragmented activity in posts taken by local people engaged in informal work who are knowledgeable about the border territory nevertheless. They are hired by intermediaries in a chain of command that ensures that employers remain anonymous if these individuals are detained (Velasco Ortiz and Contreras 2011).

Field research findings at the border region contradict the 2021 International Organization for Migration (IOM) Report, which states that subsistence smuggling prevails, independent of cartels, that is, that local impoverished people are hired in the context of informal economies in northern Mexico and Central America. The interpretation of these findings is debatable for two reasons. First, newspapers (Badillo 2021) constantly report drug cartels extorting *polleros* and migrants at the southern border and in Mexico. In this way, trafficking industry employees respond to the cartels' logic of territorial control. Second, research in Tijuana, Ciudad Juárez, and Matamoros (Velasco Ortiz and Contreras 2011; Velasco Ortiz 2016; Slack and Whiteford 2011) shows that the drug and migrant smuggling industries hire people who join the trafficking networks as an employment option. They usually do not save money or create patrimony from their working life. Hence, they take these jobs to survive trafficking, but seldom independently of organized crime. International migration management has been used to focus on the smuggling industry to relieve the state from its responsibility to protect migrants and asylum seekers.

Conclusions

The mobility regime currently in force at the Mexico–United States border is part of international and regional security policies and border control externalization. As a precarious space of mobility, the border region articulates places as distant as Brazil and Chile and shares control processes and human dilemmas with other American borders. Nevertheless, the long history of the construction of the Mexican population in terms of race and illegality by US immigration policies marks the current mobility and border control regime.

This chapter approaches this mobility regime from the standpoint of daily practices associated with surreptitious border crossing: clandestinity from below. The monopoly of the state's right to define means of border mobility faces implicit and explicit dissidence among the resident and migrant population. Tijuana or Ciudad Juárez residents with a tourist visa who notice the wage differential on the other side of the border do not have a legitimate reason not to cross to work. A person who experiences domestic or community violence in another country exercises similar reasoning in concluding they have no moral restriction against crossing as many borders as necessary to seek international protection in the United States. On the other hand, labor informality linked to organized crime and trafficking networks has permeated population strata that have found a means for survival and capitalization in cross-border mobility. Dual illegality is imposed on smuggling activities, not only because of the illegality of the crossing but also because they are part of criminal networks. All clandestine mobility practices share invisibility and masking tactics. In the smuggling or drug trafficking cases, practices of violence against other people, once dehumanized, turn into means for profit.

This chapter analyzes multiple spheres and forms of autonomous clandestine practices with different meanings for the border constitution. The logic and the categories proper to the state heavily influence the fragmented vision with which we have approached the various migration flows. In putting forward a joint vision of the various crossing modalities, I intend to underscore standard logics that only appear when these are analyzed in a cohesive manner and without disregarding the specificities of the multiple border-crossing strategies. The theory of autonomy as an analytical perspective allows for renewing the agency outlook from below. However, autonomy built as a legitimate agency makes for clearer resistance and dissidence from the moral heart of state legality.

Through twentieth- and early twenty-first-century phases of the US-Mexico border mobility regime, practices such as labor commuting or long-distance displacement, seeking asylum, become illegal—yet at the same time these different forms of mobility contest the state's legal logic. Analyzing the effects of various clandestine mobility practices on border dynamics is crucial. For example, labor mobility and the movement of asylum seekers aim to transcend the border in pursuit of a better life, defining the border as a space of hope. In contrast, smuggling and trafficking—whether involving drugs or people—serve to reinforce and redefine the border as a dangerous space.

To sum up, a dimension to theorize the border control regime is the way violence shapes and structures the various practices of clandestine mobility for ordinary people. People facing clandestine crossings and displacement often view their situation through a lens that questions the legality shaped by inadequate state protection against violence, poverty, and unemployment. As a result, they and their communities believe it is legitimate to seek protection, a life free from violence, or better employment opportunities, even at the risk of losing their lives or freedom.

NOTES

1. The US Border Patrol had 4,139 agents in 1992; two decades later, the figures had grown five times to reach 19,648 in 2019 (CBP 2020b). The Border Patrol budget increased as well: "In 1992, the federal government allocated $326 million to the agency. By 2019, its budget had ballooned to nearly $4.7 billion, increasing year-over-year since the beginning of the Trump administration" (American Immigration Council 2019, cited by D. Martínez, Heyman, and Slack 2020, 2).

2. The other ideal type is those modalities explicitly or visibly intended to sustain a state border (Parker 2020, 43).

3. Mexican internal displacement, due primarily to violence, is a growing issue. Until 2021, however, there were no official statistics or substantial field research available.

4. In 2007, there were 6.9 million, which means a significant decrease. López, Passel, and Cohn 2021.

5. The Instituto Nacional de Migración uses the term *rescue* in a general way; it means detention. Sixty-two percent are from Central and South America, mainly from Guatemala, Honduras, and El Salvador; 38 percent are from Asia, Africa, Europe, and Oceania (Segob 2022).

REFERENCES

Abraham, Itty, and Willem van Schendel. 2005. "Introduction: The Making of Illicitness." In *Illicit Flow and Criminal Things: States, Borders, and the Other Side of Globalization*, edited by Itty Abraham and William van Schendel, 1–37. Bloomington: Indiana University Press.

Agnew, John. 2020. "Dwelling Space Versus Geopolitical Space: Reexamining Border Studies in Light of the Crisis of Borders." In *Debating and Defining Borders: Philosophical and Theoretical Perspectives*, edited by Anthony Cooper and Soren Tinning, 57–69. New York: Routledge.

Alarcón Acosta, Rafael, and William Becerra. 2012. "Criminales o víctimas?: La deportación de migrantes mexicanos de Estados Unidos a Tijuana, Baja California." *Norteamérica* 7 (1): 125–48. http://www.scielo.org.mx/scielo.php?script=sci_arttext&pid=S1870-35502012000100005&lng=es&nrm=iso.

Alarcón Acosta, Rafael, and Cecilia Ortiz Esquivel. 2017. "Los haitianos solicitantes de asilo a Estados Unidos en su paso por Tijuana." *Frontera Norte* 29 (58): 171–79.

http://www.scielo.org.mx/scielo.php?script=sci_arttext&pid=S01877372201
7000200171&lng=es&nrm=iso.

Albicker, Sandra and Laura Velasco Ortiz. 2016. "Deportación y estigma en la frontera
México–Estados Unidos: Atrapados en Tijuana." *Norteamérica* 11 (1): 99–129. https://
www.revistanorteamerica.unam.mx/index.php/nam/article/view/267.

Alegría, Tito. 2002. "Demand and Supply of Mexican Cross-Border Workers." *Journal of
Borderlands Studies* 17 (1): 37–55. https://doi.org/10.1080/08865655.2002.9695581.

Andreas, Peter. 2009. *Border Games: Policing the U.S.-Mexico Divide*. Cornell University
Press.

Bada, Xóchitl, and S. Schutz. 2019. "Movilidades en América Latina en el siglo XXI."
Sociedad y Economía 34:9–10.

Badillo, Diego. 2021. "A ríos de migrantes, ganancia de delincuentes." *El Economista*, December 19. https://www.eleconomista.com.mx/politica/A-rios-de-migrantes-ganancia
-de-delincuentes-20211217-0071.html.

Basok, Tanya, Daniele Bélanger, Martha Luz Rojas, and Guillermo Candiz. 2015. *Rethinking Transit Migration: Precarity, Mobility, and Self-Making in Mexico*. London:
Palgrave Macmillan.

Bureau of Information Statistics. 2022. "Border Crossing / Entry Data: Annual Data."
Accessed October 24, 2024. https://www.bts.gov/content/us-canadian-border-land
-passenger-gateways-entering-united-states.

Bustamante, Jorge. 1989. "Frontera México-Estados Unidos: Reflexiones para un marco
teórico." *Frontera Norte* 1 (1): 7–24. https://fronteranorte.colef.mx/index.php
/fronteranorte/article/view/1666.

Chávez, Sergio. 2011. "Navigating the U.S.-Mexico Border: The Crossing Strategies
of Undocumented Workers in Tijuana, Mexico." *Ethnic and Racial Studies* 34 (8):
1320–37. https://doi.org/10.1080/01419870.2010.547586.

Chávez, Sergio. 2016. *Border Lives: Fronterizos, Transnational Migrants, and Commuters*.
New York: Oxford University Press.

CBP (US Customs and Border Protection). 2001. "U.S. Border Patrol and Office of Field
Operations Encounters by Area of Responsibility and Component." https://www.cbp
.gov/newsroom/stats/nationwide-encounters.

CBP (US Customs and Border Protection). 2017. "Written Testimony of CBP for a
House Homeland Security Subcommittee on Border and Maritime Security Hearing
Titled 'A Dangerous and Sophisticated Adversary: The Threat to the Homeland Posed
by Cartel Operations.'" https://www.dhs.gov/news/2017/02/16/written-testimony
-cbp-house-homeland-security-subcommittee-border-and-maritime.

CBP (US Customs and Border Protection). 2020a. "U.S. Border Patrol Fiscal Year
Southwest Border Sector Deaths (F.Y. 1998–F.Y. 2020)." https://www.cbp.gov
/document/stats/us-border-patrol-fiscal-year-southwest-border-sector-deaths-fy
-1998-fy-2020.

CBP (US Customs and Border Protection). 2020b. "U.S. Border Patrol Nationwide
Apprehensions by Citizenship and Sector (FY2007–FY2019)." https://www.cbp.gov
/document/stats/us-border-patrol-nationwide-apprehensions-citizenship-and-sector
-fy2007-fy-2019-0.

CBP (US Customs and Border Protection). 2022. "Nationwide Encounters." https://www.cbp.gov/newsroom/stats/nationwide-encounters.

Clavijo, Janneth, Andrés Pereira, and Lourdes Basualdo. 2019. "Humanitarismo y control migratorio en Argentina: Refugio, tratamiento médico y migración laboral." *Apuntes* 46 (84): 127–57. https://dx.doi.org/10.21678/apuntes.84.1016.

Coleman, Mathew. 2007. "Immigration Geopolitics Beyond the Mexico–U.S. Border." *Antipode* 39 (1): 54–76. https://doi.org/10.1111/j.1467-8330.2007.00506.x.

Cooper, Anthony, and Soren Tinning. 2021. *Debating and Defining Borders: Philosophical and Theoretical Perspectives*. New York: Routledge.

Coubès, Marie-Laure. 2021. "Movilidad en familias: Estudio sociodemográfico de las caravanas migrantes en Tijuana." In *Caravanas migrantes y desplazamientos colectivos en la frontera México-Estados Unidos*, edited by Camilo Contreras Delgado, María Dolores París Pombo, and Laura Velasco Ortiz, 77–102. México: El Colegio de la Frontera Norte.

Coubès, Marie-Laure, Laura Velasco Ortiz, and Oscar Fernando Contreras. 2021. "Migrantes en albergues en las ciudades fronterizas del norte de México." In *Ciencias sociales en acción: Respuesta frente al COVID-19 desde el norte de México*, edited by Oscar Fernando Contreras, 340–57. Mexico City: El Colegio de la Frontera Norte.

Das, Veena, and Deborah Poole. 2004. "State and Margin: Comparative Ethnographies." In *Anthropology in the Margin of the States*, edited by Veena Das and Deborah Poole, 3–33. Albuquerque: University of New Mexico Press.

De Genova, Nicholas. 2002. "Migrant 'Illegality' and Deportability in Everyday Life." *Annual Review of Anthropology* 31:419–47. https://www.annualreviews.org/doi/abs/10.1146/annurev.anthro.31.040402.085432.

De Genova, Nicholas. 2013. "Spectacles of Migrant 'Illegality': The Scene of Exclusion, the Obscene of Inclusion." *Ethnic and Racial Studies* 36 (7): 1180–98. https://doi.org/10.1080/01419870.2013.783710.

De Genova, Nicholas. 2017. "The Incorrigible Subject: Mobilizing a Critical Geography of (Latin) America Through the Autonomy of Migration." *Journal of Latin American Geography* 16 (1): 17–42. https://doi.org/10.1353/lag.2017.0007.

Del Monte Madrigal, Juan Antonio. 2021. "Pandemia, Biden y AMLO: Una fase más en el endurecimiento de las fronteras para las personas migrantes." *Nexos*, August. https://migracion.nexos.com.mx/2021/08/pandemia-biden-y-amlo-una-fase-mas-en-el-endurecimiento-de-las-fronteras-para-las-personas-migrantes/.

DHS (US Department of Homeland Security). 2020. *Department of Homeland Security Border Security Metrics Report 2020*. August 5. https://www.dhs.gov/sites/default/files/publications/immigration-statistics/BSMR/ndaa_border_security_metrics_report_fy_2019_0.pdf.pdf.

Dillman, Daniel. 1970. "Urban Growth Along Mexico's Northern Border and the Mexican National Border Program." *Journal of Developing Areas* 4 (4): 487–508. https://www.jstor.org/stable/4189724.

Domenech, Eduardo, and Gustavo Dias. 2020. "Regimes de fronteira e 'ilegalidade' migrante na América Latina e no Caribe." *Sociologias* 22 (55): 40–73. https://www.scielo.br/j/soc/a/t4fsJQgwWTJZLchwfJqJMtp/.

Dunn, Timothy J. 2021. "The Militarization of the U.S.–Mexico Border in the Twenty-First Century and Implications for Human Rights." In *Handbook on Human Security, Borders, and Migration*, edited by Natalia Ribas Mateo and Timothy Dunn, 35–53. Cheltenham, UK: Edward Elgar.

Fassin, Didier. 2005. "Compassion and Repression: The Moral Economy of Immigration Policies in France." *Cultural Anthropology* 20 (3): 362–87. https://www.jstor.org/stable/3651596.

Glick Schiller, Nina. 2021. "Migration, Displacement, and Dispossession." *Oxford Research Encyclopedia of Anthropology*. https://oxfordre.com/anthropology/view/10.1093/acrefore/9780190854584.001.0001/acrefore-9780190854584-e-205.

Glick Schiller, Nina, and Noel Salazar. 2012. "Regimes of Mobility Across the Globe." *Journal of Ethnic and Migration Studies* 39 (2): 1–18. https://doi.org/10.1080/1369183X.2013.723253.

Guillén, Tonatiuh. 2022. "Rutas migrantes y estructura del tráfico." *Revista Proceso*, January 18. https://www.proceso.com.mx/opinion/2022/1/18/rutas-migrantes-estructuras-del-trafico-279300.html.

Hess, Sabine. 2012. "De-Naturalising Transit Migration. Theory and Methods of an Ethnographic Regime Analysis." *Population, Space, and Place* 18 (4): 428–40. https://onlinelibrary.wiley.com/doi/10.1002/psp.632.

Heyman, Josiah. 2004. "U.S. Ports of Entry on the Mexican Border." In *On the Border: Society and Culture Between the United States and Mexico*, edited by Andrew Grant Wood, 221–40. Lanham, MD: SR Books.

Heyman, Josiah. 2012. "Construcción y uso de tipologías: Movilidad geográfica desigual en la frontera México-Estados Unidos." In *Métodos cualitativos y su aplicación empírica: Por los caminos de la investigación sobre migración internacional*, edited by Marina Ariza and Laura Velasco Ortiz, 419–54. Mexico City: Instituto de Investigaciones Sociales, Universidad Nacional Autónoma de México, El Colegio de la Frontera Norte.

Heyman, Josiah, and Alan Smart. 1999. "States and Illegal Practices: An Overview." In *States and Illegal Practices*, edited by Josiah Heyman, 1–24. New York: Oxford University Press.

Horton, Sarah B. 2020. "Introduction: Paper Trails; Migrants, Bureaucratic Inscription, and Legal Recognition. In *Paper Trails: Migrants, Documents, and Legal Insecurity*, edited by Sarah B. Horton and Josiah Heyman, 1–26. Durham, NC: Duke University Press.

INEGI (Instituto Nacional de Estadística y Geografía). 2020. "Censo de Población y Vivienda 2020." https://www.inegi.org.mx/programas/ccpv/2020/.

IOM (International Organization for Migration). 2021. *Missing Migrants: Migración en las Américas*. https://missingmigrants.iom.int/es/region/las-americas.

IOM (International Organization for Migration). 2022. *Missing Migrants Project: Annual Regional Overview 2021 (Executive Summary)—The Americas*. https://missingmigrants.iom.int/sites/g/files/tmzbdl601/files/publication/file/MMP%20annual%20regional%20overview%202021%20LAC_Executive%20Summary-ENG_0.pdf.

López, Mark Hugo, Jeffrey Passel, and De'Vera Cohn. 2021. "Key Facts About the Changing U.S. Unauthorized Immigrant Population." Pew Research Center. April 13. https://www.pewresearch.org/fact-tank/2021/04/13/key-facts-about-the-changing-u-s-unauthorized-immigrant-population/.

Martínez, Carlos. 2019. "Vuelvan todos ustedes a las sombras." *El País*, September 21. https://elpais.com/internacional/2019/09/20/america/1568989028_728880.html.

Martínez, Daniel, Josiah Heyman, and Jeremy Slack. 2020. "Border Enforcement Developments Since 1993 and How to Change CBP." Center for Migration Studies. August 24. https://cmsny.org/publications/border-enforcement-developments-since -1993-and-how-to-change-cbp/.

Menjívar, Cecilia. 2006. "Liminal Legality: Salvadoran and Guatemalan Immigrants' Lives in the United States." *American Journal of Sociology* 111 (4): 999–1037. https:// doi.org/10.1086/499509.

Mezzadra, Sandro. 2012. "Capitalismo, migraciones y luchas sociales: La mirada de la autonomía." *Nueva Sociedad*, no. 237, 159–78. https://dialnet.unirioja.es/servlet/articulo ?codigo=3984115.

Mezzadra, Sandro and Brett Neilson. 2013. *Border as Method; or, The Multiplication of Labor*. Durham, NC: Duke University Press.

Mossaad, Nadwa. 2016. "Refugees and Asylees: 2014." *Annual Flow Report*. Office of Immigration Statistics, US Department of Homeland Security (DHS). https://ohss .dhs.gov/sites/default/files/2023-12/Refugees_Asylees_2014.pdf.

Mountz, Alison. 2020. *The Death of Asylum: Hidden Geographies of the Enforcement Archipelago*. Minneapolis: University of Minnesota Press.

Ngai, Mae. 2004. *Impossible Subjects: Illegal Aliens and the Making of Modern America*. Princeton, NJ: Princeton University Press.

Orraca, Pedro. 2015. "Immigrants and Cross-Border Workers in the U.S.-Mexico Border Region." *Frontera Norte* 27 (53): 5–34. https://www.redalyc.org/articulo.oa?id =13632991001.

Pallister-Wilkins, Polly. 2017. "Humanitarian Rescue/Sovereign Capture and the Policing of Possible Responses to Violent Borders." *Global Policy* 8 (1): 19–24. https://doi.org /10.1111/1758-5899.12401.

Papadopoulos, Dimitris, Niamh Stephenson, and Vassilis Tsianos. 2008. *Escape Routes: Control and Subversion in the 21st Century*. London: Pluto Press.

París Pombo, María Dolores. 2017. *Violencias y migraciones centroamericanas en México*. Mexico City: El Colegio de la Frontera Norte.

París Pombo, María Dolores. 2018. *Migrantes haitianos y centroamericanos en Tijuana, Baja California, 2016–2017: Políticas gubernamentales y Acciones de la sociedad civil*, edited by María Dolores París Pombo. Mexico City: Comisión Nacional de los Derechos Humanos, El Colegio de la Frontera Norte. https://www.cndh.org.mx/sites/all/doc /Informes/Especiales/Informe-Migrantes-2016-2017.pdf.

Parker, Noel. 2020. "Borderwork and Its Contraries: Boundary Making and the Re-Imagining of Borders." In *Debating and Defining Borders: Philosophical and Theoretical Perspectives*, edited by Anthony Cooper and Soren Coope, 43–55. New York: Routledge.

Pew Research Center. 2006. "Modes of Entry for the Unauthorized Migrant Population: Fact Sheet." May 22. https://www.pewresearch.org/race-and-ethnicity/2006/05/22 /modes-of-entry-for-the-unauthorized-migrant-population/.

Rigoni, Flor María. 2007. "La última frontera del crimen: El secuestro del migrante indocumentado." *Migrantes: Revista de Información y Pastoral Migratoria* 13 (3): 3.

https://4dde1f4a-5fb6-414f-8ec5-93927c3946e7.filesusr.com/ugd/bd82f8_c883aeda8f ob4e009b13c823c2b827e9.pdf.

Ríos, Viridiana. 2008. "Evaluating the Economic Impact of Mexico's Drug Trafficking Industry." Paper presented at the Graduate Students Political Economy Workshop, Cambridge, MA. https://www.readkong.com/page/evaluating-the-economic-impact -of-mexico-s-drug-trafficking-3318053.

Rojas, Martha Luz, and Ailsa Winton. 2018. "Precarious Mobility in Central America and Southern Mexico: Crises and the Struggle to Survive." In *The Oxford Handbook of Migration Crises*, edited by Cecilia Menjívar, Marie Ruiz, and Ian Ness, 1–20. Oxford: Oxford University Press.

Ruiz, Olivia. 2001. "Riesgo, migración y espacios fronterizos: Una reflexión." *Estudios demográficos y urbanos* 47:257–84. https://www.redalyc.org/pdf/312/31204701.pdf.

Rumford, Chris. 2012. "Towards a Multiperspectival Study of Borders." *Geopolitics* 17 (4): 887–902. https://www.tandfonline.com/doi/full/10.1080/14650045.2012.660584.

Segob (Secretaría de Gobernación). 2022. *Rescata INM a 16 mil 740 personas migrantes irregulares en enero de 2022*. January 31, 2022. https://www.gob.mx/inm/prensa/ rescata -inm-a-16-mil-740-personas-migrantes-irregulares-en-enero-de-2022–293649? idiom=es.

Segob (Secretaría de Gobernación), Consejo Nacional de Población, Instituto Nacio- nal de Migración, Unidad de Política Migratoria-Centro de Estudios Migratorios, Secretaría de Relaciones Exteriores, Secretaría de Salud, Secretaría del Trabajo y Previsión Social and El Colegio de la Frontera Norte. 2013. *Encuesta sobre Migración en la Frontera Norte de México, 2011. Serie anualizada 2004–2011*. Government of Mexico. 2011. http://www.segob.gob.mx/work/models/SEGOB/Resource/1746/1/images /EMIF%20NORTE%202011.pdf.

Shachar, Ayelet, and Aaqib Mahmood. 2021. "The Body as the Border: A New Era." *His- torical Social Research* 46 (3): 124–50. https://www.ssoar.info/ssoar/handle/document /75562.

Shamir, Ronen. 2005. "Without Borders? Notes on Globalization as a Mobility Regime." *Sociological Theory* 23 (2): 197–217. https://onlinelibrary.wiley.com/doi/epdf/10.1111/j .0735-2751.2005.00250.x.

Slack, Jeremy, and Scott Whiteford. 2011. "Violence and Migration on the Arizona- Sonora Border." *Human Organization* 70 (1): 11–21. https://www.jstor.org/stable /44150972.

Spener, David. 2009. *Clandestine Crossings: Migrants and Coyotes on the Texas-Mexico Border*. Ithaca, NY: Cornell University Press.

Sulbarán Lovera, Patricia. 2021. "El gas usado para 'desinfectar' a mexicanos en EE.UU. que sirvió como ejemplo a la Alemania nazi." *BBC News Mundo Los Ángeles*. Septem- ber 4. https://www.bbc.com/mundo/noticias-internacional-57262972.

Torpey, Jhon. 2000. *The Invention of the Passport: Surveillance, Citizenship, and the State*. Cambridge: Cambridge University Press.

TRAC (Transaction Records Access Clearinghouse) Immigration. 2021. "Now over 8,000 MPP Cases Transferred into the United States Under Biden." https://tracreports.org /whatsnew/email.210511.html.

Varela Huerta, Amarela. 2019. "México, de 'frontera vertical' a país tapón: Migrantes, deportados, retornados, desplazados internos y solicitantes de asilo en México." *Iberoforum* 24 (27): 49–56. https://iberoforum.ibero.mx/index.php/iberoforum/article /view/124.

Varela Huerta, Amarela, and Lisa McLean. 2019. "Caravanas de migrantes en México: Nueva forma de autodefensa y transmigración." *Revista CIDOB d'Afers Internacionals* 122:163–85. https://www.cidob.org/es/articulos/revista_cidob_d_afers_internacionals /122/caravana_de_migrantes_en_mexico_nueva_forma_de_autodefensa_y _transmigracion.

Velasco Ortiz, Laura. 2016. "Cross-Border Mobility and Clandestine Practices: Scenarios of Violence in the Mexico–United States Border Region." *Human Organization* 75 (3): 269–78. https://meridian.allenpress.com/human-organization/article-abstract /75/3/269/71713/Cross-border-Mobility-and-Clandestine-Practices?redirectedFrom =fulltext.

Velasco Ortiz, Laura, ed. 2022. *Entre la espera y el asentamiento: Inserción laboral y residencial de inmigrantes y desplazados en ciudades fronterizas del norte de México (Etapa 2)*. Mexico City: El Colegio de la Frontera Norte; Los Angeles: University of California, Los Angeles.

Velasco Ortiz, Laura, and Oscar Contreras. 2011. *Mexican Voices of the Border Region*. Philadelphia: Temple University Press.

Velasco Ortiz, Laura, and Marie-Laure Coubès. 2013. *Reporte sobre dimensión, caracterización y áreas de atención a mexicanos deportados desde Estados Unidos*. Mexico City: El Colegio de la Frontera Norte.

Velasco Ortiz, Laura, Marie-Laure Coubès, María Inés Barrios de la O, and Lorena Cecilia Mena Iturralde. 2025. "La infraestructura y los espacios de la espera: Albergues en las ciudades fronterizas del norte de México." In *Entre la espera y el asentamiento: Migración y desplazamiento en ciudades fronterizas del norte de México*, edited by Laura Velasco Ortiz, Oscar Contreras, Marie-Laure Coubès, and Dolores Paris. Tijuana: El Colegio de la Frontera Norte.

Velasco Ortiz, Laura, and R. Hernández. 2021. "Salir de las sombras: La visibilidad organizada en las caravanas de migrantes centroamericanos." In *Caravanas migrantes y desplazamientos colectivos en la frontera México-Estados Unidos*, edited by Camilo Contreras, María Dolores París Pombo, and Laura Velasco Ortiz, 103–29. Mexico City: El Colegio de la Frontera Norte.

Velasco Ortiz, Laura, and Jesús Javier Peña. 2021. "Estudio cualitativo sobre la integración residencial y laboral de personas extranjeras y deportados mexicanos en Tijuana y Ciudad Juárez." In *Entre la espera y el asentamiento: Inserción laboral y residencial de inmigrantes y desplazados en ciudades fronterizas del norte de México; los casos de Tijuana y Ciudad Juárez*, edited by Laura Velasco Ortiz. Mexico City: El Colegio de la Frontera Norte; Los Angeles: University of California.

3

Subverting Internal Bordering Practices

"ILLEGAL LEGALITY" IN SOUTHERN MEXICO

Tanya Basok and Martha Luz Rojas Wiesner

Since the 1980s, nations have been securitizing their borders to prevent "unwanted" migrants from crossing into their territories (Bigo 2002; Walters 2004; Squire 2011; Rygiel 2010; Humphrey 2013). Bordering practices have also been externalized to neighboring countries (Casas-Cortes et al. 2015; Menjívar 2014; Hyndman and Mountz 2008) and have come to rely on "remote control" strategies that seek to restrict the movement of people *before* they leave countries of origin or transit (Zolberg 2003; FitzGerald 2019). A series of remote control techniques and measures have been adopted in North America, Europe, and Australia since the 1980s and have become particularly prominent since the early 2000s (FitzGerald 2019; Hyndman and Mountz 2008). Outsourcing migration control to transit countries, such as Mexico, has thus become a common and systematic practice in mobility governance (Casas-Cortes et al. 2015, 19–22). With the support of the United States, Mexico has fortified its border surveillance in the southern region and throughout the country to prevent migrants from Guatemala, El Salvador, Honduras, and other countries from reaching the border with the United States. (Isacson 2021).

Moreover, nation-states have adopted a series of *internal bordering practices* to criminalize unauthorized migrants on their territories (Mezzadra and Nielson 2013; Menjívar 2014; Balibar 2004; Rigo 2011; Pérez et al. 2019; De Genova and Peutz 2010). The internalized bordering regime defines and reinforces the boundary between "legality" and "illegality."[1] "Illegality" is (re)produced through specific legal provisions (De Genova 2013; Bosniak 2007), particular media discourses (Chávez 2013), and everyday practices of surveillance of "illegalized" bodies within the so-called deportation regime (De Genova and Peutz 2010; see also Menjívar 2014; Inda 2013; Menjívar and Kanstroom 2013; Coutin 2014; Willen 2010). In Mexico, historically and today, provisions embedded in such statutes as the various versions of the Migration Law or the General Population Law (Ley General de Población) have been used to draw boundaries between those "deserving" migrants who are to be admitted to Mexico as regular citizens and others. Reflective of Mexico's commitment to build a nation that has distanced itself from its Indigenous roots and from Indigenous populations viewed as "primitive," the earlier versions of the Mexican Migration Law gave preference to migrants from Europe (e.g., Treviño Rangel 2008; Rios-Contreras 2021).

The current Migration Law, adopted in 2011, defines deservingness mainly in economic terms (e.g., ability to obtain and hold a regular job), which tends de facto to exclude migrants from northern Central American countries, who are often prevented from meeting these eligibility requirements (e.g., Basok and Rojas Wiesner 2017), though, as we discuss below, even the ones who possess the required economic characteristics may encounter institutional racism preventing them from obtaining status. Although specific status regularization programs seem to provide opportunities to those who have been previously excluded from membership to obtain legal residency documents, in practice, many obstacles prevent migrants, particularly racialized Central American men and women, from attaining this goal. In some cases, the legal status granted to migrants may be insecure, temporary, or conditioned on compliance with certain restrictions (Landolt and Goldring 2015; Chauvin and Garcés-Mascareñas 2014; Geoffrion and Cretton 2021). Researchers have coined this type of status "precarious" (Basok and Rojas Wiesner 2017), "liminal" (Menjívar 2006), or semilegal (Kubal 2013), given that it provides no more than temporary relief from removal or deportation or prevents illegalized migrants from formally regularizing their status, or both (Menjívar and Kanstroom 2013; Bolter, Chishti, and Meissner 2021). In fact, as we have argued elsewhere (Basok and Rojas

Wiesner 2017), the rigid requirements for annual migratory status renewal in Mexico forced many "regularized" migrants from Guatemala, El Salvador, and Honduras into "illegality."

At the same time, as autonomy of migration (Mezzadra 2004, 2010; Papadopoulos and Tsianos 2008, 2013) and critical citizenship studies scholars (Nyers 2015; Isin and Nielson 2008) remind us, those who are denied entry or secure status often find ways to contest and subvert exclusions, overcome restrictions, and cross internal borders that separate them from others who have been granted full membership. One such strategy is the use of fake or falsely obtained documents (see, e.g., Chauvin and Garcés-Mascareñas 2014; Sadiq 2009; Reeves 2015; Horton 2020; and Tuckett 2018). This chapter focuses on these types of strategies in the context of other, more "legitimate" opportunities.

As we demonstrate in this chapter, internal bordering practices prevent many migrants from obtaining legal status, and even when they do receive documents, their status is precarious at best. In this context, many migrants resort to "creative" forms of legalization, such as securing substitute documents, purchasing fake documents, or falsely obtaining authentic documents. Those who do rely on these alternative means of legalization blur the line between "legality" and "illegality" and represent what we call in this chapter "illegal legality." Yet little scholarly research has addressed the lived experiences of those inhabiting the spaces of illegal legality or the degree to which the illegally obtained legality protects migrants from precarity.

This chapter is based on in-depth semistructured interviews of and focus groups with migrants from El Salvador, Guatemala, and Honduras who, until recently, constituted the vast majority of migrants residing or working in Mexico. Stories presented in this chapter have been collected since 2007 in different projects in which we participated as principal investigators, co-investigators, or collaborators, or some combination of these.[2] Through these combined studies, we conducted interviews with 179 Central American migrants,[3] along with some key informants, such as government officials, representatives of international and national organizations or agencies, and members of civil society organizations (CSOs). Most of the interviews we draw on in this chapter were conducted in Chiapas, a southern state bordering Guatemala. Some study participants had no status in Mexico; others lived there as permanent or temporary residents, authorized visitors, or naturalized Mexican citizens. We recruited study participants with the help of CSOs and by relying on snowball sampling. In each project, we asked migrants and civil society activists to comment on legal restrictions and the related processes that contributed to the illegalization of migrants, extant paths to status regularization, and the obstacles migrants experienced in obtaining secure status. In virtually every project, we identified cases of migrants who had resorted to alternative documentation processes, as reported by the migrants or key informants.

We begin by reviewing the conceptual literature on internal bordering practices and migrants' agency within those border regimes that at times blur distinctions between legality and illegality. Before documenting how migrants from northern Central American countries residing in Mexico cross the boundary between legality and illegality, we outline certain bordering practices that prevent many migrants from obtaining legal status through authorized channels. We present an overview of Mexico's temporary status regularization programs and argue that institutional racism embedded in Mexico's immigration bureaucracy, combined with migration control policies, constitutes the main reason why many migrants cannot obtain legal documents to live and work in Mexico. We then demonstrate how migrants without secure status cross the boundaries between legality and illegality by adopting one of the following three "illegal" strategies: (1) violating conditions and restrictions outlined in specific legal documents; (2) purchasing fake papers; or (3) obtaining authentic documents illegitimately. Regardless of the chosen strategy, the legal documents that migrants acquire provide them only a temporary or insufficient relief from precarity. Despite being documented, most remain in precarious conditions characterized by insecurity and uncertainty. By highlighting the precariousness, insecurity, and uncertainty of the status migrants obtain through illegal channels we shed light on the lived experiences of "illegal legality" and situate these experiences in the structural and institutional context we call "exclusionary inclusion."

Between Legality and Illegality: Delineating and Crossing Administrative Borders

In modern states, identification practices have acquired utmost importance (Torpey 1997, 842), and without identifying individuals, states would not be in a position to perform their administrative tasks (843). Identification documents allow an individual to perform many tasks such as financial transactions, tax remittance, marriage and parenting, and access to health care, while being placed in the "power/knowledge grid in which individuals are processed and constituted as administrative subjects of states" (843). By connecting individuals to the state, identity documents cement modern state administration (843). Once documented, people become "legible" (that is, categorized and standardized) to the state, which can then govern them effectively (Scott 1998). Sarah Horton

(2020, 5) refers to the processes and technologies through which individuals are integrated into official registers as "bureaucratic inscriptions."

In the context of migration, bureaucratic inscriptions are bordering mechanisms: they are expressions of state power that draw the boundary between citizens and noncitizens (Horton 2020, 4). By granting or denying documents to migrants, states perform their sovereign power to set internal borders that separate those considered deserving of recognition and social protections from those whose presence on state territory is considered undesirable and subject to surveillance and expulsion (Abarca and Coutin 2018). Jukka Könönen (2018) has identified the concept of "administrative bordering" to refer to "negotiations and processes concerning the presence and access of non-citizens that are both a fundamental part and a consequence of immigration policies" (143). Bureaucratic procedures that correspond to this administrative bordering establish and apply qualifications for residence permits as well as access to services, and actors in such institutions as local registry offices, embassies, social services, and banks use their discretionary power to interpret legislative criteria (143). Some migrants engage in border struggles, including resorting to "illicit" solutions, as discussed below, when administrative gatekeepers in the immigration bureaucracy prevent them from attaining their objectives (143).

Transitions between different statuses are rooted in what Luin Goldring and Patricia Landolt (2013) call "conditionality," comprising regulations, policies, and procedures that often draw on moral frameworks of deservingness to outline requirements that have to be met, breached, or challenged to receive authorization to stay legally in a country. Established rules and procedures are enacted by various gatekeepers through interactions among themselves and with migrants, negotiations, and discretionary decisions (Landolt and Goldring 2015, 857; see also Tuckett 2018). Thus, ironically, "illegality" is constructed through not only laws that purposefully seek to prevent the crossing of internal borders but also the administrative inadequacies of those provisions, practices, and actions that are meant to include by granting status. Various gatekeepers may use their discretionary power to deny rights to migrants or make procedures so complex, time-consuming, and costly that the applicants abandon the process.

At the same time, the analysis of decisions made by bureaucrats and gatekeepers employed in public administration or in the field of immigration needs to be situated in the corresponding structural, cultural, and institutional context. Policies that exclude immigrants and limit protection to asylum seekers, public anti-immigrant sentiments, institutional practices that deny rights and belonging to migrants seeking admission to a nation-state, racial dynamics and the understandings of race embedded in the customary morality within these institutions all undoubtedly shape bureaucrats' perceptions and impact their seemingly discretionary decisions (Alexander 1997; Fuglerud 2004). As we demonstrate below, endemic racism in the immigration bureaucracy in Mexican institutions that handle migrants' applications for secure status is responsible for the "illegalization" of many migrants in Mexico. Furthermore, the procedures for status regularization may clash with other types of bordering practices, namely, the ones that uphold the power of Mexican immigration authorities to apprehend and expel unwanted bodies.

The administrative borders that separate "legality" and "illegality" are not as clearly demarcated as may first appear. Lydia Morris (2003) points to the "increasing diversity of 'outsider' status" (79) as states set qualifying conditions of access in reference to domestic, transnational, and supranational law (77). Positing the concept of "civic stratification," she characterizes partial membership as "a system of inequality based on the relationship between different categories of individuals and the state, and the rights thereby granted or denied" (79). The concept of "differential inclusion" has also been used to describe and analyze varying degrees of subordination and segmentation to which different types of migrants are subjected (Mezzadra and Nielson 2011). "Differential inclusion" practices may operate variably at distinct regional and local levels, resulting in a multiplicity of statuses, categories, and conditions that determine opportunities and limitations in accessing protections and services (El-Kayed and Hamann 2018; Pérez et al. 2019).

Migrants may at times inhabit border zones in which legality and illegality coexist or the two are interchangeable. For instance, even those who are denied acceptance by the sovereign federal authorities may be inscribed into official bureaucratic systems and thus allowed to cross the administrative border at a different scale, for example, at the municipal level. By granting "illegalized" migrants some types of identification documents (e.g., driver's licenses, consular IDs) that authorize their access to certain rights and financial, educational, or other institutions, municipal authorities may bestow "social personhood" on the migrants who are denied legal personhood by federal authorities (Horton 2020, 3; see also Chauvin and Garcés-Mascareñas 2014). At the same time, as Susan Coutin (2020, 134) alerts us, documentation may be a "double bind," leading to legalization but also at times making it impossible to obtain secure legal status. As discussed below, the documents that some migrants obtained in southern Mexico, using creative border-crossing strategies that are not entirely "legal," have made it impossible for them to obtain more secure status through authorized federal programs.

Furthermore, in many countries, the status that states extend to migrants may be "precarious" (Basok and Rojas Wiesner 2017; Tuckett 2018, 9–11) or semilegal (Menjívar 2006; Kubal 2013). In some cases, a status may be no more than a stay from deportation, not an authorization to become permanent residents (Menjívar and Kanstroom 2013, 3–4; Castañeda 2010; De Genova 2010). The multiplicity of such legal statuses that provide temporary relief from removal but do not allow individuals to regularize their status formally obscure the lines between legality and illegality (Menjívar and Kanstroom 2013, 11) and render legalized migrants insecure.

In this chapter, we demonstrate that even though certain legal provisions establish opportunities for status regularization of nonstatus migrants in Mexico, and certain policies are put in place, the state has created no de facto infrastructure to facilitate the regularization of "illegalized" migrants. In fact, without state support for migrants or grassroots organizations that assist them, the state status regularization programs are nothing but empty promises. In particular, at the administrative level, procedural difficulties make it very difficult for many migrants to attain and retain legal status. Furthermore, similar to "street-level bureaucrats" elsewhere (see Lipsky 1980[4]), certain Mexican gatekeepers use their discretionary power to deny rights to migrants. Given that applications are so complex, and the application process so slow and costly, it is hardly surprising that migrants choose to withdraw their applications or seek other opportunities to secure their stay. The Mexican state has done little to simplify or expedite the process or reduce costs, a fact that we consider to be indicative of the consistent pattern of systemic and institutional exclusion of migrants from northern Central America and other regions. Furthermore, at times, status regularization policies may conflict with other practices, such as detentions and deportations of migrants eligible to apply for status.

The application of provisions and policies by various institutions, in different locations, and at different scales further complicates the boundary between legality and illegality and the association between status and rights. Pointing out that the state is not a monolithic entity, and that decisions regarding the boundaries between legality and illegality are the result of negotiations and power struggles, Martin Ruhs and Bridget Anderson (2010, 199) conclude that resulting policies, as well as their implementation, may be contradictory. They identify a set of political and economic concerns that impact the design of policies for governing illegality in the labor market: public opinion concerning immigration control, surveillance, and the perceived dangers of illegality; potential benefits of illegality to employers; attitudes held by organized labor toward undocumented coworkers; the costs of enforcing control and law; and the costs and benefits of illegal labor for the well-being of the domestic population (199).

Furthermore, the state is a multicentered and disaggregated institution, and its policies and bureaucratic priorities are enacted differently through the heterogenous national space. Jacques Ramírez (2017) illustrates how the regularization of regional migrants under the Mercosur visa provisions varies greatly depending on the region in Ecuador where migrants apply for legalization. As we argue in this chapter, some Mexican municipalities provide opportunities for migrants to obtain legal documents in a semilegal fashion that "bends" rules and regulations established by the federal state. In fact, by granting certain legal documents to nonstatus migrants, municipalities assume the role of federal immigration and naturalization entities, a role that they are not authorized to have.

While many state and nonstate actors, as well as gatekeepers, contribute to the porosity of the boundary between "legality" and "illegality," it is important to recognize the agency of migrants who challenge exclusionary bordering practices and contribute to the construction of "legality," "illegality," and the statuses in between. In fact, migrants challenge exclusions, claim rights, bend rules, and negotiate with gatekeepers (Landolt and Goldring 2015; Ruhs and Anderson 2010; Villegas 2017). Migrants and migrant advocates may maneuver through the laws and migrant histories to build a case that would stand up to scrutiny. It is this legal craft of migrant advocates that makes some applications for status regularization more likely to succeed (Coutin 2020). As Anna Tuckett (2018, 5) points out, "Successful navigation of the immigration bureaucracy involves taking advantage of loopholes, cultivating contacts, and knowing when and how to bend rules."

As Horton (2020, 4–5) observes, migrants can challenge state power to grant documentation by separating documents from their legal owners or borrowing and lending their documents (also see Abarca and Coutin 2018, 9). As this chapter demonstrates, some migrants who are unable to obtain legal documents resort to other means of becoming documented in the border zones of southern Mexico where such "semicompliance" practices are well tolerated. Yet, despite relatively liberal attitudes toward the crossing of the legality-illegality boundary in some municipalities, migrants who have gained "illegal legality" run the risk of losing this status, slipping into "illegality," and being pushed once again outside the administrative borders that separate them from those whose status is secure (see also Tuckett 2018, 88–91). In the following section, we discuss "administrative bordering" practices that prevent migrants from obtaining secure status in Mexico.

Documenting Illegalized Migrants: Possibilities and Limitations

The illegalization of migrants in Mexico is rooted in the racism and xenophobia prevalent in Mexican society and its immigration bureaucracy (Treviño Rangel 2016). Prior to the 1990s, many migrants residing in southern Mexico were able to move within the region in search of jobs, merchandise, and other resources and opportunities without legal papers or fear of being apprehended. Although the 1974 General Population Law (Ley General de Población) criminalized the presence of unauthorized migrants on Mexican territory (e.g., Guevara Bermúdez 2014), until the 1990s, this legal provision had not been strictly enforced (Yankelevich and Chenillo 2008; Sefchovich 2019).

However, starting in the 1990s and increasingly in the 2000s, under pressure from its northern neighbor, the Mexican government intensified its migration control provisions to contain flows of migrants, particularly from Central America, entering Mexico, staying there, or transiting the country toward the US-Mexico border. These provisions, linked to discourses around national security threats, are justified as measures required to control the trafficking or smuggling of arms, drugs, and people. Such initiatives as Operación de Sellamiento (Operation Seal Off, put in place in 1998), Plan Sur (in 2001), Plan Mérida (in 2008), and Programa Integral Frontera Sur (Southern Border Program, introduced in 2014), as well as the measures taken since 2019 to detain the so-called migrant caravans, have been introduced. Within the so-called control belts (*cinturones de contención*), immigration authorities, in collaboration with army and marine forces, have set up frequent checkpoints along the transit route, including the so-called Centers for Integrated Monitoring of Border Transit (Centros de Atención Integral al Tránsito Fronterizo), established at specific locations along the Mexican southern border, equipped with cameras and other electronic surveillance devices to inspect documents, luggage, and vehicles at ports of entry (whether by land, sea, or air) (Candiz and Basok 2021; Rojas Wiesner 2023). Between 2001 and 2021, these control measures resulted in 2.6 million deportations (or cases of "assisted return," a euphemism employed by the Mexican government), among whom 411,300 were from El Salvador, 1,123,600 from Guatemala, and 933,700 from Honduras.[5] The presence at Mexico's southern border region of the National Guard, which resorts to violence to prevent people from moving north (Isacson 2021; Moncada and Rojas 2022), has turned this area into a virtual detention center for many asylum seekers and migrants, preventing them from traveling in Mexico without documentation, such as an approved refugee status or a transit visa (*oficio de salida*). Yet these documents are not always easily available. During the first year of the COVID-19 pandemic, applications were received only virtually, making it particularly difficult for migrants without access to the internet to apply. In the case of Tapachula, while the number of migrants arriving in this city have continued to increase in the past few years, the inability of the National Immigration Institute (INM) to process a growing number of applications, combined with enhanced surveillance measures, has made it particularly challenging for many migrants without documents to avoid detention (Rojas Wiesner 2021).

At the same time, borders have remained open to some migrants, particularly transborder workers and visitors from neighboring states. To manage this flow, since the late 1990s, the federal government has been issuing legal documents to these migrants. A series of differentially inclusive policies have been put in place to grant admission to different sets of migrants, each with different sets of privileges and restrictions. In 1997, the Mexican state introduced procedures for issuing individual agricultural work permits (Forma Migratoria de Visitante Agrícola, or FMVA) to Guatemalan workers interested in working in the state of Chiapas. In 2001, a visitor's permit (Forma Migratoria de Visitante Local, or FMVL) was introduced for those coming from Guatemalan municipalities to the Guatemala-Mexico border region. In 2005, INM proposed comprehensive changes for regulating the migration of agricultural and nonagricultural workers into Mexico's southern border (INM 2005). These changes were put in place in 2008, along with changes for the admission criteria for local visitors from bordering municipalities in Guatemala and Belize.[6] These migration regulation measures were combined with some other procedures outlined in the 2011 Migration Law to authorize and document migrants entering Mexico at that time (Basok and Rojas Wiesner 2017).

Furthermore, prior to the introduction of Mexico's Migration Law in 2011, the Mexican government launched six special-status regularization programs. Civil society organizations pressured the Mexican state to approve each program and provided on-the-ground assistance to migrants who wished to apply for documentation (Sin Fronteras 2012). However, immigration status granted through these programs was valid for only one year, and on its expiration, status holders were required to renew it. Unfortunately, many migrants lost status when they could not meet certain renewal requirements, such as a job offer. In 2012, when the Migration Law became effective, requirements for status application and renewal became even more stringent, making this legal status even more precarious than before the introduction of the new law (Basok and Rojas Wiesner 2017).

Articles 133 and 134 of the Migration Law enabled some migrants to apply for permanent or temporary residency. Article 133 lists groups of individuals eligible to apply: (1) family members (i.e., spouse, common-law partner, parent, or children) of Mexican citizens or permanent or temporary residents; (2) victims of or witnesses to a serious crime committed in national territory recognized by the INM; (3) people whose degree of vulnerability make their deportation or return difficult or impossible; and (4) children and adolescents who are subject to international abduction and restitution procedures. However, many migrants from northern Central America residing in Mexico without regular status do not meet these criteria of "deservingness."

The Migration Law also clarified eligibility for temporary residency status, such as one-year renewable work permits (Tarjeta de Visitante Trabajador Fronterizo, or TVTF) for migrants from Guatemala and Belize whose labor or services were needed in the Mexican border states of Chiapas, Tabasco, Campeche, and Quintana Roo (Article 52). Furthermore, those from neighboring countries to the south were allowed to obtain a five-year multientry Regional Visitor's Card (Tarjeta de Visitante Regional, or TVR), which authorized visitors to stay, albeit not to work, in Mexico for up to seven days on each entry (Article 52, section III). However, as we discuss below, requirements for obtaining a TVTF and restrictions attached to the TVR served as barriers for many migrants, particularly domestic workers living in Mexico without legal documents authorizing them to stay and work (CDHFMC, IMUMI, and GTPM 2014, 2).

Much as in other countries where rigid immigration requirements, costs, delays, and confusion over the requirements and procedures preclude many nonstatus individuals from applying for secure status (see, e.g., Velasco 2016; Menjívar 2006), Mexico's restricted eligibility criteria outlined in the Migration Law were de facto administrative bordering mechanisms that *prevented* many migrants from legalizing their stay. Concerned about the precarity of many migrants without status, civil society organizations, citing Article 42 of the Migration Law, lobbied the government to launch new regularization programs. Eventually, the Mexican state heeded these pleas.

The first post-2011 regularization program, Programa Temporal de Regularización Migratoria (PTRM-2015) ran for ten months, February–December 2015. The earlier programs authorized status for only one year and required annual renewals, something that many migrants found difficult to do (Basok and Rojas Wiesner 2017). By contrast, the 2015 program made it possible for migrants to obtain temporary residency for a period of four years and then apply for permanent status. In this sense, the program was a step forward from the previous initiatives and promised to make legal status considerably less precarious for many migrants (Basok and Rojas Wiesner 2017).

However, this program did not come anywhere close to meeting its target of twenty thousand regularizations. Based on INM statistical reports, only 3,276 migrants were fortunate enough to be granted legal papers (CCINM 2018). Civil society activists, including the Citizen's Council, an advisory body to the INM, attributed the underperformance mainly to poor information dissemination and outreach efforts. When another regularization program, PTRM-2017, was launched, civil society organizations that supported this initiative committed themselves to assisting migrants without status to apply for status regularization by organizing fairs and engaging in other promotional activities. The fairs enabled thousands of migrants who met the PTRM eligibility requirements (i.e., nonstatus migrants who had entered Mexico prior to January 9, 2015), as well as those who met the criteria set out in the Migration Law, to obtain residency status. However, as with PTRM-2015, its achievements were lower than expected. Only 5,599 undocumented migrants were able to attain legal residency during the 2017 campaign (CCINM 2018). Institutional racism and, related to that, procedural irregularities and bottlenecks were responsible for these poor outcomes.

Migrants who wished to obtain status were faced with some internal bordering practices perpetrated by street-level bureaucrats. A representative of a nongovernmental organization (NGO) whom we interviewed for this study described the institutional racism entrenched in public offices that are well known for their differentiated treatment of those they perceive as the "other," such as low-income migrants from northern Central America. This institutional racism among civil servants is responsible for their indifference to the plight of Central American migrants and reluctance to provide adequate services to them:

> The inaction, corruption, and laziness of public officials were a major obstacle we faced at the fairs. . . . And that helped us to see who is really responsible for the lack of legal status among migrants. There is so much *institutional racism and indifference*. Public officials put up obstacles for the migrants who wish to regularize their status. The fair made it more than evident. . . . They came to the fairs to put up obstacles, and they made it clear that they were not there to help the migrants but to bother, criminalize, and harass them. . . . They made migrants look like idiots who don't know what the right documents are and how to complete an application. Of course, this classist and racist outlook on migrants is typical. They always blame migrants and civil society organizations and fail to see how

public institutions perpetuate this situation. (interview, November 8, 2017; emphasis added)

Civil society organizations continued to reach out to eligible migrants to encourage them to submit applications for status regularization. Interestingly, as many as six hundred applicants abandoned their applications in 2017, seemingly because they may have found the process to be too challenging. Among the major obstacles mentioned by some migrants and civil society activists interviewed in 2018 were excessive bureaucratic requirements, high costs, the need to absent themselves from work several times during this process, and the requirement to travel from remote areas to INM and other government offices. The application fee was to be waived for migrants whose income was below the minimum monthly levels established in Article 17 of the Federal Rights Law (Ley Federal de Derechos), and it was the responsibility of the national family welfare office (Sistema Nacional para el Desarrollo Integral de la Familia, or DIF) to review applications for eligibility. However, for those whose income exceeded the established minimum, even if only slightly, the requirement to pay fees for residency applications was a significant barrier. Since most nonstatus migrants had precarious jobs, they could not afford to cover the costs of the paperwork or transportation (CCINM 2018).

To protect migrants from discrimination in government offices, volunteers and staff from civil society organizations accompanied migrants to their appointments. Without such assistants, migrants were considerably less likely to receive adequate social services. Among the successful 2017 PTRM applicants, 22 per cent had been assisted by civil society organizations (CCINM 2018).[7] Yet, with limited resources at their disposal, these organizations were unable to reach many migrants, particularly those residing in remote communities who remained unaware of the opportunities or found it too expensive (or dangerous, as discussed below) to travel to cities like Tapachula where they could submit their applications (interview, March 25, 2018).

More important, however, the low success levels for both regularization programs can be attributed to structural factors that we call "exclusionary inclusion." Much like the pre-2011 status regularization programs (Sin Fronteras 2012), PTRM-15 and PRTM-17 were plagued by problems related to infrastructural inadequacy and bureaucratic inefficiency. The Mexican state failed to create an infrastructure to enable migrants without status to obtain regularization. Poor dissemination of information to migrants in remote communities, insufficient information, long distances to INM offices, lack of personnel to guide migrants through the processes, slow procedures, the requirement to pay fines for unauthorized entry into the country, and additional payments demanded by some bureaucrats who tried to take advantage of the migrants for their own benefit, as well as difficulties in obtaining certain required documents (e.g., proof of residence from local authorities) were among the main reasons for the poor performance of both status regularization programs.

Despite a more liberal migration law approved in 2011, Mexico continued to characterize migrants from northern Central America as a threat to be contained by fortifying surveillance and intensifying migration control. An important reason why many undocumented migrants chose not to apply for status regularization was the fear of traveling to INM offices or fairs through heavily securitized zones. For fear of apprehension and deportation, undocumented immigrants not only accepted unsafe, poorly paid, and demanding jobs (De Genova 2013; Heyman 2013; Harrison and Lloyd 2012), but also restricted their mobility and became trapped (Núñez and Heyman 2007; Heyman 2013). In recent years, increased immigration surveillance in border areas and in the so-called transit routes has had serious repercussions on the number of people seeking to cross Mexico,[8] on their mobility strategies, and on the daily life of migrants who have settled in the southern border region. Those migrants have faced risks of detention when they traveled along heavily patrolled highways.

Miguel's story provides a vivid illustration. In December 2015, Miguel, a young Salvadoran who lived in the rural area of the municipality of Tuxtla Chico, close to Tapachula, Chiapas, was arrested on two occasions when he tried to apply for status under PTRM-2015. In the first attempt, his documents were seized and destroyed at an immigration checkpoint. In the second attempt, he was sent to the Siglo XXI Migration Station, a detention center in Tapachula, from which he was deported. Although he was able to return to Mexico, once again crossing the borders without authorization, he tried to avoid running into immigration authorities by choosing to remain in remote communities where his unauthorized presence was undetected.

Although Mexico endorsed the Global Compact for Safe, Orderly, and Regular Migration (UPMRIP 2020), its actions contravene three of the agreement's twenty-three objectives, namely, to "provide accurate and timely information at all stages of migration" (objective 3); to "ensure that all migrants have proof of legal identity and adequate documentation" (objective 4); and to "enhance availability and flexibility of pathways for regular migration" (objective 5).[9] Many nonstatus migrants continue to lack the means to gain status through regular channels. Caught between the sword and the wall, migrants have no choice but to either continue to live and work without legal documents authorizing their stay or look for alternative routes to gaining status that rely on "creative" but not necessarily legal means.

Alternative Forms of "Regularization" in Border Towns

When certain administrative bordering procedures prevent migrants from northern Central America from legalizing their status in Mexico through officially approved processes and procedures, some cross these internal borders by attempting to "fix" their precarious legal situation by procuring alternative documents, buying fake documents, or falsely obtaining authentic documents. We discuss each of these strategies in turn.

First, let us consider the substitution of a required document by an alternative one. Guatemalans and Belizeans are eligible to receive a TVTF (Border Worker Card) to engage in remunerative activities in Mexico for one year. One problem they face is that this card requires a job offer by an employer registered with the INM and a fee payment of approximately US$20, an equivalent of three workdays' wages. For many domestic workers, the fee is too steep or their employers may be unwilling to register with the INM. To overcome this problem, they opt for a TVR (Regional Visitor's Card), which allows them to stay in the country legally without fear of being apprehended by the migration authorities. Even though they are entitled to stay for only seven days per visit, this rule is not enforced and can be easily bent.

Street vendors and self-employed workers (e.g., bricklayers) provide another illustration. They are ineligible to apply for a TVTF. In their attempt to limit "informality" in the economy, Mexican authorities preclude migrants in the so-called informal sector from obtaining legal status (Rojas Wiesner 2017). Without papers that grant them permission to engage in self-employment, these migrants also obtain a TVR.

In addition to domestic workers, street vendors, and other self-employed workers, other migrants who live and work in Mexico without authorization at times also opt for a TVR, a free and easily obtained legal document that offers them some protection from deportation. A TVR is not entirely free. Migrants are required to renew their TVR every five years in one of seven approved offices, five of which are located in Chiapas, one in Tabasco, and one in Quintana Roo. Guatemalan migrants interviewed in one of our research projects told us that those who found it difficult to travel to these offices during work hours paid a fee to people who kept their place in a long queue (see also Bautista 2021).[10] Still, obtaining a TVR is less expensive and complicated than getting a TVTF. Migrants thus "fix" their status by "bending" rules. Local authorities seem to tolerate this "semicompliance" (as Ruhs and Anderson [2010] have called it), though it contravenes established federal regulations. This nexus between semicompliance and state disregard or tolerance creates inherent instability; that is, semicompliance is in fact contingent on the degree of official tolerance, which can be retracted at any time if state officials choose to enforce the provisions more strictly. Thus, everyone engaged in semicompliance is susceptible to some potential recriminations.

Second, some nonstatus migrants obtain fake documents. Although in our research we did not come across any migrants who had purchased fake documents, and our key informants shared with us rumors, circulated widely in the communities in which we conducted research, concerning the presence of a migration industry specializing in the creation and sale of counterfeit documents. In fact, several municipalities of the four border states of southern Mexico have reported cases of migrants who have obtained fake documents, such as birth certificates and proof of residence statements, voter cards, and drivers' licenses (see, e.g., Domínguez 2019). The sale of false documents is not a new phenomenon in this region. As early as the beginning of the twenty-first century, a high-ranking INM official in Ciudad Hidalgo, a city in Chiapas close to the Guatemala-Mexico border, observed that false residency permits and other identity documents were easily obtained in that area.[11] Journalist accounts dating back to the early 2000s refer to the presence of a criminal network (an "industry") dedicated to the production of fake documents (e.g., *Proceso* 2003). In 2020 and 2021, when the pandemic-related restrictions made it difficult for migrants to apply for documentation required to travel within Mexico, the production and sale of false documents became widespread (see, e.g., INM 2021).

Third, some migrants obtain authentic documents in an illegitimate way (see, e.g., Domínguez 2019). For instance, they receive birth certificates for themselves (or their children) by claiming that even though they (or their children) were born in Mexico, the paperwork for birth certificates was not completed at birth (Bedoya 2021). In other cases, the local authorities or officials encourage and help migrants to become "naturalized" (that is, to obtain a voter's credential, which in practice serves as a citizen identification document) either for a fee, as political patronage, or out of compassion. In fact, as we were told, in one municipality, a former municipal president encouraged migrants to get "naturalized" by obtaining such authentic documents, charging them no more than a regular processing fee. And some suspected political patronage might have been the reason for his "generosity" toward the migrants (see also Bedoya 2021).

Lorena, a female Guatemalan street vendor residing in another municipality with her Mexican-born children, explained to us why she needed to obtain legal papers in this fashion and how she was able to do it. Her case exemplifies the nexus between what Cecilia Menjívar and Leisy Abrego (2012, 1389) call "legal violence" (i.e., the harmful consequences of legal exclusion from membership on migrants lives, including family separation, exploitation in the labor force, and denial of social supports and resources) and domestic abuse. Abused by her Mexican partner, who threatened to report her to the immigration authorities for her undocumented status, Lorena sought ways to secure her residency in Mexico: "I spoke with someone at the [municipal] presidency office. There were some kind people there, a real nice lady. She told me: 'Listen, mommy, I'm going to help you get your papers.' And that's how I did it" (interview, July 24, 2018).

In addition to public officials, lawyers and counseling agencies help migrants to access illegal documents. Migrants also borrow, rent, or buy birth certificates from relatives or friends (Bedoya 2021, 8–10). David, a Guatemalan migrant we interviewed in 2018, explained that his lawyer advised him to obtain Mexican birth certificates for his children, who had been born in Guatemala, so that he could buy land in Tapachula, something that motivates other migrants to get the falsely obtained documents:

> When I came here [to Tapachula], I couldn't buy land. . . . I contacted a lawyer, and he told me that if you had children born here, I could buy property in the name of my children. So this is what I did. I obtained birth certificates for my children, and then I bought land in the name of my son here. But the good thing is that at that time there was an opportunity to get birth certificates for my children. (interview, July 16, 2018)

With a birth certificate in hand, migrants can apply for other documents, such as voter cards. Diana, a migrant woman who participated in a focus group, links this "irregularity" to corruption among public officials:

> Here, what has harmed us is corruption. This has caused a lack of control and has allowed an increase in the number of people who reside here in an irregular manner. . . . It is so easy to obtain a birth certificate and an IFE [Federal Electoral Institute voting credential] that even those who live on that side [in Guatemala] have such documents; even if they don't live here, they have their voter credentials, your birth certificate and voter ID. (interview, July 9, 2018)

As other researchers have pointed out, the falsification of legal status may require active collaboration between state agents, the "migration industry," and migrants (see, e.g., Sadiq 2009). As Madeleine Reeves (2015) has pointed out, some state agents, such as the police, are willing to accept fake or falsely obtained documents, particularly when they receive financial compensation for their "liberal" attitudes. Reeves (2015) also recognizes that within these "spaces of ambiguity," the "tolerance" on behalf of state police is conditioned by a migrant's ability to negotiate with these agents to avoid arrest. In some cases, consultants, community organizations, and even immigration authorities encourage migrants to obtain fake papers or authentic documents containing false information, while immigration "experts" offer their full (and highly priced) services (Tuckett 2018). Similarly in Mexico, the production of "illegal legality" relies on the collaboration between migrants, corrupt officials, and the "migration industry" in the exclusionary system that precludes migrants from using authorized channels to secure their legal status in Mexico.

The Precariousness of "Illegal Legality"

Peter Schuck (2000) distinguished between the "law on the books" (i.e., the law as formally established), "law in action" (i.e., the law as implemented), and the "law in their minds" (i.e., the law as perceived by various groups and actors). Drawing on Schuck's distinction, Ruhs and Anderson (2010) have pointed out that migrants who breach certain conditions that regulate their stay in the country and access to jobs do not necessarily perceive these acts as violations that subject them to deportation. Both migrants who were authorized to stay but were not permitted to work and their employers saw such acts of unauthorized employment as "bending" rather than breaking immigration rules and therefore not as serious as immigration status violations (Ruhs and Anderson 2010, 204–5). Similarly, in our case, many migrants felt that it was legitimate to obtain birth certificates in illegitimate ways, and they were pleased with the corresponding improvements in their life circumstances.

Yet many others experienced fears and anxieties regarding their false documents. Reeves (2015) has pointed out that uncertainty about the authenticity of documents can produce a mixed feeling of excitement and anxiety among migrants. Furthermore, obtaining false documents is not without risks. Tuckett (2018, 25) has observed that even well-executed rule bending can be uncovered, and some migrants may lose status or the opportunity to obtain citizenship when their manipulations are revealed. In fact, some migrants we interviewed have had their falsely obtained documents confiscated or were arrested when immigration authorities discovered the forgery, as the following testimonies illustrate.

Dina, a Honduran migrant we interviewed in 2012, told us that her falsely documented daughter had been arrested:

> I have papers . . . illegally, let's say, because I did not get them through Migration, but a married couple registered me here in Mexico [as their daughter], and those are my documents, and my daughter is registered the same way, and my other two children are registered similarly. So my mother went to Honduras on vacation with my daughter, but my mother had a different surname, . . . and when they returned, they were captured here in Tapachula and now they are being detained. (interview, August 27, 2012)

Evernoe, a man from Honduras, who had been similarly "adopted" by a Mexican family, shared his story with us: "That's where I met Mr. Gilberto. . . . The man treated me well, and he told me that he was a good person and he helped me; he said, 'Look, I'm going to register you as my son under another name.' They went to register me and, yes, I then appeared as a Mexican, but with another name" (interview, August 27, 2012). However, when the authorities stopped him to verify his status, they found his answers to be inconsistent. During the interrogation, he confessed that he was born in Honduras. The authorities then confiscated his documents and arrested him for breaking the law.

Nancy, a Guatemalan woman who has lived in Mexico for nine years and had a TVR, expressed anxiety about the uncertainty and insecurity of having a document that did not authorize her lengthy stay and employment:

> [We] all have the migration permit, but as a visitor [TVR]. My mother, my brothers, and I have this permit . . . my Regional Visitor Card is valid until 2021. I wanted to have my papers from here. I already went to the INM in Escárcega and I went to INM of Campeche, and I went to the Ministry of Foreign Relations in Campeche, but they charge too much. . . . I tell my husband "and how can we eat without working, and for us to do this, it is already a lot." . . . And the truth is complicated, and I am sorry to be here in this country and that one day they catch me because I do not have the right papers. I've been living here for nine years now. And here no one is going to help us like this, without money, without payment. I don't know why; I don't know if that's the case or what happens. . . . Without papers we cannot do anything. . . . And so, this is how it is. (interview, February 14, 2019)

Thus, even though some migrants manage to obtain authentic documents through illegitimate means, these documents do not necessarily reduce their insecurity about their stay in Mexico, and many continue to fear that immigration authorities may detain or even deport them.

Conclusions

Responding to the exclusionary nature of internal bordering practices and limited opportunities for status regularization, many Central American migrants who reside in the southern region of Mexico employ creative strategies to seek forms of inclusion that blur the boundary between legality and illegality. In this chapter, we advance an analysis of "illegality," "legality," and what we call "illegal legality" that contributes to the understanding of "illegality" as a political, social, and cultural legal construction (Ackerman 2014; De Genova 2013; Goldring and Landolt 2013) and recognizes that multidimensional transitions between "legality" and "illegality" (Goldring and Landolt 2013; Landolt and Goldring 2015; Chauvin and Garcés-Mascareñas 2014) can blur the distinction between the two. Furthermore, we recognize that the "legality" that some migrants acquire can be not only "liminal" (Menjívar 2006), "precarious" (Basok and Rojas Wiesner 2017), or "semilegal" (Kubal 2013) but also "illegal."

Three types of migrants can be characterized as "illegally legal." First, some obtain documents, such as a TVR, that authorize their temporary stay in Mexico but not their work in remunerated activities, yet they "violate" these conditions by engaging in paid employment. Authorities in southern Mexico appear to tolerate this type of semicompliance (Ruhs and Anderson 2010). Second, some migrants obtain false documents with the help of agents of the so-called migration industry who are willing to manufacture or obtain fake documents. And, third, some migrants receive legitimate credentials (such as voter cards or birth certificates) in public registry offices, but they falsify their histories to fudge eligibility.

Migrants adopt these creative solutions in response to the administrative bordering practices in southern Mexico. The Regional Visitor's Card is used as an alternative status because certain requirements make it difficult for migrants who wish to work in Mexico to obtain a TVTF or a temporary resident card. Furthermore, the eligibility for permanent residency established in the Migration Law is restrictive and exclusionary. Likewise, the regularization programs authorized by the Mexican Ministry of the Interior were plagued by infrastructural deficiencies and bureaucratic inefficiencies. Furthermore, strict migration control measures, combined with travel and other restrictions adopted during the COVID-19 pandemic, hamper mobility within the region, making it difficult for migrants from remote communities without access to internet to travel to the urban centers to access internet or help. Under these circumstances, migrants seek alternative ways to regularize their stay that are not necessarily legal. However, as shown in this chapter, these "solutions" offer neither security nor peace of mind to the migrants. Many continue to fear that the fraud will be uncovered and they will be penalized. These fears are not unfounded. In fact, some migrants have had their fake or falsely obtained documents taken away and have been detained.

NOTES

1. We understand legality and illegality as social constructions, and as such these terms should be enclosed in quotation marks. While some academics have used *irregular migration* in place of the term *illegal*, this concept also has negative connotation, that is, as something that is incorrect and in need of correction. For this reason, we decided not to use *irregular* in this chapter.

2. Funded by El Colegio de la Frontera Sur, the National Council of Science and Technology of Mexico (CONACYT), the International Development Research Centre of Canada, and the Social Science and Humanities Research Council of Canada.

3. Of the 179 Central American migrants interviewed in various projects, there were 124 women and 55 men. Among them, 24 were from El Salvador, 113 from Guatemala, and 42 from Honduras. While some among them (very few) never attended a school, there were some who had received technical or professional training. For the vast majority of the migrants interviewed in these studies, their educational levels fell between some primary education to some secondary education.

4. Lipsky attributes the discretion exercised by "street-level bureaucrats" to the conditions they face, including a chronic shortage of resources relative to the tasks to be performed, and to rising demand for their services, unclear and contradictory policy directives, demanding performance measurements, and the need to provide services to involuntary clients. For Lipsky, these individual decisions made by "street-level" bureaucrats collectively constitute state policies.

5. Calculations made by the authors based on data reported in *boletines estadísticos* by the Unidad de Política Migratoria, Registro e Identidad de Personas (Gobierno de México, http://portales.segob.gob.mx/es/PoliticaMigratoria/Boletines_Estadisticos).

6. "Diario Oficial de la Federación," Secretaria de Gobernación, March 12, 2008, https://www.dof.gob.mx/nota_detalle.php?codigo=5031467&fecha=12/03/2008#gsc.tab=0.

7. In Chiapas, the state that processed about one-half of all the PRTM applications in 2017, as many as 40 percent of the successful applicants received assistance from civil society organizations. In the state of Chiapas, the number of beneficiaries was almost triple the number achieved by the 2015 campaign (there were 879 successful applications in 2015 and 2,990 in 2017), in large part due to the tireless work by the paid staff and unpaid volunteers of the Fray Matias Human Rights Center (CCINM 2018).

8. Annual detention figures have ranged between 170,000 and almost 440,000 migrants (Canales and Rojas Wiesner 2018). Also see various reports published in "2025 Boletín estadístico mensual," Gobierno de México, http://www.politicamigratoria.gob.mx/es/PoliticaMigratoria/Boletines_Estadisticos.

9. "Global Compact for Safe, Orderly, and Regular Migration," Refugees and Migrants, United Nations, July 13, 2018, https://refugeesmigrants.un.org/sites/default/files/180713_agreed_outcome_global_compact_for_migration.pdf.

10. "Cross-Border Mobility and Labor Insertion of the Guatemalan Population in Mexico: Regional Specificities on the Southern Border" (2018–19), coordinated by Martha Luz Rojas Wiesner.

11. This official was interviewed in the study "The Participation of Women and Minors in Guatemalan Agricultural Labor Migration to the Soconusco Region" (2000–2002), coordinated by Martha Luz Rojas Wiesner and Hugo Ángeles Cruz, with funding from the Benito Juárez Research System (SIBEJ), CONACYT.

REFERENCES

Abarca, Gray, and Susan Bibler Coutin. 2018. "Sovereign Intimacies: The Lives of Documents Within US State-Noncitizen Relationships." *American Ethnologist* 45 (1): 7–19.

Ackerman, Edwin. 2014. "What Part of Illegal Don't You Understand? Bureaucracy and Civil Society in the Shaping of Illegality." *Ethnic and Racial Studies* 37 (2): 181–203.

Alexander, Jennifer. 1997. "Avoiding the Issue: Racism and Administrative Responsibility in Public Administration." *American Review of Public Administration* 27 (4): 343–61.

Balibar, Étienne. 2004. *We, the People of Europe*. Princeton, NJ: Princeton University Press.

Basok, Tanya, and Martha Luz Rojas Wiesner. 2017. "Precarious Legality: Regularizing Central American Migrants in Mexico." *Ethnic and Racial Studies* 41 (7): 1274–93. https://doi.org/10.1080/01419870.2017.1291983.

Bautista, Marvin. 2021. "Hoteleros denuncian presunta red de corrupción en trámites de la TVR." *Diario del Sur*, January 7. https://www.diariodelsur.com.mx/local/hoteleros-denuncian-presunta-red-de-corrupcion-en-tramites-de-la-tvr-6213663.html.

Bedoya, Luis. 2021. "'Papeles' comprados: Procedimientos no ortodoxos implementados por guatemaltecos para adquirir documentos mexicanos de identificación personal." *Migraciones Internacionales* 12. https://doi.org/10.33679/rmi.v1i1.2157.

Bigo, Didier. 2002. "Security and Immigration: Toward Critique of the Governmentality of Unease." Special Issue, *Alternatives: Global, Local, Political* 27:63–92.

Bolter, Jessica, Muzaffar Chishti, and Doris Meissner. 2021. "Back on the Table: U.S. Legalization and the Unauthorized Immigrant Groups that Could Factor in the Debate." Migration Policy Institute. https://www.migrationpolicy.org/research/us-legalization-unauthorized-immigrant-groups.

Bosniak, Linda. 2007. "Being Here: Ethical Territoriality and the Rights of Immigrants." *Theoretical Inquiries in Law* 8 (2): 389–410. https://doi.org/10.2202/1565-3404.1155.

Canales, Alejandro, and Martha Luz Rojas Wiesner. 2018. "Panorama de la Migración Internacional en México y Centroamérica." Paper presented at the Reunión Regional Latinoamericana y Caribeña de Expertas y Expertos en Migración Internacional Preparatoria del Pacto Mundial para una Migración Segura, Ordenada y Regular, Santiago de Chile, 2018. Serie Población y Desarrollo, no. 124. Santiago de Chile: Comisión Económica para América Latina y el Caribe.

Candiz, Guillermo, and Tanya Basok. 2021. "Intensity and Uncertainty: Performing Border Conflicts at the US-Mexico Borderlands." *Population, Space, and Place* 27 (8): e2441. https://doi.org/10.1002/psp.2441.

Casas-Cortes, Maribel, Sebastián Cobarrubias, Nicholas De Genova, Glenda Garelli, Giorgio Grappi, Charles Heller, Sabine Hess, Bernd Kasparek, Sandro Mezzadra, Brett Neilson, Irene Peano, Lorenzo Pezzani, John Pickles, Federico Rahola, Lisa Riedner, Stephan Scheel, and Martina Tazzioli. 2015. "New Keywords: Migration and Borders." Special issue, *Cultural Studies* 29 (1): 55–87. https://doi.org/10.1080/09502386.2014.891630.

Castañeda, Heide. 2010. "Deportation Deferred: 'Illegality,' Visibility, and Recognition in Contemporary Germany." In *The Deportation Regime: Sovereignty, Space, and the Freedom of Movement*, edited by Nicholas De Genova and Nathalie Peutz, 245–61. Durham, NC: Duke University Press.

CCINM (Consejo Ciudadano del Instituto Nacional de Migración). 2018. "Informe Final: Coordinación Interinstitucional para la Implementación del Programa Temporal de Regularización Migratoria (PTRM) 2017." Grupo de Trabajo de Regularización Migratoria. Unpublished report.

CDHFMC (Centro de Derechos Humanos Fray Matías de Córdova), IMUMI (Instituto para las Mujeres en la Migración A.C.), and GTPM (Grupo de Trabajo sobre Política Migratoria). 2014. "Programa de Regularización Migratoria Como Una Acción Afirmativa: Propuesta para ampliar el acceso a la documentación migratoria con autorización para trabajar a las mujeres migrantes centroamericanas en Chiapas." IMUMI. https://imumi.org/attachments/2014/Accion-Afirmativa-regularizacion-migratoria-2014.pdf.

Chauvin, Sébastien, and Blanca Garcés-Mascareñas. 2014. "Becoming Less Illegal: Deservingness Frames and Undocumented Migrant Incorporation." *Sociology Compass* 8 (4): 422–32.

Chávez, Leo R. 2013. *The Latino Threat: Constructing Immigrants, Citizens, and the Nation*. Stanford, CA: Stanford University Press.

Coutin, Susan Bibler. 2014. "Deportation Studies: Origins, Themes, and Directions." *Journal of Ethnic and Migration Studies* 4 (4): 671–81.

Coutin, Susan Bibler. 2020. "Opportunities and Double Binds: Legal Craft in an Era of Uncertainty." In *Paper Trails: Migrants, Documents, and Legal Insecurity*, edited by Sarah B. Horton and Josiah Heyman, 130–52. Durham, NC: Duke University Press.

De Genova, Nicholas. 2010. "The Deportation Regime: Sovereignty, Space, and the Freedom of Movement." In *The Deportation Regime: Sovereignty, Space, and the Freedom of Movement*, edited by Nicholas De Genova and Nathalie Peutz, 33–65. Durham, NC: Duke University Press.

De Genova, Nicholas. 2013. "Spectacles of Migrant 'Illegality': The Scene of Exclusion, the Obscene of Inclusion." *Ethnic and Racial Studies* 36 (7): 1180–98. https://doi.org/10.1080/01419870.2013.783710.

De Genova, Nicholas, and Nathalie Peutz, eds. 2010. *The Deportation Regime: Sovereignty, Space, and the Freedom of Movement*. Durham, NC: Duke University Press.

Domínguez, Jesús Manuel. 2019. "Con documentación apócrifa, migrantes intentan tramitar INE." *El Heraldo de Tabasco*, July 3. https://www.elheraldodetabasco.com.mx/local/migrantes-falsifican-papeles-para-sacar-su-ine-3845797.html.

El-Kayed, Nihad, and Ulrike Hamann. 2018. "Refugees' Access to Housing and Residency in German Cities: Internal Border Regimes and Their Local Variations." *Social Inclusion* 6 (1): 135–46. https://doi.org/10.17645/Si.V6i1.1334.

FitzGerald, David Scott. 2019. "Remote Control of Migration: Theorising Territoriality, Shared Coercion, and Deterrence." *Journal of Ethnic and Migration Studies* 46 (21): 1–19.

Fuglerud, Oivind. 2004. "Constructing Exclusion. The Micro-Sociology of an Immigration Department." *Social Anthropology* 12 (1): 25–40.

Geoffrion, Karine, and Viviane Cretton. 2021. "Bureaucratic Routes to Migration: Migrants' Lived Experience of Paperwork, Clerks, and Other Immigration Intermediaries." *Anthropologica* 63 (1): 1–26. https://doi.org/10.18357/anthropologica6312021184.

Goldring, Luin, and Patricia Landolt. 2013. "Precarious Legal Status in Canada: Theorizing Non-Citizenship and Conditionality." In *Producing and Negotiating Non-Citizenship: Precarious Legal Status in Canada*, edited by Luin Goldring and Patricia Landolt, 3–27. Toronto: University of Toronto Press.

Guevara Bermúdez, José Antonio. 2014. "Conexiones entre los Derechos Humanos de las Personas Migrantes y la Seguridad: ¿Es Posible Afirmar que el Derecho Mexicano Criminaliza la Migración Indocumentada? *Cuestiones Constitucionales: Revista Mexicana de Derecho Constitucional* 31: 81–117.

Harrison, Jill L., and Sarah. E. Lloyd. 2012. "Illegality at Work: Deportability and the Productive New Era of Immigration Enforcement." *Antipode* 44 (2): 365–85. https://doi.org/10.1111/J.1467-8330.2010.00841.X.

Heyman, Josiah. 2013. "'Illegality' and the U.S.-Mexico Border: How It Is Produced and Resisted." In *Constructing Immigrant 'Illegality': Critiques, Experiences, and Responses*, edited by Cecilia Menjívar and Daniel Kanstroom, 111–36. Cambridge: Cambridge University Press.

Horton, Sarah B. 2020. "Paper Trails: Migrants, Bureaucratic Inscription, and Legal Recognition." In *Paper Trails: Migrants, Documents, and Legal Insecurity*, edited by Sarah Horton and Josiah Heyman, 1–26. Durham, NC: Duke University Press.

Humphrey, Michael. 2013. "Migration, Security, and Insecurity." *Journal of Intercultural Studies* 34 (2): 178–95.

Hyndman Jennifer, and Alison Mountz. 2008. "Another Brick in the Wall? Neo-Refoulement and the Externalization of Asylum by Australia and Europe." *International Journal of Comparative Politics* 43 (2): 249–69.

Inda, Jonathan X. 2013. "Subject to Deportation: IRCA, 'Criminal Aliens,' and the Policing of Immigration." *Migration Studies* 1 (3): 292–310.

INM (Instituto Nacional de Migración). 2005. *Propuesta de política migratoria integral en la frontera sur de México*. Mexico City: Centro de Estudios Migratorios.

INM (Instituto Nacional de Migración). 2021. "Presenta INM denuncia ante FGR por documentación apócrifa usada por personas migrantes para desplazarse hacia la frontera con Estados Unidos." *Boletín* 134 (March 16). https://www.gob.mx/inm/prensa/presenta-inm-denuncia-ante-fgr-por-documentacion-apocrifa-usada-por-personas-migrantes-para-desplazarse-hacia-la-frontera-con-estados-unidos.

Isacson, Adam. 2021. "Weekly U.S.-Mexico Border Update: Migrant Caravan, Biden Administration Divisions, Texas Crackdown." *Wola News*, November 5. https://www.wola.org/2021/11/weekly-u-s-mexico-border-update-migrant-caravan-biden-administration-divisions-texas-crackdown/.

Isin, Engin F., and Greg M. Nielsen, eds. 2008. *Acts of Citizenship*. New York: Zed Books.

Könönen, Jukka. 2018. "Border Struggles Within the State: Administrative Bordering of Non-Citizens in Finland." *Nordic Journal of Migration Research* 8 (3): 143–50. https://doi.org/10.2478/Njmr-2018-0018.

Kubal, Agnieszka. 2013. "Conceptualizing Semi-Legality in Migration Research." *Law and Society Review* 47 (3): 555–87.

Landolt, Patricia, and Luin Goldring. 2015. "Assembling Noncitizenship Through the Work of Conditionality." *Citizenship Studies* 19 (8): 853–69. https://doi.org/10.1080/13621025.2015.1110280.

Lipsky, Michael. 1980. *Street-Level Bureaucracy: Dilemmas of the Individual in Public Services*. Chicago: University of Chicago Press.

Menjívar, Cecilia. 2006. "Liminal Legality: Salvadoran and Guatemalan Immigrants' Lives in the United States." *American Journal of Sociology* 111 (4): 999–1037.

Menjívar, Cecilia. 2014. "Immigration Law Beyond Borders: Externalizing and Internalizing Border Controls in an Era of Securitization." *Annual Review of Law and Social Science* 10:353–69.

Menjívar, Cecilia, and Leisy J. Abrego. 2012. "Legal Violence: Immigration Law and the Lives of Central American Immigrants." *American Journal of Sociology* 117 (5): 1380–1421.

Menjívar, Cecilia, and Daniel Kanstroom. 2013. *Constructing Immigrant "Illegality": Critiques, Experiences, and Responses*. Cambridge: Cambridge University Press.

Mezzadra, Sandro. 2004. "The Right to Escape." *Ephemera* 4 (3): 267–75.

Mezzadra, Sandro. 2010. "The Gaze of Autonomy: Capitalism, Migration and Social Struggles." In *The Contested Politics of Mobility: Borderzones and Irregularity*, edited by Vicki Squire, 141–62. London: Routledge.

Mezzadra, Sandro, and Brett Nielson. 2011. "Borderscapes of Differential Inclusion: Subjectivity and Struggles on the Threshold of Justice's Excess." In *The Borders of Justice*, edited by Étienne Balibar, Sandro Mezzadra, and Ranabir Samaddar, 181–203. Philadelphia: Temple University Press.

Mezzadra, Sandro, and Brett Neilson. 2013. *Border as Method; or, The Multiplication of Labor*. Durham, NC: Duke University Press.

Moncada, Alicia, and Eduardo Rojas. 2022. *Bajo la bota: Militarización de la política migratoria en México*. Fundación para la Justicia y el Estado Democrático de Derecho (FJEDD), Sin Fronteras, Derechos Humanos Integrales en Acción (DHIA), Derechoscopio, Uno de Siete Migrando e Instituto para las Mujeres en la Migración (IMUMI). https://www.fundacionjusticia.org/bajo-la-bota-militarizacion-de-la-politica-migratoria-en-mexico/.

Morris, Lydia. 2003. "Managing Contradictions: Civic Stratification and Migrants' Rights." *International Migration Review* 37 (1): 74–100.

Núñez, Guillermina G., and Josiah Heyman. 2007. "Entrapment Processes and Immigrant Communities in a Time of Heightened Border Vigilance." *Human Organization* 66 (4): 354–65.

Nyers, Peter. 2015. "Migrant Citizenships and Autonomous Mobilities." *Migration Mobility and Displacement* 1 (1): 23–39.

Papadopoulos, Dimitris, and Vassilis Tsianos. 2008. "The Autonomy of Migration: The Animals of Undocumented Mobility." In *Deleuzian Encounters: Studies in Contemporary Social Issues*, edited by Anna Hickey-Moody and Peta Malins, 223–35. Basingstoke, UK: Palgrave Macmillan.

Papadopoulos, Dimitris, and Vassilis Tsianos. 2013. "After Citizenship: Autonomy of Migration, Organisational Ontology, and Mobile Commons." *Citizenship Studies* 17 (2): 178–96.

Pérez, Marta, Ariadna Ayala, Débora Ávila, and Sergio García. 2019. "Fronteras interiores: Las prácticas informales en el gobierno de la desigualdad en España." *Revista CIDOB d'Afers Internacionals* 122:111–35. https://doi.org/10.24241/rcai.2019.122.2.111.

Proceso. 2003. "Guatemala: Tráfico de Documentos Mexicanos." July 12. https://www.proceso.com.mx/254655/Guatemala-Trafico-De-Documentos-Mexicanos.

Ramírez, Jacques. 2017. "Etnografía del Estado: 'Visa Mercosur,' Prácticas Burocráticas y Estatus Migratorio en Ecuador." *Etnografías Contemporáneas* 3 (5): 182–212.

Reeves, Madeleine. 2015. "Living from the Nerves: Deportability, Indeterminacy, and the 'Feel of Law' in Migrant Moscow." *Social Analysis* 59 (4): 119–36.

Rigo, Enrica. 2011. "Citizens Despite Borders: Challenges to the Territorial Order of Europe." In *The Contested Politics of Mobility: Borderzones and Irregularity*, edited by Vicki Squire, 199–215. London: Routledge.

Rios-Contreras, Nancy. 2021. "Desastre Migratorio en el Tránsito México–Estados Unidos: Control de la Migración, Racismo y Covid-19." *REDER* 5 (2): 168–81.

Rojas Wiesner, Martha Luz. 2017. "Movilidad de Trabajadores Agrícolas de Guatemala a la Frontera Sur de México en Tiempos de Control Migratorio." *Entrediversidades* 8: 83–118.

Rojas Wiesner, Martha Luz. 2021. "La lucha migrante en Tapachula: Contra su inmovilidad forzada." *Gatopardo*, September 9. https://gatopardo.com/noticias-actuales/la-lucha-migrante-en-tapachula-contra-su-inmovilidad-forzada/.

Rojas Wiesner, Martha Luz. 2023. "More than a Northward Migratory Corridor: Changes in Transit Migration and Migration Policy in Mexico." In *The Routledge History of Modern Latin American Migration*, edited by Andreas Feldmann, Xóchitl Bada, Jorge Durand, and Stephanie Schütze, 353–68. New York: Routledge.

Ruhs, Martin, and Bridget Anderson. 2010. "Semi-Compliance and Illegality in Migrant Labour Markets: An Analysis of Migrants, Employers, and the State in the UK." *Population, Space, and Place* 16 (3): 195–211.

Rygiel, Kim. 2010. *Globalizing Citizenship*. Vancouver: University of British Columbia Press.

Sadiq, Kamal. 2009. *Paper Citizens: How Illegal Immigrants Acquire Citizenship in Developing Countries*. New York: Oxford University Press.

Schuck, Peter. 2000. "Law and the Study of Migration." In *Migration Theory: Talking Across Disciplines*, edited by Caroline Brettell and James Hollifield, 187–204. London: Routledge.

Scott, James C. 1998. *Seeing like a State: How Certain Schemes to Improve the Human Condition Have Failed*. New Haven, CT: Yale University Press.

Sefchovich, Sara. 2019. "De Asilo, Refugio e Inmigración." Columna Opinión. *El Universal*, November 4. https://www.eluniversal.com.mx/opinion/sara-sefchovich/de-asilo-refugio-e-inmigracion/.

Sin Fronteras. 2012. *Los Programas de Regularización Migratoria en México: Su Contribución a Favor de los Derechos Humanos de los Migrantes*. Mexico City: Sin Fronteras IAP. https://sinfronteras.org.mx/docs/inf/programas-regularizacion.pdf.

Squire, Vicki, ed. 2011. *The Contested Politics of Mobility: Borderzones and Irregularity*. London: Routledge.

Torpey, John. 1997. "Revolutions and Freedom of Movement: An Analysis of Passport Controls in the French, Russian, and Chinese Revolutions." *Theory and Society* 26:837–68.

Treviño Rangel, Javier. 2008. "Racismo y nación: comunidades imaginadas en México." *Estudios Sociológicos* 26(78): 669–694.

Treviño Rangel, Javier. 2016. "What Do We Mean When We Talk About the 'Securitization' of International Migration in Mexico?: A Critique." *Global Governance: A Review of Multilateralism and International Organizations* 22 (2): 289–306.

Tuckett, Anna. 2018. *Rules, Paper, Status: Migrants and Precarious Bureaucracy in Contemporary Italy*. Stanford, CA: Stanford University Press.

UPMRIP (Unidad de Política Migratoria, Registro e Identidad de Personas). 2020. *Informe ejecutivo 2020 sobre el seguimiento a los objetivos del Pacto mundial para una migración segura, ordenada y regular*. Mexico City: Segob. http://politicamigratoria.gob.mx/work/models/PoliticaMigratoria/CPM/DRII/INFORME_EJECUTIVO_PMM_2020.pdf.

Velasco, Juan Carlos. 2016. *El Azar de las Fronteras: Políticas Migratorias, Ciudadanía y Justicia*. Mexico City: Fondo de Cultura Económica.

Villegas, Francisco J. 2017. "'Access Without Fear!': Reconceptualizing 'Access' to Schooling for Undocumented Students in Toronto." *Critical Sociology* 43 (7–8): 1179–95. https://doi.org/10.1177/0896920516677352.

Walters, William. 2004. "Secure Borders, Safe Haven, Domopolitics." *Citizenship Studies* 8 (3): 237–60. https://doi.org/10.1080/1362102042000256989.

Willen, Sarah. 2010. "Citizens, 'Real' Others, and 'Other' Others: The Biopolitics of Otherness and the Deportation of Unauthorized Migrant Workers from Tel Aviv, Israel." In *The Deportation Regime: Sovereignty, Space, and the Freedom of Movement*, edited by Nicholas De Genova and Nathalie Peutz, 262–94. Durham, NC: Duke University. Press.

Yankelevich, Pablo, and Paola Chenillo Alazraki. 2008. "El Archivo Histórico del Instituto Nacional de Migración." *Desacatos* 26: 25–42.

Zolberg, Aristide. 2003. "The Archaeology of 'Remote Control.'" In *Migration Control in the North-Atlantic World: The Evolution of State Practices in Europe and the United States from the French Revolution to the Inter-War Period*, edited by Andreas Fahrmeir, Olivier Faron, and Patrick Weil, 195–222. New York: Berghahn Books.

4

Migrant Caravans and the Border Control Regime in Mexico

THE CASE OF THE FIFTY-DAY CARAVAN DURING THE COVID PANDEMIC

Margarita Núñez Chaim, Amarela Varela Huerta, and Valentina Glockner Fagetti

This chapter brings together two years of research on the biopolitical practices and necropolitical governance with which migrants and refugees are deported, confined, and have their human rights violated in the migration corridor linking Central America, Mexico, and the United States. It is primarily an exercise in characterizing the attempts to govern the lives of migrants and to exploit the living labor of those who seek, on the other side of the wall, a life that can be lived and celebrated. The research combines traditional ethnographic practices, participatory action research, digital ethnography, and media analysis.

We start by analyzing the migrant caravans as a specific type of migrant struggle and a defiant form of transmigration in the region between 2018 and 2022. We propose that, during 2022, caravaning people not only restructured the migration control regime in the region and social imaginaries regarding transmigration but also faced a counterinsurgency operation by the state and indirect private governments that manage migration. This counterinsurgency, we argue, sought to disarticulate the politicality of "caravanizing" the transmigration of thousands of people who sought to cross the region without using human traffickers, disobeying the frameworks of parallel legality with which migration is governed in Mexico and challenging the hospitality industry that national and transnational civil society organizations sustain in this migration corridor.

Migrant Caravans and the Border Control Regime in Mexico

Between October 2018 and spring 2019, an incalculable number of migrants participated in convening, initiating, and consolidating migrant caravans as a new political practice: walking in a group. Since then, this has become an important form of transmigration in the region. Although not unprecedented—migrant caravans have been documented since the 2000s (Varela Huerta and McLean 2019)—it is novel due to its volume. However, the 2018–22 caravans showed unprecedented political relevance, since the exoduses (as the caravanners have called them) of Central Americans, reached a mass scale due to an accumulation of factors that we explain over the course of this chapter. But, more than their size, we think it is important to analyze the caravans as episodes of migrant struggle that implied an organized, spontaneous, and profoundly political response by migrant and refugee communities, in the face of the migratory control strategies seen in the migration corridor that connects Central America, Mexico, and the United States (CA-Mex.-USA corridor). That control has been exercised through temporal, spatial, legal, and parallel legal apparatuses that we also describe.

In our perspective, the caravans are a novel form of transmigration. At the same time, they are a new type of migrant struggle that responds to the state and market violence that seeks to administer and govern migration in the region. Without wanting to reify the caravans, we argue that they are the result of the political imagination of migrant and refugee persons, while also a response to the inherent necessity, the life drive, of those who must flee from zones where extractivism, the neoliberalization of all spheres of life,[1] social and institutional violence, patriarchal violence, and even climate change force people to migrate in order to survive.

In previous work, we have each emphasized thinking about migrant caravans as a novel form of transmigration and political action, as a strategy of collective self-care, as an antiracist pedagogical tool, and as a response to state violence by the protagonists of migration (Frank-Vitale and Núñez-Chaim 2020; Varela Huerta 2020a; Glockner 2019). In this collective chapter, we think it is crucial to analyze the responses by the other group of actors that play a key role in the migration corridor reconfigured by the caravans: the state and its institutions.

From our perspective, the migrant caravans arose as a response to a series of apparatuses of migratory governmentality that had been consolidated in the transnational space. By challenging these apparatuses, the caravanners reconfigured the tactics of migratory governmentality and discipline.[2] In terms of the temporal dimension, they interrupted the perpetual waiting of undefined transience to which the Mexican visa regime subjects them, counterpoising the strategy of walking together at their own pace. Defying the apparatuses of governmentality of space by fleeing from detention centers, by not following clandestine migratory routes, and even by overflowing and reinventing the use of temporary migrant shelters run by churches and civil society.

Furthermore, the caravanners challenged the apparatuses determining the roles and functions of the key actors in the government of migration. For example, the *polleros* (smugglers) or *coyotes* lost between US$5,000 and US$14,000 for each migrant person who joined the caravans instead of using their services. The caravanners challenged Instituto Nacional de Migración (National Institute of Migration; INM) officials, local and state police, the National Guard, the agents of the Comisión Mexicana de Ayuda al Refugiado (Mexican Refugee Support Committee; Comar) of the Secretaría de Gobernación (Mexico's Ministry of the Interior; Segob). And they even challenged the technocracies contracted by international agencies such as the United Nations High Commissioner for Refugees (UNHCR) and the International Organization for Migration (IOM). All of these institutions and agencies are involved in the state management and the "savior" or humanitarianism industry of the migratory routes and strategies exercised by migrant persons, which up until that point, had been carried out on an individual or family basis. Once they recovered from the surprise, those state employees, *coyotes*, "NGOers," and humanitarian experts changed their discourses, practices, and infrastructure so as to respond, each in their own way, to the challenge posed by the caravanners and episodes of struggle.

Here we are particularly interested in the actions, discourses, practices, and structural transformations that state actors, the police, migration agents, and officials who manage asylum requests have deployed. We seek to analyze the strategies that have emerged for governing migration, reinforced by military logics. Specifically, we focus on the discourses, practices, and new infrastructure (detention centers, police, and military equipment) that seek to take back control of migratory governmentality. This restorative effort includes reestablishing guidelines for where people can migrate, how much travel over clandestine routes should cost, who can cross a territory that has been baptized as the "buffer country" without migratory authorization, and the appropriate routes and time periods for crossing Mexico. One of the central hypotheses of this chapter is that state actors of migratory governmentality have turned to old practices and techniques of transnational counterinsurgency practiced several decades ago in Latin America to disarticulate migrant caravans as a form of transmigration and a strategy of migrant struggle.

In this cartography of the logics governing human mobility in Mexico, we focus on analyzing the practices of death and counterinsurgency exercised by state institutions. We call attention to a concrete episode of migrant struggle: one of the caravans that emerged in 2021, when the COVID-19 pandemic was still at its peak, and traveled from Tapachula to Mexico City and was attacked multiple times by different state actors. We analyze this case toward the end of the chapter.

Our Site of Enunciation as Researchers of Migration

We came together as an epistemic community in 2020, when the COVID-19 pandemic confined us to our homes and "our own rooms," through the action-research collective COVID-19 and (Im)Mobilities Across the Americas. Through this work, we have focused our theoretical imagination and our political embodiment efforts on understanding the political agency of migrants and the openly military counterinsurgencies exercised by expelling, transit, and settler states.[3]

According to the Real Academia de la Lengua Española, *counterinsurgency* refers to a "military or political operation against an insurgency aiming to suffocate it." In Latin America, there is a broad theoretical tradition around these practices (see Bonavena 2011; Klare and Kornbluh 1990; Marini 1978), but here we are particularly interested in the counterinsurgencies exercised by state actors against the migrant caravans, because we are certain that they, and the very act of migrating, are a form of insurgency and anticolonial resistance to neoliberalism and its regimes of dispossession and death (Morales 2022). We define counterinsurgency as a state politics that, through discipline, apparatuses, and strategies of governmentality, seeks to take back the political hegemony that the insurrection challenges, cracks, and questions as a form of governmentality that seeks to undermine, to the point of destroying, those practices that state institutions define as political insurgencies.

We argue that counterinsurgencies have established a "war against migrant persons," demonstrated by the fact that, in 2022, there were nearly 48,000 soldiers monitoring the borders and migratory routes in Mexico, according to the last report by Andrés Manuel López Obrador's government.[4] According to data from the UNHCR office (provided through personal communication for this research), there were 137 Comar agents funded by the federal budget (Segob), 2 funded by the National Population Registry (Renapo), and 209 funded by UNHCR itself. This brings the total to 327 agents with the authority to process and authorize asylum requests in the country. In 2021 alone, those requests numbered more than 131,400, according to information provided through personal communication with the directorate of the same UNHCR Mexico Office.

We carried out interviews with migrants who participated in the caravans, accompanying them during their trajectories or through the virtual accompaniment of human rights defenders. This chapter's case study and ethnography are the result of on-the-ground accompaniment work conducted by Margarita Núñez, a member of networks of human rights defenders and migrants.

Our research and this chapter draw on traditions of participatory action-research and praxis (Fals Borda 2009), as well as situated and implicated research (Malo 2004). These traditions of research methodology propose collaboratively constructing questions with the communities with which we weave knowledge, in this case, with migrant persons. Furthermore, we built the corpus and the contextual well of this text in the middle of the COVID-19 pandemic, monitoring media and carrying out digital ethnography with organizations, native digital portals, and socio-digital networks of journalists, researchers, and migrant persons. But, above all, we used our bodies to accompany caravanners as they walked on the ground, which is an essential exercise that involves going through the experience along with the subjects who are the protagonists of the research.

We start the chapter by describing the CA-Mex.-USA corridor in order to establish the context. Next, we examine the migrant caravans as strategies of struggle and migrant insurgencies in the present moment. In the final section, we analyze a cycle of migrant mobilization that took place while we were elaborating these thoughts: the caravan "For Justice, Dignity, and Freedom for Migrant People." That episode of struggle lasted around fifty days and traveled from the city of Tapachula, Chiapas, to the country's capital, Mexico City, demanding freedom of transit and the right to refuge.

We emphasize the strategies implemented by different governmental actors in an attempt to disarticulate the caravan. We also explain the criminalization of acts of solidarity with and radical hospitality offered to caravanners, proposing an understanding of the militarization of the government of migration as a counterinsurgency strategy. At the same time, we narrate and analyze the practical responses and political imagination deployed by caravanners in order to continue advancing in a group toward northern Mexico and the southwestern United States. We close this chapter with some provisional conclusions about the processes of insurgency and counterinsurgency in the CA-Mex.-USA migration corridor.

Caravans in the "Buffer Country"

In dialogue with the ideas of Soledad Álvarez Velasco, Claudia Pedone, and Bruno Miranda (2021), and for the purposes of this article, we conceive of a migration corridor as the transnational geographic space that has been molded by shared and interconnected sociohistorical processes, the accumulation of migratory transit over time, and the unequal and tense relation between mobility-immobility and migratory control, as well as the power relations that arise at the local, national, and transnational level. Building on this definition, in general terms, we can characterize the CA-Mex.-USA corridor as composed of a "constellation of modes of migratory governance" (Agudo Sanchíz 2021) in which legal and illegal, state and nongovernmental actors come together. This combination gives rise to violent regimes of securitization and migratory governmentality that operate through policies and apparatuses of control whose rationality and main tools reveal a growing racialization and illegal-ization of people in situations of mobility, the denial of the right to asylum, and the obstruction of legal mechanisms for migration. The corollary of this regime has been the exacerbation of violence and forcing migrant persons into clandestine conditions.

The violence exercised by all types of authorities of the different countries, as well as by drug-trafficking cartels—which currently control practically all the migratory routes—has increased to the point that kidnappings, extortion, forced disappearances, massacres, arbitrary detentions, abuse of authority, and violation of judicial due process, just to name a few, have become parts of the foundation of the migratory experience. Furthermore, since 2018, we have seen an increase in the migratory flows of families, and the "family-ization of the composition of transmigrant continents," a dynamic in parallel to their walking, has affected who falls victim to these abuses. In other words, the aforementioned crimes and human rights violations are increasingly suffered by the members of a family unit (París Pombo and Varela Huerta 2021).

It is in this context that in 2018, after more than a decade of witnessing the organization of migrant caravans in Mexico, a group of families and persons, many of them deportees, self-organized and issued a call to walk the migration corridor that connects Honduras, El Salvador, and Guatemala with Mexico and the United States. There were no leaders and no collective decision-making bod-ies that managed to reflect the diversity of subjectivities that made up the so-called "Central American exodus." Nonetheless, a new form of transmigration that walked out of the shadows was given life and consolidated.

The organizational process that gave rise to the caravans, however, had been taking shape for at least a half century. They go back at least to the neoliberal reorganization of postconflict societies in Central America. It was then that a renewed regimen of the government of migrations in the North American migratory system began to emerge, a regimen that, from the 1990s to today, went from managing migrant persons as a mobile and disposable labor force to also converting them into yet another dimension of national security politics. This is what is referred to as the securitization and externalization of United States immigration policy in the region.

Thus, along with the counterinsurgency against the drive for "national liberation" and democratic change processes in Central America, the United States government responded with armed and diplomatic counterinsurgency to deactivate processes of popular organization in the region. These counterinsurgency tactics were not exempt from complex contradictions, which go beyond the objectives of this text.[5] What seems fundamental to emphasize is that US foreign policy—of meddling in the public life of the Central American countries that expel around a million people per year according to the Segob Migratory Policy Unit[6]—has occurred hand in hand with the construction of migratory confines that the criminologist Guiseppe Campesi (2012) defines as the process through which

> the confusion between internal and external security is broadened, . . .
> in such a way that the borders of internal security are projected, increasingly, toward the exterior, while the sphere of action of external security tends to penetrate the interior of the political sphere. . . . The nexus between migration and security has transformed the confines into a powerful apparatus of control that operates through the systematic reduction of rights and freedoms of migrants, subjected to a complex of powers and administrative prerogatives that, due to their nature and extension, seem to transform the border itself into a ubiquitous security technology. (3–4)

Thus, from our perspective, the caravans are not new: they have been constructed over more than a decade as a self-managed option for transmigration from Central America toward the United States. Nor was the counterinsurgency that took place during the "caravan autumn" of 2018 new. Both phenomena— the life practices crystallized in the organization of migrant families and communities on one hand and, on the other, the practices of death that we see in the responses of governments and economic elites, practices that constantly cross the border between the legal and the parallel-legal—have a long history in the North–Central American migration corridor.

Among the many relevant processes and events that would be important to explain for the 2018–22 period, here we will primarily analyze the migratory control policies implemented during those years, which allow for characterizing what we consider the most recent phase of the migratory regime: the selective closure of Mexico's northern and southern borders and the United States' de facto cancelation of the right to asylum with the complicity and participation of Mexican authorities.

For this period, we highlight the exacerbated violence and securitization of migration represented by President Donald Trump's "zero tolerance" policy,[7] which constructed legal mechanisms to make migrant persons and asylum seekers into criminals and used children's bodies as mechanisms of torture and border reinforcement through family separation (Glockner 2021). Today we know that in the first eleven months of fiscal year 2019 alone, US immigration authorities apprehended 72,873 unaccompanied migrant children and adolescents and 457,871 members of family units (Nowak 2019, 461). The number of minors deprived of freedom in the United States is higher than that of any other country in the world.

Besides the zero-tolerance policy, the caravans also came up against the "metering" policy that the United States had already been implementing in the city of Tijuana since 2016 and that was extended to other border cities in the following years. Under the pretext of a lack of staff and institutional capacity to process all the migrant persons and asylum seekers who arrived at the authorized entry points,[8] US Customs and Border Protection (CBP) placed daily limits on the number of migrant persons and asylum seekers who could enter through authorized entry points, creating a "bottleneck" that ended up becoming an extralegal strategy of border closure and legitimized the blockage, bureaucratization, and immobilization of asylum and regular migration (Torres et al. 2022).[9] Of course, this strategy could happen only with the consent and tolerance of Mexican authorities.

Later, the Trump administration—with the collaboration of the Mexican government—struck a new blow against migrant persons and asylum seekers with implementation of the Migrant Protection Protocol (MPP) in January 2019. This program forced those seeking refuge in the United States to wait in Mexico for their hearings in US immigration courts. The beginning of the MPP not only demonstrated the authoritarianism with which the United States declared Mexico as a de facto "safe third country" for people seeking asylum, but also revealed the complicity and submissiveness of Mexican authorities in blocking and immobilizing asylum seekers.

Official data show that, while the MPP was in effect, more than 80,000 people were forced to wait in Mexico, in highly dangerous and precarious conditions, in violation of international conventions regarding refuge, asylum, and international protection (Eller et al. 2020). The scenario of forced immobility, blockage, and cancelation of the right to asylum caused by metering and the MPP—in the context of supposed change under a leftist government in Mexico ushered in with the election of Andrés Manuel López Obrador—was followed by a series of governmental decisions that increased criminalization and violence through the further militarization of the borders and migration control (Calva Sánchez and Torre Cantalapiedra 2020). This militarization occurred through, among other means, the creation of the National Guard—a militarized security body—and its deployment in migratory tasks to the northern and southern borders along with tens of thousands of troops from the Mexican Army and the approval of the Presidential Agreement that provides for the participation of the armed forces in security tasks, in effect until 2028 (Brewer 2021).

Since it started in the 2010s, the *securitarian turn* of migration management (increased policing and militarization for containment and deportation) has been criticized by civil society organizations, academics, and antiracist groups, because, evidence shows, the involvement of military forces generates more violence and more human rights violations.

In 2020 and 2021, the COVID-19 pandemic served as a tool for advancing biopolitical control of migrant persons and asylum seekers (Castro Neira 2021), as it allowed for justifying and legitimizing the selective closure of the Mexico-US border, starting in March 2020. This has affected, in an unquantifiable and disproportionate way, precarious and racialized migrant persons, as well as displaced peoples and asylum seekers.

This selective closure has primarily occurred through the implementation of Title 42, whereby the CBP totally suspended the process of asylum requests in the authorized entry points (Leutert and Yates 2022). Title 42 authorizes the border patrol to immediately expel migrant persons because of a health emergency, without guaranteeing their right to due process or the evaluation (screening) under the law that would allow for determining if a person requires international protection. This measure has even affected unaccompanied children and adolescents (Amnesty International 2021). In practice, Title 42 thus functioned as an apparatus for the de facto closure of the border, blocking asylum and legitimizing rapid and extrajudicial (without official record) expulsion based on racial and biopolitical criteria for hundreds of thousands of people who attempted to request refuge in the United States through legal channels.

While these policies were being enforced along Mexico's northern border, at the southern border at the end of 2021, we saw Tapachula, Chiapas, one of the continent's most iconic border-crossing points, become a "prison city," a term that emerged from the protest discourse, that migrant persons themselves coined, and that reflects the situation of "entrapment" created by the combination of Mexican and US anti-immigrant policies (Torre Cantalapiedra 2021).

During this period, Tapachula became the Mexican symbol of the border regime, marked by externalization, excessive militarization, the brutality of immigration authorities, selective border closures, and the denial of the right to asylum. This denial was carried out through precarization of migrants, delay, and bureaucratization of legal processes, as well as through the rejection and neglect of the documents issued by Mexican government to migrants, which were ignored by the authorities responsible for migratory controls. This migration regime has shown even more violence and inhumanity toward the intra- and extracontinental Black population (Morley 2021).

It is impossible to fully describe here the impact and harm that all these policies and measures have had on the migrant and asylum-seeking population. In every moment between 2018 and 2022, however, different organizational processes and migrant caravans emerged that defied, contested, negotiated, and subverted those policies of death and dehumanization. One paradigmatic example of these migrant struggles is the Assembly of African Migrants, founded in Tapachula, which carried out various protests and emitted a written declaration in 2019 (Morley 2021; FASIC 2019).

A second paradigmatic example of defiance and contestation was the caravan of people originally from Haiti and coming not only from that country but also countries in which Haitians had settled, such as Chile and Brazil. This group crossed the continent to the border between Acuña, Coahuila (in Mexico) and Del Rio, Texas, where they were brutally repressed, exposing the racism and white supremacy of the migration regime, as well as the organizational capacity of one of the most vulnerable diasporas in the Americas (Santos Cid 2021).

The Fifty-Day Caravan: Counterinsurgency Practices to Demobilize the Caravans

I have been walking in the caravan with all my comrades for fifty days, a caravan that has been extremely painful and arduous because we have faced rain, sun, cold, hunger. Thanks to God we have found Mexican people who have given us aid, they gave us food and water. Now, the National Guard says that we cannot get on transportation for our own safety, but look at how they contradict themselves in this. They say that we cannot travel as hitchhikers, but when some people tried to take a taxi or a moto-taxi, or bus, they also made them get off. So, what safety are they talking about? They want to sacrifice every migrant, practically kill us on the way. When we left in the caravan, there were around four thousand of us, those who got out in front were grabbed and those that fell behind were also grabbed. Now, Immigration did things that they should not have done, at the least, creating xenophobia. They went from town to town and told people to lock up because migrants were coming. Then, when we reached each town, people were afraid of us, as if we were going around stealing, assaulting, making violence, but it was nothing like that. So Immigration did things it should not have done, that is their role, to create fear among the people. Since we left from Tapachula we have gone in peace. (Nicaraguan man, Ministry of the Interior, December 16, 2021, cited in UIA and Cultura Migrante 2022, 10)[10]

On December 12, 2021, the day when Mexico celebrates the Virgin of Guadalupe, the country's most important religious figure, the Basilica of Mexico City received 4 million pilgrims. That same day, the caravan of migrant persons that had left Tapachula, the "prison city," fifty days earlier, reached the Mexican capital. At the beginning, according to participants' accounts, the caravan was made up of approximately 4,000 people from different countries of Central America, the Caribbean, and South America. However, on its arrival in Mexico City, the contingent had already diminished to 500 people, as a result of the counterinsurgency strategy deployed by institutions of the Mexican state and denounced by representatives of the caravanners before various authorities with which they conversed in the Ministry of the Interior on December 16, 2021 (UIA and Cultura Migrante 2022).

As migrants told the authorities, the counterinsurgency that they faced during their transit used two central practices: wearing out and immobilizing people through extreme exhaustion, and what the caravanners recognized as physical, psychological, and emotional torture inflicted by the authorities (military and immigration authorities and representatives of the Comisión Nacional de Derechos Humanos) by forcing them to travel the entire route on foot, without letting them board any type of transportation. The authorities also actively promoted xenophobia and criminalization of people among the populations that the caravan passed through, which policy had the indirect effect of making them suffer hunger and thirst, by annihilating the everyday practices of hospitality that take place in Mexico for communities in transit.

These tactics of disciplining and governmentality are not new; they had already been tested out by the United States since the 1990s, in the policy known as prevention through deterrence (PTD). The policy has taken on diverse forms that inflict physical pain and psychological trauma on migrant persons coming from Latin America under the false hypothesis that harm would stop people from emigrating, or at least do so in fewer numbers (Gokee, Stewart, and De León 2020). At first, PTD consisted of reinforcing immigration control points in the urban areas of the border with the objective of diverting migratory transit toward the most geographically rugged area: the Arizona desert. Thus, surveillance technology, along with the desert's geography, climate, flora, and fauna, acts as a migration control strategy (De León 2015; Martínez et al. 2013).

In an interview conducted by Cameron Gokee, Haede Stewart, and Jason De León (2020), a border patrol agent declared that letting people walk in extreme climatic conditions for several days was the "best tactic" for later apprehending them, since the people were then so exhausted and desperate that it was not necessary to chase them. These practices were replicated as a counterinsurgency strategy for the Fifty-Day Caravan: forcing them to walk, forcing them to suffer hunger and thirst, promoting xenophobia, and, for those left behind because they could not keep up with the pace, detaining and deporting them without judicial due process.

As shown by the arrival of 500 people in Mexico City on December 12, 2021, and the numerical decrease of this contingent during its journey, the tactics of governmentality through dissuasion—both through wearing down and the production of xenophobia and criminalization—do not stop people from migrating. As with what happened in the Arizona desert, what these tactics of death did achieve was "the tacit objective of shaping the border zone [in this case, the Mexican territory as a whole] into a state of exception in which the state works to suspend or ignore people's rights, especially those of undocumented migrants" (Gokee, Stewart, and De León 2020, 2).

This state of exception was extended even further in that, from the perspective of migrant defenders, activists, and journalists (UIA and Cultura Migrante 2022), the Mexican institutions that are part of the global governance of migration used another counterinsurgent practice for the Fifty-Day Caravan to suspend the rights of migrant people through an illusory legal path: while they allowed them to walk, wagering on people's exhaustion and desperation, they offered them a path to temporary migration regularization in exchange for leaving the caravan. As one caravanner explained:

> I cannot believe that when we decided to walk, Immigration already wanted to give us Cards, why did they not do it in Tapachula? Why wait for us to make that dangerous decision, for our children and women to get worn out? We had to come here to demand that they follow the laws, and

we want to request that they remove that militarized chain in Tapachula because the only thing it does is incite hatred and violence. That they remove the illegal registration points in the bus stops and airports. That if they give out Humanitarian Cards that they be automatically renewable and that they give us all the corresponding documentation. (Guatemalan man, Ministry of the Interior, December 16, 2021, cited in UIA and Cultura Migrante 2022, 15)

The INM approached the contingent during the fifty days with an offer: migratory regulation in exchange for "voluntarily giving yourself up." Because of the conditions in which they were forced to travel, this became a seductive alternative for many caravanners, especially those traveling with children or sick people. However, for the 500 people who reached Mexico City, the offer was an illusion of legality that they were not willing to accept, since they knew that it did not guarantee the living conditions they were looking for: The mode of migratory regularization offered consisted of Visitor Cards for Humanitarian Reasons (TVRHS),[11] better known among migrant persons as "humanitarian visas," which, as representatives of the caravan denounced to Segob, immigration authorities themselves do not make valid on a daily basis. In fact, this was one of the primary reasons that led people to mobilize in a caravan, since even with immigration documentation, people could not leave the prison city of Tapachula:

I have witnessed, for example, in Viva México, when they got me off the bus at a checkpoint, I saw and witnessed that the cards that they give are not valid. Why are they not valid? Why did they tear them up and throw them away in front of us without giving us a chance to speak, without giving us our rights? As soon as they attacked us, I saw how they tore up a Honduran man's card, they hit him and intimidated him, they repressed him. (Guatemalan man, Ministry of the Interior, December 16, 2021, cited in UIA and Cultura Migrante 2022, 8)

It has been tough coming from Tapachula and going through what we have experienced as migrants. . . . I emigrated when they positively resolved my case in COMAR, because I went to Immigration to get my [residency] card, but they would not give it to me. Thus I went with my humanitarian [visa] and managed to get up to Sinaloa. In Sinaloa they pulled me off the transport and mistreated me, there was a police officer who hit me. I have suffered a lot of mistreatment. . . . After a lot of time in Tapachula I obtained my papers, but even so, in Sinaloa they detained me and I was held for 14 days, then they sent me back to Tapachula. (Salvadorean woman, Pilgrim's

House, Mexico City, December 16, cited in UIA and Cultura Migrante 2022, 8)

The vertical border of the Mexican territory acts as a state of exception (Varela Huerta 2019) in which the rights of impoverished and racialized migrant persons are suspended, regardless of whether or not they have documents.

> We at least need the humanitarian visa, but one that works, because the one they have given us, what is it good for? Nothing, because we show it and they always pull us off the transports. They only let you through if you have a *mordida* [bribe], excuse me for talking to you like this, but it is the truth, Immigration is all corrupt. We need documents that are legitimate. (Salvadoran woman, Secretary of the Interior, December 16, 2021, cited in UIA and Cultura Migrante 2022, 15)

This counterinsurgency practice is not new, either: Ever since the Via Crucis caravans prior to the caravan exoduses of 2018, the Mexican state, in some moment of the journey, gave members of the mobilizations "the offer of humanitarian visas," with the expectation that, once people had documents, they would no longer mobilize in caravans. At the beginning of 2019, and as the López Obrador government's first response to the migrant caravans, this practice was also a wager on demobilization.

In the Fifty-Day Caravan, once people reached Mexico City, the offer of humanitarian visas demonstrated the government's ulterior motive. The authorities used the fact that the end of the year was close and the significant backlog of files to attend to as a pretext for not complying with the caravanners' demand to be provided with visas in the capital. In the state's version of events, the INM's central offices, in the world's fifth-largest city, did not have the capacity to manage 495 procedures in the ten days that the caravanners were in Mexico City. Therefore, immigration authorities in Mexico turned to another counterinsurgent tactic tested in 2018: offering transportation to move people closer to their desired destination, the United States and, by doing so, dispersing the mobilization. On this occasion, they did so in a way similar to North American dissuasion policies: using geography as an apparatus of control, as people's desired destinations forced them to take different routes from the capital to the northern border. Thus they managed to divide the group of 500 into three: approximately half went to Hermosillo, Sonora; about 200 people went to Monterrey, Nuevo León; and the remaining 50 people went to Ciudad Juárez, Chihuahua. They all left on December 22, 2021, on buses provided by the INM.

However, just as policies of dissuasion do not significantly "reduce" migration—as the drive to live in the face of the neoliberalism of the *maquila* and the *mara* (Varela Huerta 2020b) is more powerful than the practices of death inflicted by the global government of migration—the illusion of migratory legality also does not have a significant effect in demobilizing people, since the reasons for their mobilization—precarization and the risks in the face of the government of migration and their indirect private governments—go beyond the fragile illusion of a migratory document. This was demonstrated by some Via Crucis caravans that continued their mobilization with documents, the caravans given humanitarian visas at the beginning of 2019, the Fifty-Day Caravan,[12] and other processes that have emerged in defiance of this re-elaborated counterinsurgency, including:

a The encampments of migrant persons, primarily from Haiti and Africa, outside the facilities of the Tapachula detention center between August and December 2019. This mobilization arose in response to a change in the immigration documentation that authorities provided to that population. In previous years the documents had permitted them to move freely through the national territory, but at this point the authorities began to restrict their mobility, forcing them to remain in Mexico's southern border.

b The El Chaparral encampment in Tijuana, which, following President Joe Biden's announcement that he would suspend the Migrant Protection Protocol in February 2020, arose through the movement of the migrant population, of which the majority had spent between three months and up to two years stranded in different cities of Mexico's northern border, toward the ports of entry into the United States with the intention of requesting asylum. However, due to Title 42, these people could not access that right and decided to remain in in an encampment near the Tijuana pedestrian port of entry known as El Chaparral. More than 2,000 migrant persons came to live there in tarps and tents. The encampment lasted for almost a year, after which the inhabitants were violently evicted by Mexican security forces in February 2022.

c The protests of Haitian persons in Mexico City, which took place in January 2021, in the offices of the Mexican Commission for Refugee Assistance to demand that their refugee status application procedures be expedited.

As mentioned at the beginning of this chapter, the tactics of migratory disciplining and governmentality were reconfigured in the CA-Mex.-USA corridor as a result of the caravan exoduses of 2018–19. For the following two years—from summer 2019 to summer 2021—no mobilization managed to reach the borders of the border state of Chiapas. All of the caravan attempts—or "cycles of migrant struggle" as Gina Garibó (2021) calls them—that took place during this period faced direct violence through the military deployment of security forces to completely contain them. Those security forces were remilitarized in 2019 with the deployment of the National Guard for immigration control in Mexico's vertical border,[13] along with the addition of military cadres managed by the INM.[14] Again, this was a tactic of governmentality that had already been deployed in other places, including the US southern border, and that, like the aforementioned tactics, was now applied farther south in an intensification of the externalization of borders.

As a hypothesis, we could state that the Fifty-Day Caravan did not face the complete blockage by force of its passage during its transit through the southern states of Mexico, likely because the previous escalation of militarized containment unleashed public and media scorn when the image of a Mexican INM agent kicking a Haitian man in the head went viral. This image appeared in the context of an intensive deployment, over more than five days, of militarized security forces along the highways and coastal communities of Chiapas, to contain several caravan attempts of Haitian persons between the end of August and early September 2021.[15]

These Haitian caravan attempts faced tactics of disciplining and governmentality such as kettling people on the highways; persecution with military tactics in areas along the highways; persecution of people in the communities through which they transited, which included raiding the houses of people who, following practices of hospitality (Varela Huerta 2015b), sheltered families who were fleeing and hid them from persecution; physical violence through blows with batons, shields, stones, and teargas in order to immobilize and detain people; psychological violence through family separation during detention and expulsion of migrant families from the country; and torture during detention.

After this juncture, the Fifty-Day Caravan was organized and walked to Mexico City demonstrating that, even with the war against impoverished and racialized migrant persons, the insurgent life drive defies those practices of terror of the global government of migration. However, coupled with practices to wear people down and the offer of migration regularization, the Fifty-Day Caravan was not exempt from direct violence or the massive deployment of security forces to contain them as part of the counterinsurgent strategy to demobilize it. The caravanners ran into the security forces' blockades in different state borders within Mexican territory.[16] The most violent of which was precisely on December 12, when the caravan arrived in Mexico City and a barrier of more than 300 police kettled, gassed, and beat them, leaving forty-six people injured, including children and thirteen people who required medical intervention (UIA and Cultura Migrante 2022). As a Salvadorean woman recalled:

> I was afraid when I left my country, I obtained my documents, and even so they detained me for 14 days, that's why I joined the caravan. With all my sacrifice, I have walked 1,200 km with my daughter and my grandson. With my comrades we have struggled and we have gotten this far, we only wanted to come give thanks at the Basilica of Guadalupe. And even so they received us with blows and teargas, that was the welcome we received from Mexico City. (Ministry of the Interior, December 16, cited in UIA and Cultura Migrante 2022, 12)

A Mexico City ordinance proclaims it a "sanctuary" space, and the so-called Law of Interculturality, Attention to Migrants, and Human Mobility in the Federal District,[17] implies, among other things, the prohibition of immigrant detention operations. Even so, the scenes experienced by the caravanners on their arrival in the city clearly show the deployment of direct violence as part of the counterinsurgency strategy.

The same day that this episode of war against the caravan occurred, Mexico City received 4 million pilgrims to Guadalupe from all over Mexico, offering them food and medical care as they headed, just like the caravanners, toward the Basilica of Guadalupe. Thus, the violent containment operation also functioned as a control apparatus in the form of a message through exemplary punishment: Four million people could arrive, but not if they were migrant people considered "disposable," as philosopher Judith Butler (2010) would say. It was a clear message from the city government, as well as from the governing party at the federal level, that "they are not welcome."

The message of rejection of the caravan's presence was manifested by the city's institutions, not only upon its arrival but also during the ten days that the caravan remained in the Mexican capital. The city of more than 9 million inhabitants did not have the institutional will or capacity to provide even the minimal conditions of dignity for 500 people: they did not provide food or adequate hygiene, and there was no place to sleep safe from the elements and the low winter temperatures, and no basic medical care, just to name the most egregious examples. Once again, the institutions governed through practices and apparatuses that manage death rather than governing life: this time through shelter out in the open, the dissimulation of welcome, passivity in terms of providing documents—all these forms of governing time, space, and the vital resources for migrant people, whether or not they are in caravans. All of these, if analyzed from the perspective of contemporary literature, are clearly forms of counterinsurgency.

Finally, this counterinsurgency strategy has also increasingly caused the deterioration of practices of hospitality toward migrant persons, especially those who decide to challenge the global government of migration and make themselves visible in caravans and other forms of migrant struggle. One of the most controversial dimensions of these tactics is the reproduction of discriminatory and stigmatizing discourse and practices among actors of the humanitarian industry. During the transit of the Fifty-Day Caravan, with few exceptions,[18] there was a conspicuous absence of humanitarian actors, demonstrating the effect that this counterinsurgency strategy has had in terms of isolating migrant persons from support networks.

All of this has been developed and consolidated since the caravan exoduses of 2018, as a result above all of the criminalization of human rights defenders who accompanied those exoduses.[19] Some participants in the Mexican humanitarian industry—accustomed to working based on a paternalistic logic in which migrant persons are presented as passive victims—have actively participated in the reproduction of the discourse and practices of stigmatization and criminalization. These practices happen along a spectrum that goes from veiled arguments that people, "for their own good," should not carry out any mobilization,[20] to other, explicit arguments that migrant mobilizations are actions organized by the highest rungs of power, without recognizing the agency of migrant persons.[21]

The cruelty of the sum of all these counterinsurgency tactics is manifested in the pain in participants' feet and legs after fifty days of walking, in the back pain caused by sleeping out in the cold, in the sick lungs of children, in the hungry stomachs of migrant mothers and fathers who prioritize their children in doling out the scarce amounts of food, and in the state of shock as a result of seeing mothers with babies in the arms being beaten by batons and children suffocating on tear gas, to mention just some of the clearest effects. But the cruelty of this counterinsurgency is also manifested in the way the global government of migrations constructs the spectrum of migratory illegality-legality in a gray zone that constitutes the Mexican territory as a vertical border, in which a state of exception operates that disrupts hospitality in favor of the discourse and practices of social repudiation that are gaining ground, even within the humanitarian industry of migration.

The facts of the caravan call for locating, identifying, naming, and not forgetting counterinsurgency tactics and their multiple reconfigurations. But it also forces us to take stock of the drive behind the life practices that continue to be rearticulated in confronting this global war against discarded migrant peoples. Occurring outside the traditional antisystemic ideological parameters does not make this resistance any less transgressive of the order which migrant persons, caravanners, refuse to accept as their destiny (Varela Huerta 2020b). Not recognizing this and, relatedly, the agency of migrant caravans, with all their tensions and contradictions, means not recognizing those people as political and epistemic subjects, thereby reproducing the dichotomous—victimizing and criminalizing—paternalistic logics promoted by migratory governmentality.

Conclusions

This chapter briefly outlines the recent history of the government of migration in Mexico. We trace the insurgency with which migrants and refugee persons challenged that regime of death and deportability. And, above all, we have shed light on an episode of migrant struggle, one of the most recent caravans at the time of writing, the Fifty-Day Caravan, which came from Mexico's southern border to be disarticulated in its capital, Mexico City.

We gave special attention to the practices of death, the strategies, apparatuses, and subjectivities of counterinsurgency with which, two years after the Caravan Autumn of 2018, the state responded to migrant insurgencies at the height of the pandemic. In the migration corridor that we studied, practices of death, of necropolitical governmentality, were tried out that deepened all the forms of counterinsurgency known to date. Government forces torture families; separate nuclear or chosen families; and wager on people getting sick, dehydrated, lost, kidnapped; or robbed. They rape or murder migrant people as a way of materializing the Mexican government's commitment to "safe, orderly, and regular management of migration." And, as several generations of interpreters have already documented in migration and border studies, migrant and refugee persons respond to these logics of death with practices of life. Previously they responded through migratory networks; today, they also respond through the wager of caravanizing transmigration. The caravans are a form of migrant struggle, a strategy for surviving the global border regime and a new form of transmigration in Mexico, where, along with necropolitical practices, there are also practices of solidarity and radical hospitality that, like the caravans and migrant persons, are always ungovernable.

NOTES

1. When we say "neoliberalization of life," we are referring to the withdrawal of the state from the scaffolding that makes it possible to sustain the commons—for example, through the privatization of health care, education, and even public safety. Through the overexploitation of people's living labor, in Latin America in general, we are seeing the dismantling of the commons that leaves communities on their own to manage, for example, caring for life, the territory, health care, and education.

2. We consider migratory governmentality as a form of necropolitics (Mbembe 2011) that is made up of anatomo-political and biopolitical (individual and populational) apparatuses of disciplining to control migration. By "apparatuses," drawing on the Foucauldian theoretical tradition of biopower, we refer to the practices, knowledges, discourses—and their respective translations in institutions, infrastructure, law, civil servants, and indirect private governments—that attempt to govern migration.

3. From the early 2000s to date, the governments of the states involved in this migration corridor have signed agreements of border externalization and conventions of securitization of migration management whose axis, among many other consequences, is the militarization of migration management (Varela Huerta 2015a).

4. See Presidencia de la República Mexicana, *4to Informe de Gobierno*, Cámara de Diputados, accessed October 2024, https://framework-gb.cdn.gob.mx/informe/5b8e7a9 83a893dfcbd02a8e444abfb45.pdf.

5. Describing this historical period for the subcontinent would require another exercise of synthesis. It is worth explaining that during the 1970s and 1980s, popular and armed struggles across Central America, as well as those within the field of political contention, sought to consolidate the democracies to which those peoples have always aspired. In response to social and armed resistance, local oligarchies and the US government enacted all sorts of counterinsurgency practices. For a regional panoramic of this process, see Vázquez Olivera and Campos 2016; for a historiographic point of view, see Pastor 2011.

6. "Boletines Estadísticos. I Registro de Entradas, 2022," Gobierno de México, http://portales.segob.gob.mx/es/PoliticaMigratoria/CuadrosBOLETIN?Anual=2022&Secc=1.

7. The zero-tolerance policy, which caused family separations at the border, went into effect in April 2018. However, we know that family separation had already been a constant element in certain areas of the border since at least 2015 (Danielson 2015) and that the family separation procedure that Donald Trump's executive order made official had already been implemented since mid-2017 in the state of Texas as the El Paso Program (SPLC 2019).

8. In March 2022, after the outbreak of the war in Ukraine, thousands of people from that country reached Mexico and presented themselves on the land border to request asylum. Over the course of approximately one month, the United States authorities admitted up to 550 people per day solely in the port of entry in San Ysidro, California, on the border with Tijuana. This number of admittances demonstrated the racism behind the metering system, since there was the staff and capacity to admit white people, while more than 15,000 people primarily from Central America and the Caribbean have been on the waiting lists in all the ports of entry since 2020.

9. Although a federal court ruled metering to be an illegal practice (*Al Otro Lado et al. v. Alejandro Mayorkas et al.* [S.D. Cal. 2021]), it still continues along most of the Mexico-US border.

10. The testimonies cited from the report issued by UIA and Cultura Migrante were captured by Margarita Núñez while she was accompanying the Fifty-Day Caravan.

11. The Migration Law in Mexico considers this mode of temporary migratory regularization, which is normally valid from three months to one year, under different cases related to "situations of vulnerability," such as having been a victim of a crime, being a minor, or being an applicant for refugee status. However, as we explore later, in the context of the caravans, it was used as a counterinsurgency strategy based on a provision in the law that addresses any "humanitarian or public interest cause," as determined by authorities.

12. Not only the mobilization to Mexico City, despite the fact that 39 percent of the people already had some migratory regularization (UIA and Cultura Migrante, 2022). but also, following its stay in the city, the contingent that moved toward Monterrey, Nuevo León, decided to continue its caravan route to the United States border. However, the group did not manage to reach the border, because they received threats from organized crime in the area, one of the most common tactics of migratory governmentality used by the indirect private government that operates in the CA-Mex.-USA corridor.

13. In March 2019, the National Guard was created in Mexico as a security force that replaced the Federal Police. It has a military character in that its agents currently receive military training, its operational control is subordinated to the Mexican Army, and more than 80 percent of its members come from the Mexican armed forces, to mention only some of the most significant elements (Centro Prodh 2021; Storr 2021). In addition, among the powers granted to the National Guard are immigration control and verification of foreign persons, as well as protection of migrant detention centers. Finally, in June 2019, following the threats by US President Donald Trump to impose a 5 percent tariff on Mexican products, the Mexican government deployed 15,000 National Guard agents to the northern and southern borders of Mexico.

14. Since 2019, the INM has designated staff with training in the Mexican armed forces to the head of nineteen of that institution's thirty-two state delegations at the national level.

15. In late August 2021, Haitians in the city of Tapachula started to organize diverse protests to demand that their migration regularization procedures be expedited and that they be provided nondiscriminatory treatment and dignified living conditions. After a week of protests in the city, people started to organize caravans that, for at least five days, departed continuously from Tapachula on the coastal highway of Chiapas, seeking to move toward the north of the country.

16. During their journey across Chiapas, Oaxaca, and Veracruz, the caravan encountered several blockades set up by the National Guard and the INM at the state borders. In those episodes, different confrontations took place between security forces and migrant persons in which people were injured and small groups of people detained. However, as a result of the pressure from the people, the confrontations, and different negotiations between the caravan and the authorities, the blockades were lifted.

17. Law of Interculturality, Attention to Migrants, and Human Mobility in the Federal District, Official Bulletin of the Federal District, April, 7, 2011, https://paot.org.mx /centro/leyes/df/pdf/GODF/GODF_07_04_2011.pdf.

18. The Fifty-Day Caravan was accompanied in its journey of over 1,200 kilometers by human rights defenders in different moments: in the journey across Chiapas, it was accompanied by two defenders, as well as organizations belonging to the Colectivo de Observación y Monitoreo de Derechos Humanos en el Sureste Mexicano" (Observation and Human Rights Monitoring Collective in Southeast Mexico), which monitored its advance and managed humanitarian support; later, as the caravan crossed the borders of Oaxaca and Veracruz, the Brigada Gilberto Bosques Saldívar approached and provided humanitarian support and medical aid for four days. Thus, the caravan was accompanied by human rights defenders and organizations for no more than twenty of the fifty days of its journey.

19. Following the Caravan Autumn of 2018, the region's governments unleashed a campaign of criminalization targeting people defending migrants' human rights, especially those who accompanied the caravan journeys. The organizations Frontline Defenders, the TDT Network, and the Programa de Asuntos Migratorios de la Universidad Iberoamericana (2019) documented sixty-nine acts of aggression against human rights defenders between 2018 and 2019. The most serious cases occurred in June 2019, when two defenders were detained and criminalized, the prosecutor general accused them of human trafficking, and they faced up to twenty-three years in prison.

20. For example, when the El Chaparral migrant camp was established in Tijuana, different humanitarian aid and migrant defense organizations were opposed to it, arguing that migrant persons would be exposed to serious safety and health risks by living in public space.

21. This is the case of the conspiracy theories unleashed following the explosion of the Caravan Autumn of 2018. For example, in Mexico, people working in humanitarian aid for migrant persons have publicly declared the mobilization of people in caravans is a political strategy to attack Andrés Manuel López Obrador's government.

REFERENCES

Agudo Sanchíz, Alejandro. 2021. "La provisión de bienes y servicios como acción política: Configuración de modos humanitarios y burocráticos de gobernanza en la frontera México-Estados Unidos." *Periplos Revista de Investigación sobre Migraciones* 5 (1): 53–80.

Amnesty International. 2021. *Pushed into Harm's Way: Forced Returns of Unaccompanied Migrant Children to Danger by the USA and Mexico.* https://www.amnesty.org/en /documents/amr51/4200/2021/en/.

Al Otro Lado et al. vs Mayorkas et al. 2021. "Summary Judgement on Metering September 2, 2021." Accessed December 18, 2021. https://ccrjustice.org/sites/default /files/attach/2021/09/742%20Order%20granting%20in%20part%20Plaintiffs%20 Motion%20for%20Summary%20Judgment%202021.08.02.pdf.

Álvarez Velasco, Soledad, Claudia Pedone, and Bruno Miranda. 2021. "Movilidades, control y disputa espacial: La formación y transformación de corredores migratorios en las Américas." *Periplos: Revista de Investigación sobre Migraciones* 5 (1): 4–27.

Bonavena, Pablo. 2011. "La Guerra contrainsurgente de hoy." Paper presented at IX Jornadas de Sociología, Facultad de Ciencias Sociales, Universidad de Buenos Aires. https://cdsa.aacademica.org/000–034/51.pdf.

Butler, Judith. 2010. *Marcos de guerra: Las vidas lloradas*. Barcelona: Paidós.

Brewer, Stephanie. 2021. "México militarizado: La guerra se perdió, pero la paz no llega." WOLA (Washington Office on Latin America). May 12. https://www.wola.org/es /analisis/mexico-militarizado-la-guerra-se-perdio-pero-la-paz-no-llega/.

Calva Sánchez, Luis Enrique, and Eduardo Torre Cantalapiedra. 2020. "Cambios y continuidades en la política migratoria durante el primer año del gobierno de López Obrador." *Norteamérica* 15 (2): 157–81. https://doi.org/10.22201/cisan.24487228e.2020.2.415.

Campesi, Giuseppe. 2012. "Migraciones, seguridad y confines en la teoría social contemporánea." *Revista Crítica Penal y Poder* 1 (3): 1–20.

Centro Prodh (Centro de Derechos Humanos Miguel Agustín Pro Juárez). 2021. *Poder Militar. La Guardia Nacional y los riesgos del renovado protagonismo castrense*. June 30. https://centroprodh.org.mx/2021/06/30/poder-militar-la-guardia-nacional-y-los -riesgos-del-renovado-protagonismo-castrense/.

Castro Neira, Yerko. 2021. "Viejas y nuevas formas de control migratorio en tiempos del Covid-19: El caso de la frontera de México-EE. UU." *Periplos: Revista de Investigación sobre Migraciones* 5 (1): 28–52.

De León, Jason. 2015. *The Land of Open Graves: Living and Dying on the Migrant Trail*. Berkeley: University of California Press.

Eller, Jessica, Emma Israel, Priscilla Lugo, and Juany Torres. 2020. *Migrant Protection Protocols: Implementation and Consequences for Asylum Seekers in Mexico*. Strauss Center for International Security and Law, University of Texas, Austin. https://www.strausscenter.org/wp-content/uploads/PRP-218_-Migrant-Protection -Protocols.pdf.

Fals Borda, Orlando. 2009. *Una sociología sentipensante para América Latina*. Buenos Aires: Siglo del hombre and Consejo Latinoamericano de Ciencias Sociales.

FASIC (Fundación de Ayuda Social de las Iglesias Cristianas). 2019. "De la indignación a la organización: Se conforma la Asamblea de Migrantes de África en Tapachula." September. http://fasic.cl/wp/2019/09/de-la-indignacion-a-la-organizacion -se-conforma-la-asamblea-de-migrantes-de-africa-en-tapachula/.

Frank Vitale, Amelia, and Margarita Núñez Chaim. 2020. "'Lady Frijoles': Las caravanas centroamericanas y el poder de la hipervisibilidad de la migración indocumentada." *EntreDiversidades. Revista de ciencias sociales y humanidades* 7 (1): 37–61. https://doi .org/10.31644/ED.V7.N1.2020.A02.

Frontline Defenders, Red TDT, and Programa de Asuntos Migratorios, UIA. 2019. "Defensores sin muros: Personas defensoras de derechos humanos criminalizadas en Centroamérica, México y Estados Unidos." September. https://www.frontlinedefenders .org/es/statement-report/defenders-beyond-borders-migrant-rights-defenders-under -attack-central-america.

Garibó, Gina. 2021. "Un país tapón en tiempos de pandemia." Paper presented at Seminario Interinstitucional Movilidades en Contextos Migratorios, Mexico City. Posted to YouTube, April 30, by Canal Instituto de Investigaciones Sociales. https://www .youtube.com/watch?v=9E4Q40Um2AU.

Glockner, Valentina. 2019. "Las caravanas migrantes como estrategia de movilidad y espacio de protección, autonomía y solidaridad para los adolescentes centroamericanos." *Iberoforum: Revista de Ciencias Sociales de la Universidad Iberoamericana* 14 (27): 145–74. https://iberoforum.ibero.mx/index.php/iberoforum/article/view/126.

Glockner, Valentina. 2021. "Régimen de frontera y la política de separación de familias: Racialización y castigo de la migración forzada a través de los cuerpos infantiles." In *#JóvenesyMigración: El reto de converger; agendas de investigación, políticas y participación,* edited by Mónica Valdez González and Juan Carlos Narváez Gutiérrez, 47–79. Mexico City: SIIJ, SUDIMER-UNAM.

Gokee, Cameron, Haede Stewart, and Jason De León. 2020. "Scales of Suffering in the US-Mexico Borderlands." *International Journal of Historical Archaeology* 24: 823–51. https://doi.org/10.1007/s10761-019-00535-6.

Danielson, Michael S. 2015. *Our Values on the Line: Migrant Abuse and Family Separation at the Border.* Jesuit Conference of Canada and the United States and Kino Border Initiative. https://www.kinoborderinitiative.org/wp-content/uploads/2017/11 /REPORT_2015_Our_Values_on_the_Line.pdf.

Klare, Michael T., and Peter Kornbluh, eds. 1990. *Contrainsurgencia, proinsurgencia y antiterrorismo en los 80: El arte de la guerra de baja intensidad.* Translated by Argelia Castillo. Mexico City: Grijalbo.

Leutert, S., and Caitlyn Yates. 2022. *Metering Update, February 2022.* Strauss Center for International Security and Law, University of Texas, Austin. https://www.strausscenter .org/publications/metering-update-february-2022/.

Malo, Marta. 2004. "Prólogo." In *Nociones comunes: Experiencias y ensayos entre investigación y militancia,* 13–40. Madrid: Traficantes de Sueños, https://traficantes.net/sites /default/files/pdfs/Nociones%20comunes-TdS.pdf.

Marini, Ruy Mauro. 1978. "El Estado de Contrainsurgencia: Intervención en el debate sobre 'La cuestión del fascismo en América Latina.'" *Cuadernos Políticos* 18: 21–29.

Martínez, Daniel E., Robin C. Reineke, Raquel Rubio-Goldsmith, Bruce E. Anderson, Gregory L. Hess, and Bruce O. Parks. 2013. "A Continued Humanitarian Crisis at the Border: Undocumented Border Crosser Deaths Recorded by the Pima County Office of the Medical Examiner, 1990–2012." Binational Migration Institute, University of Arizona, Tucson.

Mbembe, Achille. 2011. *Necropolítica: Sobre el gobierno privado indirecto.* Barcelona: Melusina.

Morales, Ana María. 2022. "Migrar es resistencia anticolonial: Entrevista a Amarela Varela Huerta y Soledad Álvarez Velazco." *Revista Amazonas,* January 5. https://www.revistaamazonas.com/2022/01/05/migrar-es-resistencia -anitcolonial-entrevista-a-amarela-varela-y-soledad-alvarez/.

Morley, Priya, et al. 2021. *'Nos tienen en la mira': el impacto del racismo anti-negro sobre las personas migrantes africanas en la frontera sur de México.* IMUMI (Instituto para las

Mujeres en la Migración). https://imumi.org/nuestras-publicaciones/nos-tienen-en-la
-mira/.

Nowak, Manfred. 2019. *United Nations Global Study on Children Deprived of Liberty*.
United Nations High Commissioner on Human Rights. July 11. https://www.ohchr
.org/en/treaty-bodies/crc/united-nations-global-study-children-deprived-liberty.

París Pombo, Dolores, and Amarela Varela Huerta. 2021. "Caravanas de migrantes, nueva
forma de lucha migrante en Mesoamérica." *(Trans)Fronteriza: movilidades y fronteras
desde una perspectiva interseccional* 8: 59–65.

Pastor, Rodolfo. 2011. *Historia mínima de Centroamérica*. Mexico City: El Colegio de
México.

Santos Cid, Alejandro. 2021. "Más de 10.000 migrantes haitianos, retenidos en un cam-
pamento precario bajo un puente en el sur de Texas." *El País*, September 17. https://
elpais.com/mexico/2021-09-17/mas-de-10000-migrantes-haitianos-retenidos-en-un
-campamento-precario-bajo-un-puente-en-el-sur-de-texas.html.

SPLC (Southern Poverty Law Center). 2019. "Family Separation Under the Trump Administration—A Timeline." September 24. https://www.splcenter.org/news/2019/09
/24/family-separation-under-trump-administration-timeline.

Storr, Samuel. 2021. "Descifrando la conferencia de prensa presidencial; Qué es la Guardia Nacional?" Seguridad Ciudadana. August 25. https://seguridadviacivil.ibero.mx
/2021/08/25/que-es-la-guardia-nacional/.

Torre Cantalapiedra, Eduardo. 2021. "'Ciudad cárcel' y el discurso de protesta de los
migrantes." *Nexos*, October 2021. https://migracion.nexos.com.mx/2021/10/ciudad
-carcel-y-el-discurso-de-protesta-de-los-migrantes/.

Torres, Rebecca Maria, Valentina Glockner, Nohora Niño-Vega, Gabriela García-
Figueroa, Caroline Faria, Alicia Danze, Emanuela Borzacchiello, and Jeremy Slack.
2022. "Lockdown and the List: Mexican Refugees, Asylum Denial, and the Feminist
Geopolitics of *Esperar* (Waiting/Hoping)." *Environment and Planning C: Politics and
Space* 41 (8): 1503–20. https://doi.org/10.1177/23996544221118906.

UIA (Universidad Iberoamericana) and Cultura Migrante. 2022. *La caravana migrante en
la Ciudad de México, del 12 al 22 de diciembre de 2021*. PRAMI (Programa de Asuntos
Migratorios. January. https://prami.ibero.mx/wp-content/uploads/2022/01/Informe
-Caravana-CDMX.pdf.

Varela Huerta, Amarela. 2015a. "La 'securitización' de la gubernamentalidad migratoria
mediante la 'externalización' de las fronteras estadounidenses a Mesoamérica." *Contemporánea* 2 (4): 5–19. https://con-temporanea.inah.gob.mx/del_oficio/amarela_varela
_num4.

Varela Huerta, Amarela. 2015b. "'Luchas migrantes': Un nuevo campo de estudios para la
sociología de los diseños." *Andamios* 12 (28): 145–70. https://doi.org/10.29092/uacm
.v12i28.37.

Varela Huerta, Amarela. 2019. "México, de 'frontera vertical' a 'país tapón': Migrantes, deportados, retornados, desplazados internos y solicitantes de asilo en
México." *Iberoforum: Revista de Ciencias Sociales de la Universidad Iberoamericana*
14 (27): 49–76. https://iberoforum.ibero.mx/index.php/iberoforum/article/view
/124.

Varela Huerta, Amarela. 2020a. "Caravanas de migrantes y refugiados centroamericanos: Un feminismo para abrazar las fugas de quienes buscan preservar la vida." *Revista de Antropología Social* 29 (2): 245–55. https://doi.org/10.5209/raso.71669.

Varela Huerta, Amarela. 2020b. "Introducción." In *Necropolítica y migración en la frontera mexicana: Un ejercicio de conocimiento situado*, 1–12. México: Instituto de Investigaciones Jurídicas-Universidad Nacional Autónoma de México.

Varela Huerta, Amarela, and Lisa McLean. 2019. "Caravanas de migrantes en México." *Revista CIDOB d'Afers Internacionals* 122: 163–86. https://doi.org/10.24241/rcai.2019.122.2.163.

Vázquez Olivero, Mario, and Fabian Campos. 2016. *México ante el conflicto centroamericano: testimonio de una época*. Mexico City: Bonilla Artigas Editores.

5

The Indeterminacy of Transit Through Latin America as Seen from the Colombia-Panama Border

Juan Thomas Ordóñez and Jonathan Echeverri Zuluaga

For several weeks between May and August 2021, more than ten thousand migrants, mostly Haitians, got stuck in Necoclí, a port town on the Gulf of Urabá, Colombia. Tonny came to Necoclí thinking he would stay a day or two while he bought boat tickets and supplies, only to end up living there almost four months. At thirty-one, he had spent part of his youth in the Dominican Republic, then some months in Brazil, and had finally moved to Chile where he worked and studied for six years with a temporary residency. He left when his permanent residency was denied. With excellent Spanish and a slight Chilean accent, he told us about his day-to-day life on the Gulf, explaining that he dealt with getting stuck in Colombia by making friends, finding a room to rent from a local family, and getting to know how things worked there. He made a living by taking advantage of Necoclí's dual role as a hub in the transit toward North America and as a tourist town. He catered to other Haitian migrants by exchanging currency and selling lemonade on the boardwalk in the mornings and did other odd jobs in restaurants catering to tourists in the evenings. Tonny even dated a local woman and introduced her to us one evening when we bumped into him in the restaurant district in town. Like thousands of Haitians at that time, Tonny was forced to interrupt his journey north due to a series of circumstances (border closures, infrastructure problems, and migration policies instated during the pandemic) that made it impossible to continue across the Colombia-Panama border.

Migrants waited in Urabá, the region around the Gulf that carries the same name, ready to cross the Darién jungle. Their presence usually goes unnoticed in the national media until something happens and their transits are blocked, as they were that August and in 2016 when more than a thousand Cubans were stuck in the neighboring port of Turbo for several months (Palomino 2016; Sánchez 2016). Because they enter Colombia through informal crossings, their lack of visibility is also institutionalized; they are "irregular" migrants whom the Colombian state considers to be on their way to the United States.[1] Yet some, like Tonny, are curious about opportunities to stay, as many Cubans, Haitians, and some Africans have lived legally for years in other South American countries. Tonny assumed getting a residence permit in Colombia would be easy; after all, he got one in Chile and worked and studied there for more than six years. But, as we explained to him, there was no legal way of remaining in Colombia, other than marrying a Colombian citizen and paying almost US$500 in fees to the Ministry of Foreign Affairs. And, even then, he might have to leave the country and reenter via an official checkpoint. Tonny didn't believe us. "The Venezuelan guy selling dollars at the port says it's easy; he says I can get a Venezuelan ID for eighty thousand pesos."

But in truth there was no way for him to legally stay; no policy in the country would regularize him in his current situation. He just had to wait until he could continue his journey. Transit migration in Colombia is governed in the interstices of a seemingly indifferent state and the region's armed actors who control the informal crossings between the two countries and have influence over commerce, tourism, and transportation. After living in Necoclí for months, Tonny finally moved on, spent two weeks in Tapachula, Mexico, and then made his way across the country to the United States in November, only to be deported back to Haiti. Not one to accept his lot, he borrowed money and managed to return to Chile a short time later. Other Haitians we spoke to that August entered the United States and are processing asylum claims after extended stays—some several months long—in Tapachula, Mexico City, and Tijuana.

Their stories illustrate the multiple experiences migrants have as they wander through South America, sometimes for years or even decades. We met many Africans with Brazilian immigration status and Haitians with temporary residencies in Chile. With a favorable exchange rate for sending remittances back home and a job market hungry for manual labor in these two countries, they stayed and even considered settling there permanently. But over the past few years many have become frustrated or disappointed with the weather, racism, and bureaucratic barriers to permanent residency and decided to look for opportunities in North America. They make their way up through Peru and Ecuador, usually by land, and enter Colombia via informal border crossings either in the Andean highlands or the lowlands of Putumayo. Then they must travel to Necoclí, where boats take them to the isthmus, and they cross into Central America.

In the Colombia-Panama border zone, interruptions of migrant flows, which we here call bottlenecks, occur sporadically when tensions over the volume of migrants between the two countries emerge, when Colombia's internal conflict affects movement throughout the region, or when local politics leads communities to block their territories. Many times, these factors all coincide at given moments of "crisis" and have important effects on local communities. In the case we present in this chapter, for example, Necoclí's urban population of about twelve thousand (Gobernación de Antioquia 2021) almost doubled when the more than ten thousand migrants got stuck there in 2021.[2] In 2021 Haitians were the main cohort in this population, and we could hear Creole spoken throughout the town as they made their way to grocery stores, the beaches, and hotels. Many were stuck there for days and weeks, waiting for the boat company to sell them the tickets they needed to continue up north.

On their transcontinental journeys, migrants encounter a variety of national migration systems, some (like Ecuador's) that allow movement and others that "tolerate" it, or respond to their presence through policies of contention and control. The latter is the case in Colombia, which sees migrants like Tonny as complete strangers, foreigners in the country by geographical happenstance. The Colombian state, through its migration agency Migración Colombia, both irregularizes these migrants by constructing their presence as transitory and disengages from its responsibilities to this population through haphazard policies aimed at allowing the flow but not facilitating it in any way.

This chapter explores the transit of migrants through Urabá and the Darién, areas in the northwestern tip of Colombia, focusing on the bottleneck of mid-2021 that emerged after border closures related to the COVID-19 pandemic ended and thousands of people tried to migrate by land to North America. This, along with other factors, led to the interruption of migrants' journeys toward Central America and, eventually, the US-Mexico border.

We argue that the Colombian state governs transit migration through *indeterminacy*, a legal and social condition that renders this type of transit vague. Indeterminacy is also tied to the historical marginalization of the areas these migrants' journeys traverse and of the complex configurations of sovereignty in the border regions of the country. A distinct border regime emerged in Necoclí from this state of vagueness. It both hindered migrants' movement and opened the doors to highly effective responses from local actors like hotel and hostel owners and the inhabitants around town, especially the neighborhood closest to the port, *barrio Caribe*.

Border regimes are systems of regulation that emerge from the encounter of different actors and geographic scales. They are valid only within limited space-time coordinates, which means that they vary from one leg of the journey to the next. For instance, in the regime that prevailed in Necoclí, no single actor monopolized and managed migrant movement; rather, an array of actors responded to different aspects of the problem. This multiplicity created opportunities for migrants to manage their journeys and deal with the delays and gave locals chances to make profits in a post-COVID depressed economy. Conditions changed once migrants crossed the Gulf and landed in Capurganá, where ethnic communities and armed groups cooperated to organize tight control of migrant circulation (Sarrut, Echeverri Zuluaga, and Valenzuela 2023). The border regime there, in the last town before the jungle crossing, was connected to the one we described for Necoclí, but operated under different logics tied to the ways the actors there are present and act on the economy and social organization.

Migrants have been passing through Urabá and the Darién on their way north at least since the 1970s, as hostel owners told us in Turbo—until 2019, before the pandemic, the main port where migrants embarked to cross the Gulf of Urabá. Initially, most of the foreigners were from other South American countries, but with more stringent US immigration policies in the twenty-first century, the flow has diversified to include people from across the globe, especially Africa, Asia, and the Caribbean. Flows also increased dramatically after Ecuador lifted most visa requirements in 2007, following a political doctrine of universal citizenship (Echeverri Zuluaga and Acevedo Sáenz 2018; Ruiz Muriel and Álvarez Velasco 2019). Ecuador thus became a point of entry, and Chile, Argentina, and Brazil became new destinations (Winders 2014) for migrants from Africa and the Caribbean during progressive governments in the past two decades. Haitians also came to countries like Brazil and Chile after the 2010 earthquake, when these nations lifted visa requirements as part of a tacit trade of humanitarian relief for labor.

Unlike the US-Mexico border or the borders of the European Union, with their massive infrastructures and state-of-the-art surveillance technology, the borders in Colombia, and especially the border with Panama, are not militarized or systematically controlled (Niño González and Jaramillo 2018, 84; Ramírez 2008, 139). These are also highly porous borders, marked by informal crossings known as *trochas*. The Colombia-Panama border is the country's shortest land border (266 kilometers), and it is shaped by the Darién rainforest. Necoclí, the closest port accessible by road to the Darién rainforest, lies between 55 and 65 kilometers away, a one-and-a-half-hour ride on a high-power boat, from Capurganá or Acandí. These two small ports on the Colombian side of the border, inaccessible by land, are points that migrants need to reach before making the days-long trek through the jungle. During the 2021 bottleneck in Necoclí, migrants had to organize their stay and prepare for crossing the jungle by negotiating with local actors such as hostel and hotel owners, boat companies, street vendors, "guides," and mestizo communities—armed actors and people who provide a variety of travel-related services.

During the 2021 bottleneck, these local actors challenged state policies and responded to the "humanitarian crisis" that Migración Colombia was unable or unwilling to deal with effectively. Furthermore, the sudden appearance of thousands of Haitians also generated ethnic solidarity among some of Necoclí's inhabitants whose African heritage and local identity politics led them to feel affinity toward them because of a perceived common history. Solidarity also worked hand in hand with the entrepreneurial spirit of many of Necoclí's inhabitants who were quick to accommodate Haitians in different ways, as we illustrate below.

This chapter is based on ethnographic research we conducted in Necoclí at the beginning of 2019 and throughout 2021. Methods consisted of ethnographic observations of Necoclí's dock and boardwalk, in the Caribe neighborhood (located across the boardwalk). and in the hotel where we stayed. We also had informal, unrecorded conversations with various locals who were part of the tourist industry, with state officials, and with migrants. Maintaining ties with migrants in this situation is difficult, as contact after they cross the Darién depends on their use of social apps such as WhatsApp and Facebook. Most of our interlocutors had lived in Brazil, Chile, or Argentina and hailed mainly from Haiti and Cuba but also from Nigeria and Namibia. We have anonymized their names and, in some cases, created composites of their experiences to guarantee their privacy.

Transit Migration and Border Regimes

Scholarly works have tended to view migration as relocating from point of departure A to point of destination B, a rationale that state policy and the media replicate. When migrants' journeys cover ample geographical areas across many states, the countries of transit get subsumed into these linear imaginings as places people traverse "on the way" (Crawley and Jones 2021; Papadopoulou 2004). Many studies thus tend to ignore how migrants experience or even inhabit the journey (Mainwaring and Brigden 2016; Dumans 2013). Methodological nationalism has naturalized the nation-state as the key locus of inquiry in many studies of migration (Wimmer and Glick Schiller 2003), thereby emphasizing the ways national policies inform migrant experience at their destination or looking at their continued ties to home countries. The ways the countries they traverse affect their lives and journeys remains understudied even as transit migration has become a political problem and has thus been included in the concerns of many countries through which migrants cross to get to the European Union (Crawley and Jones 2021). Turkey is a case in point, but transit migration, because of its irregular nature, is hard to study, and estimates tend to fall short of reality in many instances (İçduygu and Sert 2014).

Whereas the European emphasis lies within a wider debate about which host country becomes the country of residence for refugees and asylum seekers, in the Americas, most scholarship has focused on the transit of Latin Americans through Central America and Mexico with the intent to reach one destination, the United States. Here, scholars have tied US politics to the production of increasingly dangerous migration routes through the externalization of its borders (Ruiz and Álvarez Velasco 2019, 697), but also to the multiple ways that these transits reshape social relations along the journey (Brigden 2018; Mainwaring and Brigden 2016; Vogt 2018). Scholarship centering on Mexico has also emphasized how US politics, drug trafficking, and other elements come together in violent and unpredictable ways to hinder, threaten, and challenge movements (Basok et al. 2015; Rizzo Lara 2022).

From countries like Ecuador establishing a human rights–based legal paradigm for governing migration, to shifts toward more stringent forms of control with the rise of center-right and right-wing governments, migration has become a key issue in Latin America (Domenech 2017). Transit migration in the region is starting to garner some attention as migratory trends have shifted in the past few decades (Cerrutti and Parrado 2015). Some scholarship on transit has focused on single countries. For example, Isabel Berganza (2017) identifies routes and costs among migrants from Haiti, Senegal, Colombia, and the Dominican Republic traversing Peru; and Santiago Valenzuela (2019) describes ways of managing needs and demands of the journey among Cubans and South Asians in Urabá. Regarding transit through Mexico and Central America, Nanneke Winters and Franziska Reiffen (2019) have explored the links that Africans create during their stays in local communities, and Pedro Roa Ortega (2021) looks at how religious narratives serve to make sense of the journey. Other works combine a more regional and continental scope with a focus on routes, border crossings, temporary hubs, and points of blockage. For example, Bruno Miranda (2021) follows the trajectories of Haitians between Brazil and the US-Mexico border; and Gustavo Dias, Joao Carlos Jarochinski, and Sidney da Silva (2020) analyze the circuit of interconnected cities in Latin America and beyond that foregrounds Haitian migrant networks.

In the case of Colombia, which has historically been a country of emigration due to the armed conflict and economic conditions (Ramírez and Mendoza 2013; Palma Gutiérrez 2015), the government's migration policy is heavily shaped by the response to the almost 3 million Venezuelans who have settled in the country over the past decade and hundreds of thousands more who enter Colombia in transit toward other destinations in South America (R4V 2022; Migración Colombia 2023). Based on a discourse of generosity and brotherly care (Palma Gutiérrez 2021), Colombia has governed Venezuelan migration by decree (Del Real 2022) and avoided establishing structural migration policies, preferring temporary stay permits like the one Tonny wanted to get. What this means is that Colombia recognizes Venezuelans and "regularized" foreigners (Latin Americans and citizens from the Global North), who can thus be considered temporary residents, tourists, businesspeople, and those with family ties to the country. African, Asian, and Caribbean migrants on the move, on the other hand, are not part of the equation, cannot legally enter the country, and thus become "irregular" when they cross informal *trochas* into Colombia. *Migrante irregular* is the official label for migrants with unauthorized status, a designation that contributes to rendering them hyperforeign in the eyes of state officials.

Along with these developments comes a long history of government neglect of the country's border areas, which in Colombia's national narratives have been constructed as empty and impoverished, in need of development plans, or as wild and governed by criminal actors. Media and official accounts of transit across the Colombia-Panama border construct the Darién as a wild and pristine jungle or as a battlefield where guerrillas, paramilitaries, and other illegal groups fight for control of migration and the drug and arms trade, thus neglecting its history as a region. Indeed, these forms of representation ignore peripheral areas as social and economic hubs for local and regional actors (Serje 2005) that in the Darién include Indigenous, Black (Peralta 2012), and mestizo communities on both sides of the border. The region has a rich history of legal and illegal commerce that connected to the Andean interior through the natural waterways of the Gulf and the Atrato River. In recent decades, these activities have intensified and induced high rates of deforestation, turning considerable areas of the Darién into grassland for cattle.

Theoretical discussions in the field of critical border studies suggest that locations such as this one are unique spaces in which to question commonsense assumptions about borders. The distinction between migration systems and migration regimes is a case in point. While the former refers to a central organizing logic, the latter emerges from the actions of an array of actors whose practices are variably determined in a complex struggle with "fluid, streamlined, clandestine, multidirectional, multipositional and context-dependent forms of mobility" (Papadopoulos, Stephenson, and Tsianos 2008, 163). Human movement is not a mere reaction to state endeavors to control a sovereign space, but an active force that catches state power "off guard" (something especially pertinent in the case of the Darién) and shapes the way such endeavors evolve. In the case of the mid-2021 bottleneck in Necoclí, it was local entrepreneurs, citizens, and migrants themselves who responded to the blockage that government institutions could not deal with.

Commonsense understandings of borders take them as spatial and geopolitical entities that exclude and separate and as exclusive tools of state sovereignty. Critical border studies challenge this perspective through key ideas, of which we elaborate on three. First, these studies understand borders as temporal entities. Their ability to speed and slow down movements enhance the regulation of people and labor (Mezzadra and Neilson 2013, 135). In the European Union, detention centers are a visible mechanism that allows this regulation, as they modulate the pace of movement like a gear box or a decompression chamber (Papadopoulos, Stephenson, and Tsianos 2008; Andrijasevic 2010). The bottleneck of 2021 was also highly mediated by state regulations—including a national registration system for all nonresident foreigners, border closures, tax audits, and port controls—that restricted migrants' ability to move. Transportation companies, hotels, and hostels developed for tourism also affected migrants' ability to move on to the next stage of their journey.

Second, borders serve parallel sovereignties in the sense that different jurisdictions intervene in their operation. Some are state jurisdictions, but the border regime is not necessarily limited to them. Migrant indeterminacy is articulated both through the state's indifference and Urabá's history and marginalization. Various criminal groups tied to paramilitary organizations control or influence different aspects of everyday life in places like Necoclí. Their relation to migrants is mostly indirect, as it is businesses, guides, and others that pay them in order to operate. Furthermore, as in other countries in the region (Krupa 2010), state sovereignty in Colombia is often outsourced. Many border areas not only are controlled or disputed by guerrilla and paramilitary groups but may also be militarized or rendered as zones of humanitarian crises where state responsibilities are transferred to humanitarian organizations and nongovernmental organizations (NGOs) (Ordóñez and Ramírez Arcos 2024; M. Ramírez 2015; Tate 2015). Organizations to which the state delegates the provision of assistance also contribute to reproducing the conditions of marginality and exclusion rather than overcoming them, because in many ways they do not bring structural solutions to the regions (Serje 2012, 110). While these institutions were originally limited to the Catholic Church, the past few decades of violence and drug trafficking have seen the emergence of humanitarian aid, which in Colombia initially targeted the victims of the armed conflict and, more recently, has included the Venezuelan diaspora. Besides the Catholic Church, the presence of humanitarian organizations and NGOs dealing with transit migration toward Panamá is very recent.

Finally, at stake in the functions that borders perform are producing otherness and governing subjects on the move (Mezzadra and Neilson 2013, 183). Borders transform those who cross them. Irrespective of how they do it, border crossers come to be seen as foreign others in opposition to citizens (Balibar 2002). In the case of those who cross without legal documents, foreignness gets magnified. In the words of Nathalie Peutz and Nicholas De Genova (2010), migrants "serve the sovereign state through their embodiment of the elementary distinction between citizens and others, 'insiders' and 'outsiders'" (14). The Colombian state has constructed specific representations of Venezuelan migrants (both regular and irregular) (Ordóñez and Ramírez Arcos 2019), and many policies construct transit migrants as either smuggled migrants or migrant smugglers in the sense that state authorities see their migration networks as suspect (Echeverri Zuluaga et al. 2023; Echeverri Zuluaga and Ordóñez 2023). But on the ground, in everyday interactions, the Colombian state and its authorities disengage from defining migrants like Tonny in any way. They are simply rendered vague through the concept of *migración irregular*. In fact, as we show below, the few haphazard policies that affect these transits reinforce their legal and social illegibility.

The configurations of state bordering here lead to the production of indeterminacy in how these migrants move and the way local and national authorities understand their governance. But, while it might appear to be the product of purposeful inaction by the state, this indeterminacy is also haphazard; it intersects local logics and idiosyncrasies and the ways migrants affect them. In this sense, indeterminacy is highly productive and creates opportunities for migrants and locals alike to manage migration on their own terms.

Before the COVID-19 pandemic, a constant trickle of migrants, many Haitians but also African and South Asian, passed through Urabá. To cross the Colombia-Panama border, these migrants had to visit Migración Colombia offices either in Ipiales (as most migrants arrived from Ecuador), Medellín, or Turbo in order to "regularize" their entry into the country. Here they would present themselves, register, and get a *salvoconducto*, a document of safe passage designed to temporarily regularize the immigration status of someone who has entered the country irregularly or whose visa has expired (Guerra Restrepo 2016, 152). The Colombian government started issuing this document to migrants in transit to Central America in 2015 to allow them to legally leave the country. The *salvoconducto* stated it was issued because the person was being deported—something migrants did not usually realize at the time they applied for it. In fact, they were getting deported at no cost to the state. It was also practical for the state to dispense with identifying people needing protection as recognized by international law. Indeterminacy was thus present even in the state's inscription, which a self-deportation order presented to migrants as regularizing their transit.

For five years, migrants used the *salvoconducto* to reach the border with Panama (Ocampo González and Arboleda Cardona 2016). It allowed them to buy tickets on formal means of transportation and, especially, to legally stay in hotels and hostels that are required by law to report foreigners to Migración Colombia. The COVID-19 pandemic, however, led to border closures and mobility restrictions throughout the Americas, including Colombia. Due to the circumstances, Migración Colombia closed its offices and even extended the expiration dates of all visas and residency permits. A few months before the 2021 bottleneck became national news, one of the institution's officials explained to us matter-of-factly that Migración Colombia simply stopped issuing the *salvoconducto* during the pandemic because the borders closed and people were not officially supposed to be crossing them. To him it was an obvious measure. That land border "closures" in Colombia simply meant limiting the flows of people and things to clandestine paths (Ordóñez and Ramírez Arcos 2024) seemed not to be an issue. Without the *salvoconducto*, migrants were forced to turn to smugglers the moment they entered the country, as they could not buy bus tickets or hire transportation without legal migration status. In Necoclí "closure" also meant turning to local people who could ferry them across the Gulf in small and unstable boats. In September 2020, after COVID restrictions were slowly lifted, a steady trickle of migrants began to appear on the border with Ecuador. Once some transportation was allowed, they managed to move toward the border with Panama, paying locals to informally hire buses, taxis, and even Uber drivers to make the more than twenty-two-hour ride from Ipiales to Necoclí. A little over 1,200 kilometers on paved roads and highways, this journey entails crossing the western part of the country and can take longer by bus. In the absence of any state measures to assist these transits, migrants found help from and paid people in Colombia whose services could solve their transportation problems. The trickle of people reaching Necoclí only to find the border still closed slowly became a torrent. By early July 2021, the media started reporting ten thousand migrants crowding the town's streets and beaches. Both media and the local politicians began to describe the situation as a "humanitarian crisis." The town's mayor almost declared a health emergency due to encampments on the beach, water shortages, and the collapse of the sewage system (*El Tiempo* 2021a; Osorio Montoya 2021).

The bottleneck was at its height when we arrived in mid-August, and the media had daily been portraying migrants as victims in need of humanitarian aid and at the mercy of trafficking networks (*El Tiempo* 2021b; *France 24* 2021). These reports did not mention that the cancelation of the *salvoconducto* increased the number of cases of corruption and state violence. Yet walking up and down the boardwalk and the market in Necoclí, the crowds of migrants notwithstanding, we got a general feeling of being in a bustling border town. Migrants were flooding in by the hundreds every day, and police officers took advantage of the moment to fish in troubled waters. They set up roadblocks, stopped vehicles with migrants, and charged a US$20 bribe for not arresting each migrant or returning them to Ecuador. This led drivers to leave migrants far from Necoclí's urban area for fear of being stopped at checkpoints or roadblocks. Local people waited at these points to offer cheap housing in town. Around the docks and ATM machines were long lines of people struggling to withdraw money and purchase boat tickets. However, amid the turmoil, we also found migrants relaxing and enjoying themselves. Along the beach, the beer stands and restaurants that cater to tourists had shifted their business to better suit Haitian customers, playing Tony Mix and other Haitian music well into the night. Migrants took part in impromptu football matches and ate fried fish. Rather than a "crisis," it was an environment that heavily resembled Necoclí's tourist season.

In the mornings, groups of people walked up and down the boardwalk, changing money and looking for equipment for their trip through the jungle. The local formal and informal markets in Necoclí were offering camping supplies like machetes, gas stoves, pots and pans, rain parkas, insect and snake repellants, tents, and boots. Migrants walked down toward the port daily, catching glimpses of those finally leaving or hearing news about the trek. The Venezuelan who offered to procure papers for Tonny introduced him to the money exchange business on the boardwalk, one of his multiple jobs in town: he sold lemonade, worked nights at a hot dog stand, and was interviewing at another fast-food place, where he would likely sign a contract. Tonny's "Ji sitwon, ji sitwon" ("lime juice, lime juice"), broadcast to thirsty fellow Haitians was unique; all the other entrepreneurs were locals or Venezuelans. In the neighborhood across the boardwalk, ads in Haitian creole offered photocopies and other services. Occasionally, two officials from Migración Colombia in charge of supervising migrant circulation drove through town in a pickup truck on the main street along the boardwalk. A couple of times, we saw these officials stepping out of the truck to snap pictures amid the crowds of migrants. Was this a "crisis," or was this business as usual? Were the migrants "in transit" or were they tourists? Indeterminacy had given the bottleneck these locally shaped contours and was helping to revive the COVID-depressed economy.

All hotels, hostels, and many private homes in town were working to full capacity. Don Fernando, the owner of our hotel, told us that seeing thousands of people camping on the beach with money to pay for rooms, led to a decision among hostel and hotel owners to receive migrants at a fixed rate of US$10 a night. This was supposedly not allowed since the *salvoconducto* had disappeared and there was no way to register undocumented migrants in the system. "Once we got people off the beach and into the hotels, we wrote Migración Colombia and asked them what we should do; we asked them to tell us if this was illegal," don Fernando explained as he was registering a group of Nigerians in his guest book. Migración Colombia had to accept the fact that private entrepreneurs had managed to house most of the people on the street and in beach encampments.

This approval encouraged local homeowners to openly rent out rooms or entire houses to large groups of migrants for US$6 to US$8 a night. Catalina, don Fernando's granddaughter, had been unemployed before she started hosting people from Haiti. Adapting her house to receive migrants was an opportunity to make ends meet. Acknowledging that their presence revived Necocli's economy, she described their arrival as a small blessing, "*una bendición chiquita.*" She also helped them find guides for trekking through the Darién rainforest and developed close ties of friendship with some of her tenants. However, again, one of the warnings from Migración Colombia to local hosts was not to broker tickets for their irregular clients, and Catalina became increasingly afraid that she would be accused of migrant smuggling.

A similar situation occurred with the only boat company in Necoclí. The main reason the bottleneck formed was that in response to Colombia opening its borders after COVID-19 restrictions were lifted in May 2021, Panama closed its borders

(Ministerio de Relaciones Exteriores 2021). But once the border opened again, the Colombian government's restrictions on the number of people the boat company could transport became an issue. Because authorities could interpret exceeding the government cap as migrant smuggling or money laundering, the company initially had to limit ticket sales, thus contributing to the blockage. After hundreds and then thousands of migrants were forced to wait weeks for tickets, the company came to an agreement with Migración Colombia to transport higher numbers, but it did not have enough boats with the required safety certificates to cover demand, and migrants kept accumulating in the town. The company eventually came up with a more effective solution: creating a second boat company with the assets from the former and a new fleet of boats. By mid-August 2021, this innovation had helped ease the bottleneck, and the two companies managed to reduce the waiting time to a week or less.

Unlike Necoclí's hotel and boat transport businesses, state institutions like Migración Colombia did not contribute to reducing the bottleneck, but rather seemed to make things more difficult and offered no pragmatic solutions. The Migración Colombia officer at one meeting we attended that August epitomized the institutional approach. The officer stressed that the agency did not want people dealing in dollars and were warning everyone interacting with the migrants from the Ecuadorian border to Necoclí to deal only in Colombian pesos. "We don't want to affect the financial sector with this money; you know that the people in the United States—*los americanos*—don't like their money circulating outside their country." Two blocks away from the room where this man was speaking, money changers at the seafront boardwalk, including Tonny, were openly buying and selling dollars, Colombian and Chilean pesos, and Brazilian reales. You could see the makeshift signs a block away. We also saw exchanges in dollars in small neighborhood shops and in one national chain supermarket.

Much of what Colombian authorities do for migrants contrasts with a discourse at the international level that takes up the standard of contention and struggle against migrant trafficking (Miranda 2021, 123). There is no intention to either contain or facilitate the transit of this population, and since the pandemic, there hasn't even been a pretense of temporarily regularizing their status. Ironically, bottlenecks in Necoclí are part of the domino effect of contention policies implemented in Central American countries such as Panama and Nicaragua (Miranda 2021). Other actors, such as paramilitary groups, and contingencies like shipwrecks in the border region call attention to the problem for the Colombian government, but in the absence of coherent policies, all responses end up producing indeterminacy that, in turn, creates the conditions of possibility for other types of responses. It was the Necoclí tourist industry that set the pace in solving the "humanitarian" and "health" crises. This border town came together to both help people in need and reactivate the local economy, precisely because the indeterminacy concerning transit made it possible to develop responses inscribed in local practices.

Catalina's experience embodies the entrepreneurial spirit that took Necoclí by storm. It also illustrates how migrants themselves were active in facilitating a movement that the governments of Panama and Colombia were so intent on curbing or constraining. From the onset of the "crisis," Catalina felt empathy and kinship with many of the Haitians and developed a close friendship with some of the people who stayed in her house. Gabriel was probably among the closest. "My Haitian friend Gabriel told me one day that he knew everyone because he had been a social leader either in Haiti or Chile, I can't remember," she said one evening as we ate pizza. Thinking he was just boasting, she was surprised one day as they walked down the street to see that everyone, in fact, knew him by name. Gabriel proposed they go into business together. With her knowledge of the region and her acquaintance with boat owners in Necoclí and Capurganá, Catalina could organize early-morning informal passage to the isthmus. With his ties to the other migrants, Gabriel organized the groups and got payment on good faith based on his previous work with the Haitian community. Catalina knew a boatman who paid the fees to paramilitary intermediaries for each migrant and who could manage the passage in the predawn hours. The first two trips went smoothly, but after word got around that there were boats leaving for the Darién in the early mornings, the two got into trouble. Gabriel's charisma was not enough to keep other migrants from storming the hired boats in disorder, many not having even paid. The boatmen had to leave the beach and wait offshore while he tried to calm people down. But in the end, they had to stop the business for fear of drawing the attention of authorities. The endeavor was a failed investment of Catalina's money since the boatman paid fees on several shipments that never materialized. Gabriel made it to Orlando, Florida, Catalina told us. "We still chat every once in a while, but I ended up in debt and am only getting back on my feet a year later."

What had suddenly brought so many people to the town, however, was not completely clear to Catalina and other local entrepreneurs. They just repeated what many of the migrants had told them, simply reducing it to the idea that, at least for Haitians, there was a time limitation to their entry into the United States. Most of the Haitian migrants, in fact, were traveling under the impression that the Biden administration's renewal of Temporary Protected Status (TPS) for Haitians would make their entry into the United States easy. They ignored the fact that people arriving in the United States after July 29, 2021 (USCIS 2021), could not benefit from the measure. Some Cubans, Africans, and South Americans were also trapped in the bottleneck. One Ecuadorian family we talked to on the dock was under the impression that the TPS for Haitians also applied to people from their country. "They're only receiving families," the man told us, "not single men or anything like that." He was traveling with his wife and two small children, his sister with five-year-old twins, and a nephew who was about sixteen.

Slowly but surely, all these local responses, along with the boats that the new company added, made the transits efficient again, and by October, don Fernando told us he wasn't taking in as many Haitians and Africans in his hotel. Migrants in fact went back to waiting only a day or two to embark for the isthmus. Even the money exchange stands were gone. Catalina had stopped housing migrants in her home, as demand for rooms had dropped significantly. She had also become very concerned about being accused of migrant smuggling as Migración Colombia officers constantly warned that anyone "facilitating" these transits was legally liable. Many of the local responses then reverted to the way things were before the pandemic, but a few locals like Catalina nevertheless continued their ties of friendship with the migrants they had helped, many of whom remained in contact with them via WhatsApp and Facebook.

With tourism going back to normal at the end of 2021, the beach took on its old contours, with bars, restaurants, and hotels playing Latin American music and catering to mostly Colombian tourists. By January 2022, during Necoclí's famous Coconut Festival, it was even hard to find Haitians or Africans on the street. But for the months the town was the epicenter of this bottleneck that caught government and local institutions off guard, it was local citizens, entrepreneurs, and migrants themselves who set in motion pragmatic responses to the problem. In doing so, they challenged the state's ability to irregularize these movements by recognizing that migrants were there and that the town could incorporate them into the local economy. Locals, in fact, resuscitated Necoclí's pandemic-depressed economy through these practices in a way the government's lethargic policies could not. During the bottleneck, local responses shaped the experiences of migrants on the ground. Border policies across the hemisphere might have set the conditions for the blockage, but the border regime that emerged escaped the politics and practices of control that were supposed to be in place. The border regime also created ties of solidarity and friendship that further connected this region to the US, Haiti, and Chile, the last being the country from which most of the migrants had departed.

Conclusions: A Border Regime

Tonny's ramblings about staying in Colombia, seeking temporary jobs, or even settling there are unimaginable within the rationale of apathy through which the Colombian state governs the circulation of these migrants toward the Panamanian border. State-sponsored actions avoid any compromise that lets them stay, which would entail conferring them a legal or regular status or speeding up their trajectories, which would amount to engaging in smuggling in the Colombian state's logic. The *salvoconducto* is a good example of this as it guaranteed partial recognition only for the purpose of self-deportation. State indeterminacy concerning transit instated by unrealistic policies and disinterest makes people illegible, irrevocably foreign, and obscure. But questions like Tonny's about how to acquire legal Colombian papers catch the government off guard, and his life arrangements in Necoclí, with several jobs and later a Colombian girlfriend, helped his own interests to prevail despite the government's apathy, at least for a certain time. His indeterminacy also made his actions and local responses to the bottleneck part of a productive response beyond the government's reach.

The accounts in this chapter illustrate that transit migration on the Colombia-Panama border is more than just the flow of people with little or no agency who cross an inhospitable jungle full of dangers—a narrative deeply ingrained in media, government, and academic reports and in public debate (Echeverri Zuluaga et al. 2023). Instead, a variety of actors at local, national, and international levels react to transit-producing border regimes that vary from one leg of the journey to the next. National laws, policies, and the institutions that enforce them are among these actors but do not shape the regime on their own. Rather than enforcing an agenda, we see the state reacting haphazardly or lagging in its responses as it faces the moves of neighboring states, small-business owners, smugglers, paramilitary groups, and local communities. These other actors often seem, at least in the Colombian borderlands, to be more efficient or pragmatic in responding to the situations generated by migrants circulating, crossing, and waiting. Interactions can be tense, but local actors manage to keep the movement going. Furthermore, interactions are entwined and unstable. The circulation of money is a good entry point for understanding the ways interactions unfolded. Money changing comprised relatives of hotel owners; local people working for undisclosed bosses; Venezuelans and Colombians from the city of Montería, up the Gulf; and Tonny, who told us the "powers that be" were watching but allowed him to work because he bought dollars only from fellow Haitians. These were not legal currency exchanges (of which there were a few in town), but they operated in the open and were part of the informal commerce of the boardwalk. The boardwalk itself has internal dynamics of control tied to local gangs that answer to paramilitary groups and take cuts from most formal and informal entrepreneurs. In a sense, Tonny working there shows that even these traditional "dark powers" were making concessions to allow migrants to survive. And while the Migración Colombia officer, disconnected completely from reality a block away, thought that using dollars on the streets of Colombia would create problems with the United States, many small businesses and even one national chain were informally accepting the currency.

The 2021 bottleneck in Necoclí offers insight into the dynamics of a "context dependent" or situated border regime. From a large-scale point of view, the way the border regime operates in the Darién area resonates with trends described in other locations. Take, for example, the gearbox effect that modulates the pace of movement. One could read the circulation across the Darién as the result of global, regional, and national factors, such as changes in US politics and migration laws, economic and public health issues tied to the pandemic, and the haphazard measures of Migración Colombia.

However, the way the border was enacted during the 2021 bottleneck in Necoclí shows a different configuration of the phenomenon, one that ultimately raises questions about control on a global scale. Border authorities, armed illegal groups, ethnic jurisdictions, migrants with different origins and backgrounds, and the local tourist industry and communities all actively participated in shaping the contours of this event. The pandemic, infrastructure, and the shared sense of so many migrants that *now* was the time to travel were crucial to causing people to arrive in large numbers. Divergent standards of legality emerged during this time as entrepreneurs reacted to a public health "crisis" that local and national officials could not understand or did not want to recognize. The actions of local hotel and hostel owners, ignoring state laws and directives, made waiting convenient for migrants, reactivated the economy in Necoclí, and eventually pushed the state to help the boat company accommodate the high volume of passengers. By canceling the *salvoconducto*, on the other hand, the state created instances of corruption where the national police could "catch" migrants traveling illegally and transporters moving them without authorization. Thus, rather than controlling movement, the state actually generated instances when migrants had to bribe police officers or turn to "traffickers" who could move them surreptitiously.

Migrants we met in 2021 went on eventually and entered Central America. Many of those we spoke with described encountering other border regimes that blocked their paths in Tapachula and Tijuana, cities in the southern and northern borders of Mexico. In Tapachula delays were associated with getting papers to legally travel in Mexico, which is the only country in Latin America to operationalize the Cartagena Declaration. This agreement amplifies the definitions of the circumstances that merit consideration for special protection of refugees to include economic hardship and thereby permits migrants to remain in Mexico and work for a given amount of time. Such documentation thus enabled migrants to respond to the border regime in Tijuana. One woman we met during the bottleneck in Necoclí told us five months later in Tijuana that crossing to the United States had become very difficult. "*Cambió*," she said, meaning that the border crossing had changed, and it wasn't as easy as before. While she waited for entry into the United States to become easier, she worked in a tortilla factory and legally rented a room in a building with other migrants and a few Mexicans.

The temporality and geographic specificity of border regimes form key factors in determining the mobility of migrants in transit. These factors shape migrant experience and set the parameters for the decisions they make about how and when to move or stay put. They also affect how local inhabitants respond to these junctures as they emerge.

NOTES

1. *Migrante irregular* is the official category the Colombian migration agency, Migración Colombia, uses to label people who enter the country via unofficial border crossings or who overstay the legal time limits of their entry. The agency also uses the verb *regularizar* in reference to migrants who have acquired a legal status after being undocumented in the country, especially in the case of Venezuelans.

2. Since 2022, the bottlenecks in Necoclí have mainly affected Venezuelan migrants, many leaving Colombia and other Latin American countries after living there for years with different immigration statuses.

REFERENCES

Andrijasevic, Rutvica. 2010. "From Exception to Excess: Detention and Deportations in Contemporary Europe." In *The Deportation Regime: Sovereignty, Space, and the Freedom of Movement*, edited by Nicholas De Genova and Nathalie Peutz, 147–65. Durham, NC: Duke University Press.

Balibar, Etienne. 2002. *Politics and the Other Scene*. London: Verso.

Basok, Tanya, Daniele Bélanger, Martha Luz Rojas Wiesner, and Guillermo Candiz. 2015. *Rethinking Transit Migration: Precarity, Mobility, and Self-Making in Mexico*. London: Palgrave Macmillan.

Berganza, Isabel. 2017. "Los flujos migratorios mixtos en tránsito por Perú: Un desafío para el Estado." In *Migración haitiana hacia el sur andino*, edited by Nicolas Rojas and Jose Koechlin, 41–64. Lima: Servicio Jesuita a Migrantes.

Brigden, Noelle. 2018. *The Migrant Passage: Clandestine Journeys from Central America.* Ithaca, NY: Cornell University Press.

Cerrutti, Marcela, and Emilio Parrado. 2015. "Intraregional Migration in South America: Trends and a Research Agenda." *Annual Review of Sociology* 41 (1): 399–421. https://doi.org/10.1146/annurev-soc-073014-112249.

Crawley, Heaven, and Katherine Jones. 2021. "Beyond Here and There: (Re)Conceptualising Migrant Journeys and the 'In-Between.'" *Journal of Ethnic and Migration Studies* 47 (14): 3226–42. https://doi.org/10.1080/1369183X.2020.1804190.

Del Real, Deisy. 2022. "Seemingly Inclusive Liminal Legality: The Fragility and Illegality Production of Colombia's Legalization Programmes for Venezuelan Migrants." *Journal of Ethnic and Migration Studies* 48 (15): 1–22. https://doi.org/10.1080/1369183X.2022.2029374.

Dias, Gustavo, Joao Carlos Jarochinski, and Sidney da Silva. 2020. "Travellers of the Caribbean: Positioning Brasília in Haitian Migration Routes Through Latin America." *Vibrant: Virtual Brazilian Anthropology* 17:1–19. https://doi.org/10.1590/1809-43412020v17d504.

Domenech, Eduardo. 2017. "Las políticas de migración en Sudamérica." *Terceiro Milênio: Revista crítica de sociologia e política* 8 (1): 19–48.

Dumans, Andre. 2013. *O trecho, as mães e os papeis: Etnografia de durações e movimentos no norte de Goiás.* São Paulo: Garamond.

Echeverri Zuluaga, Jonathan, and Liza Acevedo Sáenz. 2018. "Pensando a través de la errancia: Travesías y esperas de viajeros africanos en Quito y Dakar." *Antípoda: Revista de Antropología y Arqueología* 32: 105–23. https://doi.org/10.7440/antipoda32.2018.05.

Echeverri Zuluaga, Jonathan, Juan Thomas Ordóñez, Jorge Raul Álvarez Posada, and Nicolas Henao Bard. 2023. "Reflexiones sobre la construcción del tráfico de migrantes en Colombia a partir del caso de Urabá." *Secuencia: Revista de Historia y Ciencias Sociales* 116:1–26 https://doi.org/10.18234/secuencia.v0i116.2077.

Echeverri Zuluaga, Jonathan, and Juan Thomas Ordóñez. 2023. "Discerning Networks: Distortions of Human Movement in Urabá, Colombia." *Journal of Latin American and Caribbean Anthropology* 29 (1): 1–10. https://doi.org/10.1111/jlca.12694.

El Tiempo. 2021a. "Crisis sanitaria en Necoclí, Antioquia, por más de 10 mil migrantes varados." July 27. https://www.eltiempo.com/colombia/otras-ciudades/migrantes-en-necocli-hay-crisis-sanitaria-por-10-mil-personas-varadas-606284.

El Tiempo. 2021b. "Crisis migratoria." July 2. https://www.eltiempo.com/opinion/editorial/crisis-migratoria-editorial-606694.

France 24. 2021. "Ombudsman colombiano pide 'plan de choque' en crisis migratoria en frontera con Panamá." July 30. https://www.france24.com/es/minuto-a-minuto/20210730-ombudsman-colombiano-pide-plan-de-choque-en-crisis-migratoria-en-frontera-con-panam%C3%A1.

Gobernación de Antioquia. 2021. "Necoclí: Ficha Municipal 2019–2020." https://www.antioquiadatos.gov.co/territorio_antioquia/index.php/municipios/.

Guerra Restrepo, David. 2016. "Los requisitos de entrada, permanencia y salida del territorio nacional aplicables a los inmigrantes y emigrantes en Colombia y su marco normativo." *Justicia* 29:131–57. http://dx.doi.org/10.17081/just.21.29.1238.

İçduygu, Ahmet, and Deniz Sert. 2014. "Migrants' Uncertainties Versus the State's Insecurities: Transit Migration in Turkey." In *Transit Migration in Europe*, edited by Frank Duvell, Michael Collyer, and Irina Molodikova, 37–54. Amsterdam: Amsterdam University Press. https://doi.org/10.1515/9789048523160-004.

Krupa, Christopher. 2010. "State by Proxy: Privatized Government in the Andes." *Comparative Studies in Society and History* 52 (2): 319–50. https://doi.org/10.1017/S001041751000006X.

Mainwaring, Ċetta, and Noelle Brigden. 2016. "Beyond the Border: Clandestine Migration Journeys." *Geopolitics* 21 (2): 243–62. https://doi.org/10.1080/14650045.2016.1165575.

Mezzadra, Sandro, and Brett Neilson. 2013. *Border as Method; or, The Multiplication of Labor*. Durham, NC: Duke University Press.

Migración Colombia. 2023. "Distribución de Migrantes Venezolanas(os)." *Informe Agosto 2023*. Ministerio de Relaciones Exteriores, República de Colombia.

Ministerio de Relaciones Exteriores 2021. "Panamá cierra temporalmente frontera con Colombia." República de Colombia. https://mire.gob.pa/panama-cierra-temporalmente-frontera-con-colombia/.

Miranda, Bruno. 2021. "Movilidades haitianas en el corredor Brasil-México: Efectos del control migratorio y de la securitización fronteriza." *Periplos: Revista de Investigación sobre Migraciones* 5 (1): 108–30.

Niño González, Cesar A., and Felipe Jaramillo. 2018. "Una aproximación geopolítica a la política binacional de seguridad fronteriza entre Colombia y Panamá." *Opera* 23:81–96.

Ocampo González, Melina, and Sebastián Arboleda Cardona. 2016. "Colombia y los flujos mixtos de migrantes en el derecho internacional de los refugiados." *Opinión Jurídica* 15 (30): 93–108.

Ordóñez, Juan T., and Hugo E. Ramírez Arcos. 2019. "(Des)orden nacional: La construcción de la migración venezolana como una amenaza de salud y seguridad pública en Colombia." *Revista Ciencias de La Salud* 17:48–68.

Ordóñez, Juan T., and Hugo E. Ramírez Arcos. 2024. "Border Jobs: The Business of Work on the Colombia/Venezuela border." *Journal of Borderlands Studies* 39 (5): 975–92. https://doi.org/10.1080/08865655.2023.2261471.

Osorio Montoya, Miguel. 2021. "Crisis en Necoclí: 11.000 personas represadas y el hospital al borde del colapso." *El Colombiano*, September 10. https://www.elcolombiano.com/antioquia/hospital-de-necocli-esta-a-punto-de-colapso-por-paso-de-migrantes-GC15605571.

Palma Gutiérrez, Mauricio. 2015. "¿País de emigración, inmigración, tránsito y retorno? La formación de un sistema de migración colombiano." *Oasis* (21): 7–28.

Palma Gutiérrez, Mauricio. 2021. "The Politics of Generosity: Colombian Official Discourse Towards Migration from Venezuela, 2015–2018." *Colombia Internacional* 106:29–56. https://doi.org/10.7440/colombiaint106.2021.02.

Palomino, Sally. 2016. "Colombia intensifica la presión a los migrantes cubanos." *El Pais*, August 9. http://internacional.elpais.com/internacional/2016/08/08/colombia/1470614253_379305.html.

Papadopoulou, Aspasia. 2004. "Smuggling into Europe: Transit Migrants in Greece." *Journal of Refugee Studies* 17 (2): 167–84. https://doi.org/10.1093/jrs/17.2.167.

Papadopoulos, Dimitris, Niamh Stephenson, and Vassilis Tsianos. 2008. *Escape Routes: Control and Subversion in the Twenty-First Century*. London: Pluto Press.

Peralta, Jaime A. 2012. "De lo 'doméstico/manso' a lo 'lejano/arisco': Un recorrido por la cartografía simbólica del territorio negro de Chocó." *Antípoda: Revista de Antropología y Arqueología* 14:113–37.

Peutz, Nathalie, and Nicholas De Genova. 2010. "Introduction." In *The Deportation Regime: Sovereignty, Space, and the Freedom of Movement*, edited by Nicholas De Genova and Nathalie Peutz, 1–29. Durham, NC: Duke University Press.

R4V (Inter-Agency Coordination Platform for Refugees and Migrants from Venezuela). 2022. *Regional Refugee and Migrant Response Plan (RMRP), January–December 2022*. https://www.r4v.info/en/document/rmrp-2022.

Ramírez, María C. 2015. "The Idea of the State in Colombia: An Analysis from the Periphery." In *State Theory and Andean Politics: New Approaches to the Study of Rule*, edited by Christopher Krupa and David Nugent, 35–55. Philadelphia: University of Pennsylvania Press.

Ramírez, Clemencia, and Laura Mendoza. 2013. *Perfil migratorio de Colombia 2012: OIM Colombia*. OIM (Organización Internacional para las Migraciones). https://repository.iom.int/handle/20.500.11788/222.

Ramírez, Socorro. 2008. "Las zonas de integración fronteriza de la comunidad andina. Comparación de sus alcances." *Estudios Políticos*, no. 32, 135–69.

Rizzo Lara, Rosario, D. L. L. 2022. "Managing Irregularized Migration in Mexico: Rhetoric of a Renewed Approach." *Journal of Borderlands Studies* 39 (3): 433–54.

Roa Ortega, Pedro. 2021. "Éxodos contemporáneos del África occidental a la frontera norte de México." *Revista nuestrAmérica* 9 (17). https://doi.org/10.5281/zenodo.5644602.

Ruiz Muriel, Martha. C., and Soledad Álvarez Velasco. 2019. "Excluir para proteger: La 'guerra' contra la trata y el tráfico de migrantes y las nuevas lógicas de control migratorio en Ecuador." *Estudios Sociológicos* 37 (111): 689–725. http://dx.doi.org/10.24201/es.2019v37n111.1686.

Sánchez, Juan. A. 2016. "CIDH expresó 'profunda preocupación' por situación de migrantes en Turbo." *El Colombiano*, August 8. https://www.elcolombiano.com/antioquia/cidh-expreso-profunda-preocupacion-por-situacion-de-migrantes-en-turbo-AF4733983.

Sarrut, Marilou, Jonathan Echeverri Zuluaga, and Santiago Valenzuela. 2023. "Briser le mythe de la 'jungle qui tue': Analyse du rôle des intermédiaires dans la traversée du Darién (frontière Colombie-Panama)." *Revue Européenne Des Migrations Internationales* 39(4): 15–42. https://doi.org/10.4000/remi.24401.

Serje, Margarita. 2005. *El revés de la nación: Territorios salvajes, fronteras y tierras de nadie*. Bogotá: Universidad de los Andes.

Serje, Margarita. 2012. "El mito de la ausencia del Estado: La incorporación económica de las 'zonas de frontera' en Colombia." *Cahiers es Amériques Latines* 71:95–117.

Tate, Winifred. 2015. "The Aspirational State: State Effects in Putumayo." In *State Theory and Andean Politics: New Approaches to the Study of Rule*, edited by Christopher Krupa and David Nugent, 234–53. Philadelphia: University of Pennsylvania Press.

USCIS (US Citizenship and Immigration Services). 2021. "Temporary Protected Status." https://www.uscis.gov/humanitarian/temporary-protected-status.

Valenzuela, Santiago. 2019. *Ayudando a los chilangos: Solidaridad, políticas, redes y subjetividades en Turbo, Antioquia*. Bogotá: Editorial Universidad del Rosario.

Vogt, Wendy A. 2018. *Lives in Transit: Violence and Intimacy on the Migrant Journey*. Berkeley: University of California Press.

Wimmer, Andreas, and Nina Glick Schiller. 2003. "Methodological Nationalism, the Social Sciences, and the Study of Migration: An Essay in Historical Epistemology." *International Migration Review* 37 (3), 576–610. https://doi.org/10.1111/j.1747-7379.2003.tb00151.x.

Winders, Jamie. 2014. "New Immigrant Destinations in Global Context." *International Migration Review* 48:149–79.

Winters Nanneke, and Franziska Reiffen. 2019. "Haciendo-lugar vía huellas y apegos: Las personas migrantes africanas y sus experiencias de movilidad, inmovilidad e inserción local en América Latina." *REMHU* 27 (56):11–33.

6

Illegalized in the Country of "Universal Citizenship"

Soledad Álvarez Velasco

Since the late twentieth century, South American countries have embraced an approach favoring more open borders and migrant rights. Freedom of movement and residency policies for mobile populations have been part of regional debates materialized in important mobility agreements like those contemplated under the Andean Community or the MERCOSUR[1] (Stang 2009). The twenty-first-century South American immigration reforms were thus not a mere coincidence but part of a much longer regional quest for a human rights and nondiscriminatory approach to migration (Acosta Arcarazo 2016). The new migratory legal frameworks adopted in Argentina (2004), Uruguay (2008), Ecuador (2008), and Bolivia (2013) during the previous decade's "postneoliberal" turn (Ruiz Muriel and Álvarez Velasco 2019) could be seen as an attempt to lessen the hegemony of the globally reinforced border regime.

As discussed elsewhere in this volume, this regime—orchestrated by the United States and the European Union since the 1990s (Mezzadra and Neilson

2013)—has focused on the national security of those major global destinations, taking the form of selective and racist visa and deportation schemes, advanced border surveillance technology, and programs to strengthen policies to control mobility based on the suspicion and criminalization of migration (Bigo and Guild 2005). Those programs have relied on the "legal production of migrant illegality and deportability" (De Genova 2002) and equally on the externalization of US and EU borders southward and their internalization in transit countries so as to contain unwanted migrant mobility coming from the Global South (Faist 2017; Andersson 2017).

In the face of tightening antimigrant controls, the twenty-first-century South American legal immigration reforms were inevitably coated with a halo of supposed "exceptionalism." Some, if not all, of those legal reforms were internationally recognized as benchmarks of a reputedly "new model" for governing migration based, among other things, on the freedom of movement and respect of migrant rights (Ceriani Cernadas 2018; Acosta Arcarazo 2016). That halo, however, did not last very long. As Eduardo Domenech (2017) suggests, twenty-first-century South American "exceptionalism" has been riddled with significant setbacks and paradoxes.

When examining the micropolitics of regional migration, it is possible to unveil, for instance, the limits of that alleged "exceptionalism." Legal contradictions, the inapplicability of progressive legal frameworks, the incompatibility between open-border immigration policies and repressive border agents' practices, and the adoption of securitization measures[2] within immigration policies have been coupled with the extremely complex daily living conditions for migrants and asylum seekers, thus providing new empirical material for critical migration studies (see Domenech 2011, 2017; Stefoni 2011; Trabalón 2018; Ruiz Muriel and Álvarez Velasco 2019; G. Herrera and Cabezas 2019; Correa 2019; Gómez and Malo 2019; Magliano and Clavijo 2011; Pereyra 2018). This renewed scholarly focus has demonstrated how South American legal "progressivism" in migration matters has paradoxically coexisted alongside punishment, surveillance, and violence, thus questioning the role that the continent plays in the geopolitics of contemporary migration.

The Ecuadorian case is especially instructive in this regard. This Andean country adopted what is still considered the most radical constitutional reforms in migration matters. The 2008 Constitution, approved during the Citizens' Revolution government recognized, among other rights, the right to seek asylum and refuge (Article 41), the right to migrate, and the principle that "no human being shall be identified or considered as illegal because of his/her migratory status" (Article 40). It also advocated for "the principle of universal citizenship, the free movement of all inhabitants of the planet, and the progressive extinction of the status of alien or foreigner as an element to transform the unequal relations between countries, especially those between North and South" (Article 416). In that same year, President Rafael Correa eliminated by presidential decree any visa requirement for worldwide visitors to Ecuador for stays of up to ninety days.[3] All these reforms were accompanied by a vigorous official discourse promoting national sovereignty and resisting foreign intervention in national affairs, particularly by the United States (Pugh 2017; Álvarez Velasco 2020). In such an open migration context, the mechanisms typically deployed as part of the current, neoliberal global border regime would seem to have no place. In this chapter, evidence is presented to the contrary.

By drawing on ethnographic data from a qualitative investigation conducted in Ecuador between 2015 and 2018, I analyze how, in the framework of greater constitutional progressivism on migration, other legal and social practices paradoxically coexisted, producing "migrant illegality, deportability and disposability" (De Genova and Roy 2020, 355). These practices included professional disqualification, social and economic segregation, systemic racism, legal locks that impeded migrants' regularization, and even raids, detentions, and deportations. I argue that these practices—which in some cases are reminiscent of historical racist legacies present since the nineteenth-century immigration laws—have been implemented de jure or de facto, or both (Didi-Huberman 2018), targeting the most impoverished migrants and asylum seekers from certain Caribbean, African, and Asian countries, stripping them of their most basic rights and confining them to everyday hyperprecarity. It is the paradoxical coexistence of a highly progressive constitution and these practices of racialized migrant illegalization that have ended up producing migrant disposability by accelerating their deportability or their enforced departure from Ecuador—a place that transitioned from a promising destination to an unbearable place to live—to some other place, mainly the United States.

This chapter comprises four sections. I first develop the theoretical perspective that guides my analysis, then explain, in the second and third sections, why Caribbean, African, and Asian immigrants have chosen the Andean country as their destination; the main setbacks and inconsistencies in Ecuador's migration policy; and how these setbacks and inconsistencies have affected the daily lives of migrants in a way that triggers their subsequent departure. The chapter concludes by reflecting on how the paradoxical coexistence between a highly progressive constitutional framework and practices of racialized migrant illegalization outlines Ecuador's complex and perverse present role in the geopolitics of contemporary migration across the Americas.

The Global Neoliberal Border Regime and the Legal
Production of Migrant Illegality

The limitations of Ecuadorian progressivism concerning migration have been examined from a variety of theoretical and methodological perspectives. From a state-centric approach, historical reviews have shown that since the end of the nineteenth century, Ecuadorian migration policy has transitioned from a selective openness (Ramírez 2013) to contemporary rights-based openness (Araujo and Eguiguren 2009); throughout the past century, a national security approach and selective and racist parameters have persisted in allowing or denying the entrance of certain groups of foreigners (Eguiguren 2011; Ramírez 2013). Research has also shown the coexistence and incompatibility of the 1971 Migration Law— designed and implemented during Ecuador's latest dictatorship under a national security doctrine—and the 2008 Constitution (Valle Franco 2009; Arcentales Illescas 2012b; Feline Freier 2013). Other studies have analyzed the political disputes in Correa's administration (2007–17) and their impact on how migration was managed by national institutions, including the 2013 dissolution of the National Secretariat for Migrants (SENAMI), which was responsible for designing and implementing a rights-based policy (Margheritis 2011; Herrera Ríos 2016). The production of the discourse of universal citizenship and its purpose (aside from its actual implementation) in political calculations has been examined (Pugh 2017), as have the paradoxes of a supposed open border policy that welcomes migrants while whitewashing its rejection of them (Acosta Arcarazo and Feline Freier 2015). In addition, the daily dynamics of state bureaucracy and their impact on the construction of foreign others have been examined (Ackerman 2014), as well as the tension between humanitarian interventions and policies targeting human trafficking and disciplining migrants (Ruiz Muriel and Álvarez Velasco 2019).

Using a migrant-centered approach, other research has demonstrated that inconsistencies between the constitutional framework and its praxis have a significant impact on regional and transcontinental migrants and asylum seekers (Correa 2019; Moscoso 2016; Álvarez Velasco 2016, 2020; Ménard Marleau 2018). And a historical structural approach has also explained the limitations to achieving genuine openness and the praxis of universal citizenship as the consequence of asymmetrical global interdependencies that have created contradictions, such as the selective reimposition of visas, and unforeseen impacts such as irregularized transit from Ecuador to other destinations (Góngora-Mera, Herrera, and Müller 2014).

This chapter contributes to that renewed critical scholarship by analyzing how such legal inconsistencies and migration policy setbacks lead to the legal and social production of migrant illegality embodied in racialized subjects from impoverished and in-conflict countries (De Genova 2002). Beyond a state-centered analysis, such a critical framework leads us to understand the role that Ecuador has had in the geopolitics of contemporary migrations. As part of a transnational dialogue, this reflection aligns with critical migration studies (Walters 2010; De Genova 2002; De Genova 2012; Mezzadra and Neilson 2013; see ref. cite p. 189; Mountz 2011)[4] that have provided key concepts for reconceptualizing current migration dynamics, which I now review.

Controlling the mobility of "desirable and undesirable" populations has been a sine qua non duty of nation-states since their inception (Scott 1998). Foucault's (2007) theoretical contribution on governmentality inspired researchers to critically analyze the shift to securitization, which has taken place since the 1990s and been exacerbated particularly since 9/11. Foucault saw governmentality as a heterogeneous assemblage of power materialized in institutions, mechanisms, and diverse practices and discourses designed to control populations. This heterogeneous assemblage produces both docile, governable bodies and "counter conducts," or behavior outside this order, which needs to be tamed (Foucault 2007, 29–32). "Migration governmentality" (Tazzioli 2014) therefore implies that that heterogeneous assemblage is designed to discipline migrants and tame their counterconducts so as to govern their unruly mobility (see also Walters 2010; Bigo and Guild 2005). From this perspective, the global border regime is seen as a set of "multifarious practices of 'subjectivation'" (De Genova et al. 2015) in which the "legal production of migrant illegality" (De Genova 2002) is a nodal mechanism.

De Genova (2002) argues that migrant illegality is not a "natural condition" embodied in mobile subjects. Illegality is a legal, political, and social construct. Through highly restrictive laws, policies, and programs, the state produces the migrant illegality it claims to combat. Our institutions and social practices (such as racism, xenophobia, and a suspicion of nonnational others) then socially reinforce the legal production of migrant illegality (Tazzioli 2014). This is why racialized bodies are "normally" illegalized, criminalized, and deported (Mountz 2011). De Genova (2002) insists that it is not deportation but deportability, or the fact that those bodies carry the latent threat of being deported, which acts as the power mechanism that tames illegalized migrant labor and transforms it into a disposable commodity (438–39).

In current uneven geographical development, illegalization practices target other categories of marginalized populations inside national territories. Nicholas De Genova and Ananya Roy (2020) point out that while the figure of the illegalized migrant is a "constitutive obsession of the border, immigration, and asylum regimes," it is less well known but no less important that the production of illegality also serves to subjugate different categories of marginalized and impoverished citizens (353–54). This would confirm how the production of illegality reinforces hierarchical citizenship (Castles 2005) as de jure or de facto mobile, racialized, impoverished subjects are increasingly stripped of the basic human right to have rights (Arendt [1951] 1998). Georges Didi-Huberman (2018) lucidly points out this double-process *continuum* from *de jure*, because there are legal explicit practices targeting migrants to *de facto*, because there are simultaneously social practices that contribute to making their lives increasingly precarious while turning them into "disposable" subjects. The global border regime sustains its expansion by multiplying geopolitical, legal, social, and economic borders that reinforce the legal and social production of migrant illegality as a constituent element of its operations and spatial impact on multiple scales.

In line with this conceptualization, my analysis in this chapter arises from a qualitative investigation conducted in Ecuador between 2015 and 2017. Inspired by George Marcus's (2001) multisited proposal, I "followed the tracks of" twenty migrants to reconstruct their migration trajectories.[5] Sixteen of them were from Cuba, the Dominican Republic, Haiti, Iraq, Nigeria, Syria, or Zimbabwe, and four were Ecuadorians who had been deported from the United States. I worked with migrants of different genders, ages, professions, and class origins. I accompanied them on their urban journeys to their informal jobs, while completing immigration procedures in state offices, and in their daily struggles. I complemented my analysis with a digital ethnography of multiple websites used by migrants and of migrant's digital space, press review and historical research (1960–2017), and a review of migration policy literature (2007–17). I interviewed a total of 180 parties, including civil servants, representatives of nongovernmental organizations (NGOS), people working in international organizations, and migrants and their families. This chapter focuses on the sixteen immigrants' intricate trajectories coming from Caribbean, African, and Asian countries and their everyday lived experiences in Ecuador and sheds ethnographic light on the conceptual approach outlined above.

Destination: The Country of "Universal Citizenship"

The sixteen migrants I met in Quito between 2015 and 2018 had left their countries of origin because of the brutal effects of various forms of violence on their lives. Some fled war. Others escaped from democratic contexts in which the everyday violence of "peace-time crimes," to echo Nancy Scheper-Hughes (1997, 472–73), had made their lives unbearable. The civil wars in Syria and Iraq; religious conflicts in Sudan; Mugabe's dictatorship and political persecution in Zimbabwe; Boko

Haram's urban terror in Nigeria; the violence of poverty in the Dominican Republic and Cuba; or the devastating effects of the latest earthquake in Haiti triggered the departures of Danah, Abd ar-Rahman, Osama, Ali, Mustafa, Ebu, Charles, Duniel, Odelia, Idalmis, León, Ángela, Carmen, Claude, and Wislene.

The digital space was crucial in putting Ecuador on their migrant trajectories. By "Googling," "Facebookeando," and "WhatsAppeando," as they said, they accumulated strategic information that allowed them to decide to migrate to the Andes. Through an unceasing exchange of messages through these social networks, mostly with acquaintances of acquaintances, some learned that the country name *Ecuador* existed, others confirmed the short or long distance via air it would take them to get there, and all acknowledged extremely appealing national conditions that turned the Andean country into an apparently promising destination.

The fact that Spanish is Ecuador's official language was attractive for the Cuban and Dominican migrants I worked with, while its dollarized economy was one of the most favorable conditionalities pointed out by all sixteen of my interlocutors. Before reaching Ecuador, they had already pictured themselves earning and saving in dollars and sending remittances back home. And the fact that "Ecuador was in the same continent as *America* [the U.S.]," as Ali, a twenty-seven-year-old Iraqi migrant, once told me, was not a minor quality. Even though they all departed intending to try their luck in Ecuador, they never ruled out a subsequent trip to the United States, so Ecuador's geographical position seemed ideal if they ever decided to remigrate to the United States.

In addition to these already attractive conditionalities, a further defining one was Ecuador's apparently progressive stance on migration. Using Wikipedia, the Visa Mapper, and similar apps, they confirmed that, at that time (between 2008 and 2015), Ecuador did not require a tourist visa for arrivals from any of their countries of origin for stays of up to ninety days. Those coming from war zones such as Iraq and Syria, or from countries with other religious and political conflicts such as Nigeria, Sudan, and Zimbabwe, also confirmed that they had the right to seek asylum on arrival and be recognized as refugees in Ecuador. My African and Asian interlocutors double-checked the Ecuadorian government's official websites in English, including those of the Ministry of Tourism and the Ministry of Foreign Affairs and Human Mobility, while those coming from Cuba and the Dominican Republic had even listened to speeches given by former president Rafael Correa and his ministers on YouTube. In these speeches directed to Ecuadorian migrants in Spain or in the United States, Ecuadorian authorities asserted that Ecuador had turned into a "country of open borders where no human being is 'illegal.'"[6] Although the institutional discourse built around the constitutional principle of "universal citizenship" (Article 416) was mainly part of a political calculation to win votes from the Ecuadorian diaspora (See Pugh 2017), it also had an unquestionable direct impact on global immigrants who translated that principle as a real opportunity for recognition of their right to migrate and to pursue a decent life in Ecuador. In fact, the open border and pro-migrant policy completed the package of the "Ecuadorian dream."

Once my sixteen interlocutors were fully aware of the apparent immigration advantages that Ecuador offered them, they embarked on regional and transcontinental air routes. They all mentioned that they were excited to know that they could enter the country without a visa and that they were going to rebuild their lives in a place whose constitution guaranteed the right to asylum and to migrate and "universal citizenship." In their own words:

> By investigating on the Web, I learned that I could travel to Ecuador as a *normal* passenger, carrying my passport, in a plane, and not camouflaged, like my people do when trying to reach Europe. (Mustafa, age thirty-six, from Sudan)

> When I heard about Ecuador, a country that I did not know existed before, I concluded that I was not obliged to cross the Mediterranean to reach Europe or to risk my life to find a new home when fleeing war. . . . Ecuador was that alternative for me; it was somewhere I wouldn't have to die in order to arrive and where I was certain I could enter and be given asylum. (Danah, age thirty-eight, from Syria)

> Few countries allow Cubans to *enter freely*. I came because the door was open, and because I didn't have to travel by boat or guided by a *coyote* [human smuggler] like so many Cubans who travel to the US do. (Idalmis, age forty-three, from Cuba; translated from Spanish for this chapter)

As their testimonies show, from the outset these migrants rejected the idea of becoming an illegalized migrant in order to travel from their home countries. They rejected the possibility of being illegalized and exposed to the risk of death. In a way they rejected one of the defining features of the neoliberal border regime and its incessant "production of death and grief at sea" (Stierl 2016). Not becoming an illegalized migrant was a way to escape the threat of disposability en route to the United States or Europe. This escape also showed the "imperceptible care involved in migrant resistance" (Papadopoulos and Tsianos 2013)—in this case, care for their own lives in deciding to head for Ecuador and not putting their lives at risk for the sake of reaching Europe or the United States.

Traveling as a *"normal* passenger" and "carrying my passport," as Mustafa mentioned, implied something else: that they were traveling as full citizens, not second- or third-class citizens doomed to traverse clandestine routes, a conditionality that would be present also when entering Ecuador and starting a new (temporary or permanent) life as an immigrant or refugee with full rights as established by a set of constitutional articles. Even though they were able to travel as full citizens, from the moment they arrived in Ecuador and had to pass Ecuadorian checkpoints, the reality they confronted turned out to be far from what they had imagined or what had been promised to them by the country of "universal citizenship."

Buttressing Controls on Mobility

The postneoliberal government in Ecuador lasted a decade (January 2007–May 2017). As previously mentioned, those years were marked by inconsistencies and setbacks that threw the sixteen immigrants' Ecuadorian dream overboard. This section of the chapter analyzes the swing toward securitization and its impact on the legal and social production of migrant illegality in Ecuador.

Like Aléx Valle Franco (2009) and Javier Arcentales Illescas (2012a, 2012b), I see as one of the biggest problems that the 1971 Migration Act remained in force for almost the entire duration of Correa's government, as the Constitutional Law on Human Mobility was approved only in February 2017, three months before the end of his tenure as president. The 1971 Migration Act was entirely antithetical to the 2008 Constitution. It resulted from the last dictatorship, a time dominated by the doctrine of national security. As Daniel Feierstein (2010) has observed, this doctrine is a legacy of the Cold War, in which the United States frequently interfered in Latin American governance. A shared ideology of fighting external and internal enemies in the form of left-wing militants and insurgents was expanded through training centers for Latin American officials, including the Escuela de las Américas (School of the Americas) in Panama (Feierstein 2010, 223–26). The 1971 act was part of the regulations that permitted this fight in Ecuador (Rivera 2001). It makes no sense that this act remained untouched by a left-wing government, as it implicitly reaffirmed mechanisms of US interference in national affairs (something the official discourse rejected) and gave explicit carte blanche to the legal production of illegality embodied in the historical presence of racialized migrants. Article 5 of the 1971 law stipulated that "the decision to grant, deny or revoke a foreign citizen's visa in spite of full compliance with legal and regulatory requirements is a sovereign power at the discretion of the Executive Powers through the competent bodies" (Migration

Act 1971; translated from Spanish into English for this article). In other words, during the years of the progressive swing, migration officers had legal grounds to arbitrarily grant rights or withhold them from migrants on their arrival in Ecuador.

This practice is confirmed by multiple human rights reports and press coverage, warning that immigrants, particularly Black migrants, from certain African, Asian, and Caribbean countries were being unconstitutionally denied their rights on entering the country and detained or deported.[7] Testimony by the director of the Strategic Litigation Department of one of the main migrant rights organizations working in Quito provides an idea of how this arbitrary form of control operated: "Immigration officers' decisions are based on prejudice. According to their own individual criteria, anyone who seemed 'dangerous' was unconstitutionally denied the right of entry. They were protected by the 1971 act! We haven't worked for a single European or United States citizen denied the right of entry. We work with Cubans, Haitians, and Africans. Too much individual discretion and racism is allowed."[8] The director's perceptions were corroborated by other interviewees, who insisted that citizens from poor countries or war zones were often subject to long interrogations or rejected on entering Ecuador. The experiences of Charles (a thirty-seven-year-old from Nigeria) and Duniel (a forty-year-old from Cuba), both participants in my research, are exemplary. Even though they were not required to have a visa because of their nationality, after a long period of initial questioning they were led to an office at Quito's Mariscal Sucre airport. According to them, their nationality and "skin color" made them suspicious: "I think the police suspected I might be a member of Boko Haram. And you know what, they don't like Black people around here. Skin color is a problem," affirmed Charles. "It's tough being from Cuba, and, believe me, being a Black Cuban is terrible. I learned that as soon as I got off the plane," said Duniel.

In Ecuador, the selective and racist construction of nondesired versus desired migrants has prevailed since the first normative immigration framework, legislated in the nineteenth century. The first Ley de Extranjería (Immigration Law) of 1886, the second in 1892, and the Constitution of 1897 explicitly stated that Europeans and North Americans were welcome but not so other foreigners, such as people from China and those categorized as "gypsies," who were inadmissible, rejected, and even expelled (see Ramírez 2013; Carrillo 2012). Selectivity and racism have persisted over time, being present in the different immigration laws, including that of 1971, in force during the period of my research. This legal framework has been nourished by local racism that gave rise to the legal and social production of migrant illegality. Racist practices are in fact part of a "shared grammar" (De Genova 2016) that sustains the global neoliberal border control regime in which bodies of certain colors and origins can be de jure and de facto illegalized, criminalized, and deported (Didi-Huberman 2018).

In Ecuador this "shared grammar" has been reinforced by another factor. Under bilateral cooperation agreements, migration officers have never stopped training in the detection of migration profiles and border control, at both the International Law Enforcement Academy (ILEA),[9] run by the US State Department (this process inevitably harks back to the former Escuela de las Américas in Panama), and at the US embassies in Quito and Guayaquil during the "postneoliberal" government, as the national director of migration control units at the Ecuadorian Interior Ministry and the national coordinator in the General Prosecutor's Office Against Migrant Trafficking confirmed in interviews.[10] Immigration officer training is part of the process of externalizing the US border to the south. Ecuador thus incorporates the shared grammar that legitimizes the fight against racialized migrants who are construed as threats to national security (Mountz 2011).

The legal and social production of migrant illegality during the Citizens' Revolution government didn't just happen at the gateways into the country. Under the legal protection of the 1971 act, raids and arbitrary arrests were also carried out inside Ecuador. Human rights reports, documentaries, various news media investigations,[11] and academic research articles confirm that the police patrolled migrant neighborhoods. According to Cecilia Menjívar (2014), the progressive government practiced "the internalization of the border into national space" to guard urban spaces and identify illegalized and deportable migrants (364). The unconstitutional deportation of Cuban migrants in July 2016 is one conclusive example. Because I was able to carry out an ethnography of this event in situ, it is possible to explore the operation in more depth to demonstrate its analytical and political relevance.

The Cuban deportees were part of a group of 800 regularized and irregularized Cubans who were publicly camping out in Quito to campaign for a "humanitarian bridge" (or direct flights) to Mexico and to request asylum in the United States under the former Dry Feet/Wet Feet policy (Colectivo Atopía 2016).[12] The Interior Ministry used the pretext of maintaining order to send snipers, dog patrols, more than 500 police officers, and an armored water cannon truck to clear the camp. Around 200 Cubans were detained (*El Comercio* 2016; Álvarez Velasco 2016). The spectacle of having internalized the border to a central area of Quito was a highly repressive mechanism that legally criminalized and punished the Cuban population and simultaneously reinforced the deportability of anyone who was irregularized in Ecuador.

Under the anachronistic 1971 act, the constitutional judges in this case ruled that 121 of the over 200 detained Cuban citizens were to be deported. Subsequent reports by human rights organizations confirmed that those deportees included Cuban asylum seekers as well as others who had regularized their situation in the country of universal citizenship (Colectivo Atopía 2016). The 1971 act legally but unconstitutionally produced illegalized, deportable, and disposable subjects. National and international human rights organizations openly questioned this action,[13] and, as shown below, instead of holding back irregularized mobility, the operation actually catalyzed it, multiplying irregularized departures along the extensive migratory corridor from the Andean region, through Central America and Mexico, to the United States.

The examples analyzed effectively show that the coexistence of the 1971 act and the 2008 Constitution was highly functional in producing migrant illegality, deportability, and disposability. How should we interpret this unquestionable negation of Ecuador's progressive swing? The answer given in an interview by the former interior minister (2007) and subsequent pro-government member of the National Assembly (2009–17) is revelatory in this respect: "We were under pressure from the party and the media. Also, directly from the [US] embassy. . . . As a society, we weren't and still aren't ready to recognize foreigners as equals. Which is why we were unable to enforce the Constitution."[14]

As the former minister noted, internal and external pressure on the government carried significant weight. On one hand, there was considerable resistance to the pro-migrant constitution within the parties that supported the government, as noted by Ana Margheritis (2011) and Jacques Ramírez (2017). This opposition posed a major hurdle for an effective progressive swing in migration policy. Moreover, restrictive measures like those adopted are popular in highly racist contexts like Ecuador. According to the data from the national survey of public opinion carried out by Beatriz Zepeda and Francisco Carrión Mena (2015), 65 percent of the Ecuadorians surveyed believed that foreigners create insecurity, 93 percent were in favor of border controls, and 73 percent favored deportation (Zepeda and Carrión Mena 2014, 164–74). While the constitutional principle of universal citizenship positioned Ecuador internationally as having a discourse against the hegemony of the global neoliberal border control regime, internally, at home, this discourse seems to have been paused to maintain order, national security, and above all selective control of mobility, which was and is a social and governmental priority that generated subsequent electoral returns.

Going back to the former minister's words: US pressure didn't stop either. WikiLeaks cables published in the international press (*BBC News Mundo* 2012) confirm that Washington forced Ecuador to reestablish control of its borders and therefore to stop being a space of global transit for unwanted irregular-ized migration in the Americas (Álvarez Velasco 2020). In 2010, geopolitical inequality between Ecuador and the United States resulted in visa requirements being reimposed on eleven countries in Africa, Asia, and the Middle East that were classified as alleged threats to national security (Feline Freier 2013; Ruiz Muriel and Álvarez Velasco 2019).[15] In 2015, in the run-up to the so-called migra-tion crisis, visas were also reimposed on Cubans, supposedly as a way to reduce irregularized migration and fight migrant trafficking. But, as Manuel Góngora-Mera, Gioconda Herrera, and Conrad Müller demonstrate (2014), China's political weight and the strengthening of bilateral economic cooperation with the United States were decisive in its removal from the list only a few months later.

Moreover, the maintenance of the 1971 Migration Act and selective visa reimpositions were not the only measures under Correa. Although these were the most important, an additional control measure was adopted practically every year. The period between 2009 and 2016 saw asylum application pro-cessing delays and reductions in approval rates (Asylum Access and Refugee Work Rights Coalition 2014), while raids, detentions, and deportations con-tinued (Global Detention Project 2015). The migrant detention center known euphemistically as Hotel Hernán was created in 2011 (Yépez Arroyo 2016). In 2012, Decree 1182 reduced the window of opportunity for submitting asylum applications to just fifteen days after first arrival. This decree became null and void in 2014 thanks to the lawsuit filed by human rights organizations that as-sailed its constitutionality (Ubidia Vásquez 2015). In 2013, the so-called Hotel Carrión, a second detention center, was created (Yépez Arroyo 2016). And in the same year, SENAMI was dissolved as the result of internal political tensions, corruption allegations, and a failure to achieve planning objectives (Herrera Ríos 2016). To slow their influx, Cuban citizens were required to present a "letter of invitation from a notary" on arrival (MREMH 2013). And in 2016, the processing fee for a migration status change was increased without reason (MREMH 2016).

Actions to fight migrant smuggling networks and allegedly to protect the victims were carried out in parallel to control reinforcement (Ruiz Muriel and Álvarez Velasco 2019). Some of the most significant measures included the unconstitutional deportation of sixty-seven migrants from India, Iraq, and Pakistan in 2010. These people were inconclusively accused of illegal activities, including migrant smuggling to the United States (*El Universo* 2020). And in 2015, the Haitian Tourist Registration System was created on the grounds of a need to fight migrant trafficking (MREMH 2015).

One final inconsistency stems from the fact that two governing bodies, with two seemingly incompatible approaches—security and human rights—had the power to intervene in migration issues. The first, the Interior Ministry, is responsible for "the police, national security and the implementation of a comprehensive policy for citizen security" (MI 2018). The second, the Vice Ministry for Human Mobility, belonged to the MREMH. After the 2013 dissolution of SENAMI, the Vice Ministry had to "plan, manage and assess the management of human mobility policy in the field of emigration, immigration, transit, return and asylum, in compliance with the principles of the constitution and the standards of international law" (MREMH 2018a; my translation). However, as a specialist human rights lawyer and member of the Coalición para las Migraciones y el Refugio (Coalition for Migration and Asylum) affirmed, "The lack of institutional continuity has meant that migration policy, albeit consistent with the constitutional framework, is not supported by dedicated programs for each type of migrant, and above all is subject to the security approach imposed by public policy."[16] This observation was shared by the vast majority of NGO representatives and members of international organizations interviewed, all of whom, through their daily work with emigrants, immigrants, migrants in transit, and refugees, notice that the emphasis was on migratory control and that the lack of an integral policy on migration had a negative impact on successful implementation of the promising Ecuadorian Constitution. This made the situation of the mobile population in Ecuador more precarious, as we will see next.

Illegalized, Deportable, and Precarious

The sixteen immigrants I worked with lived in Ecuador between 2008 and 2015, which coincided with the period of reinforced control. Of all the measures analyzed, two had the most impact: (1) delays in the process of granting asylum; and (2) requirements for changing migration status. Both factors contributed to the legal production of their migrant illegality in legal and/or social terms, and to making their situation increasingly precarious. Only three of these migrants had managed to regularize their status when I met them. Danah from Syria, Mustafa from Sudan, and Joseph from Zimbabwe all held refugee cards. This official document reduced their risk of being deported because they were not de jure illegalized. But de facto, it did not necessarily guarantee their social and economic rights, as we will see later. Two others, Abd ar-Rahman from Syria and Ali and Osama from Iraq were condemned to a long wait. Over ten months had passed since they submitted their asylum application between September and December 2015; apparently, the National Directorate for Refugees in the Ministry of Foreign Relations and Human Mobility (MREMH) "unusually ran out of supplies," as the then director confirmed in an interview.[17] This meant that they could not access a refugee card, so they were given an "official letter" certifying that each one "was an asylum seeker," as the public authority I interviewed explained.

Because this letter was an official document, it supposedly prevented deportation. But it was useless in everyday life. While the official refugee card made it exceedingly difficult to achieve a social position guaranteeing a decent life, most Ecuadorians were unfamiliar with the *papel blanco* (white paper), as they referred to the official letter, which made it impossible to get a decent job, open a bank account, and rent housing. Even when, de jure, they were in the middle of the legal process to obtain asylum, they were de facto confined to a socially illegalized and clearly precarious existence.

Delays in processing asylum applications are not unusual. International organization and NGO representatives whom I interviewed noted that this is a serious problem in Ecuador. As analyzed by Francisco Hurtado Caicedo and colleagues (2020, 7), drawing on data from the Ministry of Foreign Affairs and Human Mobility, Ecuador received 243,974 applications for refugee status between January 1, 1989, and July 31, 2020. Of these, only 57,138 individuals were formally recognized as active refugees. While Colombian nationals constitute the overwhelming majority—78 percent of applicants, of which 97 percent were granted refugee status—individuals seeking asylum have arrived from 148 countries across all continents. This means that less than 25 percent of asylum seekers have been granted refugee status, leaving a large population in a state of legal limbo that, to paraphrase Cecilia Menjívar (2014), effectively relegates them to a condition of migrant illegality.

The other immigrants I worked with came from Cuba, the Dominican Republic, Haiti, and Nigeria. When their ninety-day tourist visa expired, they were unable to meet the requirements for obtaining a work or temporary visa and became irregularized. They argued that two of these requirements were impossible to achieve. First, they needed to "submit original criminal records certificates issued both by the country of origin and by the Interior Ministry of Ecuador" (MREMH 2018a). To obtain this certificate from afar, they needed to grant power of attorney to a family member, authorizing them to complete the process, which was beyond the means of most migrants. Because they were irregularized, they also feared being deported if they requested a criminal records certificate from Ecuador's Interior Ministry.

Second, they had to "demonstrate legal ways of making a living that would allow the applicant and their dependent family members to survive" or an employment contract, together with certificates of having paid taxes and of their employer having registered them with Ecuadorian Social Security (MREMH 2018a). These requirements were simply unattainable, as they had worked in the informal economy since their arrival in Ecuador and the state does not consider this to be a "legal way of making a living." They also needed to pay a standard fee of US$450 to have their migration status changed, plus approximately US$1,158 as a fine for having been irregularized (MREMH 2018a). On average, they earned between US$200 and US$250 a month, which made paying nearly US$1,600 impossible. As they were prevented from fulfilling these requirements, their biggest fear became a reality: they came to embody the figure of an illegalized migrant inside the country of alleged universal citizenship.

This is why they felt so misled by Ecuador's migration policy. For them, the free visa and constitutional principles formed part of a uniform policy. They assumed that if they were allowed to enter without a visa, there would be mechanisms guaranteeing their rights by virtue of their presumed universal citizenship inside Ecuador. They imagined Ecuador as a country of free residence. While this idea was mistaken, it sprang out of the widely broadcast image of universal citizenship that, as I have explained, largely convinced them to emigrate. Instead, as in any other country, the number of irregularized migrants grew as the Ecuadorian state reinforced its control.

Because, legally and socially, they embodied the position of the illegalized migrant, de facto the only labor market open to them was in the informal economy. They would indeed earn dollars, but very few and in highly precarious conditions. In Ecuador, 35 percent of the population lives below the poverty line, and the informal market employs 45 percent of the economically active population (INEC 2018). The formal economy is incapable of absorbing all the migrant population, which means they have to work without contracts, social security, or heath care, and all of these denials increase their precarity.

This was true for the sixteen international migrants who shared their stories with me. Many of them were overqualified for the jobs they had found. For example, Osama from Iraq, who was an economist and a refugee, sold smuggled goods in the street. Danah from Syria, also a refugee, had a degree in communications but sold Arab food. Idalmis from Cuba, an irregularized migrant and a nurse, worked as a hairdresser, and Claude from Haiti was an agricultural engineer working as a builder, car minder, and toilet paper street seller. Their monthly income was below the US$386 minimum wage (INEC 2018) and barely covered their needs.

All sixteen international migrants also mentioned racism and xenophobia as among the main impediments to full socioeconomic inclusion, and the final triggers that accelerated their transit to the United States. Here are some testimonies: "They called me a 'terrorist' because I wore my Hijab. I learned what it means to be Black in this country, not in Africa," said Danah. "They cross over to the other side of the street when they see me," said Mustafa. "I have to fake my accent; Ecuadorians don't like Cubans," said Idalmis. "I was beaten at work because I was Black," recounts Claude. These stories show how the migrants have been socially abused. They state that these were common experiences. Racism and xenophobia were added to the fact that they embodied the figure of an illegalized, deportable, precarious migrant. This situation definitely did not allow them a safe place to live in Ecuador.

Their plan to move on to the United States took shape as their daily lives became unsustainable. The constant online exchange of success stories perpetuated the image of the United States as a promised land. And so, as their Ecuadorian dream came to pieces, it was replaced by Cuban, Dominican, Haitian, Nigerian, Sudanese, and Zimbabwean versions of the *American Dream*: this unquestionable element of the postcolonial migratory imaginary drew them on, despite the risks en route.

The violent deportation of Cubans from Ecuador in 2016 had a multiplying effect on several of the sixteen immigrants. Some Cubans, Dominicans, and Haitians anticipated their potential deportation and set off as irregularized migrants. Other, African migrants paid *coyotes* and left as well. Some went via Peru, others via Colombia, and all were irregularized and entered the extended corridor that connects the Andean region with Mexico via Central America. Far from reducing irregularized transit and migrant smuggling as proclaimed by the national authorities, deportation as a form of internal control triggered their departures.

Illegalized, deportable, disposable, and precarious, the migrants left the country of "universal citizenship." Their departure from Ecuador was a prelude to a violent journey that involves much more than the clandestine crossing of seven national borders. Their stories tell how they crossed the Loma de la Muerte (Hill of Death) in the Darién jungle between Colombia and Panama. They faced extreme climates and violence. Then they crossed Central America into Mexico, where things got more violent as they faced the risk of bribery, abuse, rape, torture, group kidnappings, disappearances, and even murder perpetrated with complete impunity by those who operate along the corridor. Because crossing the extended Andean region–Central America–Mexico–US migratory corridor is a matter of life and death, not all of the sixteen immigrants left. Danah, Wislene, Abd ar-Rahman, Ebu, Charles, and Duniel feared losing their lives in an attempt to reach the United States, and so they extended their stay in Ecuador until they found an opportunity to leave or the strength to face the long corridor's dangers.

Conclusions

This chapter demonstrates the ways in which the legal and social production of migrant illegality, deportability, precarity, and disposability happened in the context of greater constitutional progressivism in Ecuador. Because this analysis is based on the lived experiences of African, Caribbean, and Asian migrants, it is possible to discern the spatial interconnections of their journeys and the role Ecuador plays in the geopolitics of contemporary migration.

The dynamics of the South–South influxes to South America (featuring migrants and refugees) cannot be understood without recognizing the violence they involve. As we have seen, contemporary migration is triggered by structural, religious, political, and military violence. This violence places extreme demands on recipient countries like Ecuador because they require responses not found in the shared grammar of control. The demands require responses that allow the construction of a countergrammar based on the right to have rights, as Hannah Arendt ([1951] 1998) wrote, especially when violence spreads in wartime and peacetime.

When a notable and exceptional historic opportunity arose in Ecuador, the so-called postneoliberal government refined its ability to legally produce the illegality, deportability, precarity, and disposability of various categories of migrants who arrived in Ecuador escaping from violence, instead of making decisive progress toward this highly complex construction. As I explain, in reinforcing or adopting mechanisms analogous to the global neoliberal border control regime, the Ecuadorian state's ability to punish and violate immigrant and refugee rights in various ways far exceeded its general inability to protect their rights.

This chapter also confirms that asymmetric global interdependencies were decisive in understanding the shift to securitization in Ecuador. The externalization of the US border southward did not cease during the postneoliberal swing. However, this mechanism was not only vertically imposed by the United States; externalization is not "copied and pasted" from a central country to a peripheral country, as Ruben Andersson (2017) has observed. Peripheral states that internalize control, in this case Ecuador, are not simply passive players. The means of controlling mobility take other local forms in the geopolitics of contemporary migration, because they are determined by historical and geographic contexts and by local political rationales. Moreover, the changing nature of mobility means that forms of control are locally shaped and readapted in response to these movements. In the current context of the globalization of violence, choosing a Global South destination does not mean escaping the contemporary neoliberal border control regime. It means facing the local forms used by this regime, as these were present in Ecuador during the progressive swing.

The inconsistencies between the constitutional framework and its applicability and the adoption of various control mechanisms undid the promise of "universal citizenship" in practice. In the long term, these mechanisms reinforced hierarchical citizenship in which migrants and refugees became de jure or de facto second-class citizens stripped of many rights. Although my analysis focuses on a particular historical moment—namely, the peak of the progressive turn in Ecuador during the Correa government—it clearly shows the limitations that this political project had in terms of migration. As I have shown, the inconsistencies and setbacks impacted migrant lives, prompting transits to the United States. After the Correa administration's patent right turn in 2017, the governments of Lenin Moreno (2017–21) and Guillermo Lasso (2021–23) sustained the same pattern of *correismo*: the paradoxical and perverse coexistence between a highly progressive constitutional and legal framework regarding migration and a practice that conversely reinforces securitization and criminalization of migrants. In the ensuing years, most new arrivals in Ecuador have been Venezuelans as part of that massive exodus. State response has given continuity to the legal production of Venezuelans' illegality, confining them to long waits in their never-solved regularization processes, and limitations on the recognition of asylum. In 2019, the government imposed visas on Venezuelans to discourage their arrivals. In fact, the legal and social production of Venezuelan illegality, disposability and precarity is an everyday dynamic in Ecuador, something that, as several investigations have confirmed, has expelled this population into continental transits to the south and north (see G. Herrera and Cabezas 2019; Gandini, Rosas, and Lozano-Ascencio 2020).

Thus far in the twenty-first century, Ecuador has played a clearly paradoxical role in the geopolitics of contemporary migration. It is a selective and racist "open door" that stimulates the arrival of regional and extracontinental refugees and illegalized migrants, or cheap, irregularized labor traveling to the United States. This fact confirms how it operates as a hub in a much broader and complex system of neoliberal mobility control. The legal production of migrant illegality confirms a violent process that is endemic to the neoliberal regime of border control. Sandro Mezzadra and Brett Nielson (2013) refer to it as "differential inclusion," a process in which marginalized groups such as illegalized migrants are indeed included in the social and economic sphere but only as subordinate, deportable, and disposable subjects. This production of illegality begins in Ecuador and is reinforced all along the extended Andean region–Central America–Mexico–US corridor, where a "state of emergency" reigns, affecting increasing numbers of illegalized, deportable, disposable, and precarious migrants.

Still, as I have shown, regional and transcontinental migrants continue to deploy strategies to improve their lives as part of their daily struggle. That is why, in line with Abdelmalek Sayad (2008), we should understand migrant mobility as a heretical response, or in the words of Foucault (2007), as "counter-conduct" continuously deployed by migrants to break into the national orders to which they don't belong, where they don't have the right to have rights, and where they hope to achieve their migratory plans, which are their life plans, despite these disadvantages. It is only in glimpsing the power of the heresy of their mobility that we can identify the ever-present cracks in that heterogeneous assembly of power that fruitlessly aims to tame uncontrollable migrant mobility.

NOTES

1. MERCOSUR stands for Mercado Común del Sur or Southern Common Market.

2. The securitization of migration, as several authors suggest (Huysmans 2000; Bigo and Guild 2005), accounts for the process through which certain actors (such as state institutions, the media, international organizations, and even social organizations) construct supposed threats, military and nonmilitary, that put national security at risk. This construction is what supports the deployment of certain emergency measures to justify the legitimate use of public force and the adoption of control and deterrence techniques. Since the end of the twentieth century, and in an exacerbated manner after the September 11, 2001, attacks in the United States, international migration, particularly from impoverished countries or countries in conflict, has come to embody this alleged threat to national security. In response, as Huysmans (2000) has shown, a sustained security policy has been unleashed as an instrument to protect the state, its society, and the domestic market from the threats, that is, migrants or asylum seekers (756–58).

3. See the Presidential Decree published on June 20, 2008, in News Bulletin No. 398 of the Ministry of Foreign Affairs, Trade, and Integration.

4. In the South American context, the works of Domenech (2011, 2017) have contributed to opening a transnational dialogue with critical migration and border studies.

5. This investigation was part of my doctoral thesis, "Trespassing the Visible: The Production of Ecuador as a Global Space of Transit for Irregularized Migrants Moving Towards the Mexico-U.S. Corridor," defended at King's College London in June 2019.

6. Quotation translated for this article. See the speech that Correa made to Ecuadorian migrants in Milan, July 14, 2007. YouTube, http://www.youtube.com/watch?v=gQXde1OTtq0&feature=related.

7. For monitoring reports on the fulfilment or violation of migrant rights in Ecuador, including holdups, arrests, and deportations, see Coalición por las Migraciones y el Refugio (Coalition for Migrations and Asylum), "Documento análisis Proyecto de Ley de Movilidad Humana," October 2015, https://movilidadhumana.wordpress.com. See also Benavides 2008; Arcentales Illescas 2012a, 2012b; and "Cubanos viven en aeropuerto de Quito," *Martí Noticias*, April 20, 2014, http://www.martinoticias.com/content/Cubans-viven-en-airport-de-quito/34293.html.

8. Personal interview with the author, Quito, April 2016 (translated for this chapter).

9. ILEA San Salvador is part of a network of international academies that former US President Bill Clinton created to combat transnational crimes. Training courses operate by direct invitation to participating countries. See International Law Enforcement Academy, San Salvador, accessed March 11, 2025, https://sansalvador.ilea.state.gov.

10. Personal interviews with the author, Quito, October 2016; Quito, January 2016.

11. See Coalición por las Migraciones y el Refugio (Coalition for Migrations and Asylum), "Documento análisis Proyecto de Ley de Movilidad Humana"; Global Detention Project 2015; Calvo 2010; Correa 2019; Moscoso 2016; and the documentary *Migrantes, los otros nosotros—cubanos* (Them-Us Migrants), posted to YouTube by Pocho Alvarez, February 14, 2016, https://www.youtube.com/watch?v=udEYHMVobxo.

12. The Dry Feet/Wet Feet policy was a US immigration rule (1995–2017) allowing Cuban migrants who reached US soil by land (dry feet) to stay and pursue residency, while those intercepted at sea (wet feet) were detained and returned to Cuba. It was part of the 1995 revision to the 1966 Cuban Adjustment Act, and it ended under President Obama in 2017. See Anguiano Téllez and Rodríguez Chávez 2018.

13. See, for example, "IACHR Expresses Concern Regarding Detentions and Deportations of Cuban Migrants in Ecuador" (press release), OAS (Organization of American States), July 26, 2016, https://www.oas.org/en/iachr/media_center/PReleases/2016/102.asp; and Collectivo Atopia 2016.

14. Personal interview, Quito, September 2016 (translated for this chapter).

15. The eleven countries are Afghanistan, Bangladesh, China, Eritrea, Ethiopia, Kenya, Nepal, Nigeria, Pakistan, Somalia, and Senegal (*El Comercio* 2010).

16. Personal interview, Quito, February 2016 (translated for this chapter).

17. Personal interview with the author via Skype, Quito, October 2016 (translated for this chapter). "Quedarse sin especies" (to run out of supplies) is the colloquial expression used to mean that national institutions in Ecuador have run out of material for printing official documents, in this case refugee cards.

REFERENCES

Ackerman, Alana Sylvie. 2014. *La ley, el orden y el caos: Construcción social del Estado y el inmigrante en Ecuador.* Quito: Instituto de Altos Estudios Nacionales.

Acosta Arcarazo, Diego. 2016. "Free Movement in South America: The Emergence of an Alternative Model?" *Migration Policy Institute.* https://www.migrationpolicy.org/article/free-movement-south-america-emergence-alternative-model.

Acosta Arcarazo, Diego, and Luisa Feline Freier. 2015. "Turning the Immigration Policy Paradox Upside Down? Populist Liberalism and Discursive Gaps in South America." *International Migration Review* 49 (3): 659–96.

Álvarez Velasco, Soledad. 2016. "Control y violencia ante la migración irregularizada por la Región." *Revista Seguridad y Sociedad* 14 (6): 30–39. https://www.ieepp.org/publicaciones/derechos-humanos/revista-seguridad-y-sociedad-no-14-migraciones/.

Álvarez Velasco, Soledad. 2020. "From Ecuador to Elsewhere: The (Re)Configuration of a Transit Country." *Migration and Society* 3 (1).

Andersson, Ruben. 2017. "Rescued and Caught: The Humanitarian-Security Nexus at Europe's Frontiers." In *The Borders of "Europe": Autonomy of Migration, Tactics of Bordering*, edited by Nicholas De Genova. Durham, NC: Duke University Press.

Anguiano Téllez, María Eugenia, and Ernesto Rodríguez Chávez. 2018. "Crisis de flujo y permanencia en la emigración cubana a la luz de la restauración de las relaciones entre Cuba y Estados Unidos." In *El mundo a través de las fronteras: El difícil viaje de los migrantes en tránsito*, edited by María Eugenia Anguiano Téllez, Rafael Alonso, and Daniel Villafuerte, 45–80. Mexico: El Colegio de la Frontera Norte y la Universidad de Ciencias y Artes de Chiapas.

Araujo, Lorena, and María Mercedes Eguiguren. 2009. "La gestión de la migración en los países andinos: Entre la securitización y los vínculos diaspóricos." *Boletín Andina Migrante*, no. 3, 2–10.

Arcentales Illescas, Javier. 2012a. *Las políticas de deportación en el ecuador: Análisis desde un enfoque de derechos humanos*. Programa andino de derechos humanos especialización superior en derechos humanos. Quito: Universidad Andina Simón Bolívar.

Arcentales Illescas, Javier. 2012b. "Ejercicio de los derechos de las personas inmigrantes y refugiadas en Ecuador durante el año 2012." In *Horizonte de los derechos humanos, Ecuador, 2012*. Quito: Universidad Andina Simón Bolívar.

Arendt, Hannah. (1951) 1998. "The Perplexities of the Rights of Man." *Headline Series*, no. 318 (Winter): 88.

Asylum Access and Refugee Work Rights Coalition. 2014. "Global Refugee Work Rights Report: Taking the Movement from Theory to Practice." http://asylumaccess.org /work/global-initiatives/refugee-work-rights-coalition/.

BBC News Mundo. 2012. "Los Cables que WikiLeaks Filtró Sobre Ecuador." June 2. https://www.bbc.com/mundo/noticias/2012/06/120620_ecuador_wikileaks_assange _correa_cables_pea.shtml.

Benavides, Gina. 2008. "Procesos de deportación en Ecuador." Programa Andino de Derechos Humanos (PADH), Universidad Andina Simón Bolívar. April. https://www .uasb.edu.ec/wp-content/uploads/2021/04/Informe-DDHH-2011.pdf.

Bigo, Didier, and Elspeth Guild. 2005. "Policing at a Distance: Schengen Visa Policies." In *Controlling Frontiers: Free Movement into and Within Europe*, edited by Didier Bigo and Elspeth Guild. Aldershot, UK: Ashgate.

Calvo, O. 2010. "El hotel de los sin papeles." https://www.planv.com.ec/miradas/el-hotel -sin-papeles.

Carrillo, Ana. 2012. "Comerciantes de fantasías: El Estado ecuatoriano ante la inmigración china." In *Ciudad-Estado, inmigrantes y políticas: Ecuador, 1890–1950*, edited by Jacques Ramírez. Quito: Instituto de Altos Estudios Nacionales, Instituto de la Ciudad.

Castles, Stephen. 2005. "Hierarchical Citizenship in a World of Unequal Nation-States." *PS: Political Science and Politics* 38 (4): 689–92.

Ceriani Cernadas, Pablo. 2018. "Migration Policies and Human Rights in Latin America: Progressive Practices, Old Challenges, Worrying Setbacks, and New Threats." Policy brief. Global Campus Open Knowledge Repository. https://repository.gchumanrights .org/server/api/core/bitstreams/1b1fb459-46b8-42f3-8059-e3b2f2926600/content.

Colectivo Atopía. 2016. "Bitácora de Una Expulsión." February 23. https://colectivoatopia.wordpress.com/2017/02/23/bitacoraexpulsion/.

Correa, Ahmed. 2019. "Deportación, tránsito y refugio: El caso de los Cubanos de El Arbolito en Ecuador." *PERIPLOS: Revista de Investigación sobre Migraciones* 3 (2): 52–88.

De Genova, Nicholas. 2002. "Migrant 'Illegality' and Deportability in Everyday Life." *Annual Review Anthropology* 31:419–47.

De Genova, Nicholas. 2012. "Border, Scene and Obscene." In *A Companion to Border Studies*, edited by Thomas M. Wilson and Hastings Donnan. Sussex: John Wiley and Sons.

De Genova, Nicholas, and Ananya Roy. 2020. "Practices of Illegalization." *Antipode: A Radical Journal of Geography* 52 (2). https://doi.org/10.1111/anti.12602.

De Genova, Nicholas, Sandro Mezzadra, and John Pickles, eds. 2015. "New Keywords: Migration and Borders." Special issue, *Cultural Studies* 29 (1): 55–87.

Didi-Huberman, Georges. 2018. *Pasar cueste lo que cueste*. Barcelona: Contracampo.

Domenech, Eduardo. 2011. "Crónica de una 'amenaza' anunciada: Inmigración eilegalidad; visiones de Estado en la Argentina contemporánea." In *La construcción social del sujeto migrante en América Latina: Prácticas, representaciones y categorías*, edited by Bela Feldman-Bianco, Liliana Rivera Sánchez, Carolina Stefoni, and Marta Villa. Quito: Facultad Latinoamericana de Ciencias Sociales–Ecuador, Consejo Latinoamericano de Ciencias Sociales, Universidad Alberto Hurtado.

Domenech, Eduardo. 2017. "Las políticas de migración en Sudamérica: Elementos para el análisis crítico del control migratorio y fronterizo." *Terceiro Milênio: Revista Crítica de Sociologia e Política* 8 (1): 19–48.

Eguiguren, María Mercedes. 2011. "Sujeto migrante, crisis y tutela estatal: Construcción de la migración y modos de intervención desde el Estado ecuatoriano." Serie Tesis. Quito: Facultad Latinoamericana de Ciencias Sociales.

El Comercio. 2010. "El Gobierno fijó otra vez la visa para nueve países de África y Asia." September 7. https://www.elcomercio.com/actualidad/seguridad/gobierno-fijo-vez-visa-nueve.html.

El Comercio. 2016. "Ecuador busca la deportación de cubanos sin documentos." July 7. https://www.elcomercio.com/actualidad/ecuador-deportacion-cubanos-visa-humanitaria.html.

El Universo. 2020. "Estados Unidos subraya 17 puntos de acuerdo y trabajo con Ecuador desde la reactivación de la relación bilateral." February 13. https://www.eluniverso.com/noticias/2020/02/13/nota/7737363/estados-unidos-subraya-17-puntos-acuerdo-trabajo-ecuador.

Faist, Thomas. 2017. *The Moral Polity in Migration: Mechanisms in Externalization*. Working paper presented at workshop Beyond External Borders: Multi-Level Analysis and Comparative Perspectives on Migration Governance, Bielefeld University, Bielefeld, Germany.

Feierstein, Daniel. 2010. "National Security Doctrine in Latin America." In *The Oxford Handbook of Genocide Studies*, edited by Donald Bloxham and A. Dirk Moses. http://www.oxfordhandbooks.com/view/10.1093/oxfordhb/9780199232116.001.0001/oxfordhb-9780199232116-e-25.

Feline Freier, Luisa. 2013. *Open Doors (for Almost All): Visa Policies and Ethnic Selectivity in Ecuador*. Working Paper 188. Center for Comparative Immigration Studies. May. https://ccis.ucsd.edu/_files/wp188.pdf.

Foucault, Michel. 2007. *Security, Territory, Population: Lectures at the Collège de France, 1977–78*. New York: Picador.

Gandini, Luciana, Victoria Prieto Rosas, and Fernando Lozano-Ascencio. 2020. "Nuevas movilidades en América Latina: La migración venezolana en contextos de crisis y las respuestas en la región." *Cuadernos Geográficos* 59 (3): 103–21.

Global Detention Project. 2015. "Ecuador Immigration Detention." https://www.globaldetentionproject.org/countries/americas/ecuador.

Gómez, Carmen, and Gabriela Malo. 2019. "Un recorrido por la literatura sobre refugio y desplazamiento forzado en América Latina y el Caribe: Abordajes principales y nuevos ejes críticos de estudio." *Migraciones* 3 (2): 4–21.

Góngora-Mera, Manuel, Gioconda Herrera, and Conrad Müller. 2014. "The Frontiers of Universal Citizenship: Transnational Social Spaces and the Legal Status of Migrants in Ecuador." Working Paper 71. desiguALdades.net (International Research Network on Interdependent Inequalities in Latin America). https://www.desigualdades.net/Working_Papers/Search-Working-Papers/working-paper-71-_the-frontiers-of-universal-citizenship_/index.html.

Herrera, Gioconda, and Gabriela Cabezas. 2019. "Ecuador: De la recepción a la disuasión; políticas frente a la población venezolana y experiencia migratoria, 2015–2018." In *Crisis y migración de la población venezolana: Entre la desprotección y la seguridad jurídica en Latinoamérica*, edited by Luciana Gandini, Fernando Lozano Ascencio, and Victoria Prieto Rosas, 125–55. Mexico City: Universidad Nacional Autónoma de México.

Herrera Ríos, William. 2016. "S'emparer des 'absents': La construction du Secrétariat national du migrant de l'Équateur (2007–2013)." PhD diss., Université Paris I Panthéon-Sorbonne.

Hurtado Caicedo, Francisco, Carmen Gómez Martín, Soledad Álvarez Velasco, Manuel Bayón Jiménez, Lucía Pérez Martínez, Camilo Baroja, and Jesús Tapia. 2020. *(Des)protección de las personas refugiadas en Ecuador*. Quito: FES-ILDIS y Colectivo de Geografía Crítica de Ecuador. https://geografiacriticaecuador.org/justiciamigrante/wp-content/uploads/2021/04/Cartilla-Refugio.pdf.

Huysmans, Jef. 2000. "The European Union and the Securitization of Migration." *Journal of Common Market Studies* 38 (5): 751–77.

INEC (Instituto Nacional de Estadísticas y Censos). 2018. Encuesta Nacional de Empleo, Desempleo y Subempleo. June. http://www.ecuadorencifras.gob.ec/empleo-junio-2018/.

Magliano, María José, and Janneth Clavijo. 2011. "La trata de persona en la agenda políca sudamericana sobre migraciones: La securitización del debate migratorio." *Análisis político* 24 (71): 149–63.

Marcus, George. 2001. "Etnografía en/del sistema mundo: El surgimiento de la etnografía multilocal." *Alteridades* 22: 111–27.

Margheritis, Ana. 2011. "'Todos Somos Migrantes' (We Are All Migrants): The Paradoxes of Innovative State-Led Transnationalism in Ecuador." *International Political Sociology* 5:198–217.

Ménard Marleau, Andrée. 2018. "¿Irse o quedarse? Las formas y dinámicas de movilidad de los migrantes senegaleses en América del Sur (2007–2016)." Master's thesis, Facultad Latinoamericana de Ciencias Sociales, Ecuador.

Menjívar, Cecilia. 2014. "Immigration Law Beyond Borders: Externalizing and Internalizing Border Controls in an Era of Securitization." *Annual Review of Law and Social Science* 10:353–69.

Mezzadra, Sandro, and Brett Neilson. 2013. *Border as Method; or, The Multiplication of Labor*. Durham, NC: Duke University Press.

MI (Ministry of Interior). 2018. "Valores/misión/visión." https://www.ministeriodegobierno.gob.ec/valores-mision-vision/.

Moscoso, Raúl. 2016. *"Ciudadanos universales" en el Comité del Pueblo*. Quito: Universidad Andina Simón Bolívar.

Mountz, Alison. 2011. "Refugees—Performing Distinction: Paradoxical Positionings of the Displaced." In *Geographies of Mobilities: Practices, Spaces, Subjects*, edited by Tim Cresswell and Peter Merriman. London: Ashgate.

MREMH (Ministerio de Relaciones Exteriores y Movilidad Humana). 2013. "Ecuador requerirá carta de invitación para ingreso de ciudadanos Cubanos." El Nuevo Ecuador, Cancillería del Ecuador. https://www.cancilleria.gob.ec/ecuador-requerira-carta-de-invitacion-para-ingreso-de-ciudadanos-cubanos/.

MREMH (Ministerio de Relaciones Exteriores y Movilidad Humana). 2015. "Bolivia, Brasil, Ecuador, Haití y Perú reconocen logros en aplicación de medidas cooperativas para promover la migración segura de ciudadanos haitianos en la región." El Nuevo Ecuador, Cancillería del Ecuador. https://www.cancilleria.gob.ec/bolivia-brasil-ecuador-haiti-y-peru-reconocen-logros-en-aplicacion-de-medidas-cooperativas-para-promover-la-migracion-segura-de-ciudadanos-haitianos-en-la-region/.

MREMH (Ministerio de Relaciones Exteriores y Movilidad Humana). 2016. "Costo de visados en Ecuador." El Nuevo Ecuador, Cancillería del Ecuador. https://www.cancilleria.gob.ec/visa-.

MREMH (Ministerio de Relaciones Exteriores y Movilidad Humana). 2018a. "Misión/vision/valores." El Nuevo Ecuador, Cancillería del Ecuador. https://www.cancilleria.gob.ec.

MREMH (Ministerio de Relaciones Exteriores y Movilidad Humana). 2018b. "Requisito para solicitud de visado." El Nuevo Ecuador, Cancillería del Ecuador. https://www.cancilleria.gob.ec/requisitos-para-solicitud-de-visas-no-inmigrantes-e-inmigrantes/.

Papadopoulos, Dimitris, and Vassilis S. Tsianos. 2013. "After Citizenship: Autonomy of Migration, Organisational Ontology and Mobile Commons." *Citizenship Studies* 17(2): 178–96.

Pereyra, Silvana Estefanía Santi. 2018. "Biometría y vigilancia social en Sudamérica: Argentina como laboratorio regional de control migratorio." *Revista mexicana de ciencias políticas y sociales* 63 (232): 247–68.

Pugh, Jeffrey D. 2017. "Universal Citizenship Through the Discourse and Policy of Rafael Correa." *Latin American Politics and Society* 59 (3), 98–121.

Ramírez, Jacques. 2013. *La Política Migratoria del Estado Ecuatoriano: Rupturas, Tensiones, Continuidades y Desafíos*. Cuaderno de Política Pública 3. Quito: Instituto de Altos Estudios Nacionales.

Ramírez, Jacques. 2017. "Lo crudo, lo cocido y lo quemado: Etnografía de la ley de movilidad humana de Ecuador." In *Migración, Estado y Políticas: Cambios y Continuidades en América del Sur*, edited by Jacques Ramírez. La Paz: Vicepresidencia de Bolivia.

Rivera, Fredy. 2001. "Democracia Minimalista y Fantasmas Militares en el Ecuador Contemporáneo." In *Las Fuerzas Armadas en la Región Andina: ¿No deliberantes o actores políticos?*, edited by Martín Tanaka. Lima: Comisión Andina de Juristas.

Ruiz Muriel, Martha Cecilia. and Álvarez Velasco, Soledad. 2019. "Excluir para proteger: La 'guerra' contra la trata y el tráfico de migrantes y las nuevas lógicas de control migratorio en Ecuador." *Revista Estudios Sociológicos* 37 (111). http://dx.doi.org/10.24201/es .2019v37n111.1686.

Sayad, Abdelmalek. 2008. "Estado, nación e inmigración: El orden nacional ante el desafío de la inmigración." *Apuntes de Investigación* 13.

Scheper-Hughes, Nancy. 1997. "Specificities: Peace-Time Crimes." *Social Identities* 3 (3): 471–98.

Scott, James C. 1998. *Seeing like a State: How Certain Schemes to Improve the Human Condition Have Failed*. New Haven, CT: Yale University Press.

Stang, María Fernanda. 2009. "El dispositivo jurídico migratorio en la Comunidad Andina de Naciones: Migración y política: el Estado interrogado." *Procesos actuales en Argentina y Sudamérica*, 301.

Stefoni, Carolina. 2011. "Ley y política migratoria en Chile: La ambivalencia en la comprensión del migrante." In *La construcción social del sujeto migrante en América Latina: Prácticas, representaciones y categorías*, edited by Bela Feldman-Bianco, Liliana Rivera Sánchez, Carolina Stefoni, and Marta Villa, 79–111. Quito: Facultad Latinoamericana de Ciencias Sociales–Ecuador, Consejo Latinoamericano de Ciencias Sociales, Universidad Alberto Hurtado.

Stierl, Maurice. 2016. "Contestations in Death: The Role of Grief in Migration Struggles." *Citizenship Studies* 20 (2): 173–91.

Tazzioli, Martina. 2014. *Spaces of Governmentality: Autonomous Migration and the Arab Uprisings*. London: Rowman and Littlefield.

Trabalón, Carina I. 2018. "Política de visado y regulación de las fronteras: Un análisis desde la movilidad de haitianos en Sudamérica." *POLIS: Revista Latinoamericana* (51).

Ubidia Vásquez, Daniela. 2015. "La inconstitucionalidad parcial del Decreto 1182 sobre el derecho a solicitar refugio en el Ecuador: Análisis y efectos." *USFQ Law Review* 2 (1). http://revistas.usfq.edu.ec/index.php/lawreview/article/view/880.

Valle Franco, Aléx Iván. 2009. "El derecho a tener derechos." *Los Derechos en la movilidad humana: Del control a la protección*. Quito: Ministerio de Justicia.

Walters, William. 2010. "Rezoning the Global: Technological Zones, Technological Work, and the (Un-)Making of Biometric Borders." In *The Contested Politics of Mobility: Borderzones and Irregularity*, edited by Vicki Squire, 51–76. London: Routledge.

Yépez Arroyo, Cristina. 2016. "El Hotel Carrión: Resistencias y contradicciones un acercamiento a experiencias de detención y deportación." Bachelor's thesis, Universidad San Francisco de Quito.

Zepeda, Beatriz, and Francisco Carrión Mena. 2015. *Las Américas y el mundo: Ecuador 2014*. Quito: Facultad Latinoamericana de Ciencias Sociales, Ecuador.

7

Border Control, COVID-19, and the Criminalization of Irregularized Migration in Chile

Daniel Quinteros, Romina Ramos, and Roberto Dufraix-Tapia

As in other countries, the border control regime in Chile underwent a series of transformations in the context of COVID-19. Indeed, the available evidence indicates that the closure of borders implemented due to the pandemic allowed the deployment of a number of restrictive strategies on human mobility that have caused an unprecedented increase in migratory irregularities. According to official reports, in 2019 there were 8,048 entries registered as unauthorized border crossings. In 2020, this figure more than doubled to 16,848, and by September 2021 it stood at 33,503, which represents more than twenty-two times the annual mean for 2011–15 (Leal 2021).

More than three-quarters of this migratory flow corresponded to Venezuelan nationals who were displaced as a result of the humanitarian emergency taking place in their country (Stefoni, Cabieses, and Blukacz 2021). The general increase in armed violence, the violation of human rights, and, in general, the economic collapse along with that of public services pushed more than 5.9 million

Venezuelans into a situation of forced displacement (R4V 2021), leading to the second-largest of forced-mobility operation in recent years, surpassed only by the refugee crisis in Syria.

At the beginning of the pandemic, the flow of Venezuelan people ran up against significant hurdles throughout South America, mainly due to the closure of land border crossings (Brumat 2021). Such had been the case of the Chilean-Peruvian border in 2019, when a consular visa was imposed on all Venezuelan nationals wishing to enter Chile (Olavarría 2019), with said border closure triggering a full humanitarian crisis on the Chilean northern frontier at the beginning of 2021 (Cociña, Ramos, and Ravetllat 2021; Tapia, Quinteros, and Ramos 2021). In response to this humanitarian emergency, the Chilean state adopted a wide range of control measures to prevent the entry of displaced people through any of the *trochas*, or illegal migratory trails, that traverse the Andean highlands (Cociña and Quinteros 2021). Thus, the pandemic represented a scenario of opposites, in which, on one hand, intense restrictive measures (border closures) were implemented, yet on the other, there was a massive flow of forced migrants whose final destination was Chile.

This chapter describes the historical configuration of migration control in Chile and the changes it underwent during the pandemic. For this purpose, it first considers the criminology of mobility, which may be especially useful for analyzing the growing interrelation observed between the rationale and foundations of the criminal justice system toward migration management (Bhui 2013; Stumpf 2006, 2013). Second, we present historical and empirical background information to describe (and understand) the various measures of immigration and border restrictions that have been implemented in Chile over the past few decades. We complement this analysis with the measures adopted in response to border closures as a result of the pandemic, and finally, we offer our study's main conclusions.

Criminology of Mobility, Crimmigration, and Instrumentalism

The growing relationship between criminal, migration, and border policies can be understood as part of a broader strategy of social control, which tends to increase the number and reach of surveillance devices, privatize public services, make working conditions more precarious, and impoverish important segments of the population. In this sense, measures such as restricting access to regular forms of migration, as well as intensifying border control or implementing broad deportation processes, are the mechanisms of a strategy of control aimed at disciplining the new global proletariat by promoting processes of differential or subordinate inclusion in the labor market, the political sphere, and social life in general (De Giorgi 2010). In this respect, Mary Bosworth, Katja Franko, and Sharon Pickering (2018), for example, have analyzed the progressive precariousness of the legal status of the migrant population, whereby criminal control and migration control play an essential role in regulating the relationship between the state and individuals.

Consequently, it has been argued that the state seeks to maintain not only internal supremacy through a policy of criminalization but also external autonomy through immigration policies and border protection (Franko 2013). For this reason, Bosworth, Franko and Pickering (2018) point out that given the fact that detentions and deportations are applied and experienced as a punishment, it is possible to understand their role in the control of mobility not merely as auxiliary to the criminal process but as a constitutive part of the transformations that can be observed in the field of criminality (Pickering, Bosworth, and Franko 2017). However, and despite the fact that such a punitive rationale should have no place in an efficient migration system (Aliverti 2015), the incorporation into the ambit of border control of various police, judicial, and penal practices has led to an intense process of criminalization of migration (Wacquant 1999) and a racialization of mobility through the rejection of the other based on the perception of their inferiority (Tijoux and Córdova 2015).

This relationship has been condensed by the idea of *crimmigration*, which seeks to precisely describe the recently observed fusion between criminal law and migration law. In her work, Juliet Stumpf (2006) has imagined a memorandum to the president of the United States in 2017 that comments on the tension between two social representations of migrants: one that aims for their inclusion, considering them as full members of the society, and the other, which, after reducing them to the category of criminal subjects, is strongly oriented to their exclusion. In this sense, the general concept of *crimmigration law* seeks to describe both the increase in the reasons why it is possible to criminally expel a foreigner and the creation of new criminal categories in terms of administrative regulations, such as those associated with irregular or clandestine border crossings (Stumpf 2013). Thus, the literature has warned us that this overlap between administrative law and criminal law is being carried out under conditions of interchangeability and mutual reinforcement (Bowling and Westenra 2018), thereby causing a system of control geared toward the exclusion of immigrants. However, this exclusionary approach with which immigration control is being designed is not based solely on the circumstance of having or not having the necessary documentation. Behind this approach, it has also been possible to observe logics of exclusion based on xenophobia or racism, or both (García Hernández 2013) that impact the work undertaken by criminal justice operators and in the collective imagination.

Although the origin of the concept is restricted to the historical and political specificities of the US context (García Hernández 2013), the term *crimmigration* has served as a general frame of reference for investigating these new configurations of control and surveillance (Stumpf 2013). In South America, for example, scholars have used this thesis particularly to review the relationship between criminal policy and migration policy, such as the case of Brazil (De Moraes 2015, 2018). In the case of Argentina, it has also been recently used to analyze the expulsions of foreigners and other modifications, which have sought to extend migration control and border surveillance (García 2015; Penchaszadeh and García 2018). In the case of Chile, researchers have studied the application of administrative sanctions (Quinteros 2016), the priority given to criminal expulsions (Brandariz, Dufraix, and Quinteros 2018), and the tensions created in Chilean constitutional matters (Navarro 2021).

Crimmigration has also been used as a frame of reference in the context of the COVID-19 pandemic. Here, investigations were focused on the changes produced by the pandemic regarding the detention and expulsion of migrants (Brandariz and Fernández-Bessa 2021; Schiriro 2021; Stefanelli 2021), as well as on the criminalization processes where the migrant is seen as a danger to public health (McNeill 2021). It is important to note the reaction of South American countries to the significant increase in the Venezuelan migratory flow, which has oscillated between two extremes: on one hand, those that have tried to protect and regularize the flow with a long-term outlook, as has been the case of Argentina, Brazil, Colombia, and Uruguay; and, on the other, those countries where security-oriented discourse and policies predominate and where, in the best of cases, a series of ad hoc and short-term regularization mechanisms have been adopted, as has occurred in Ecuador, Peru, and Chile (Brumat 2021).

In this sense, the evidence shows that crimmigration accounts for a broader process of instrumentalization of legal norms and legal procedures. As David Sklansky (2012) has noted, this ad hoc instrumentalization consists precisely of the possibility that control agents have to use these tools in an interchangeable way that achieves the highest possible levels of effectiveness. Moreover, this way of operating has contributed to the fusion between immigration and criminal law, allowing both the selectivity of its operators and the opacity of their actions. Despite the global influence of instrumentalization, however, José Brandariz (2021b) acknowledges that there is not a common pattern to all scenarios and that, at least for the European context, far from being ad hoc for each particular case, the result is to prioritize migratory control measures. Thus, what is identified as crimmigration instrumentalism would present a series of advantages for control agencies, such as reducing the workload, avoiding costly criminal investigations, and legitimizing efforts to prevent crime. On the whole, this set of measures reinforces the idea of immigrant criminality against which social exclusion, the closure of borders, the use of force, and the power to punish appear as a natural and obvious response. Thus, as Katja Franko (2020) observes, under these control dynamics, immigrants are no longer considered as people who need protection or as potential sources of labor, but rather have been transformed into transgressors and criminal offenders, that is to say, the "crimmigrant other."

Historical Background of Border Control in Chile

Despite how groundbreaking many of these transformations might appear, migration policies seeking to control and restrict the mobility of foreigners have a long history in Chile. In fact, the first formal migration regulation in the country dates back to 1918, when the aim was to prohibit the entry of "undesirable elements." The "undesirable" or "unadaptable" people were those foreigners who were convicted or charged with common crimes, who did not have a profession or occupation, or who could not practice their occupations to earn a living, along with those who, by any means, propagated doctrines that were incompatible with the "Spiritual Unity of the Nation." Likewise, Law 3,446 included the impediment to enter or reside in the country of those people who might alter the social, political, or economic order of the nation (Lara Escalona 2014; Plaza Armijo and Muñoz Cortés 2013).

Reflecting the health emergency caused by the 1918 flu pandemic, Law 3446, in its first article, barred anybody who suffered from any of the diseases listed in the Health Code of the time from entering or residing in the country (Durán Migliardi and Thayer 2017; Norambuena, Navarrete, and Matamoros 2018). Since then, the successive regulations in the Decree in Force of Law 69 (1953), Legislative Decree 1094 (1975), and the New Immigration and Foreign Nationals Act of April 2021 (Law 21.325) have explicitly obliged the state to expel and prevent the entry of people who suffer from specified diseases.

The situation prior to the COVID-19 pandemic in Chile already included various measures that complicated the administrative procedures for entering, residing in, and staying in the country. During the military dictatorship (1973–90), the number of foreigners residing in Chile reached a historic low, representing less than 1 percent of the population (Tapia 2012). Following the transition to democracy, an increase in immigration flows was observed, part of various migratory processes in the region that were administered rather ambivalently by the successive postdictatorial governments. As Undersecretary of the Interior Belisario Velasco stated at the time, it was precisely from 1988 that the number of foreigners arriving in Chile began to show a sustained increase, "attracted by the benefits of the prevailing system in Chile" (*El Mercurio* 1991, A1).

Indeed, along with the waves of Chilean nationals who returned from exile during the early 1990s (Llambias-Wolff 1993; Martínez 1997), there was a progressive arrival of international migrants, mostly from other South American countries, in concordance with the intense process of acceleration and diversification of intraregional migratory flows observed in Latin America and the Caribbean at the time. Such was the case of the Peruvian nationals who, despite the historical presence of foreigners in the northern border regions, began moving toward the center of the country in search of job opportunities in commerce and the service sector (Solimano and Tokman 2006). From then on, and during the first decades of the new century, Chile began to receive intraregional migrants from nonbordering South American countries, especially Ecuador and Colombia. According to some estimates, while the number of Ecuadorians doubled between 2005 and 2014, there was a fivefold increase in the number of Colombians, with just these two groups representing 10.8 percent of Chile's foreign population (DEM 2016). During the past decade, migrants and refugees have begun to arrive from Caribbean countries such as Haiti, Cuba, and the Dominican Republic. More recently, an intense process of human mobility has been observed emanating from Venezuela, with a flow that began around 2015 and has steadily increased since then. As official figures show, even though the 2017 Census recorded a total of 83,045 Venezuelans (INE 2018), subsequent updates show that their presence increased notably during the years 2018 (334,386), 2019 (441,495) and 2020 (448,138) (DEM 2021; INE AND DEM 2020, 2021).

What, then, was the response of the Chilean state when it was faced with a scenario of growing and changing migratory flows? According to Carmen Norambuena (2013), it is possible to observe a certain progress in terms of migration management among the postdictatorship governments until 2010. In this regard, he explains, the regularization processes carried out under the administrations of Eduardo Frei, in 1998, and Michelle Bachelet, in 2007, are usually the ones referred to (Stefoni 2011b). Likewise, some pivotal events are mentioned, such as the ratification of the Palermo Convention and its complementary protocols in 2004, as well as the publication of Refugee Law 20.430 in 2010, along with the promulgation in 2005 of the International Convention on the Protection of the Rights of all Migrant Workers and Their Families. In 2008, President Bachelet issued Presidential Instruction 9, which regulated migratory movements and provided specific actions for the protection of such peoples (Norambuena 2013). In short, during this first period it was possible to observe a series of welcoming initiatives and policies to open up migration, providing guarantees of admission, rights, and protection.

However, this greater formal opening to international migration was also accompanied by increased restrictions on some specific mobilities, with an increasing enforcement of control and surveillance mechanisms. Indeed, the statement made by Undersecretary Velasco in 1991 regarding the presence of a greater number of foreigners in the country was accompanied by the announcement of a significant increase in the Immigration Department's budget. In his own words, these greater resources would make it possible to exercise "strict control of foreigners," for which a computer system would be implemented and oriented not only toward the "facilitation of visa and residence procedures" but also toward the ability to "take better control of who enters Chile and what activities they carry out" (*El Mercurio* 1991, A1).

Thus, since the 1990s, a highly contradictory migration policy has taken shape in Chile, a policy that says what it does not do and does what it does not say. On one hand, even when it states the need to defend and promote migrants' rights by adopting a series of instruments and intergovernmental forums, the strategy is questionable, considering how it was implemented. Certainly, and as discussed in several investigations (e.g., Stefoni and Stang 2017), the situation of the foreign population was highly precarious and marked by a series of barriers to accessing basic social services, a strategy summarized by Stefoni (2011a) as "the policy of the non-policy." On the other hand, as various news reports show, during those first years, the migration laws would be applied discretionally and selectively to control people or specific cases. Throughout the 1990s, deportation was effectively imposed only in high-profile cases, as, for example, on members of a Peruvian sect accused of polygamy and other crimes of a sexual nature, who were expelled for "acts against morality and good customs" (*El Mercurio* 1996, C9). Consequently, and despite their greater public notoriety, cases like this were isolated and specific, which typified a period in which control devices played a secondary and exceptional role in regulating migration flows.

Border Securitization and the Production
of Irregularity in Chile, 2010–2019

Since the turn of the century, measures such as deportation have become increasingly more frequent and relevant in migration policy. As shown in figure 7.1, in addition to being applied in exceptional cases, during this period there was also a considerable increase in expulsion orders. An important turning point in Chilean politics, in which many aspects of migration and border control would change, corresponds to the victory of the right wing in the presidential elections at the end of 2009. Grouped in the Alliance for Chile, headed by former president of the republic Sebastián Piñera, the right-leaning parties implemented a punitive agenda in terms of migration control, which acquired much more force during their second four-year term, from 2018 to 2022. These changes in the political arena influenced the trajectory of migration policy as political leaders employed a discourse that did not recognize the right to migrate, as when the Chilean government refused to sign the Global Compact for Migration (the Marrakech Pact) in 2018 and imposed mobility restrictions on certain nationalities that were subjected to control. In short, far from welcoming and promoting the integration of the thousands of foreign nationals who arrived in Chile during this period, the emphasis was placed on restrictions, lack of protection, and criminalization of certain migrant groups.

Under the repeated discourse of safe, orderly, and regular migration, the government began to implement a series of mechanisms and instruments oriented to restricting the mobility especially of nationals from Haiti and Venezuela (Ramos and Tapia 2019; Dufraix-Tapia, Ramos, and Quinteros 2020). This can be verified by the reinforcement of border controls since 2011, especially in the northern zone of Chile. Within this context, the launch of the Northern Border Plan 2011–2014, with its purported aim of fighting crime and drug trafficking in the far north of Chile (García Pinzón 2015), led to a greater deployment of human and material resources on the border, as provided for by this policy. In fact, according to the final audit report issued by the Contraloría General de la República (Comptroller General of the Republic) (2014), the Northern Border Plan allocated more than 5 million Euros for the acquisition of X-ray equipment, fiberscopes, densitometers, thermal cameras, night vision devices, and drug incineration furnaces. Also, the plan enabled the incorporation of the armed forces as an auxiliary but relevant actor in the area of border control, which until then had been the exclusive responsibility of the Chilean police. This approach to control would progressively expand during the decade through the creation of the Safe Border Plan, which basically extended the Northern Border Plan to all five regions of northern Chile (Ramos, Brandariz, and Dufraix-Tapia 2021, 352).

Furthermore, during the past decade there has also been a notable expansion in migration control with the introduction of restrictions for migrants to regularize their status. As clearly shown in figure 7.1, the administrative expulsion orders increased sharply toward 2020. Despite the slight differences observed between the data presented by Caterine Galaz, Gabriela Rubilar, and Claudia Silva (2016) and the data obtained directly from the Undersecretariat of the Interior via the Law of Transparency (Dufraix-Tapia, Ramos, and Quinteros 2020), the graph allows us to splice two time series together and thus accurately describe a trend in the application of expulsions between 2005 and 2020.[1] As can be observed, up until 2015 the average number of expulsions per year remained relatively constant at around 2,200, which shows a limited capacity of the state bureaucracy to manage the flow of infractions and administrative sanctions. However, as of 2016 there has been a sustained growth in the number of people receiving expulsion orders, with an annual increase recorded of between 12 percent and 16 percent during the three years up to 2018, when there were 3,307 expulsions. This upward trend continued at a relatively constant rate, with the exception of 2019 when expulsions tripled compared to the average for the previous decade, reaching 6,702; this represented an unprecedented figure in the history of migration control in Chile.

This trend in the number of expulsions can be better understood by focusing on the context in which the variations occurred. First, after the rise in the expulsions between 2005 and 2007, a slight increase can be noted in the expulsions decreed during 2014. A large part of this rise could be the consequence of the imposition of consular visas on citizens from the Dominican Republic in 2012. This measure, based on the idea that migratory flows could be addressed or stopped through administrative mechanisms, far from discouraging the arrival of Dominican nationals, ended up dividing the migration flow between those who could access regularity and those who could enter only through unauthorized bordering crossings (Galaz et al. 2017). In effect, after representing a marginal proportion in the historical total of deportations, from 2012 onward the number of expulsions of Dominicans sharply increased. For example, while for the period 2010–12, twelve, thirty-one, and twenty-seven expulsions were issued for the respective years, the rate of expulsions witnessed a dramatic increase from 2013 onward, reaching almost 900 deportation orders by 2017. This is reaffirmed by Galaz, Rubilar, and Silva (2016), who recognize that "from the imposition of the consular visa requirement, the number of expulsions decreed begins to increase, as does the representation of Dominican Republic nationals in the total number of expulsions decreed" (6).

Second, the sharp increase during the years 2018–19 can be explained by two different processes, which were interconnected and occurred simultaneously in terms of migration control. One of these processes is related to the measures announced in April 2018 that, among other things, included a series of modifications in the entry requirements for groups of specific nationalities.

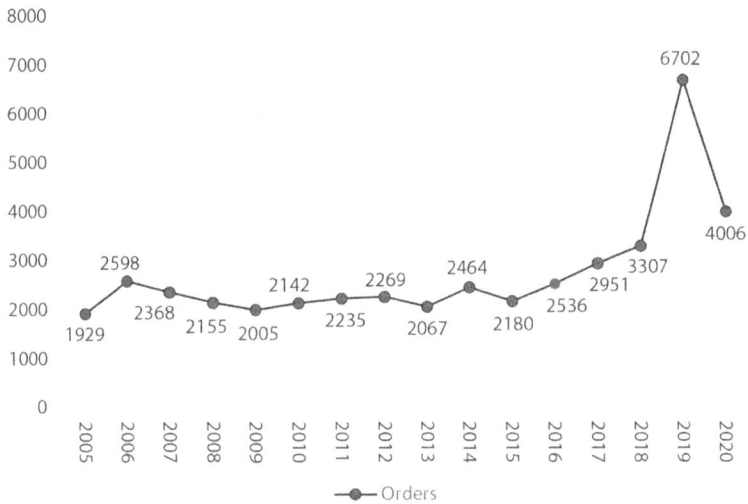

FIGURE 7.1. Number of administrative deportation orders in Chile, 2005–2020. Sources: For 2005–2009, Galaz, Rubilar, and Silva 2016; for 2010–2020, Undersecretariat of the Interior, Government of Chile (2020a, 2020b).

An example was the case of Haitian nationals and the imposition of a consular tourist visa, while at the same time they were granted a family reunification visa for spouses, civil partners, minors, or children who were studying up to age twenty-four, which even allowed access to permanent residency after twelve months (Ministerio de Relaciones Exteriores 2018). Furthermore, in the case of Haiti, the strategy included a Humanitarian Plan for Orderly Return, which consisted of voluntary return flights but also included a clause that prohibited their reentry into Chile for nine years, one year less than the ten years of no return imposed by legal expulsions.

The other process that explains the explosive increase observed in 2019 is mainly related to the state response when managing the Venezuelan migration flow. As expected, and given the scenario of social and political crisis in Venezuela, the state initially opened the country's doors to those who wanted to settle in Chile. In a well-publicized visit by President Piñera in 2018 to Cúcuta, a city in Colombia on the border of Táchira-Norte de Santander, the head of state invited all those who wished to settle in Chile, announcing the creation of a special visa for this purpose, the Democratic Responsibility Visa. Basically, this visa was to be requested at Chile's foreign consulates and allowed the holders and their family members and dependents to acquire "a temporary residence permit for one year, extendable just once and [with] the possibility of obtaining Permanent Residency" (Ministerio de Relaciones Exteriores 2018). However, from the data presented by the Jesuit Migrant Service (Servicio Jesuita a Migrantes 2021), obtained directly from the undersecretariat of foreign relations, of the 441,253 Democratic Responsibility Visas requested between April 2018 and June 2021, only 61,096 were granted (13.8 percent), and the remaining 376,720 (85.4 percent) were simply rejected.

The aforementioned extensive rejection of applications for the Democratic Responsibility Visa coincides with the second moment identified in the trajectory of the migratory policy response to Venezuelan immigration. Following the decision of Peru and Ecuador to impose visas issued at their consular bureaus abroad for Venezuelan nationals (Brumat 2021), Chile also adopted this policy and in the same week imposed the same requirement. Decree 237, of June 20, 2019, required "every Venezuelan citizen who wishes to enter the country, without the purpose of immigration, residency or undertaking of a paid occupation" to obtain a "Consular Visa for Basic Tourism with the right to enter and remain in Chile in such a capacity, for a maximum period of 90 days" (Ministerio del Interior y Seguridad Pública 2019). In practice, however, and despite the fact that the same decree admitted, in its sixth item, that "the stay in Chile, beyond the time provided for tourists, is a situation that exposes migrants and their families to violations derived from their irregular situation in the country" (Ministerio del Interior y Seguridad Pública 2019), the results once again showed a massive rejection of such applications. According to the Jesuit Migrant Service (Servicio Jesuita a Migrantes 2021), nine out of ten applications were denied, with only 11.5 percent (11,117) of the 96,480 applications submitted between June 2019 and June 2021 receiving the tourist visa.

Taken together, these measures resulted in an exponential increase in expulsion orders issued to Venezuelan nationals, rising from just 5 such decrees in 2017 to more than 2,000 between 2019 and 2020 (Dufraix-Tapia, Ramos, and Quinteros 2020). Moreover, the available data allow us to corroborate that the sharp increase in the number of deportations ordered, which mainly affected Venezuelans, coincided with the location of the first major crisis in June 2019, linked to the change in requirements for those entering the country as tourists.

The region of Arica and Parinacota, a bi-border area of intense mobility in the far north of Chile, boasts the highest number of authorized land entries registered at the national level (Tapia, Liberona, and Contreras 2017). It was precisely on the Arica-Tacna border that the first critical moment in the history of Venezuelan migration to Chile took place that was directly linked to the increase in the expulsions issued by the Arica y Parinacota Regional Administration, which passed from an annual average of 667 expulsion orders between 2010 and 2018 to 3,126 expulsion orders during 2019. According to Isaldo Bettin, a member of the Chilean Catholic Migration Institute in Arica, these sudden changes to the entry requirements resulted in people "stranded" between the Santa Rosa (Peru) and Chacalluta (Chile) border posts: "There are two highways, one heading to Peru and another in the direction of Chile. In between, there is a space, and there they remain . . . they use blankets to protect themselves from the sun and the cold, and there they stay" (Bettin quoted in Olavarría 2019).

Third, the unprecedented increase in deportations issued in 2019 must also be understood as the result of another measure adopted in the context of migration governance: the 2018 Immigration Regularization Process. Formally, this process sought to resolve the situation of all foreigners who had an irregular immigration status and who had entered the country prior to April 8, 2018 (Ministerio de Relaciones Exteriores 2018). Although this group was originally estimated to be at least 300,000 people, only 155,707 applications were submitted and 131,399 visas were issued, mainly to nationals of Haiti, Venezuela, and Peru. However, in practice only 90,000 visas could actually be stamped due to a number of impediments, problems, and difficult-to-fulfill requirements, such as the obligation to obtain an apostilled criminal-record certificate (Dufraix-Tapia, Ramos, and Quinteros 2020), the excessive delay in the issuing of the residence permits, inadequate information strategies during the implementation of the measure, and the impossibility of accessing formal jobs while the applications were being processed (Valencia and Ramos 2021).

Thus, although the process allowed thousands of people to access administrative regularity, it also implied the irregular status of all those who could not obtain a visa stamp or meet all the requirements. The 12,000 people whose regularization requests were rejected and who were automatically issued a standing expulsion order thus saw their permanent condition of deportability perpetuated.

Finally, even though deportations had shown an upward trend since the 2014, the most significant increases were observed after the measures were announced in April 2018. Paradoxically, while the number of expulsion orders rose, the number that actually occurred decreased, producing a significant deportability gap (Brandariz 2021a,).[2] As we have shown elsewhere (Dufraix-Tapia, Ramos, and Quinteros 2020), although during the period 2010–15 approximately 40 percent of expulsion orders were implemented, that percentage dropped to below 10 percent between 2018 and 2020. In short, the deportation policy whose configuration is described above, aside from the organizational capacity that it exhibits in terms of the administrative process of each case, has left unexecuted a high percentage of expulsion orders issued. Based on the foregoing analysis, it is possible that far from regularizing, registering, and "ordering the house," these security policies have ended up producing the irregular status of thousands of migrants, exposing them to greater risks and worse living conditions. Though constructed on the basis of an orderly, safe, and regular migration, this strategy has thus ended up generating a total of more than twenty thousand unexecuted administrative expulsions between 2010 and 2019, thereby perpetuating a situation of irregularity that intensifies "the condition of vulnerability of thousands of people who will not be able to access State protection" (Dufraix-Tapia, Ramos, and Quinteros 2020, 18).

The analysis presented up to this point allows us to reconstruct the recent and contradictory past of Chilean migration policy, which is vital to understanding the most recent mutations in this matter. As may be observed, these control policies "with a human face" (Domenech 2013) include contradictory measures that, discursively legitimized by a narrative of humanitarian and rights protection (Ruiz and Álvarez Velasco 2019), end up strengthening the control and surveillance devices at the country's borders, while at the same time conditioning and restricting access to regularity (Stang, Lara, and Andrade 2020). In this sense, we believe that the Chilean state has opted for a trend in migration management identified by Nicholas De Genova (2017) as a legalized production of migratory irregularity, where the border, and its "externalized perimeter" (Álvarez Velasco 2016), has been key in the domain of migration management. The foregoing makes it possible to describe, as we show below, how the effects of this form of migration management are not only reduced to the expulsion of "noncitizens" and practical consequences in terms of the efficient management of racialized migrants, culturally constructed as "undesirables," but also "keep them [migrants] under extreme control, exclusion and extreme vulnerability, and always with the possibility of banishing them when necessary" (Aquino 2015, 77).

Border Control Mutations During the Pandemic: Self-Incrimination, Detention, and Pushbacks

In February 2021, with borders closed due to the pandemic, the small village of Colchane became the center of national and international attention. Colchane is a border village located in the Andean highlands at 3,650 meters above sea level, with fluctuating temperatures that can drop to as low as −8 degrees Celsius at night. The town was founded in 1970 as part of a strategy oriented to "establishing a permanent settlement and to control the border" (Municipalidad de Colchane 2015, 6). This rural commune forms part of the ancestral

Aymara territory, which was partitioned after the War of the Pacific (1879–83). In the 2017 Population and Housing Census, the village registered only 1,728 inhabitants (INE 2018). However, between the end of 2020 and February 2021, thousands of Venezuelans arrived in a context of clandestine migratory transit (Ramírez and Álvarez Velasco 2009; Álvarez Velasco 2009), entering the country through nonauthorized border crossings. At the peak of this crossing, the number of migrants far outnumbered local inhabitants (Paredes 2021). A Venezuelan woman who entered in a nonauthorized crossing and was in Colchane told the local press: "I am here with my husband; we left our three children in Venezuela. I came here looking for a better future . . . we decided to embark on this risky journey, but nothing has been like we were told. It's been horrible" (Soy Iquique 2021, 1). During this period the situation in the village took a dramatic turn for the worse, with hundreds of families, including children, searching for water, food, and a place to sleep and to escape the cold (Cociña, Ramos, and Ravetllat 2021).

In response to the humanitarian crisis in the Chilean highlands, the authorities responded at different levels and through various actions. On January 27, for example, a constitutional protection action was filed against the Chilean president, the local mayor, and the interior and defense ministers for illegal and arbitrary omissions in safeguarding the population against the health threat posed by the mass transit of foreign nationals through unofficial border crossings (Case No. 25529-2021). Then, despite the disturbances between migrants and the police, the government claimed on February 2 that the situation was under control and that all public services in Colchane were working normally, referring specifically to the Carabineros (Chile's national police force), the PDI (Policía de Investigaciones de Chile, the investigative police force) and the armed forces (*Meganoticias* 2021a). A week later, on February 9, the ministers of the interior, defense, and foreign relations visited the area and, together with the mayor and senator of the region, announced the creation of the "Colchane Plan" (*Cooperativa.cl* 2021).

However, this plan, far from providing humanitarian aid and protection, consisted of specific measures aimed at providing more resources to the police and extending the role of the armed forces in border control and surveillance. In this sense, Decree 265 (2019) was particularly relevant, as it allowed the military to assume tasks related to drug trafficking and organized crime on the border (Ministerio de Defensa Nacional 2019). This combined effort was reinforced during the pandemic through Decree 3 (2021), which permitted the expansion of military support to controlling the smuggling of migrants (Ministerio de Defensa Nacional 2021). As can be noted in the details of Decree 3, the vast territory, climatic conditions, and extreme geographical characteristics of this border zone require the reinforcement of certain border sectors in order to prevent, detect, and control crimes associated with drug trafficking, transnational organized crime, and migrant smuggling. Furthermore, as the document indicates, such measures would be based on the obligation of the state to safeguard national security and protect the population, as well as on "the good results obtained from the collaboration provided by the Armed Forces in its joint interagency work in the border zones of the national territory" (Ministerio de Defensa Nacional 2021, 2). Indeed, between January and September 2021, control agencies detected more than 33,000 entries through unauthorized crossings—double the number in 2020 and far exceeding the total for irregular crossings during the whole decade of 2010–2019 (Leal 2021).

In addition, the government coordinated with the health authority and the Municipality of Iquique to accommodate people who had arrived in the city along different routes. Indeed, during the weeks prior to the announcement of the Colchane Plan, the head of national defense of the Tarapacá region sent multiple requests to the municipality for authorization to use different facilities as shelters or places to accommodate people undergoing their fourteen-day quarantines, thus preventing them from being left on the streets. It is worth noting that during the pandemic, all formal transportation services between Colchane and Iquique were suspended, leaving people two options. The first was to report themselves to the police and then be registered by the health authority and wait for one of the few buses to take them to the reception centers, where they would receive medical attention and food. The second option, in order to escape the cold, the high altitude, and the scarcity of food, was to negotiate exorbitant prices with informal transporters, or risk a 265-kilometer walk, crossing the highlands and desert for days on foot until reaching Iquique or some other nearby town. The vast majority had no choice but to agree to the condition established by the Chilean authorities so as to access health care (León 2021).

In this context, on the morning of Wednesday, February 10, 2021, eighty-six Venezuelans were expelled from Chile in a Chilean Air Force flight that took off from Iquique airport. Each person was escorted onto the plane by a police officer, and despite the fact that they all had a negative test for COVID, were forced to wear white overalls, which they were told to put on in the airport minutes before boarding. They were then taken to the plane under the gaze of the media. They had been notified of their expulsion order at the Centennial School at 3 a.m. on Tuesday, the 9th, and were arrested twenty-four hours later. As one of the Venezuelans deported told the press that day (TVN 2021), they were expelled without the possibility of receiving legal assistance or appealing the measure. And even though fourteen of said nationals were being expelled as a result of convictions for committing minor crimes, the remaining seventy-two had not committed any crime; rather they had entered the country in an irregular manner. Nonetheless, in a press conference held at the airport while the deportees were being put on the plane, the minister of the interior stated that "this administrative expulsion includes people who entered the country less than three months ago, and who entered clandestinely through irregular crossings, all of which makes them, obviously, subjects of expulsion" (24 Horas 2022). However, their only mistake was having thought that going to the police would eventually allow them to regularize their immigration status in the country, without knowing that in Chile, anyone who reports themselves to the police in such circumstances always ends up receiving an expulsion order. As one of the expelled Venezuelans who had crossed the border at Colchane regretfully noted: "The police told us that it was best to report ourselves because that would lead to a regularization process. I did everything they said voluntarily. My pregnant wife is staying at a shelter right now and they're expelling me. The only thing I ask is that she can travel back with me" (*Meganoticias* 2021b, 1).

Two months later, on Sunday, April 25, another fifty-five Venezuelans were expelled, again wearing white overalls. Forty of them had reported themselves to the police for entering via nonauthorized border crossings and were notified of their expulsion while held in the former Cavancha Stadium, which at the time operated as a Transitory Health Lodging after the modifications made to the COVID-19 protocols in March. This new expulsion started on Friday, April 23, at 6 a.m., when dozens of officers from the PDI burst into the temporary health facilities set up next to a soccer field and handed out deportation orders. Once again there was no access to legal assistance or opportunity to appeal the measure, and these people were then arrested on Saturday, the 24th, and transferred to a police station, where they were held in the auditorium, their mobile phones confiscated, until the next morning. In spite of all these communication barriers, that afternoon, some migrant legal support groups, in coordination with local organizations, managed to file a writ of habeas corpus in favor of fifteen people, which would be heard by the Court of Appeals of Iquique in a special session during the morning of Sunday, the 25th (Rol 209-2021). However, the applicants' petition to quash the expulsion orders and to suspend the removals through an injunction was rejected by the court, even though the migrants were already being held on the airport tarmac awaiting deportation. The plane carrying all fifty-five migrants was thus permitted to take off at around 1 p.m. on a nonstop flight to Maiquetía Airport in Venezuela.

Along with the similarities between both flights, the latter represents a second important turning point in the history of migration control deployed during the pandemic. It was the first time a private charter flight had been used in Chile for the purpose of expulsions, thanks to a service that the government had been trying unsuccessfully to tender since October 2020, even before announcing the so-called Colchane Plan. Afterward, the foreign minister said, "Chile's response to illegal entries will be a persistent policy of administrative expulsion," for whose purpose, according to the defense minister, the government was opening "a bidding process for private companies, which are the ones to fulfill this role" (*Meganoticias* 2021b). Such an agreement was finally made with Sky Airlines only four days before the takeoff, in a contract signed by the undersecretary of the interior and approved on April 21 by Decree 92 (2021). According to the decree's first clause, the service was contracted in response to the "increase in the clandestine entry of foreigners . . . through unauthorized border crossings," which had generated "a significant increase in the number of administrative expulsions by the Regional Government and consequently, a large accumulation of foreign nationals who are waiting for the expulsion measures to be implemented" (Ministerio del Interior y Seguridad Pública 2021, 2). Likewise, the document established a maximum budget of US$1.6 million to carry out at least fifteen such flights, whose final destination would be countries of South and Central America with a maximum capacity of 180 passengers per flight, consisting of those being deported and security escorts.

Furthermore, this second turning point also stands out for the modification made to the maximum time of detention to execute expulsions, which was established the same week in April 2021. On Thursday, the 22nd, the minister of the interior and the PDI director signed Exempt Decree 1128 (2021), which extended the detention period from twenty-four to forty-eight hours. As described in the decree, the extension took into special consideration the health alert implemented in the country and the Constitutional State of Exception that allowed the closure of borders, thus affecting both free movement across the borders and the carrying out of expulsions (Ministerio del Interior y Seguridad Pública 2021, 1). The exempt decree led to verbal instructions being given that same day to several control agencies, though the document was not officially processed until Monday, April 26 (Rol 206-2021). However, this delay was crucial, as it permitted the detention to be declared illegal and the canceling of the expulsion orders for 31 people in the city of Arica. These people had been detained on Friday, the 23rd, and were to be transferred to Iquique airport and put on board a flight scheduled for Sunday, April 25 (Case No. 142-2021). As stated in the presentation of the appeal, despite the fact that all these persons had roots and family ties in Chile, the PDI had arrested them on the Friday when they were simply fulfilling their obligation to report to said police, at which time their identity documents and mobile phones were confiscated.

Based on these regulatory and operational modifications, at least four other flights with similar characteristics took off during 2021. However, as a result of various judicial, media, and political interventions carried out by social and academic organizations, among other actors, the control agencies were forced to modify some of their strategies. In this regard, for example, the action presented by the public criminal defender of Tarapacá stands out in response to the probable illegal detention of those who already met the requirements to leave the quarantine facilities, which consisted of having a negative result from a COVID test taken five days after their arrival at the Transitory Health Lodging. At the same time, legal practices, social organizations, and activist lawyers based in the region filed various judicial demands to denounce the illegal and arbitrary nature of the collective expulsions in progress. Although, for several reasons, many of these appeals were not accepted, others effectively forced the state agencies to be transparent with their protocols and modify their criteria for implementing them. In this respect, it is worth mentioning, for example, the flight scheduled for Sunday, May 9, which was eventually canceled, as the National Institute of Human Rights pushed strongly for the release of people who had been arrested in their own homes even though judicial rulings had been issued that had revoked their expulsion orders.

As a result of the situation we have described, however, nearly 200 people were deported on these flights in 2021, the majority of them Venezuelan nationals who never had the chance to request asylum, or apply for a visa, or even obtain fair treatment or due process during the processing of their expulsion orders. Social organizations, international agencies, and academia, among others, have denounced these expulsions. Moreover, and with a couple of exceptions, most of the writs of habeas corpus filed against these measures have been accepted by the courts of appeals or by the Supreme Court, though almost always after the person concerned had been deported. Ultimately, all the discretionary measures adopted during this period have contributed to tightening the mechanisms of control and surveillance but have not managed to stop the flow of migrants into the country. On the contrary, the strategy deployed has not only resulted in an unprecedented crisis and serious violations of the human rights of migrants but has also claimed the lives of at least eighteen people who have been forced to take more dangerous routes (TVN 2021), including "a nine-month-old baby who stopped breathing after crossing the border with her family" (*La Tercera* 2021, 1).

Conclusions

The increase in intraregional immigration that Chile has experienced in recent decades has been managed based on a punitive, exclusive, and selective agenda of migration governance, influenced by racial, sovereign, and political factors. As discussed in this chapter, prior to the pandemic, the Chilean migration and border control system already presented some conditions that pointed to a hardening approach. After the return to democracy in 1990, the postdictatorship governments gradually developed a contradictory model of migration policy that proclaimed more rights but in practice increasingly restricted access to processes of regularization. Then, with the turn of the century, immigration flows rose sharply but were accompanied by restrictions imposed on entering, circulating or residing in the country. As a result, and except for some tepid modifications during the second administration of the socialist Michelle Bachelet, between 2014 and 2018, this way of considering migration and mobility management would intensify significantly during the second Piñera government, between 2018 and the 2021.

Thus, during the latter period, a political model was built that, contrary to the discourse of order, security, and regularity that was declared, in practice produced and perpetuated disorder, insecurity, and undocumented migration. Here, the series of restrictions deployed by the Chilean state to prevent the regular entry of foreigners and thereby amplify their "subordinate inclusion" (Melossi 2018) and vulnerability stand out. Among these measures are the imposition of new visas, the delay and subsequent rejection of a significant proportion of visa applications, the barriers to requesting and accessing refugee status, and more recently, the closure of land border crossings as part of the health strategy in response to the pandemic. As a consequence, during the past decade the number of people denied the option of entering the country regularly, or of regularizing their immigration status, increased considerably, which also produced an increase in the number of people detected entering through unauthorized border crossings, a number that reached its historical maximum during the pandemic.

Faced with this scenario, the reorganization of Chilean immigration and border control experienced during the pandemic allowed the border limits and their logic of surveillance to be extended into the interior of the national territory. Despite the difficulties the state encountered in preventing entry through unauthorized crossings, particularly of Venezuelan citizens, the renewed registration and control strategy that was founded on the basis of "self-reporting to the police" generated a favorable scenario for the implementation of administrative expulsions. Other modifications were also relevant in this sense, such as the increase in the legal period of detention, the hiring of commercial flights to carry out deportations, and the presence of the military at the borders. Likewise, the implementation of Transitory Health Lodgings, initially intended for quarantine purposes, became an instrumental mechanism that combined sanitary measures with administrative migration control. In practice, this assemblage enabled the execution of collective expulsions, which are prohibited under international law, while circumventing judicial oversight by higher courts. Furthermore, these measures reinforced misconceptions surrounding irregular migration (Dufraix-Tapia, Ramos, and Quinteros 2023). In fact, at a symbolic level, the measures implemented by the Chilean state constituted an authentic "border spectacle" (De Genova 2017, 158) that was carried out through the dissemination of mass expulsions of foreigners dressed in white overalls, thus transmitting a message of efficiency and effectiveness that certainly did not find a correlation in the available data (Mascayano and Vergara 2022). All this underlines a control strategy that, along with adapting to the context, finds its greatest strength in the messages it disseminates concerning the "crimmigrant other" and that helps generate a collective consensus that manages to divert attention away from the real problems (the violation of human rights, economic recession, corruption, the increase in violence in general, etc.). Despite the aforementioned problems, it is important to recognize that civil society supported various strategies and resistance mechanisms that emerged for the protection of the human rights of migrants subject to control in the context of a pandemic. Although these efforts are not the subject of analysis in this chapter, the practices that made it possible to counteract the measures applied by the state, on the basis of collaboration and civil protection, undoubtedly represent an important field of research to investigate in the future.

NOTES

This chapter was written between 2021 and 2022, within the framework of the Fondecyt Regular Project No. 1240286, funded by the National Agency for Research and Development (ANID). We gratefully acknowledge their support. Please note that the temporal scope of the analysis reflects the available information up to that period.

1. The differences are mainly due to the fact that in their report, Galaz, Rubilar and Silva counted "people with expulsion orders," while the request to the undersecretariat of the interior was for the number of "administrative acts that impose expulsion," which may eventually involve more than one person.

2. This gap between the expulsions issued and the expulsions executed reached its greatest distance in 2020, with barely 5 percent of effectiveness. Specifically, of 4,006 expulsion

orders issued, only 202 were executed (Dufraix-Tapia, Ramos, and Quinteros 2023). This low effectiveness can be explained, in part, by the border closures caused by the pandemic and the difficulties in the registration that occurred because of undocumented people.

REFERENCES

24 Horas. 2022. "Declaraciones ministro Delgado: Crisis migratoria en Colchane." You-Tube, March 17. https://www.youtube.com/watch?v=5wv5CMlEaMk.

Aliverti, Ana. 2015. *Crimes of Mobility. Criminal Law and the Regulation of Immigration*. London: Routledge.

Álvarez Velasco, Soledad. 2009. "Transitando en la clandestinidad: Análisis de la migración indocumentada en tránsito por la frontera sur mexicana" (Transiting clandestinely: Analysis of undocumented migration on the Mexican border). *Dossier central: Andina migrante* 4:2–10.

Álvarez Velasco, Soledad. 2016. "¿Crisis migratoria contemporánea? Complejizando dos corredores migratorios globales" (Contemporary migration crisis? Making two global migratory corridors more complex). *Ecuador Debate* 97 (April): 155–71.

Aquino, Alejandra. 2015. "Porque si llamas al miedo, el miedo te friega: La ilegalización de los trabajadores migrantes y sus efectos en las subjetividades" (If you summon the fear, the fear beats you: The illegalization of migrant workers and its effect on their subjectivities). *Estudios fronterizos* 16 (32): 75–98.

Bhui, Hindpal. 2013. "Introduction: Humanizing Migration Control and Detention." In *The Borders of Punishment: Migration, Citizenship, and Social Exclusion*, edited by Katja Franko and Mary Bosworth, 1–18. Oxford: Oxford University Press.

Bosworth, Mary, Katja Franko, and Sharon Pickering. 2018. "Punishment, Globalization, and Migration Control: 'Get Them the Hell Out of Here.'" *Punishment and Society* 20 (1): 34–53. https://doi.org/10.1177/1462474517738984.

Bowling, Ben and Sophie Westenra. 2018. "Crimmigration." In *The Routledge Companion to Criminological Theory and Concepts*, 253–57. London: Routledge.

Brandariz, José Ángel. 2021a. "Crimigración y Deportation Gap, en una perspectiva global" (Crimigration and deportation gap, in a global perspective). In *Securitización de las fronteras y criminalización de las migraciones* (Securitization of borders and criminalization of migrations), edited by Roberto Dufraix-Tapia, Romina Ramos, and Daniel Quinteros, 351–74. Santiago: Ediciones Jurídicas de Santiago.

Brandariz, José Ángel. 2021b. "Criminalization or Instrumentalism? New Trends in the Field of Border Criminology." *Theoretical Criminology* 26 (2): 136248062110091. https://doi.org/10.1177/13624806211009158.

Brandariz, José Ángel, and Cristina Fernández-Bessa. 2021. "Coronavirus and Immigration Detention in Europe: The Short Summer of Abolitionism?" *Social Sciences* 10 (6): 226.

Brandariz, José Ángel, Roberto Dufraix, and Daniel Quinteros. 2018. "La expulsión judicial en el sistema penal chileno: ¿Hacia un modelo de Crimmigration?" (Judicial expulsion in the Chilean penal system: Towards a Crimmigration model?) *Política criminal* 13 (3): 739–70. https://scielo.conicyt.cl/pdf/politcrim/v13n26/0718-3399-politcrim-13-26-00739.pdf.

Brumat, Leiza. 2021. "Gobernanza migratoria en Suramérica en 2021: Respuestas a la emigración venezolana durante la pandemia" (Migration governance in South America in 2021: Responses to Venezuelan emigration during the pandemic). *Análisis Carolina* 12:1–28.

Cociña, Martina, and Daniel Quinteros. 2021. "Las consecuencias de la respuesta del Gobierno ante la crisis humanitaria: Migración desordenada, altamente insegura y masivamente irregular" (The consequences of the government's response to the humanitarian crisis: Disorderly, highly insecure, and massively irregular migration). *El Mostrador*, February 15. https://www.elmostrador.cl/noticias/opinion/2021/02/15/las-consecuencias-de-la-respuesta-del-gobierno-ante-la-crisis-humanitaria-migracion-desordenada-altamente-insegura-y-masivamente-irregular/.

Cociña, Martina, Romina Ramos and Isaac Ravetllat. 2021. "La obligación de resguardar la infancia en la crisis humanitaria" (The obligation to protect children in the humanitarian crisis). *The Clinic*, February 22. https://www.theclinic.cl/2021/02/22/columna-de-martina-cocina-romina-ramos-e-isaac-ravetllat-la-obligacion-de-resguardar-la-infancia-en-la-crisis-humanitaria/.

Contraloría General de la República (Comptroller General of the Republic). 2014. *Informe en investigación especial n° 10, de 2013, sobre presuntas irregularidades en adquisiciones de equipamiento para el plan frontera norte, en el ministerio del interior y seguridad pública* (Special investigation report No. 10, of 2013, on alleged irregularities in the acquisition of equipment for the northern border plan, in the Ministry of the Interior and Public Security).

Cooperativa.cl. 2021. "'Plan Colchane': Gobierno explica cómo controlará la inmigración ilegal" ("Colchane plan": Government explains how it will control illegal immigration). *Cooperativa.cl*, February 9. https://cooperativa.cl/noticias/pais/poblacion/inmigrantes/plan-colchane-gobierno-explica-como-controlara-la-inmigracion-ilegal/2021-02-09/162732.html.

De Genova, Nicholas. 2017. "Movimientos migratorios contemporáneos: Entre el control fronterizo y la producción de su ilegalidad; un diálogo con Nicholas De Genova" (Contemporary migratory movements: Between border control and the production of its illegality; a dialogue with Nicholas De Genova). *Revista ICONOS* 58. http://revistas.flacsoandes.edu.ec/iconos/article/view/2718.

De Giorgi, Alessandro. 2010. "Immigration Control, Post-Fordism, and Less Eligibility: A Materialist Critique of the Criminalization of Immigration Across Europe." *Punishment and Society* 12 (2): 147–67. https://doi.org/10.1177/1462474509357378.

DEM (Departamento de Extranjería y Migración) (Department of Immigration and Migration). 2016. *Migración en Chile 2005–2014* (Migration in Chile, 2005–2014).

DEM (Departamento de Extranjería y Migración) (Department of Immigration and Migration). 2021. *Tercera estimación de población extranjera residente en Chile* (Third estimate of the foreign population residing in Chile).

De Moraes, Ana Luisa. 2015. "Crimigração: A relação entre política migratória e política criminal no Brasil" (Crimmigration: The relationship between migration policy and criminal policy in Brazil). http://hdl.handle.net/10923/7787.

De Moraes, Ana Luisa. 2018. "The Non-Criminalization Principle in Accordance to the New Brazilian Migration Law." *Panorama of Brazilian Law* 5 (7–8): 113–36. https://doi.org/10.17768/pbl.v5i7-8.p113-136.

Domenech, Eduardo. 2013. "'Las migraciones son como el agua': Hacia la instauración de políticas de 'control con rostro humano'; La gobernabilidad migratoria en la Argentina" ("Migrations are like water": Toward the establishment of "control policies with a human face"; migration governance in Argentina). *Polis (Santiago)* 12 (35): 119–42. https://doi.org/10.4067/s0718-65682013000200006.

Dufraix-Tapia, Roberto, Romina Ramos, and Daniel Quinteros. 2020. "'Ordenar la casa': Securitización y producción de irregularidad en el norte de Chile" ("Tidying up the house": Securitization and production of irregularity in northern Chile). *Sociologias* 22 (55): 172–96. https://doi.org/10.1590/15174522-105689.

Dufraix-Tapia, Roberto, Romina Ramos, and Daniel Quinteros. 2023. "Sobre las dinámicas (y funcionalidades) del control de la movilidad humana en tiempos de pandemia: El caso de las expulsiones en Chile y su relación con la tesis de la crimmigration" (About the dynamics [and functionalities] of human mobility control in times of pandemic: The case of expulsions in Chile and their relationship with the crimmigration thesis). In *XVII Jornadas Chilenas de Derecho Penal y Ciencias Penales*. Tirant Lo Blanch: Valencia.

Durán Migliardi, Carlos, and Luis Thayer. 2017. "Los migrantes frente a la ley: Continuidades y rupturas en la legislación migratoria del estado chileno (1824–1975)" (Migrants facing the law: Continuities and ruptures in the immigration legislation of the Chilean state [1824–1975]). *Historia 396* 7 (2): 429–61. http://www.historia396.cl/index.php/historia396/article/view/212/101.

El Mercurio. 1991. "Gobierno hará severo control de extranjeros: Por aumento de flujo." *El Mercurio*, November 3, A1.

El Mercurio. 1996. "Notifican a secta peruana de expulsión: Trámite policial." *El Mercurio*, April 10, C9.

Franko, Katja. 2013. "The Ordered and the Bordered Society: Migration Control, Citizenship, and the Northern Penal State." In *The Borders of Punishment*, edited by Katja Franko and Mary Bosworth, 21–39. Oxford: Oxford University Press.

Franko, Katja. 2020. *The Crimmigrant Other*. London: Routledge.

Galaz, Caterine, Gabriela Rubilar, Catalina Álvarez, and Susana Viñuela. 2017. *Promesas (In)Cumplidas* (Promises [un]fulfilled). Área de Trabajo Social de la Facultad de Ciencias Sociales de la Universidad de Chile.

Galaz, Caterine, Gabriela Rubilar, and Claudia Silva. 2016. *Boletín Informativo Nº 2: Migración dominicana en Chile* (Information Bulletin No. 2: Dominican migration in Chile). https://colab1.facso.cl/ficha/recursos/20.

García, Lila. 2015. "Política migratoria y delitos: Expulsión por causas penales y derechos bajo la actual Ley Argentina de Migraciones" (Immigration policy and crimes: Expulsion for criminal causes and rights under the current Argentine Migration Law). *REMHU: Revista Interdisciplinar da Mobilidade Humana* 23 (45): 197–214. https://doi.org/10.1590/1980-85852503198800045l0.

García Hernández, César. 2013. "Creating Crimmigration." *Brigham Young University Law Review* 13. https://doi.org/10.2139/ssrn.2393662.

García Pinzón, Viviana. 2015. "Territorios fronterizos: Agenda de seguridad y narcotráfico en Chile; El Plan Frontera Norte" (Border territories: Security and drug trafficking agenda in Chile; The Northern Border Plan). *Estudios Internacionales* 47 (181): 69–93. http://www.jstor.org.ezproxy.eafit.edu.co/stable/44821616.

INE (Instituto Nacional de Estadística) (National Statistical Institute), and DEM (Departamento de Extranjería y Migración) (Department of Immigration and Migration). 2020. "Estimación de personas extranjeras residentes habituales en Chile al 31 de diciembre 2019: Informe técnico" (Estimation of foreign persons habitually residing in Chile as of December 31, 2019: Technical report). INE, March. https://www.ine.cl /docs/default-source/demografia-y-migracion/publicaciones-y-anuarios/migración -internacional/estimación-población-extranjera-en-chile-2018/estimación-población -extranjera-en-chile-2019-metodología.pdf?sfvrsn=5b145256_6.

INE (Instituto Nacional de Estadística) (National Statistical Institute) and DEM (Departamento de Extranjería y Migración) (Department of Immigration and Migration). 2021. "Estimación de personas extranjeras residentes habituales en Chile al 31 de diciembre de 2020" (Estimate of foreigners habitually residing in Chile as of December 31, 2020). https://www.ine.cl/estadisticas/sociales/demografia-y-vitales/demografia-y-migracion.

INE (Instituto Nacional de Estadística) (National Statistical Institute). 2018. "Síntesis de resultados Censo 2017" (Summary of 2017 census results). https://www.ine.gob.cl /docs/default-source/censo-de-poblacion-y-vivienda/publicaciones-y-anuarios/2017 /publicaci%C3%B3n-de-resultados/sintesis-de-resultados-censo2017.pdf.

La Tercera. 2021. "Tercera víctima migrante en Colchane: Bebé habría muerto tras el cruce de fronteras" (Third migrant victim in Colchane: Baby would have died after crossing the border). *La Tercera*, October 11. https://www.latercera.com/nacional /noticia/tercera-victima-migrante-en-colchane-bebe-habria-muerto-tras-el-cruce-de -fronteras/2HFUJOKLWRD5VDTQFPVB5CBQRY/.

Lara Escalona, María Daniela. 2014. "Evolución de la legislación migratoria en Chile: Claves para una lectura" (Evolution of immigration legislation in Chile: Keys for Reading). *Revista de Historia del Derecho* 47:46.

Leal, Ignacio. 2021. "PDI registra 50.351 ingresos clandestinos a Chile durante la pandemia" (PDI records 50,351 clandestine entries to Chile during the pandemic). *La Tercera*, November 5. https://www.latercera.com/la-tercera-sabado /noticia/pdi-registra-50351-ingresos-clandestinos-a-chile-durante-la-pandemia /UAOXGP6R4RGZPAZD4HV4YZSHCM/.

León, Rosario. 2021. "Investigador de la U. Arturo Prat revela qué les espera a los venezolanos repatriados" (Researcher from the Arturo Prat University reveals what awaits repatriated Venezuelans). *Pauta*, February 12. https://www.pauta.cl/nacional /daniel-quinteros-inmigrantes-venezolanos-colchane.

Llambias-Wolff, Jaime. 1993. "The Voluntary Repatriation Process of Chilean Exiles." *International Migration* 31 (4): 579–99. https://doi.org/10.1111/j.1468-2435.1993 .tb00684.x.

Martínez, Jorge. 1997. *Situación y tendencias de la migración internacional en Chile* (Situation and trends of international migration in Chile). Repositorio CEPAL. https://hdl .handle.net/11362/7388

McNeill, Henrietta. 2021. "Dealing with the 'Crimmigrant Other' in the Face of a Global Public Health Threat: A Snapshot of Deportation During COVID-19 in Australia and New Zealand." *Social Sciences* 10 (8): 278.

Mascayano, Camila, and Stephanie Vergara. 2022. "El control penal de la migración en tiempos de pandemia: Un estudio exploratorio sobre el caso de la región de Tarapacá (Chile)" (The criminal control of migration in times of pandemic: An exploratory study on the case of the Tarapacá region [Chile]). Undergraduate thesis, Universidad de Tarapacá, Iquique, Chile.

Meganoticias. 2021a. "Incidentes entre migrantes y carabineros por ingreso masivo de extranjeros en Colchane" (Incidents between migrants and police due to massive entry of foreigners in Colchane). February 2. https://www.meganoticias.cl/nacional/326031 -colchane-carabineros-migrantes-venezuela-acx08.html.

Meganoticias. 2021b. "'Fuimos engañados': Las denuncias de migrantes irregulares antes de ser expulsados" ("We were deceived": The complaints of irregular migrants before being expelled). February 11. https://www.meganoticias.cl/nacional/326880-expulsion -de-migrantes-chile-extranjeros-denuncias-gobierno-mgx17.html.

Melossi, Dario. 2018. *Controlar el delito, controlar la sociedad: Teorías y debates sobre la cuestión criminal, del siglo XVIII al XXI* (Controlling crime, controlling society: Theories and debates on the criminal question, from the 18th to the 21st century). Buenos Aires: Siglo Veintiuno Editores.

Ministerio de Defensa Nacional (Ministry of National Defense). 2019. *Decreto Nr. 265 que autoriza colaboración y delega en el Ministro de Defensa Nacional las facultades en materia que indica* (Decree No. 265 that authorizes collaboration and delegates to the Minister of National Defense the powers in matters indicated). *Diario Oficial*. https:// www.diarioficial.cl.

Ministerio de Defensa Nacional (Ministry of National Defense). 2021. *Decreto Nr. 3 que modifica el Decreto Supremo Nr. 265 de 2019, que autoriza colaboración y delega en el Ministro de Defensa Nacional las facultades en materia que indica* (Decree No. 3 that modifies Supreme Decree No. 265 of 2019, which authorizes collaboration and delegates to the Minister of National Defense the powers in matters indicated). *Diario Oficial*. https://www.diarioficial.cl.

Ministerio de Relaciones Exteriores (Ministry of Foreign Relations). 2018. *Minuta bases y componentes de la nueva política y reforma migratoria en Chile* (Minutes bases and components of the new immigration policy and reform in Chile). https:// www.camara.cl/verDoc.aspx?prmID=157413&prmTIPO=DOCUMENTO COMISION.

Ministerio del Interior y Seguridad Pública (Ministry of the Interior and Public Security). 2019. *Decreto 237 Establece Visto Consular de Turismo a Nacionales de la República Bolivariana de Venezuela. Diario Oficial* (Decree No. 237 establishing a tourist consular visa requirement for nationals of the Bolivarian Republic of Venezuela). https://www .diarioficial.cl.

Ministerio del Interior y Seguridad Pública (Ministry of the Interior and Public Security). 2021. *Decreto Nr. 92. Gobierno de Chile* (Decree No. 92. Government of Chile). https://www.diarioficial.cl.

Ministerio del Interior y Seguridad Pública (Ministry of the Interior and Public Security). 2021. *Decreto Exento Nr. 1128 que aprueba modificación de protocolo de actuación
para expulsión de extranjeros infractores, suscrito entre el Ministerio del Interior y
Seguridad Pública y la Policía de Investigaciones. Gobierno de Chile*. (Exempt Decree
No. 1128 that approves modification of the action protocol for the expulsion of foreign
offenders, signed between the Ministry of the Interior and Public Security and the
Investigative Police. Government of Chile).

Municipalidad de Colchane (Municipality of Colchane). 2015. *Plan de Desarrollo Comu-
nal 2015–2018* (Community Development Plan, 2015–2018).

Navarro, Roberto. 2021. "Prohibición de la crimigración por la irrelevancia de la condición de extranjero en el derecho chileno" (Prohibition of crimmigration due to the
irrelevance of the status of a foreigner in Chilean law). In *Securitización de las fronteras
y criminalización de las migraciones*, edited by Roberto Dufraix-Tapia, Romina Ramos,
and Daniel Quinteros, 333–50. Santiago: Ediciones Jurídicas de Santiago.

Norambuena, Carmen. 2013. "Amenazas sin fronteras: Nuevas periferias en la circulación
de personas" (Threats without borders: New peripheries in the movement of people).
Cuadernos de Historia 39:147–68.

Norambuena, Carmen, Bernardo Navarrete, and Rodrigo Matamoros. 2018. "Entre
continuidades y rupturas, mejor la continuidad: Política migratoria chilena desde
comienzo de siglo XX" (Between continuities and ruptures, continuity is better: Chilean immigration policy since the beginning of the 20th century). *Revista Austral de
Ciencias Sociales* 34:217–37. https://doi.org/10.4206/rev.austral.cienc.soc.2018.n34–13.

Olavarría, José. 2019. "Venezolanos en la frontera: Director de Incami en Arica advierte
que decisión del Gobierno de pedir visa consular se tomó sin medir las consecuencias"
(Venezuelans on the border: Director of Incami in Arica warns that the government's
decision to request a consular visa was made without measuring the consequences).
El Mostrador, June 25. https://www.elmostrador.cl/noticias/pais/2019/06/25
/venezolanos-en-la-frontera-director-de-incami-en-arica-advierte-que-decision-del
-gobierno-de-pedir-visa-consular-se-tomo-sin-medir-las-consecuencias/.

Paredes, Norberto. 2021. "La crisis 'sin precedentes' de la pequeña Colchane, el pueblecito
chileno que tiene más migrantes que habitantes" (The 'unprecedented' crisis of small
Colchane, the Chilean community that has more migrants than inhabitants). *BBC
News*, February 6. https://www.bbc.com/mundo/noticias-america-latina-55950140.

Penchaszadeh, Ana Paula, and Lila García. 2018. "Política migratoria y seguridad en
Argentina hoy: ¿El paradigma de derechos humanos en jaque?" (Migration policy and
security in Argentina today: The human rights paradigm in check?). *URVIO: Revista
Latinoamericana de Estudios de Seguridad* 23:91–109. https://doi.org/10.17141/urvio
.23.2018.3553.

Pickering, Sharon, Mary Bosworth, and Katja Franko. 2017. "The Criminology of
Mobility." In *The Routledge Handbook on Crime and International Migration*, 382–98.
London: Routledge.

Plaza Armijo, Camilo, and Víctor Muñoz Cortés. 2013. "La Ley de Residencia de 1918 y la
persecución a los extranjeros subversivos" (The Residence Law of 1918 and the persecution of subversive foreigners). *Revista de Derechos Fundamentales* 10:107–36.

Quinteros, Daniel. 2016. "¿Nueva 'crimigración' o la vieja economía política del castigo? Dos aproximaciones criminológicas para entender el control punitivo de la migración en Chile" (New 'crimigration' or the old political economy of punishment? Two criminological approaches for understanding the punitive control of migration in Chile). *Astrolabio: Nueva Época* 17 (17): 81–113.

R4V (Plataforma Regional de Coordinación Interagencial para Refugiados y Migrantes de Venezuela) (Regional Interagency Coordination Platform for Refugees and Migrants from Venezuela). 2021. "Nota explicativa de la actualización de las cifras de refugiados y migrantes venezolanos de octubre—Oct 2021" (Explanatory note on the October update of Venezuelan refugees and migrants figures). Report. https://www.r4v.info/es/document/nota-explicativa-de-la-actualizacion-de-las-cifras-de-refugiados-y-migrantes-venezolanos

Ramírez, Jacques, and Soledad Álvarez Velasco. 2009. "'Cruzando Fronteras': Una aproximación etnográfica a la migración clandestina ecuatoriana en tránsito hacia Estados Unidos" ("Crossing Borders": An ethnographic approach to Ecuadorian clandestine migration in transit to the United States). *Confluenze. Rivista di studi iberoamericani* 1 (1): 89–113.

Ramos, Romina, José Ángel Brandariz, and Roberto Dufraix-Tapia. 2021. "Heterogeneous borders: migrant workers in northern Chile." In *Handbook of Migration and Global Justice*, edited by Leanne Weber and Claudia Tazreiter, 352. Cheltenham, UK: Edward Elgar. https://doi.org/10.4337/9781789905663.

Ramos, Romina, and Marcela Tapia. 2019. "Una mirada heterogénea del espacio fronterizo: el caso de la frontera tarapaqueña (Chile)" (A heterogeneous look at the border space: The case of the Tarapacan border [Chile]). *Revista CIDOB d'Afers Internacionals* 122: 187–212. https://doi.org/10.24241/rcai.2019.122.2.187.

Ruiz, Martha, and Soledad Álvarez Velasco. 2019. "Excluir para proteger: La 'guerra' contra la trata y el tráfico de migrantes y las nuevas lógicas de control migratorio en Ecuador" (Exclude to protect: The "war" against trafficking and smuggling of migrants and the new logic of migration control in Ecuador). *Estudios Sociológicos* 38 (111): 689–725.

Schiriro, Dora. 2021. "On the Other Side of the Looking Glass: COVID-19 Care in Immigration Detention." *Social Sciences* 10 (10): 353.

Servicio Jesuita a Migrantes (Jesuit Migrant Service). 2021. "Cifras claves de la migración en Chile." (Key figures of migration in Chile). *Migración en Chile.* https://www.migracionenchile.cl/.

Sklansky, David. 2012. "Crime, Immigration, and Ad Hoc Instrumentalism." *New Criminal Law Review* 15 (2): 157–223. https://doi.org/10.1525/nclr.2012.15.2.157.

Solimano, Andrés, and Víctor Tokman. 2006. "Migraciones internacionales en un contexto de crecimiento económico: el caso de Chile" (International migrations in a context of economic growth: The case of Chile). Comisión Económica para América Latina (CEPAL) (Economic Commission for Latin America and the Caribbean), United Nations. August https://www.cepal.org/sites/default/files/events/files/victortokman.pdf.

Soy Iquique. 2021. "Crudo testimonio de venezolana en Colchane: 'Prácticamente vinimos engañados'" (Raw testimony of a Venezuelan woman in Colchane: "We were practically deceived"). February 4. https://www.soychile.cl/Iquique/Sociedad/2021/02/04/692684/VIDEO-Crudo-testimonio-de-venezolana-en-Colchane-Practicamente-vinimos-enganados.aspx.

Stang, Fernanda, Antonia Lara, and Marcos Andrade. 2020. "Retórica humanitaria y expulsabilidad: Migrantes haitianos y gobernabilidad migratoria en Chile" (Humanitarian rhetoric and expulsion: Haitian migrants and migration governance in Chile). *Si Somos Americanos* 20 (1): 176–201.

Stefanelli, Justine. 2021. "Detained During a Pandemic: Human Rights Behind Locked Doors." *Social Sciences* 10 (7): 276.

Stefoni, Carolina. 2011a. "Ley y política migratoria en Chile: La ambivalencia en la comprensión del migrante" (Immigration law and policy in Chile: Ambivalence in the understanding of the migrant). In *La Construcción Social del Sujeto Migrante en América Latina: Prácticas, representaciones y categorías* (The social construction of the migrant subject in Latin America: Practices, representations, and categories), 1:79–110. Facultad Latinoamericana de Ciencias Sociales–Ecuador, Consejo Latinoamericano de Ciencias Sociales, and Universidad Alberto Hurtado.

Stefoni, Carolina. 2011b. *Perfil migratorio de Chile* (Migratory profile of Chile). International Organization for Migration, IOM Chile. https://www.red-iam.org/sites/g/files/tmzbdl2386/files/2021-01/Perfil%20Migratorio%20Chile.pdf.

Stefoni, Carolina, and Fernanda Stang. 2017. "La construcción del campo de estudio de las migraciones en Chile: Notas de un ejercicio reflexivo y autocrítico" (The construction of the field of study of migrations in Chile: Notes from a reflective and self-critical exercise). *Íconos: Revista de Ciencias Sociales* 58:109. https://doi.org/10.17141/iconos.58.2017.2477.

Stefoni, Carolina, Báltica Cabieses, and Alice Blukacz. 2021. "Migraciones y COVID-19: Cuando el discurso securitista amenaza el derecho a la salud" (Migrations and COVID-19: When the securitist discourse threatens the right to health). *Simbiótica Revista Electrónica* 8 (2): 38–66. https://doi.org/10.47456/simbitica.v8i2.36378.

Stumpf, Juliet. 2006. "The Crimmigration Crisis: Immigrants, Crime, and Sovereign Power." *American University Law Review* 56 (367): 1689–99. https://doi.org/10.1017/CBO9781107415324.004.

Stumpf, Juliet. 2013. "The Process is the Punishment in Crimmigration Law." In *The Borders of Punishment: Migration, Citizenship, and Social Exclusion*, edited by Katja Franko and Mary Bosworth, 58–75. Oxford: Oxford University Press.

Tapia, Marcela. 2012. "Frontera y migración en el norte de Chile a partir del análisis de los censos de población: Siglos XIX–XXI" (Border and migration in northern Chile based on the analysis of population censuses, nineteenth–twenty-first centuries). *Revista de geografía Norte Grande* 53:177–98. https://doi.org/10.4067/s0718-34022012000300011.

Tapia, Marcela, Nanette Liberona, and Yasna Contreras. 2017. "El surgimiento de un territorio circulatorio en la frontera chileno-peruana: Estudio de las prácticas socio-espaciales fronterizas" (The emergence of a circulatory territory on the Chilean-Peruvian border: Study of border socio-spatial practices). *Revista de geografía Norte Grande* (66), 117–41. https://dx.doi.org/10.4067/S0718-34022017000100008.

Tapia, Marcela, Daniel Quinteros, and Romina Ramos. 2021. "Colchane en el centro de la noticia: La crisis con rostro humano" (Colchane at the center of the news: The

crisis with a human face). *Edición Cero*, February 13. https://edicioncero.cl/2021/02/
colchane -en-el-centro-de-la-noticia-la-crisis-con-rostro-humano/.

Tijoux, María Emilia, and María Gabriela Córdova. 2015. "Prólogo: Racismo en Chile;
colonialismo, nacionalismo, capitalismo" (Prologue: Racism in Chile; colonialism,
nationalism, capitalism). *POLIS Revista Latinoamericana* 42:7–13.

TVN (Televisión Nacional). 2021. "18° muerte en Colchane: Fallece hombre venezolano
de 64 años tras intentar cruzar frontera con Bolivia" (18th death in Colchane:
64-year-old Venezuelan man dies after trying to cross the border with Bolivia).
24horas, November 9. https://www.24horas.cl/regiones/tarapaca/18-muerte-en
-colchane-fallece-hombre-venezolano-de-64-anos-tras-intentar-cruzar-frontera-con
-bolivia-5053140.

Undersecretariat of the Interior, Government of Chile. 2020a. Response to Public Information Access Request No. AB001C0004251.

Undersecretariat of the Interior, Government of Chile. 2020b. Response to Public Information Access Request No. AB001T0001403.

Valencia, Pilar, and Romina Ramos. 2021. "Análisis crítico del proceso de (des) regularización migratoria extraordinaria en Chile (2018–2019)" (Critical analysis of the
extraordinary migration (de)regularization process in Chile [2018–2019]). *Diálogo
andino* 66 (2021): 399–417.

Wacquant, Loic. 1999. "'Suitable Enemies': Foreigners and Immigrants in the Prisons
of Europe." *Punishment and Society* 1 (2): 183–205. http://hjb.sagepub.com.proxy.lib
.umich.edu/content/9/2/183.full.pdf+html.

8

The Politics of Hostility in Argentina

DETENTION, EXPULSION, AND BORDER REJECTION

Eduardo Domenech

During the past decade, after the first migratory reforms carried out by some national governments recognized as "progressive" or "postneoliberal," and after various efforts at constructing regional consensus around migration, a significant reconfiguration occurred in the field of South American migration policies. Thus, in a regional context with important mutations in migration movements and a changing political stage due to the coming to power of parties or coalitions of a "new right," the expansion and intensification of migration and border control were expressed through the increase of state violence toward migrants and the proliferation of punitive and repressive practices under new justifying narratives. This chapter analyzes the transformations produced in migration control policies in the current Argentinian context. I maintain that the main changes experienced in migration control relate to the reconfiguration of the control regime of migrant "illegality," which took place through specific interventions in detention, deportation, and rejection at the border. Furthermore, I suggest that in the framework of an official strategy of spectacularization of migration control, which is part of a process of criminalization and securitization of migration with a scope that goes beyond Argentina, the detention, deportation, and border rejection practices acquired an unusual preeminence, establishing multiple disputes with organizations and groups that historically or occasionally act in defense of migrants.

Based on the proposed "politics of hostility,"[1] I also seek to account for the expansion and intensification of migration control in the Argentinian context. These processes relate to events that reorganized the struggles around the migration issue, which contributed decisively to establishing a politics of deportation. There were two crucial government measures in this direction: creating a detention center for migrants in an administrative "irregular" situation and a decree focused on the concept of deportation. Rejections at the border also played an essential role in producing unrest among some migrant collectives, though they did not cause significant confrontations between migration authorities and migrant rights organizations. I also explore and analyze the spatial-temporal dimension involved in the migration control expansion and intensification processes and policies. Therefore, I suggest that the transformation of the control regime of migrant "illegality" took on new spatialities and temporalities of control in the Argentinian context. By investigating some of the forms that the exercise of control has taken, I intend to indicate that, although the intensification of migration and border control is a question of magnitude, it is so not only in quantitative terms. It is about the diversification and multiplication of specific control practices, executed on different spatial scales and in variable time intervals. To develop these suppositions, the chapter is organized as follows: The first section provides some theoretical and methodological details on securitization, illegality, and hostility. The second section describes in general terms the politics of hostility toward migrants in the Argentinian national context. The subsequent three sections reconstruct and analyze some processes, stages, events, actions, and conflicts related to detention, deportation, and border rejection to shed some light on the most recent transformations in the field of migration control policies. The last section provides some final considerations on the findings of this chapter.

Securitization, Illegality, and Hostility

In recent years, the notion of *securitization* has been widely used to explain some of the changes in migration policies in the South American context, particularly those national experiences that illustrate an intensification of migration and border control and state violence against migrants. Hence, it is common to find references to migration criminalization processes and to tightening border controls and, in some cases, to the link between those and a notion of "security" generally labeled as national. Although this article does not explicitly scrutinize the migration securitization process in Argentina, the analysis of certain control practices necessarily refers to this concept. The category "politics of hostility" is linked to the way the (in)securitization of migration occurs (Bigo 2002). The approach here to the notion of securitization is based on some central propositions of critical studies of security (Balzacq et al. 2010; Bigo 2002; Bigo and McCluskey 2018; Huysmans and Squire 2009). Thus, discourses, practices, or representations without a punitive or repressive connotation are also assumed as part of the production of (in)securitization. The attention to securitization in these terms assumes other spatialities and temporalities in analyzing migration and border policies and practices. For this reason, I avoid using the criterion of spatial-temporal delimitation of the chronological periods imposed by the succession of governmental administrations, and eschew making interpretations in terms of continuities and ruptures in specific periods. Instead, I am more inclined to apprehend the different spatialities and temporalities of migration control policies and practices.

The exploration of migration control policies and practices developed in this chapter follows the critical theoretical-methodological approaches that propose the concept of *regime* for studying migration and borders (Hess 2012; Hess and Kasparek 2017; Sciortino 2004; Tsianos and Karakayali 2010). Thus, from the perspective of critical migration and border studies, the concept of regime refers to a space of conflict, negotiation, and resistance to movement control. This chapter starts from the premise that migration policies were, and are, constituted around the tension between the control and freedom of movement in specific national frameworks that are part of international mobility regulation processes. Together with the contributions of the view of autonomy of migration, the notion of regime makes it possible to challenge those approaches to the study of migration policy that view migration from a sedentary conception, which reproduces the perspective of the so-called receiving society. On the other hand, the notion of regime allows for the incorporation of a multiplicity of actors whose practices are related but not organized according to a central logic or rationality; that is, it makes it possible to understand regulation as an effect of social practices (Hess 2012). Similarly, the concept also leaves room for interstices, ambiguities, and tensions: a regime is the result of constant repair work through practices (Sciortino 2004).

From this perspective, migrant struggles (De Genova, Mezzadra, and Pickles 2015) are also constitutive of migration policies. They are not just responses or reactions to the official policies or any new form of migration regulation; they actively participate in their configuration. In tune with the propositions of the autonomy of migration, I understand migration policies as shaped and organized based on how they are challenged by the multiple forms and continuous transformations that migration movements acquire, and the diverse struggles triggered by the search for control. Here, I pick up again the notion of an "illegal" migration control regime, used previously to analyze the historical production of the "illegal migrant" figure in Argentina (Domenech 2011). This regime includes practices of control of those mobilities that do not respond to state parameters (e.g., those that infringe migration laws or that do not follow the technocratic formula of "secure, orderly, and regular migration"), as well as regulation practices of diverse character (punitive, repressive, assistential, humanitarian) explicitly related to detention, deportation and deportability, border rejection, regularization, and "voluntary assisted return," among other possibilities. Similarly, it can include practices of negotiation and response to control such as struggles for documentation, denunciations of human rights violations, legal defense of migrant rights, mobilizations against detentions and deportations, and "struggles for movement,"[2] among others.

This chapter proposes the notion of a *politics of hostility* to give an account of a dominant form that the power relationship acquires from the disputes that various actors in the field of migration and borders maintain and the specific forms the exercise of migration control takes. A politics of hostility is not limited to, nor does it necessarily have to coincide with, a period of government; it can precede it, exceed it, or determine a moment of varying durability. In this sense, a politics of hostility as a dominant form does not pretend to ignore practices that give an account of other categories such as so-called selective hospitality, targeting specific national groups.

In analytical terms, it is not a matter of opposing one with the other but understanding their connections and mutual constitution. Similarly, by assuming that migration and border control practices are heterogeneous, changing, and dynamic, I seek to examine their configuration in relational terms; that is, I avoid isolating a practice from the set of practices directed at regulating migration and borders. Although the focus is on detention and deportation practices, the intent is to understand them from their relationship with other control practices in certain contexts and specific circumstances. Furthermore, to more fully understand the exercise of migration and border control, attention is given to how the actors strategically use space and time while producing certain spatialities and temporalities from their actions. Authors of critical migration and border studies with diverse disciplinary origins have drawn attention to the space-time interrelation and to the spatial and temporal categories in order to understand the functioning of the border regimes and the crucial role that borders play in the control of movement (Bigo 2010; Conlon, Hiemstra, and Mountz 2017; Griffiths, Rogers, and Anderson 2013; Khosravi 2014; McNevin 2022; Mezzadra and Neilson 2017; Tazzioli 2018).

This chapter uses material from fieldwork carried out in different periods between mid-2013 and the end of 2019. The fieldwork began when deportation and migration control practices, in general, were not considered a significant research topic and had not gained much public visibility or exposure in Argentina.[3] Even in the migrant activism circles that I frequented, these practices did not constitute a priority in collective actions. The time interval between the invisibility of the deportations and the appearance of measures such as the initiative of creating a detention center for foreigners with a deportation order and the reform of the migration and citizenship law—which contributed decisively to reinstating deportation as a topic in public debate—was fundamental to understanding the transformations in the field of migration policies in terms of a politics of hostility and evoking the need to speak of a "politics of deportation" and not only of deportation practices.

During these years, I conducted several interviews with migrants of different nationalities, met or contacted them in occasional encounters, and shared social or political spaces and personal ties. I also held conversations and interviews with representatives of migrant and social organizations and employees, technicians, and government officials of the National Directorate of Immigration (NDI) during the administration of Cristina Fernández de Kirchner (2007–15) and Mauricio Macri (2015–19). In all cases, the interviewee selection criteria were based on the formal link or experiences related to the policies or practices under study. To reconstruct specific processes and events, it was necessary to use bibliographic, newspaper, and audiovisual documentary sources of various kinds: journalistic notes, working papers and yearbooks of civil organizations, statements by groups or networks of organizations, institutional statements, official press releases, national regulations, verbal testimonies, and public discussions. I also used an archive compiled during the past seven years that included newspaper articles and official documents linked with migration and border control and detentions and deportations in various South American countries.

A politics of hostility condenses multiple practices and representations of actors whose actions bring about the criminalization and securitization of migration and borders. These are openly hostile actions, originating from government and media sectors that have produced collective states of unease, fear, and dread among migrants. Some national groups are often exposed or affected by individual narratives, initiatives, or measures that associate migration with criminality or delinquency. A politics of hostility is imbued with a spectacularization of migration and border control[4] to capture public attention through the dissemination of statements and images related to the strengthening of border control, the hardening of migration policy, the fight against "irregular migration," the intensification of administrative and police controls in various social spaces, and the detention and deportation of "criminal aliens." Simultaneously, a politics of hostility sheds light on a series of political decisions and administrative and legislative measures that have received greater or lesser public attention, making the daily lives of various sectors or groups of the migrant population more precarious or difficult.

In the current context, two government measures are examples of this politics of hostility: first, the announcement of the creation of a detention center and, a few months later, the signing of the Necessity and Urgency Decree (Decreto de Necesidad de Urgencia, or DNU) No. 70, which modified Migration Law No. 25.871 and introduced a substantial change to Citizenship Law No. 346. Organized migrant activists challenged both of these measures, as illustrated later in this chapter, particularly activists from organizations with a long history of promoting and defending migrant rights in Argentina and those concerning new spaces and networks of migrant and social organizations. It is necessary to understand these two measures as part of a broader process of producing hostility toward migrants that includes exponential enhancement of controls on permanence; institutional persecution and violence toward migrant street vendors; bills aimed at restricting access to health and higher education; an increase in the number of deportations and deportation orders; information campaigns via social networks against "irregular migration"; creation of a digital application used by security forces to control "irregularity"; exponential increase in migration rates; temporary extension of the requirement for criminal records; and implementation of a remote electronic system for residence procedures that caused enormous difficulties and delays for migrants.

A politics of hostility involves much more than hostile actions or episodes of hostility against migrants in a particular social context. It recognizes a heterogeneity of practices that combine historical constructions about migrants as illegitimate presence, anomaly, or "exteriority" (Sayad 2008), associated with illegality, deportability, dangerousness, or criminality, with new narratives about security and protection. A politics of hostility supposes a twofold movement as a product of migration and border criminalization and securitization processes. On one hand, it makes out specific individuals or groups to be a threat, danger, or risk. On the other hand, it seeks to provide protection or security to the rest of society or those established as victims. The figure of the delinquent or criminal foreigner as a deportable subject is intrinsic to the politics of hostility produced in recent years. It is mobilized as a way of disciplining all migrants. Here, as indicated by Tanya Basok (2019), DNU No. 70 can be interpreted as a disciplinary technique directed at deterring or preventing, under threat of detention and deportation, participating in protests, resisting authorities, or engaging in informal or illegal economic activities.

A decade after the approval of Migration Law No. 25.871, the association between migration, crime, and security was reestablished as the dominant representation through the "criminal alien." In 2014, the deportation of foreigners and the control of migration, in a pre-electoral context marked by the discussion of "public safety," became relevant in the public debate once more. Secretary of Security Sergio Berni appeared in front of the cameras in several episodes in which migrants or foreigners were accused of being criminals and their deportation demanded. Many other leaders of different political parties expressed themselves in the same vein. In the context of the reform of the National Code of Criminal Procedure (NCCP), the presidential announcement established a direct link between foreigners and crime, in addition to justifying the modification of one of the articles based on the "protection that we Argentinians deserve." The Center for Legal and Social Studies (Centro de Estudios Legales y Sociales, CELS), one of the human rights organizations with the most significant influence on migration policies, questioned the introduction of the "expulsion of foreigners" in the bill and advocated eliminating the article in question.[5] In this context, some concerns and fears about their precarious immigration status and their deportability began to emerge among migrant families in working-class neighborhoods. With the NCCP reform project already started in Congress, the secretary of security once again condemned "foreign criminals" and urged deporting them. In these circumstances, the national director of immigration, Martín Arias Duval, distanced himself from the secretary of security's statements and the presidential position on the reform of the NCCP. However, a few weeks later, the NDI approved one of the measures that generated the most unrest among migrant and social organizations: the procedure involving justified suspicion in the tourist subcategory, a figure better known as the "false tourist," whose history goes back to the 1980s.[6]

These crossovers between national officials demonstrate that a politics of hostility can also be a product of the struggles between competing government sectors to monopolize migration control. This competition feeds the securitization process of migration. At times some institutional activities and certain statements by government officials in the media respond to the interests and strategies they deploy in the face of the confrontations they maintain to develop their political projects or survive bureaucratic restructuring. Thus, the "false tourist" procedure in 2014 was part of the disputes between the NDI, as an agency of the Ministry of the Interior, and the Ministry of Security. The differences between NDI Director Martín Arias Duval and Secretary of Security Sergio Berni reflected this situation. The disputes between these two government sectors recurred, with different connotations, in the succeeding administration. The initiative to create the detention center, which existed before the new leadership of the NDI, was part of the struggle to transfer the NDI to the Ministry of Security. Multiple rumors long circulated about the transfer of this agency to the security sector. In the end, the transfer never materialized. According to some interviews with key actors, the DNU, which was created within the NDI, contributed to keeping the agency in charge of migration within the sphere of the Ministry of the Interior. These battles were part of the securitization process of migration during the administration of Mauricio Macri.

Finally, although the figure of the criminal foreigner is central to the production of a politics of hostility, its legitimization requires a counterpart: a politics of selective hospitality. As demonstrated by the recent experience of several South American countries, narratives justifying control do not just exploit the migrant or foreign figure as a criminal or delinquent but *simultaneously* operated on the division between desirable and undesirable migrants. The presence of the "good migrant" is celebrated, and the arrival of the "criminal foreigner" is rejected, at the same time that, in a nationalist key, the opening or closing of the "doors" to the country is postulated for those who would come to produce, work, or study in contrast to those who would arrive to commit crimes. Thus, official bodies propose residence facilities for the former and detention, deportation, or border rejection for the latter. This aspect became evident in the current Argentinian context with the high visibility that Senegalese, Haitian, and Venezuelan migration acquired. On one hand, Senegalese street vendors have been subjected to various criminalization practices, persecution, and police violence in different urban contexts. On the other hand, the more significant influx of Haitian nationals in the leading international airports of Argentina generated a great deal of speculation among migration authorities about their possible intentions and behaviors. This suspicion at airport migration control posts translated into a systematic practice of selectivity: in a few months, there was an exponential increase in rejections at the border based on the category of "false tourists." At the same time, Venezuelan nationals arriving in Argentina were favored with "humanitarian" measures.

Detention

In August 2016, the NDI communicated through its website that it had signed an agreement with the national Ministry of Security and the Ministry of Justice and Security of the city of Buenos Aires to use a building destined for "people detained for infractions of the *Migration Law*." It was a statement "against migration irregularity," and it announced the upcoming opening of a detention center for migrants who had been served with a deportation order. This measure was in line with the punitive and police vision of migration that the statements of government officials and the intensification of daily control practices had demonstrated in previous months. Nevertheless, this official vision did not respond only to a particular conception of migration regulation but also involved struggles between different state agencies that explained, in part, one of the dimensions of the securitization process of migration in the Argentinian context. Thus, the Ministry of Security expressed a particular interest in extending its sphere of intervention and taking over migration affairs. Furthermore, according to some testimonies gathered in formal and informal exchanges with NDI officials, the idea of creating the detention center had circulated in the last years of the previous administration; however, it was discarded in the end.[7] In its argumentative strategy, based on the confrontation with organizations that defend the rights of migrants, the NDI also drew on the recommendations made by civil organizations about places of detention in the alternative report presented in previous years before the Committee on the Protection of the Rights of All Migrant Workers and Members of Their Families.[8]

However, through the agreement, not only was the property handed over, but the security forces would also be in charge of the daily administration of the detention center. Specifically, under the Ministry of Security, the Federal Police, as Auxiliary Immigration Police, would be responsible for "the guard, custody, and security of detained foreigners," in addition to dealing with transfers. Based on the criticism and pressure received, the securitization strategy turned toward the humanitarian: The Red Cross would assume the functions initially intended for the Federal Police. The appearance of this international organization in the field of humanitarianism on the national scale was evidence of the transnational dimension of the migration and border control processes. Thus, the project of creating a "detention center" expresses the local materialization of a global expansion process of detention as an unprecedented way of governing migration (De Genova 2016), which institutes new spatialities and temporalities of migration and border control. In some countries, such as Australia, the Red Cross has been in charge of monitoring migrant detention centers, under "humanitarian" precepts, for more than twenty years. In an interview in 2018, one of the arguments with which an NDI official defended the opening of the detention center and minimized its punitive aspects pointed to the role of the Red Cross and its humanitarian character as a guarantee of protection for the detainees.[9]

A detention center is a centerpiece in producing a politics of deportation since it makes official the practices of detention and expulsion from the national territory. Due to its material and symbolic implications, the agreement between the NDI, the national Ministry of Security, and the Buenos Aires Ministry of Justice and Security as an "act of institution" (Bourdieu 1999a) of detention was a crucial element in the reconfiguration process of the control regime of migrant "illegality" in current times. "Irregular migrants," who as nonnationals are intrinsically deportable, also become *detainable* subjects, deprived of "ambulatory freedom," thus creating new spatialities of control. This confinement also acquires a particular temporality: This is a detention, as the agreement says, "for the reasonable and necessary time to fulfill the purposes and scope set by the migration authority." In the migration control sphere, the practice of detention demonstrates the most evident relationship with time: waiting (Griffiths, Rogers, and Anderson 2013). In the case of administrative detention, the migration authority exercises its power by depriving people of their mobility and making them wait, using their time: The prolonged waiting for deportation means *not being in time with others* (Khosravi 2014).[10] Therefore, seen from the perspective of state power, waiting is a delay, a multiuse practice of controlling people's movement. Detention stops being exceptional to become routine, mundane, even inevitable (De Genova 2016). Although detention is concomitant to any act of deportation, in a space destined specifically for "irregular" migrants as "detainees," through its daily use it produces a new spatiality of control that reaffirms illegalization and gives a material form to the "irregular" migrant, and the deprivation of ambulatory freedom becomes proof of their social dangerousness.

The official announcement also revived the circles of migrant activism. A week after the announcement of the NDI, organizations that defend migrant human rights had already spoken out against the creation of the detention center.[11] In general, explicitly or implicitly, they opposed or rejected its creation and demanded respect for migrant human rights. The reasons were based on the linking of migration and crime, the treatment of migration as a "security problem," and the violation of human rights. They also demanded regularization as an urgent response to "irregularity" and vigorously defended the Migration Law and the national migration policies' human rights approach. One of the announcements invoked perhaps the most effective slogan in the international fight against the criminalization of migration: "No human being is illegal." In the course of the week, an international human rights organization also appeared that until then had not been present in the disputes over the political definition of migration in Argentina: Amnesty International expressed its concern and stated its opposition to the use of detention as "a form of punishment or deterrence" (Amnistía Internacional n.d.).

In this conflict between the government and social organizations, the project to create a detention center came into prominence and became a "controversy:" On the same day that several organizations demonstrated against the detention center, the most widely circulated newspaper in the country dedicated several articles to the issue. The article entitled "A Prison for Foreigners" read: "Beyond euphemisms, it will be the first prison for migrants in the country" (Abrevaya 2016). In the following days, the national subdirector of the NDI responded through a statement entitled "False Controversy About Supposed 'Prison' for Immigrants." He sought to disprove that the government would criminalize migration by creating a detention center and argued against the appellation of "prison." Over the following months, the organizations' struggle against the center used the notion of a prison to symbolize xenophobia and state violence against migrants. In retrospect, the NDI official intended to discuss a political claim on a technical level beyond legal clarifications and technicalities. In their argument in favor of the center, they appealed to the notion of "protection," a common resource for legitimizing security practices: The center was supposedly designed to "provide greater protection and comfort" to detained foreigners "during the time it took until their departure to their place of origin."[12] Numerous social organizations did not take long in questioning these statements and were intransigent in holding to their positions on the initiative. In those days, academics, activists, and migrants who identified with the defense of migrant rights launched a campaign against the detention center and promoted the signing of a petition entitled "No to the Creation of Detention Centers for Migrants in Argentina." Since its announcement in 2016, the detention center has never been inaugurated.

Deportation

During 2016, several announcements promised a tightening of migration policy. The initiative to create a detention center in the city of Buenos Aires had already alerted migrant rights organizations to the punitive character of the upcoming state measures. However, NDI officials' response to the various consultations they made through formal and informal channels regarding the modification of the Migration Law did not seem to augur a measure that would reinforce the punitive and coercive aspects of the law. The national government flatly denied that there was a project to repeal or modify it. In various spaces and meetings of migrant activism, this possibility was frequently addressed. The law reform was drawn up in absolute secrecy. In January 2017, the national government issued a DNU, citing a critical security situation. As Basok (2019) has noted, the notion of "crisis" was mobilized to justify an exceptional measure that would supposedly alleviate the current situation. The DNU modified the migration law under fallacious arguments that sought to show the close relationship between migration and "organized crime" in order to justify the strengthening of the detention and deportation procedures. The DNU was the most significant act of the politics of deportation taking shape, and it hegemonized the symbolization of the criminalization of migration.[13] Over time, this measure led to an increase in the number of deportations. However, above all, it (re)activated deportability among various migrant groups by multiplying deportation orders and different daily control practices. Like the agreement to create the detention center, the DNU officialized a regular state action that, due to the criticisms, tensions, or conflicts it can trigger, is often hidden. Unlike the limited impact of some control measures that go mostly unnoticed because they operate in the field of humanitarianism or electronic surveillance, the explicit violence of detention and deportation subjects governments to the scrutiny of local and international actors and can occasionally lead to collective mobilizations.

In the context of a politics of hostility, with the initiative to create the detention center in 2016 and DNU No. 70 in 2017, struggles were reactivated, and migrant activism spaces reorganized. Cancelation of DNU No. 70 became the pivotal point of the migrant struggles during the following two years, which reactivated the memory of the collective struggles based on mobilizations in support of migrants as understood by Martina Tazzioli (2020): the temporality of solidarity. The fight against the DNU meant that migrant rights organizations recovered the practical knowledge acquired over the years, developed different advocacy strategies, activated their national and international networks, established alliances with new actors, and formed new work and discussion spaces. In this context, based on a specific deportation measure, there emerged the most representative figure of the campaign for the repeal of the DNU, which gained many followers: Vanessa Gómez Cueva, a Peruvian woman who had been living in Argentina for more than fifteen years and who in early 2019 was deported with her baby and separated from her other two young children as a result of a criminal case for which she had served her sentence in 2014.[14] Her removal from national territory became a symbol of the regressive policy of the national government regarding the human rights of migrants that the organizations sought to denounce. Somehow, it was to be expected that, in an environment openly hostile to migrants where deportation was used to demonstrate the state's sovereign power, an emblematic figure would be produced. These emblematic figures illuminate the tension between the practices of control and those of opposition: They are the product of the conflicts and confrontations between political or security professionals and activists from social organizations. Moreover, in the heterogeneous universe of migrant activism, these figures produce cohesion beyond the differences and disagreements about the means of struggle.

In Argentina, the politics of hostility in the 1990s also had a representative figure: Juan Carlos de la Torre, an Uruguayan citizen who was summarily deported after living twenty-two years in Argentina. At that time, in a context of open criminalization of migration from neighboring countries, the practices of persecution, detention, and deportation were also justified as part of the fight against "illegal migration." The case of Juan Carlos de la Torre was one of the most important lawsuits in the history of CELS. In a context of institutional reconversion and professionalization of legal work, litigation before international bodies became an effective internationalization strategy for influencing national migration policies. In 1999, CELS presented a petition on de la Torre's behalf before the Inter-American Commission on Human Rights (IACHR). In addition to other international actions, the claim and the amicable settlement reached before the IACHR were part of the strategy in the fight for the repeal of the migration law passed during the previous military dictatorship (CELS 2008, 2013). In the wake of the amicable settlement reached shortly after the new law's approval, the Argentinian state committed itself to protect migrants' rights more broadly. This case also became a fundamental precedent for future international claims.

The gradual diversification of the field of migrant activism has condensed multiple spatialities and temporalities of migrant struggles in Argentina. In the "struggles for rights" (Caggiano 2011), particularly at times of open hostility toward migrants from official bodies, organizations of different types carried out specific actions and invented spaces that did not last for long: Whether because they fulfilled their purpose or because they did not have the necessary funding or participation to sustain them, they merged with other initiatives, or conflicts of interests and views affected their viability. Other collective organization experiences gave rise to spaces and links relatively stable over time and favored the development of advocacy strategies at the local and international levels. Since the DNU was issued in early 2017, the universe of migrant activism has reorganized, with important agreements and convergences between organizations of diverse types, beyond the expected differences and disputes in collective construction spaces. Some social organizations carried out various actions of encounter, mobilization, and street protest as part of their "Migration Is Not a Crime" campaign, whose slogan was "Migration Is a Right."[15] On the other hand, with the slogan of "Coordinated Activism," as CELS called it, human rights organizations, civil associations, migrant organizations, and research centers at public universities established new alliances. In turn, some of the migrant rights organizations, such as CELS and CAREF, drew on their extensive experience and expertise to fight for the repeal of the DNU. In addition to bringing the matter to the national courts, their fight against the DNU included an internationalization strategy that had already been effective in the past. On other occasions, CELS and CAREF, together with other national and international organizations, had already turned to bodies of the inter-American human rights system and the United Nations system to influence local policy.

Based on the experience of CELS in international litigation, the organizations sought the intervention of the IACHR to involve and exert pressure on the Argentinian government. At the request of a group of organizations, the IACHR summoned the Argentinian state to a hearing regarding the changes to the Migration Law made by the DNU. At the hearing, the representatives of the four organizations presented their arguments against the DNU and requested its annulment. The Argentinian state officials sought to justify the measure with a harmonizing notion of the relationship between control and human rights. For their part, the IACHR commissioners expressed their "extreme concern" about the regression of the Argentinian migration policy away from protecting migrant rights. Later, a larger group of organizations described for the IACHR the deportations that the Argentinian state was carrying out, among other issues. Beyond deportation statistics and legal arguments, among so many issues not considered in the deportation decisions, one that is fundamental for those who experience it is the removal of time lived or what Khosravi (2018) calls "stolen time." Vanessa Gómez Cueva had lived more than fifteen years in the country before her deportation. Khosravi uses the notion of *stealing* to highlight the fact that migrants are deprived of the time they have *saved, spent,* and *invested.* In this way, he repoliticizes "the concepts of borders and deportations that have been naturalized and depoliticized by the ideology of the nation state" (Khosravi 2018, 41). The campaign against Gómez Cueva's deportation was effective and made the state return part of the "stolen time" to her: Seven months after her deportation, the NDI lifted the reentry ban based on "exceptional humanitarian reasons" so that she could return to Argentina.[16]

As has happened in other national contexts where the migration issue has been involved in securitization processes, the DNU represented the blurring of the line between migrant law and criminal law in Argentina. This phenomenon, known as *crimmigration* (Stumpf 2006), has been analyzed in some South American countries such as Chile (Brandariz, Dufraix, and Quinteros 2018). In Argentina, some recent publications have analyzed the changes in national migration policy carried out by the political coalition of the "new right" led by President Macri. They have also analyzed thoroughly and in detail the context of the creation of the DNU, the modifications it introduced to the Migration Law, and its implications for migrant rights (Canelo, Gavazzo, and Nejamkis 2018; CELS 2017; García and Nejamkis 2018; Monclús Masó 2017; Penchaszadeh and García 2018). These works demonstrate that the duration of the administrative and legal processes was a central aspect of the reform carried out. The modifications eloquently indicated the transformation that the temporalities of the migration and border control regimes are experiencing. Thus, the DNU is an expression of the importance that time and time management have on the exercise of state control over migration and borders. At the same time, it sheds light on the struggles among various actors over the definition of its temporal dimension. The specificity of the temporality of deportation comes from the combination of the infinite prolongation in time of the deportation order, due to its lack of an expiration date, and the disputes about the possibilities of limiting or extending the time limits of the procedure. Time and the temporalities of migration and border control have received substantial theoretical discussion in recent critical literature (Griffiths, Rogers, and Anderson 2013; Mezzadra and Neilson 2017; Tazzioli 2018). For the analysis of the temporality of control, the difference established by Tazzioli (2018) between time as an object of mechanisms of control ("control *over* time") and time as a means and technology for managing migration ("control *through* time") is productive for the analysis of the specificities of the DNU.

The question of time is a central aspect of migration control and the carrying out of deportations. According to Tazzioli (2018), the key is control *over* time. The DNU refers to the duration and deadlines of the administrative procedures and legal proceedings concerning migration issues, which would be too long and would not adjust to a criterion of reasonability. According to the migration authority, the excessive length of time of "a complex recursive procedure" would have brought to the national state "severe difficulties in enforcing expulsion orders issued against people of foreign nationality." Consequently, the DNU seeks to establish a shortening of time, a moving up of deadlines through the implementation of a "special migratory procedure of a summary character" for foreigners who have been part of criminal acts and have entered "in a clandestine manner into the national territory, eluding migration control." Similarly, it seeks to lengthen the duration of detainment and reduce the time of the recursive channels to make the administrative procedure "faster," that is, increase the *tempo*. In short, the DNU seeks to regulate the temporality of the act of deportation by compressing the duration of the procedure and the time limits set for the defense, increasing the speed of the whole deportation process. Reducing the time of the recursive channels to a minimum and increasing the time of detention reveal with greater starkness the arbitrariness and the violence of this state act.

The explication in the DNU about the difficulties that the national migration authorities have in enforcing deportations is an indicator of the struggles being waged in the field of migration control and, in particular, in the realm of the judiciary. These "severe difficulties" result from a historical antagonism instituted through different conflicts between various state actors. In Argentina, since 2010, the Migration Law's *regulatory decree* has entrusted to the Ministry of Defense the legal representation of migrants in the case of denial of entry or expulsion from the national territory. With the modification introduced by DNU No. 70, the Migration Law would guarantee free assistance in administrative procedures, but it must be expressly requested. In September 2018, I met with two professionals from the Public Ministry of Defense. In the meeting, one of the defense attorneys made a statement suggesting that the DNU viewed cases through the prism of time: through what the attorneys call "interposition of resources," migrants "gain time." Extending time by filing appeals is part of the defense attorneys' strategy. The passing of time has legal effects, modifying legal relationships. Time is a valuable asset, and its accumulation can change the defended migrants' situation to their benefit. Thus, a struggle is established for the control of time that defines the temporalities of deportation in different contexts and situations: Migrant authorities invent measures to shorten the time of the deportation procedure, seeking to influence the time limits of the recursive channels, while defense attorneys generate strategies to lengthen it. The recurrent visits by NDI officials to judges and prosecutors to influence their decisions make sense in the context of these disputes.

Border Rejection

In 2013, after the celebration of Migrant Day at the central plaza of the city of Córdoba, I went to lunch at a Peruvian restaurant on the invitation of the president of the Union of Migrant Communities of Córdoba (Unión de Colectividades de Inmigrantes de Córdoba, OR UCIC). Here, I met a young Colombian man who was in Córdoba to study and work. During the conversation, I remembered some Colombian nationals rejected at the border when trying to enter Argentina and asked him if he knew of any. He spoke of his border crossing from Peru to Chile. Along the way, he spent a few days in Arica, where a friend lived and worked in a nongovernmental organization that assisted migrants, and had spoken with some of them. He explained that it was necessary to have a residence in the country to enter with no problems. Without documentation that certified residence in Argentina, entry presented more significant difficulties since the control was then stricter. As an alternative, some chose to enter Argentina through Bolivia because they were less likely to be rejected at the border.

In May 2014, I met one of the principal figures of the Haitian community in Córdoba. It had been three years since he had arrived in the city. In our first meeting, he spoke of the difficulties Haitian nationals faced in entering and residing in Argentina. He explained that even though they did not need a visa to enter, they were still "returned," and that they "returned" several Haitian men and women every week. In the case of his brother, who had arrived in Córdoba just a few days before, the authorities kept him apart and interrogated him for four hours at Ezeiza. Although he had missed his flight, he was able to continue that same day to Córdoba. Soon after, I met an NDI adviser and asked him about the border rejections. Some episodes with Haitian nationals at the border with Bolivia and Colombian nationals at the border with Chile had come to light. He explained that they were orders "from above," referencing both the Ministry of the Interior and the presidency. At the end of 2014, I met in Brasilia with a migration policy specialist with whom I had maintained a bond of trust for several years. Among other issues, we spoke about the border rejections at the airport in Quito. Employees and migration officials had told him that they kept "migrant profiles" in order to detect "false tourists" at the border control points. They used a set of criteria based on specific characteristics of foreigners that they had learned in "instruction courses." Haitian nationals were the most affected by this type of control by border agents. In 2018, rejections at the airport in Córdoba became recurrent; thereafter, these isolated conversations and exchanges began to take on other meanings and another dimension. Those rejections occurring at

Argentina's land and air borders reflected recent transformations in the South American migration and border regime.[17]

Border closures, stranded migrants, detentions, deportations, border rejections, humanitarian visas, and protests in public spaces became frequent manifestations of the changes that South American migration and border control policies were experiencing. The various border conflicts that arose from the incursion of new movements and border crossings associated with "irregularity" were represented by national and international bureaucracies as "migration crises" within the framework of action and thought schemes associated with the "governance" of migration flows. In a few years, "extraregional" migration convulsed the scene of cross-border mobilities and became a major political issue. Since the early 2010s, the turbulence generated by migration from various Asian and African countries and the Caribbean—particularly Haiti and Cuba—has disrupted the institutional arrangements of the South American migration and border regime. These moments, which had not gone unnoticed by the migration authorities of different national governments during previous years, quickly became a matter of regional interest when they began to perceive their expansion and "irregular" character.

The expansion of "extraregional migration" in the South American space as a new and recent phenomenon gave rise to various struggles for a movement that involved Caribbean and African migrants as illegalized and racialized subjects. The dispersion of Haitian migrants in the region increased considerably after the visa exemption came into force in Ecuador in 2008, the earthquake in Haiti in 2010, and the changes in the admission policy of French Guiana in 2012. These transformations in the South American space derived from struggles for movement had a fundamental impact on the renewal of the uses and justifications of the consular visa requirement to prevent movement from the places of origin and to decrease the arrival of Haitian, Senegalese, and Dominican migrants, among other "extraregionals." In this context, in 2018, after a period that saw an enormous number of rejections at international airports, the governments of Chile and Argentina began to demand, almost simultaneously, a consular visa for Haitian citizens under the pretext of humanitarian protection for the migrant population (cf. Trabalón 2018). Similarly, in Chile, as a measure complementary to the consular visa, the national government organized, with the support of the International Organization for Migration, a "humanitarian plan of orderly return" aimed explicitly at illegalized Haitian migrants (cf. Stang, Lara, and Andrade 2020). This action was justified by "the national interest in providing the country with an orderly, safe, and regular migration," from "a global perspective of migration governance." In Argentina, Haitians' consular visa requirement was established a year and a half after the NDI initiated a migration regularization process "for humanitarian reasons" aimed explicitly at Haitian nationality citizens for six months.[18] The sequence of measures revealed the changing and contingent character of control in the face of movement: regularization, border rejections, and visa imposition. Based on the statements made by officials in the press, it is possible to notice the recurrence of the notions of "protection" and "prevention" in the means of legitimizing security measures: The visa application process was intended to protect them from becoming victims of human trafficking and smuggling, and to prevent possible crimes.

The reasons that migration authorities provided for imposing a visa were the "increase in passenger flow" from Haiti and the increasing rejections based on the concept of the "false tourist."[19] On the day the measure was officially announced, several media outlets published absolute and relative figures on the entries and rejections of Haitian nationals during the previous years and estimates for 2018 that would support the official argument. However, it is not necessarily the absolute quantity of migrants of one nationality or its proportion concerning other nationalities that determines the activation or deactivation of certain control practices. Instead, it is the accumulated volume of certain nationalities in a limited space-time interval. In these cases, the rejections are related to the speed of people's movement, expressed in the daily, weekly, or monthly growth rate. What counts is not the annual statistics the NDI produces but the daily register handled by inspectors, supervisors, and heads of regional offices. In turn, the logic of control receives feedback and leads to the intervention of agents from various spheres of the state: Those in charge of verifying the documentation and identification of persons generate "rejections," and then that accumulation of rejections serves as the basis for higher authorities to resolve visa imposition "inward" and negotiate it "outward" with the diplomatic counterpart. The accumulation of "rejections at the border" is not the result of an individual or random practice. It is an increase not only in the "flow of passengers" but also in the flow of travelers with certain preestablished national origins viewed as suspicious or subject to criminalization and racialization processes that are concomitant with the border control regimes. In May 2018, a memorandum from the NDI required staff to "take extreme care with the entry of Haitian nationals and any other sensitive nationality (Middle Eastern, Colombian, African, among others) to the Republic of Argentina." It established that "a lack of examination or deficient examination" would be considered "major offenses."[20] This memorandum confirmed the intensification and selectivity of the migration controls that Haitian nationals were already experiencing at airports in Argentina.

Airports have become part of detention geographies (Martin and Mitchelson 2009) and the deportation infrastructure (Walters 2018b). In Argentina, the country's main airport terminals have adopted biometric technology and adapted their facilities according to international recommendations for movement control and surveillance. Innovations in airport security have led to substantial changes in spatial and temporal control practices, which exacerbate the anxieties experienced by travelers who are suspected of being "false tourists." An episode at the Córdoba city airport reveals specific details about how the spatialities and temporalities of control are usually experienced at the time of entry through confinement, waiting, and separation of individuals or groups in a state of total uncertainty. On the night of April 17, 2018, accompanied by Jean, I met with Willy, who had arrived in Córdoba from Haiti around two years before. Willy was a street vendor. He had the temporary residence he had obtained the year before through the migration regularization plan. Ruth, his partner, had just arrived from Haiti with their youngest daughter. Both were on the verge of being rejected at the border. In the end, after waiting several hours, they were allowed to enter. Nobody could explain the confusing situation they had experienced or what had finally helped authorize their entry.

The Copa Airlines flight had landed a half hour after midnight. Ruth and her daughter got off the plane and went to the documentation checkpoints. Haitian women and men—"*Black people*," emphasized Willy—were made to line up separately from the rest. When Ruth went to the checkpoint and presented their passports and the letter of invitation her partner had sent her, the inspector asked her to wait right there. She was then taken aside and escorted to a room where her wait was prolonged. Meanwhile, Ruth communicated via WhatsApp with her partner, who was waiting outside with a friend. Other Haitians were also waiting there. Hours passed, and no one informed them of anything. It was a period filled with anguish, loneliness, and uncertainty. Furthermore, there was no interpreter or inspector at the airport who spoke French. Ruth did not understand Spanish; she spoke Creole and French. Since Willy's friend was better at Spanish, he asked to speak to the inspector on the phone to explain the situation. However, she refused to talk to him. Later, an airline employee informed Willy that his partner was not being allowed entry due to a (legal) "cause" stemming from a conflict he had had with a municipal agent on a public thoroughfare while selling merchandise.

After a few hours, Ruth and her daughter were taken upstairs and placed in line for the next flight. It was only then that she learned they were being sent back to Haiti. At one point, an NDI employee came for her and took her and her daughter out of the line. Finally, after more than four hours since their airplane had landed, they were allowed entry. About ten Haitians were not allowed entry and were sent back. During the conversation, I asked Willy how he explained what had happened. He answered, smiling, "It is not my country . . ." Compared to the time when Willy had entered the country two years before, he and Jean agreed that it had become more difficult to enter now. A friend of Willy's mentioned an acquaintance who had been rejected at the airport the previous Saturday and another who had arrived in Buenos Aires on the day of our meeting. During the meeting, I noticed that they were a bit disconcerted: they wondered what was necessary to enter and pointed out that the requirements were not clear because they were always changing. At times, it seemed that the letter of invitation was enough, and at others, it seemed that a hotel reservation would make it easier for them to gain entry. Willy's friend was waiting for arrival of his partner, who had a ticket for May 19. With the increase in the number of border rejections at the airport, he was afraid she would not be allowed entry. The NDI memorandum notifying inspectors of "sensitive nationalities" such as Haitians was already in circulation.

Conclusions

Since the approval of the migration law that came into force in early 2004, there has seemed to be a certain *objective complicity* between the various actors involved in the control of migration and borders to maintain the universe of detentions, deportations, and rejections at the border on the plane of the unspoken, the invisible, and the exceptional. In addition to the tasks of legitimizing violence carried out by states, the omissions and silence surrounding punitive and coercive state actions has indicated an effective work of concealment. Although in those years, specifically in 2014, there were already some indicators of the changes that the field of migration control was experiencing, it was difficult to foresee what was to come. Later, the spectacularization of migration and border control, whose deployment was linked to the initiative of creating a detention center and the approval of a provision that sought to tighten the restrictive and punitive aspects of the current migration law, prompted the consideration that, in terms of process, this was the configuration of a politics of hostility toward migration. Under this policy, in a regional context that had already demonstrated the intensification of state violence toward migrants for some years, there was a redefinition and a strengthening of the division between "desirable" and "undesirable" migrants whose most evident manifestation was the figure of the criminal foreigner. This chapter seeks to demonstrate that this politics of hostility was not the result of the accumulation or sum of hostile actions and attitudes toward migrants, but that it was a specific mode of intervening politically in the field of migration control. While its production is based on migrant "illegality," the condition of deportability, determined by the division between nationals and nonnationals, was differentially and effectively exploited by state and nonstate actors. The politics of hostility also created conditions forming new spatialities and temporalities of migration or border control and migrant struggles.

This chapter aims to contribute to understanding the intensifying process of migration control in the Argentinian context in a brief period at different scales. These changes are attributable to the actions, strategies, and struggles of multiple actors interested in imposing their definition of the *things to be done* and how they should be done. The Argentinian national experience provides numerous elements with which to observe the long-term transformation of the control regime of migrant "illegality," the formation of a politics of deportation, and the overlap between securitization practices and humanitarian narratives. These far-reaching processes are intertwined with the forms and justifications that control practices acquire in specific contexts or situations. In the deployment of a politics of hostility, there were moments of the exaltation of punishment or "punitive pride" through the theatricalization of detentions and deportations. On the other hand, the exploration of the space-time relationship makes it possible to notice transformations in the political field of migrations and borders linked with the production of new spatialities and temporalities of control: a detention center destined for "irregular" migrants with a deportation order; specific waiting places for suspicious travelers at airports; dissimilar spatial practices of migrant struggles; measurement of the speed of "migration flows"; disputes over the definition of administrative deadlines and waiting periods; delays and interruptions in the detention and deportation processes. Finally, the changing spatial and temporal character of control demonstrates the need to understand the heterogeneity of migration and border control practices in an articulated and relational manner, based on the stability or instability demonstrated by the measures that seek to facilitate or impede the entry or residential status of one person or others.

NOTES

This chapter began to be developed during a stay at King's College London in 2019, made possible through an external scholarship from the National Scientific and Technical Research Council (Consejo Nacional de Investigaciones Científicas y Técnicas, or Conicet), Argentina. Special thanks to some of the people who made my stay in London a special moment in my personal and professional life: Didier Bigo, Elspeth Guild, Martina Tazzioli, Simone Vegliò, and Emma McCluskey. I would also like to thank four important people for carrying out the fieldwork: Marta Guerreño, Youby Jean-Baptiste, Valeria Roldán, and Rosa Quiroga. Thanks also to all those people who dedicated their time and who, on occasion, received me for long conversations and interviews. This chapter was also enriched by conversations with Paul Hathazy in the framework of a joint project on migration and security policies. Further thanks to Lourdes Basualdo for the careful reading and review of a preliminary version of this text. Finally, I dedicate this chapter to the memory of the anthropologist Daniel Etcheverry.

1. Without an exhaustive development, I have previously used the notion of "politics of hostility" in Domenech 2019 and París Pombo, Domenech, and Bélanger 2020.

2. I use "struggles for movement" in the sense proposed by Papadopoulos and Tsianos (2013), Martignoni and Papadopoulos (2014), and Tazzioli (2015).

3. This statement does not intend to ignore research carried out at that time that addressed the issue of deportations in the recent Argentinian context. The dissertation of García (2013), for example, on the new migration policy in Argentina, is worthy of note.

4. The notion of spectacularization is used here following De Genova (2013), who speaks of "spectacles of migrant 'illegality.'" These "spectacles" confer visibility on migrant "illegality."

5. The center presents in detail its arguments against Article 35 of the document in "Proposals and Observations on the Reform of the National Code of Criminal Procedure" (November 2014), https://www.cels.org.ar/web/wp-content/uploads/2016/06 /CELS-Propuestas-y-observaciones-CPPN-final.pdf.

6. By applying this procedure, the migration control agents decide on the admission of a foreigner suspected of intending to enter or remain in the national territory or to obtain a "tourist" visa, without the "real intention" of pursuing "rest" or "leisure" activity. In the case of "justified suspicion," the inspector must notify the supervisor, who will decide on the "rejection of the foreigner." In the case of rejection, "redirection," as it is known in administrative jargon, takes place. For an analysis of the "false tourist" figure in Argentina, see Alvites Baiadera 2018.

7. The formal interview took place in October 2016 in the city of Buenos Aires, together with Janneth Clavijo.

8. Alternative report for the Committee on the Protection of the Rights of All Migrant Workers and Members of Their Families, 15th session, Evaluation on Argentina, CELS, Comisión Argentina para Refugiados y Migrantes (CAREF), Universidad Nacional de Lanús (UNLA), 2011. One of the issues this document notes is that no "structure" in the country could "be used by the migration authority and judges who issue detention orders, in accordance with the mandates established in the law and the regulations."

9. This interview was held in the office of a regional delegate of the NDI in August 2018.

10. In this brief text, Khosravi reflects on the meaning of waiting for "undocumented" migrants, asylum seekers, and other displaced people. He draws on Bourdieu's (1999b) analysis of time in his book *Meditaciones pascalianas* (Pascalian meditations).

11. In the days following the announcement, the program on immigration and asylum of UNLA, CELS, the Argentinian Commission for Refugees and Migrants (CAREF), the Office

of the Ombudsman of the City of Buenos Aires, Amnesty International, and Abogadas y Abogados del Noroeste Argentino en Derechos Humanos y Estudios Sociales (Andhes) spoke out.

12. "False Controversy About Supposed 'Prison' for Migrants," National Directorate of Migration, Buenos Aires, August 29, 2016.

13. Although this section focuses on deportation, it is necessary to mention that DNU No. 70 modified the requirements for access to Argentinian nationality by excluding the possibility that the required years of residency be considered regardless of the applicant's administrative situation. The DNU now states that foreigners must prove their residence as "permanent residents" or "temporary residents." This modification clearly manifests the reconfiguration of the control regime of migrant "illegality."

14. An important aspect of the case of Vanessa Gómez Cueva, which cannot be fully addressed here due to space constraints, concerns the political effectiveness of the campaign based on her status as a woman and a mother. Her case and the arguments used against her deportation provide various elements for the discussion of the legitimization and normalization of deportation based on the division between those who deserve or do not deserve such punishment. Cf. Lecadet 2018; Walters 2018a.

15. On the new configurations of migrant struggles in Argentina between 2016 and 2019, see Rho 2020.

16. Provision No. 3.767 (August 30, 2019), National Directorate of Migration, Buenos Aires.

17. On the South American migration and border regime, see Domenech 2019.

18. Provision No. 1.143 (March 20, 2017), National Directorate of Migration, Buenos Aires.

19. On August 21, several articles were published in national and regional newspapers that referred to the "increase in the flow" of Haitian passengers or migrants. See, for example, "Tourist Visa Will Be Required for Haitians Who Want to Enter the Country," *Clarín*, August 21, 2018; and "The Government Imposes a Tourist Visa for Haitians Who Want to Enter the Country in Order to Regulate the Entry of Migrants," *La Nación*, August 21, 2018.

20. Memorandum No. 192 (May 10, 2018), National Directorate of Migration, Buenos Aires.

REFERENCES

Abrevaya, Sebastian. 2016. "Una cárcel para extranjeros." *Página 12*, August 26.
Alvites Baiadera, Angélica. 2018. "Extranjeros bajo la lupa: La figura del 'falso turista' en Argentina." *Horizontes Decoloniales* 4 (4): 39–62.
Amnistía Internacional. n.d. "Amnistía Internacional observa con preocupación la creación de un centro de detención para personas migrantes." Accessed August 26, 2016. https://amnistia. org.ar/amnistia-internacional-observa-con-preocupacion-la-creacion-de-un-centro-de-detencion-para-personas-migrantes/.
Balzacq, Thierry, Tugba Basaran, Didier Bigo, Emmanuel-Pierre Guittet, and Christian Olsson. 2010. "Security Practices." In *Oxford Research Encyclopedia of International Studies*. Oxford: Oxford University Press; International Studies Association.

Basok, Tanya. 2019. "Regional Migration and Argentina's 'Hospitality' in Crisis." In *The Oxford Handbook of Migration Crises*, edited by Cecilia Menjívar, Marie Ruiz, and Immanuel Ness. Oxford: Oxford University Press.

Bigo, Didier. 2002. "Security and Immigration: Toward a Critique of the Governmentality of Unease." *Alternatives* 27 (1): 63–92.

Bigo, Didier. 2010. "Freedom and Speed in Enlarged Borderzones." In *The Contested Politics of Mobility: Borderzones and Irregularity*, edited by Vicki Squire, 51–70. Abingdon, UK: Routledge.

Bigo, Didier, and Emma McCluskey. 2018. "What Is a PARISS Approach to (In)Securitization? Political Anthropological Research for International Sociology." In *The Oxford Handbook of International Security*, edited by Alexandra Gheciu and William C. Wohlforth, 116–30. Oxford: Oxford University Press.

Bourdieu, Pierre. 1999a. *¿Qué significa hablar? Economía de los intercambios lingüísticos*. Madrid: Akal.

Bourdieu, Pierre. 1999b. *Meditaciones pascalianas*. Barcelona: Anagrama.

Brandariz, José A., Roberto Dufraix, and Daniel Quinteros. 2018. "La expulsión judicial en el sistema penal chileno: ¿Hacia un modelo de crimmigration?" *Política Criminal* 13 (26): 739–70.

Caggiano, Sergio. 2011. "Migrantes y lucha por los derechos: Posibilidades y limitaciones de la articulación entre organizaciones." Paper presented at the IV Congreso de la Red Internacional de Migración y Desarrollo, Facultad Latinoamericana de Ciencias Sociales–Ecuador, Quito, May 18–20.

Canelo, Brenda, Natalia Gavazzo, and Lucila Nejamkis. 2018. "Nuevas (viejas) políticas migratorias en la Argentina del cambio." *Si Somos Americanos*, 18 (1): 150–182.

CELS (Centro de Estudios Legales y Sociales). 2008. *La lucha por el derecho: Litigio estratégico y derechos humanos*. Buenos Aires: Siglo XXI.

CELS (Centro de Estudios Legales y Sociales). 2013. *Migrantes*. Buenos Aires.

CELS (Centro de Estudios Legales y Sociales). 2017. *Derechos humanos en la Argentina: Informe 2017*. Buenos Aires: Siglo XXI.

Conlon, Deirdre, Nancy Hiemstra, and Alison Mountz. 2017. "Spatial Control: Geographical Approaches to the Study of Immigration Detention." *Global Detention Project Working Paper* 24: 1–17.

De Genova, Nicholas. 2013. "Spectacles of Migrant 'Illegality': The Scene of Exclusion, the Obscene of Inclusion." *Ethnic and Racial Studies* 36 (7): 1180–98.

De Genova, Nicholas. 2016. "Detention, Deportation, and Waiting: Toward a Theory of Migrant Detainability." *Global Detention Project Working Paper* 18: 1–10.

De Genova, Nicholas, Sandro Mezzadra, and John Pickles, eds. 2015. "New Keywords: Migration and Borders." *Cultural Studies* 29 (1): 55–87.

Domenech, Eduardo. 2011. "Crónica de una 'amenaza' anunciada: Inmigración e ilegalidad; visiones de Estado en la Argentina contemporánea." In *La construcción social del sujeto migrante en América Latina: Prácticas, representaciones y categorías*, edited by Bela Feldman-Bianco, Liliana Rivera Sánchez, Carolina Stefoni, and Marta Villa, 31–77. Quito: Facultad Latinoamericana de Ciencias Sociales–Ecuador, Consejo Latinoamericano de Ciencias Sociales, AND Universidad Alberto Hurtado.

Domenech, Eduardo. 2019. "Contested Spaces of Mobility: The South American Migration and Border Regime." Paper presented at the First International Workshop on Contested Territories, University of Leeds, Leeds, May 20–21.

García, Lila. 2013. "Nueva política migratoria y derechos de la movilidad: Implementación y desafíos de una política basada en derechos humanos a través de las acciones ante el Poder Judicial (2004–2010)." PhD diss., Universidad de Buenos Aires.

García, Lila, and Lucila Nejamkis. 2018. "Regulación migratoria en la Argentina actual: Del 'modelo' regional al recorte de derechos." *Autoctonía: Revista de Ciencias Sociales e Historia* 2 (2): 219–41.

Griffiths, Melanie, Ali Rogers, and Bridget Anderson. 2013. "Migration, Time, and Temporalities: Review and Prospect." *COMPAS Research Resources Paper* 3: 199–217.

Hess, Sabine. 2012. "De-Naturalising Transit Migration: Theory and Methods of an Ethnographic Regime Analysis." *Population, Space, and Place* 18 (4): 428–40.

Hess, Sabine, and Bernd Kasparek. 2017. "Under Control? Or Border (as) Conflict: Reflections on the European Border Regime." *Social Inclusion* 5 (3): 58–68.

Huysmans, Jef, and Vicki Squire. 2009. "Migration and Security." In *Handbook of Security Studies*, edited by Myriam Dunn Cavelty and Victor Mauer, 185–95. London: Routledge.

Khosravi, Sharam. 2014. "Waiting." In *Migration: The COMPAS Anthology*, edited by Bridget Anderson and Michael Keith, 74–75. Oxford: Centre on Migration, Policy, and Society (COMPAS).

Khosravi, Sharam. 2018. "Stolen Time." *Radical Philosophy* 2 (3): 38–41.

Lecadet, Clara. 2018. "Deportation, Nation State, Capital: Between Legitimisation and Violence." *Radical Philosophy* 2 (3): 28–32.

Martignoni, Martina, and Dimitris Papadopoulos. 2014. "Genealogies of Autonomous Mobility." In *Routledge Handbook of Global Citizenship Studies*, edited by Engin Isin and Peter Nyers, 38–48. London: Routledge.

Martin, Lauren L., and Matthew L. Mitchelson. 2009. "Geographies of Detention and Imprisonment: Interrogating Spatial Practices of Confinement, Discipline, Law, and State Power." *Geography Compass* 3 (1): 459–77.

McNevin, Anne. 2022. "Mobility and Its Discontents: Seeing Beyond International Space and Progressive Time." *Environment and Planning C: Politics and Space* 40 (5): 994–1011.

Mezzadra, Sandro, and Brett Neilson. 2017. *La frontera como método o la multiplicación del trabajo*. Madrid: Traficantes de Sueños.

Monclús Masó, Marta. 2017. "La reforma de la Ley de Migraciones mediante Decreto de Necesidad y Urgencia: Un retroceso en la política de derechos humanos." *Revista Argentina de Teoría Jurídica* 18:166–79.

NDI (National Directorate of Immigration). 2016. "Complementación estatal en aplicación de la ley migratoria. Un inmueble será destinado al alojamiento de infractores a la Ley 25.871 (State support in enforcing immigration law. A property will be used to house people who break Law 25.871). August 19.

Papadopoulos, Dimitris, and Vassilis S. Tsianos. 2013. "After Citizenship: Autonomy of Migration, Organisational Ontology, and Mobile Commons." *Citizenship Studies* 17 (2): 178–96.

París Pombo, Dolores, Eduardo Domenech, and Daniele Bélanger. 2020. "Refugios y refugiados." *Encartes* 3 (5): 238–55.

Penchaszadeh, Ana Paula, and Lila García. 2018. "Política migratoria y seguridad en Argentina hoy: ¿El paradigma de derechos humanos en jaque?" *URVIO: Revista Latinoamericana de Estudios de Seguridad* 23:91–109.

Rho, María Gabriela. 2020. "De las luchas por una nueva ley de migraciones al Paro Migrante: Nuevas configuraciones de las luchas migrantes en Argentina." *REMHU: Revista Interdisciplinar da Mobilidade Humana* 28 (58): 127–45.

Sayad, Abdelmalek. 2008. "Estado, nación e inmigración: El orden nacional ante el desafío de la inmigración." *Apuntes de Investigación del CECYP* 13:101–16.

Sciortino, Giuseppe. 2004. "Immigration in a Mediterranean Welfare State: The Italian Experience in Comparative Perspective." *Journal of Comparative Policy Analysis: Research and Practice* 6 (2): 111–29.

Stang, Fernanda, Antonia Lara, and Marcos Andrade. 2020. "Retórica humanitaria y expulsabilidad: Migrantes haitianos y gobernabilidad migratoria en Chile." *Si Somos Americanos: Revista de Estudios Transfronterizos* 20 (1): 176–201.

Stumpf, Juliet. 2006. "The Crimmigration Crisis: Immigrants, Crime, and Sovereign Power." *American University Law Review* 56 (2): 367–419.

Tazzioli, Martina. 2015. "Which Europe? Migrants' Uneven Geographies and Counter-Mapping at the Limits of Representation." *Movements: Journal for Critical Migration and Border Regime Studies* 1 (2).

Tazzioli, Martina. 2018. "The Temporal Borders of Asylum: Temporality of Control in the EU Border Regime." *Political Geography* 64:13–22.

Tazzioli, Martina. 2020. "What Is Left of Migrants' Spaces? Transversal Alliances and the Temporality of Solidarity." *Political Anthropological Research on International Social Sciences (PARISS)* 1 (1): 137–61.

Trabalón, Carina. 2018. "Política de visado y regulación de las fronteras: Un análisis desde la movilidad de haitianos en Sudamérica." *Polis: Revista Latinoamericana* 51:163–86.

Tsianos, Vassilis, and Serhat Karakayali. 2010. "Transnational Migration and the Emergence of the European Border Regime: An Ethnographic Analysis." *European Journal of Social Theory* 13 (3): 373–87.

Walters, William. 2018a. "Expulsion, Power, Mobilisation." *Radical Philosophy* 2 (3): 33–37.

Walters, William. 2018b. "Aviation as Deportation Infrastructure: Airports, Planes, and Expulsion." *Journal of Ethnic and Migration Studies* 44 (16): 2796–2817.

9

Wolf in Sheep's Clothing

TRANSFORMATIONS OF REFUGE THROUGH
THE PROTECTION-CONTROL RELATIONSHIP
IN THE SOUTH AMERICAN SPACE

Janneth Clavijo

Asylum regulation in the Latin American context, and particularly in South America, shows multiple transformations at different historical moments linked to socio-political conflicts that have had repercussions on the volume and dynamics of displacement throughout the region, including the crisis in Nicaragua and El Salvador in the 1980s, the armed conflict in Colombia and its impact on border countries, and the increase and centrality of migrations of Venezuelan origin since 2015. The configuration of regional protection policies shows a constant production and redefining of concepts, practices, and categories for the management of refuge, together with the coexistence of long-standing notions such as territorial asylum (specific to the Inter-American system). At the same time, the political treatment of the refugee issue in the region resonates, and has increasingly converged, with global guidelines associated with the 1951 Convention Relating to the Status of Refugees, the 1967 Protocol, and the actions of the UN High Commissioner for Refugees (UNHCR), especially since the Cartagena

Declaration (UNHCR 1984). The declaration is a key instrument that established new criteria for defining refugee status and has served as a basis for subsequent political agreements and action plans at the regional level.[1]

In the field of international migration policies, particularly those movements categorized as forced, the relationship among the origins, causes, and conditions of displacement is constantly being redefined, as are the criteria that operate in the selection of people recognized as deserving international protection. Just as displacement is characterized by its dynamism, the categorical systems that nominate and differentiate it are constantly being renewed and (re)interpreted. This chapter explores the transformations—of policies and the figure—of refuge in South America by analyzing the relationship between protection and control of mobility on one hand and the reconfiguration of the notion of protection at different historical moments on the other.

The construction of diagnoses and responses elaborated by various actors in answer to questions of why and how people are displaced or should be displaced reveals a constant political dispute. This dispute encompasses definitions of and intervention in populations and their displacement based on the assignment of categories such as *refugee, migrant, displaced person*, and *asylum seeker*. At the same time, the classificatory exercise leads to the establishment of criteria that privilege some aspects of migrants' trajectories and conceal others. Therefore, in this analysis, the categorical system is taken up again as part of the field of inquiry in order to understand the transformations of the refugee question in South America.

The notion of protection has been central to the construction of asylum systems and refugee status at global, regional, national, and local levels. Access to so-called international protection has involved at least two initial issues: first, establishing selection criteria and diagnostic bodies for the discernment of qualified causes for the validation of the request for protection and the justification of displacement; and, second, determining to what extent a threat or danger exists of which one is a victim and from which one needs to be protected. The definitions and representations surrounding protection (or its denial) are linked to other variables in the swarm of categories and relations in what I understand as the regime of migrations and borders in the South American space (Domenech 2019). In this sense, one quality of the notion of protection is its polysemic nature and its connection to the forms that control takes in the management of displacement. Although the asylum systems in the different countries of the region have unique historical features, and their development has been heterogeneous and variable, understanding how they work increasingly involves paying attention to the connections with regional and global refugee and protection policies.

In this sense, as Domenech (2019, 2021) argues, the configuration of the regional migration and border regime is associated with the processes of regionalization and internationalization of migration control policies and practices and the construction of a South American space as a "border zone" (Domenech 2021).

In this chapter, I explore the production and political use of definitions, categories, and practices of control of displacement categorized as forced. Particularly, I examine the transformations in the political treatment of refuge on a regional scale, based on three key moments that enable us to problematize the ways in which protection and control have been mutually constituted: In the first moment, during the 1980s, the expanded definition of the condition of refuge took shape and the Cartagena Declaration (UNHCR 1984) was adopted. During this turning point, the leading role of the UNHCR was established and subsequent regional instruments for refugee management were founded. The second moment refers to the centrality of the notion of *mixed flows* during the early years of this century and its implications for the processes of selection and categorization of displacement. The third moment is the recent context, in which migrations of Venezuelan origin and the notion of temporary protection as a way of managing the presence of migrant populations are especially relevant. Two questions that guide this problematization are: How is the movement controlled by the asylum system and access to mechanisms associated with protection in South America? And what effects has this movement control had on the migration and border regime?

It is important to clarify that beyond the trajectories and self-perceptions of migrants, I seek to question the exercise of categorizing migrants and their displacements. This implies questioning the contingent readings and interpretations that have been constructed about the populations and the contexts of origin, transit, and destination. These readings are inextricably linked to the ways of differentiating, qualifying, and weighing certain attributes, which operate in the modes of political legitimization in the assignment of migratory categories.

From this analysis I argue: (1) that the meanings and modalities that protection has acquired at different times reveal the dynamism and permanent transformation of asylum systems, in terms not only of access and recognition of refugee status but also of the guarantees that this status entails; (2) that there is a dynamic relationship between protection and control of mobility that adopts diverse folds and that underlies the safeguarding of national order; and (3) that the dynamics of displacement, as movement for the preservation of life, overflow the frameworks imposed for its management, shake up the border regime, and induce new sutures—new arrangements and adjustments in the exercise of reconfiguration and permanent reaction of the regime—such as the production of categories that diversify the forms of *protection and control*, in some cases dissociated from asylum and the figure of the refugee.

This chapter is has two parts. First, I clarify the theoretical-methodological lens I use to investigate the relationship between protection and control, as well as the ways in which protection is produced and entwined with state order and security. Far from understanding this protection-control relationship as fixed or monolithic, I seek to understand it as dynamic within the framework of the migration and border regime. Second, I examine three moments that reveal transformations in the narratives, rationalities, and practices of access to international protection and refugee status in regional policies.

For the development of this work, I opted for a qualitative methodology based on the analysis of a documentary corpus that recovers various materials referring to the guidelines, definitions, and practices of institutional actors involved in the issue of refuge and international protection, in particular, the United Nations High Commissioner for Refugees, as the lead agency for the protection of asylum-seeking and refugee populations; declarations and guiding instruments addressing the refugee issue in the region, including the Cartagena Declaration (1984); the Mexico Plan of Action (PAM 2004); the Brasilia Plan of Action (2014); the 100 Points Brasilia document (2018); and information gathered in the fieldwork of the collective research project "Borders in Dispute: Policies of Control, Practices of Containment, and Strategies and Experiences of Mobility in the South American Space."[2] Furthermore, in the final section, I recover materials that allow us to illustrate the multiscale production of the protection-control relationship between different actors and spheres of government associated with the regulation of mobility, in particular, the Interagency Group on Mixed Migratory Flows (GIFMM), the Regional Interagency Coordination Platform for Refugees and Migrants from Venezuela (or R4V platform), and the Temporary Protection Statute for Venezuelan Migrants (ETPV), adopted in the Colombian context.

Tools for (Re)Thinking the Relationship Between
Protection and Control in the Field of Refuge

This analysis is inspired by the problematization that critical migration and refugee studies have raised in relation to protection (Bigo 2006; De Genova 2021; Federico and Hess 2021; Hess and Kasparek 2017; Huysmans 2006; Picozza 2017; Scheel, Garelli, and Tazzioli 2015; Scheel and Ratfisch 2013; Scheel and Squire 2014; Tazzioli and Garelli 2019) and to the configuration of the South American migration and border regime (Domenech 2013, 2019), understood as a space of "conflict, negotiation and contestation between various actors who dispute the political definition of migration and border" (Domenech and Dias 2020, 2).

Framed within a critical perspective of the regime (Hess 2012; Sciortino 2004), this research focuses on the production of intervention categories associated with the notion of protection. Categories have been linked to different statutes, actors, and practices in the complex and dynamic assemblage of the migration and border regime. From this perspective, far from being the product of a preestablished and static order—as it is usually proposed at the normative level—the regime is mutating. Rather than explaining transformations along an evolutionary or predictable line, this perspective focuses on the changes in the dynamics of displacement and the emerging conflicts and treatments for the regulation of movements. This focus implies understanding categorization (in this case, linked to refuge and protection) as a political act and, at the same time, detaching oneself from the categories in order to denaturalize their meaning and functioning.

A first matter to problematize is the classification of migrations as forced or economic; at this point I resort to the idea of "preservation migrations" (Clavijo, Ceballos, and González 2022) as a way of naming the displacements that people undertake to guarantee and reproduce life through movement. While all movements may involve some form of preservation, in this analysis, I focus on displacements that take place from and in contexts that are marked by the deepening of violence and various forms of precariousness, situations that coerce the ways and times of mobility. This concept is in dialogue with Varela's (2020) ideas about care strategies and the forms of organization—individual and collective—associated with migration in order to preserve life (247). The idea of preservation migrations allows us to problematize the assignment of categories associated with forced migration as given, eminently apolitical categories, detached from the dynamics and effects of the state order.

From the notion of preservation migrations, it is possible to examine the narratives that are constructed around suffering, compassion, vulnerability, and the political practices that reproduce them, rather than assuming them as natural characteristics of migrants and contexts of origin. Likewise, understanding displacement as strategies of preservation emphasizes movement as a process prior to the assignment of governmental categories and practices of control over the lives of those who move. In other words, the political treatment of migration has a direct and daily impact on these populations, because their lives take place in movement, and are transformed and preserved through movement. People who are displaced share conditions of precariousness and violence articulated with the increased use of restrictive practices on their displacement. Despite these restrictions, they also find themselves in the mechanisms of protection and in the strategies to sustain their lives in movement. In this sense, displacement as a form of preservation can also be thought of as a way of protecting life and the freedom (with greater or lesser leeway) to choose how and where to sustain it.

Likewise, I examine forced migration and refuge as institutional categories of life administration through the control of movement. Categories that subordinate populations to certain positions of entreaty (Butler 2006; Fassin 2010, 2016) assimilate them to *burdens* on which discourses and instruments based on cooperation and shared responsibility are based. The labeling of migrations as forced (Zetter 2007) emphasizes the idea of emergency, exceptionality (Ticktin 2015), and the unpredictability of movements (Zolberg 1983), that is, the overflow that disrupts the productivity and nationalist logics to which migration dynamics have been pressed to conform. If movement is a strategy for the preservation of human life, the categories that operate in protection policies reveal a tension—in permanent reconfiguration—between the migrations of preservation and the ways sought to control and order displacements within the framework of the migration and border regime.

Protection policies associated with the recognition of refugee status can be understood as ways of managing the *overflow* that certain displacements entail within the confines of the state. As the analyses of Domenech and Dias (2020) in South America evidence, movements exceed the margins of bureaucratic categories; thus, the exercise of recategorization reveals the circumstantial nature of the regime, in which expectations about the purposes and conduct (appropriate, positive, legitimate) of people on the move are constantly created and disputed—between different actors and alliances. Following Huysmans (2006), the way in which political agency is structured and organized in protection policies affects the validation of demands, rationales, and who, how, and by whom they deserve to be protected (Huysmans 2006, 2). Considering protection policies as dynamic terrains of a dispute between actors (with different interests) within the migration regime puts under scrutiny the capacity for intervention and the hierarchies between the different bodies involved in the exercise of administering protection instruments and thus controlling asylum systems.

According to Huysmans (2006) the notion of protection policy highlights the politically contested nature of protection claims, both in their legitimacy and in the techniques for administering them. Protection policies in asylum systems can be understood as part of the control mechanisms that reinstitute state order. Therefore, instead of thinking of protection and control as parallel or antagonistic notions, I suggest delving into the way in which they are co-constituted and entwined in the *protection-control* relationship, which not only problematizes the separation between protection and control but also highlights the existence of an interlocking link in which protection and control function as a unit associated with migrations produced as *forced*. At the same time, this protection-control relationship is linked to—and influences—historical changes in the regional migration and border regime and is consequently a dynamic relationship that takes on particular forms in different historical contexts and operates as part of the regional migration and border regime.

In the case of international protection policies, the notion of protection is also characterized by its nationalistic nature (Scheel, Garelli and Tazzioli 2015; Bigo 2006). In other words, protection is produced in—and at the same time reproduces—the "national order" (Malkki 1995) and the "border order" of territories (Naranjo Giraldo 2015). If, as Sharma and Gupta (2006) have argued, the state can be understood as "an *effect* of everyday practices, representations and multiple modalities of power" (165), the narratives and practices that operate under the protection-control relationship of mobilities also result in the production of state order.

Protection as a form of control is based on an asymmetrical relationship between the protector and the protected; this unequal relationship (Bigo 2006; Fassin 2010, 2016), which is (re)re-created in various forms and scales, leads to a hierarchization of migrants in the selection of those *deserving* protection. This asymmetry in the framework of asylum systems is expressed in parameters of dependency and obedience (Scheel, Garelli, and Tazzioli 2015). Eligibility processes as *state rituals* (Clavijo 2018) re-create the institutional structure and selectivity that involves different conditions in the regulation of the entry and stay of migrants in *national territories*, as well as a series of behavioral expectations; that is, "it implies a counter-gift in the form of an obligation that binds the recipient to his or her benefactor" (Fassin 2016, 14). In the analysis of protection as a nodal category, it is necessary to attend, as Huysmans (2006) warns, to different ways in which political agency understood as "the capacity to intervene meaningfully in the political dispute of protection demands" (6) structures the scope of protection and the definition of the *well-founded fears*[3] against which access is *legitimized*. Thus, protection claims "are not simply constructed through discourse and bureaucratic routine, but remain embedded in fields of contestation structured by asymmetrical power relations" (5).

Finally, with regard to the South American space, some analyses of the issue of refuge have focused on the particular conflicts and gray areas present in the classifications that operate in the regulation of so-called forced migration and refugee status (Riaño 2008; Vidal 2005; Gómez 2021), as well as on the relationship between national borders and differential access to protection (Naranjo Giraldo

2015; González Gil 2015). In the recent context, in which other mechanisms for the regulation and recategorization of displacement are emerging in the region, the "ambivalent character" that characterizes the interactions between migration authorities and migrants (Moulin and Magalhães 2020, 2) and the improvisation in the production of institutional categories for the management of migrant populations (17) gain relevance.

From Inter-American Asylum to the UN System

In this section, I examine a moment of transformation in the governance of refuge at the regional level that took place in the 1980s. This iconic moment was associated with the increase and management of displacement from Central American countries—especially Nicaragua, Guatemala, and El Salvador—and the adoption of the Cartagena Declaration as the basis for subsequent regional instruments. To problematize this transformation, I examine the changes that the protection-control relationship underwent during this period, linked to three aspects within the framework of regional refugee policies: massiveness as a characteristic of refugee populations; access to recognition of refugee status under other hypotheses of persecution and of flight; and the UNHCR's leading role in the adoption of new protection-control policy responses to the overflow of refugee movement in the region, and under the notions of burden and responsibility sharing for states.

An antecedent to consider—as a particular feature of the Latin American context—is the coexistence of the Inter-American asylum system and the framework established in the 1951 Convention and its 1967 Protocol. The reference to the Inter-American asylum system is relevant to understanding the first connotations of asylum in South American countries. A long-standing reference is the Treaty on International Criminal Law (1889), which insists on the relevance of the *political* character as a basis for the mobility of the asylum seeker, which evidences the political use that, since that time, the statute has had in interstate relations, marking affinities or tensions between governments. The 1889 treaty establishes that "asylum is inviolable for those persecuted for political offences." Along these lines, the Convention on Territorial Asylum (adopted in Caracas in 1954) reiterates that "no State is obliged to surrender to another State or to expel from its territory persons persecuted for political reasons or offences."[4] Thus, the granting of asylum during this period was mostly associated with individual and exceptional cases that stood out for their militancy.

At the same time as the adoption of instruments referring to territorial asylum, the path of convergence with the United Nations system was being forged, based on the parameters of the 1951 Convention and the actions of the UNHCR. However, given the preponderance of the Inter-American system of territorial asylum, there was initially little participation among Latin American countries in the preparatory bodies of the 1951 Convention. In fact, only four countries (Brazil, Colombia, Cuba, and Venezuela) sent delegations to the Conference of Plenipotentiaries on the Status of Refugees and Stateless Persons, where work was carried out prior to the 1951 Convention. Some documents that reconstruct this period (Franco and Santiesteban 2011) attribute this situation, in large part, to the quest for autonomy by the states of the region, as an attempt to avoid the supervision of an international body; at the same time, the Inter-American asylum system was considered an adequate and satisfactory response for the Latin American context, as it had its own instruments and customary practices.

Those documents refer to the tendency to prioritize regional agreements that lasted until the Cartagena Colloquium in 1984. However, since the 1960s, the Inter-American asylum system had begun to show transformations and fractures. The first UNHCR regional office opened in Buenos Aires in 1965. The initial objective of UNHCR's activities was to assist European postwar refugees. However, during the military dictatorships in the Southern Cone, in the 1960s and 1970s, there was "a drastic change in the work and challenges of the Office, as well as in the profile of the beneficiaries of its protection activities" (UNHCR 2014). In this regard, some documents mention that in the 1960s, mass movements began to be generated among the countries of the region, linked to "socio-political crises" in various contexts, including the conflicts in Central America in the 1980s. "In the following decades, mass movements continued to increase in Central America, due to the conflicts and conditions of violence in countries such as Nicaragua, El Salvador, and Guatemala" (Parliamentary Procedure, 1998, N° 128, "Draft General Refugee Law," Argentina, 6565).

Displacement associated with refuge (beyond its formal recognition) acquired new visibility and volume and implied a reformulation of the hypotheses of conflict, the causes of persecution, and the fears considered to be "well founded" as triggers for displacement. From the 1980s onward, a rapprochement with the United Nations system became evident—a turnaround that involved the accession and ratification of the 1951 Convention and its 1967 Protocol by several countries in the region, redefining the concept of refugee, protection demands, and protection policies.

With the adoption of the Cartagena Declaration (UNHCR 1984), three features outlined the transformations in the connotation and regulation of asylum. First, displacement was characterized as a *mass influx of people*, which meant that the conception of asylum as an exceptional and singular guarantee, granted particularly to people of outstanding political militancy, lost its preponderance. Some texts even argue that this situation of mass influx "allowed the advantages offered by the United Nations system to become evident" (San Juan 2004, 29). The recognition of refugee status, in this period, was associated with hypotheses of persecution of various kinds, incorporating, as part of the legitimate causes of flight, "generalized violence, foreign aggression, internal conflicts, massive violation of human rights or other circumstances that have seriously disturbed public order" (Cartagena Declaration, UNHCR 1984, 3): situations in which people were involved beyond their political participation. Thus, establishing an expanded definition of refugee status changed the eligibility guidelines and the treatment of displacement linked to the issue of asylum and refuge. In the review of preparatory documents for the Cartagena Declaration, the mass influx was a basis not only for rapprochement with the United Nations system but also for regional harmonization in the definitions and management of the population recognized as refugees in the different countries of the region. This harmonization process involved the adoption of regional guidelines in national legislative frameworks, along with the installation and development of programs promoted by the UNHCR.

With the expanded definition, other protection demands are contemplated within the framework of the treatment of populations recognized as refugees, and notions such as international protection and humanitarian protection are combined. These forms of protection converge in considering refugees not only under situations of persecution but also as victims of armed conflict or situations of generalized violence that oblige forced displacement.

Second, the mass influx was also a priority argument for the adoption of other mechanisms associated with international protection, for example, the implementation of the criterion of prima facie recognition as a way to manage access to refugee status.

This mechanism refers to recognition in conditions of large-scale influx,[5] under which, given the difficulty of individual selection and assessment, states are encouraged to grant refugee status collectively based on knowledge of armed conflicts or crises in the places of origin. After collective recognition, one form of management of displaced populations was the installation of refugee camps and settlements,[6] which became central at the International Conference on Central American Refugees (CIREFCA), held in 1989. Refugee camps or settlements, defined as temporary protection spaces, were mechanisms for containing and controlling displaced populations under the assumption of possible repatriation. At that time, return to places of origin was the preferred option among the range of solutions promoted by the UNHCR. References to the conditions of settlement in these refugee camps show—in addition to the precariousness of life in these spaces—differential treatment according to the national origins of the people confined there. Honduras, for example, with funding from the US government, received Sandinista refugees from Nicaragua, but treated Salvadorans differently; thus, "while Nicaraguan refugees could leave and enter their camps freely, Salvadorans were forced to remain in closed camps, guarded by the Honduran armed forces" (Franco and Santiesteban 2011, 133).

Third, in regional spaces, displaced populations are represented as a *burden* for states, a burden that must be managed through cooperation and shared responsibility as mechanisms for distributing responses to the demands that the massive movements of refugees brought with them. The figure of the refugee, as opposed to the political asylum seeker, became associated with representations that allude to groups of impoverished victims, whose demands for protection not only referred to entry and stay in host territories but also to access to basic services and goods.

Mixed Flows: Refuge in the Framework of the
Fight Against Irregular Migration

A second moment that illustrates the transformations of the refugee figure and the modalities of the protection-control relationship in the region is the adoption of the concept of "mixed flows" during the first decade of the twenty-first century. This notion takes on special relevance in the context of the rise of the *governance* approach[7] and *migration management*. According to UNHCR, mixed flows "involve various categories of people travelling along similar routes and using the same methods of transport but with different needs, profiles and motivations" (UNHCR 2011, 24). This definition encompasses various bureaucratic categories in the orbit of so-called *irregular migration*, emphasizes the increase in migratory irregularity as the main disorder to be addressed, and (re)produces the imperative of selection under dichotomous criteria on the people who are displaced. From the logic of international organizations, the idea of mixed flows assumes that irregular—irregularized—movements, which include people who could be recognized as refugees, are a source of lack of protection and, therefore, that new mechanisms are required to manage migrant movements and populations.

Various regional instruments—in synchrony with the International Organization for Migration (IOM) and UNHCR—established the category of mixed flows as a diagnostic concept for the definition and treatment of migratory dynamics. The dissemination of this notion is framed in the context of the primacy of the migration governance approach together with the processes of internationalization and regionalization of migration policy (Domenech 2013). The idea of mixed flows is taken up again in various interstate bodies and regional consultative spaces and brings together different actors while reiterating the differentiation of the fields of intervention based on categorization procedures.[8] Under the imperative of managing mixed flows, other forms of linkage between international organizations and interinstitutional spaces are produced. In a document entitled "Refugee Protection and Migration Control: UNHCR and IOM Perspectives" (UNHCR and IOM 2001), UNHCR and IOM recognize the need for a coordinated approach "to address the displacement situations that affect the respective mandates of both organizations." "The challenge for the international community," the document continues, "is to find ways to respond adequately to the needs of refugees and asylum seekers, including access to protection, within the context of migration management" (3). The notion of mixed flows is included in the UNHCR's Agenda for Protection (2002), which, along with its recognition, raises the difficulties of caring for asylum systems. Premises are then used to validate control mechanisms legitimized by the need to identify false refugees in the context of mixed flows. Thus, the UNHCR program explicitly expresses concern about "difficulties in preventing abuse of asylum systems and in excluding and repatriating those who are not entitled to or do not require international protection" (UNHCR 2002, 3).

In South America, the notion of mixed flows gained prominence on a regional scale with the Mexico Declaration and Plan of Action (PAM 2004), which recognizes "the existence of mixed migratory flows within which there are people who may qualify as refugees who require specific treatment with the necessary legal safeguards to ensure their identification and access to refugee status determination procedures" (PAM, 3). Concern about the increase in mixed flows and the development of protocols for the identification of refugees continued to be among the fundamental points in subsequent declarations and action plans established in the region, including in regional integration spaces such as the Common Market of the South (MERCOSUR).

However, the tendency to define migration dynamics in the region using the concept of mixed flows did not operate homogeneously for all movements, nor did it have the same impact on the asylum systems across the different countries. The political reading of the contexts of origin continued to be a central aspect in the classification of displacement and control practices. For example, in this period, emphasis was placed on the need for international protection for displaced populations of Colombian origin. In 2007, the UNHCR's presentation

"Inter-American Programme for the Promotion and Protection of the Human Rights of Migrants" (UNHCR 2007) mentioned the increased presence and monitoring of border areas in the Andean region as part of the actions undertaken to respond to mixed flows and the regional strategy in the face of "the humanitarian needs of Colombian nationals in need of international protection" (4). Another emblematic response to the increase in displacement of Colombian origin was the Expanded Registry for the recognition and documentation of refugees (2009) carried out by the Ecuadorian government—with UNHCR support—through mobile brigades in border areas. At the same time, in the framework of responses to mixed flows, temporary regularization and residence programs were adopted for humanitarian reasons,[9] rejecting the asylum route, particularly for migrants from countries *outside* MERCOSUR, such as Senegal and Haiti, nationalities that are prominent in the number of asylum applications, in countries such as Argentina and Brazil, but not in the recognition as refugees.

The reconfigurations of the migration regime and asylum systems in this period are based on discourses that define the overflow of unauthorized displacement as the main problem, thus making explicit the association between refuge and irregularity. Under these assumptions, institutional responses are aimed to promote and implement a series of practices linked to interception schemes, identification, classification, and verification. Irregularity, defined as a characteristic of displacement or of migrants, makes invisible the process of irregularization as a condition produced within the framework of state regulation—within what Nicholas De Genova (2002) posits as "the legal production of illegality"; therefore, following Domenech (2011), "without ignoring the implications it has for migrants in their daily lives, it could be said that *illegality* is not a problem in itself, but a problem *for* the state" (61). As Scheel and Squire (2014) argue, under the logic of migration governance, "illegality" has become the interpretive fabric of migratory movements, including those of "forced migrants."

Here, the protection-control relationship manifests itself in a double sense, both for refugees through identification and selection processes, and for the safeguarding of states in the administration of populations under the argument of sovereignty and national security. Access to international protection is subordinated to migration control, as the priority objective is to order and combat irregular—irregularized—migration and the dangers it brings with it. Thus, the humanitarian argument in the selection of those deserving of protection is one of the gears in the processes of securitization of migrations (Bigo 2006). The close relationship between protection and control in the framework of mixed flows is made explicit in institutional documents where they state that "refugees may also move—and this is happening more frequently—within a broader mixed flow. . . . Therefore, the line between migrant and asylum seeker is increasingly blurred. Equally, the distinction between migration control and refugee protection is difficult to draw in the policies of some states" (UNHCR and IOM 2001, 3).

In contexts of mixed flows, the category that precedes recognition of refugee status is that of irregular migrant. Concern in asylum systems is therefore centered on reception and eligibility procedures for the identification of *genuine* asylum seekers, those whose *well-founded* reasons justify their *unauthorized* movement. The notion of mixed flows amalgamates, through the condition of *irregularity*, categories associated with refuge that are considered parallel and that refer to different and specific forms of protection and stay in national territories. This concern for reception and identification procedures is reflected in *institutional strengthening projects* as part of *operational actions* to respond to mixed flows. Examples include the decentralization and regionalization of the functions of the Refugee Office of the Ecuadorian Foreign Ministry, and the decentralization refugee status determination procedure to strengthen decision making at the border.

From an institutional perspective, people whose situation merits recognition of refugee status represent a minority within the framework of mixed flows; indeed, the UNHCR (2008) states that "the new context of international refugee protection is based on an understanding of migratory flows, in which refugees represent only a small proportion of the large number of people seeking entry into a given country" (354). Thinking of asylum as an exceptional resource has enabled various mechanisms of inquiry and surveillance of subjects, such as the construction of *profiles* and reference cases, in the face of the influx of mixed flows. In this sense, "instances of initial determination" are proposed in order to ascertain the causes and motivations that people have for leaving their country of origin (UNHCR 2011, 16).

Now, then, the double meaning of the protection-control relationship also refers to the status of refuge as an institution that deserves to be protected, particularly by the guarantee of the principle of non-refoulement, a central element in the ideal differentiation between refugees and migrants. The protection argument for the institution of asylum is combined with the emergence of voluntary return programs for those who, in the opinion of institutional actors, do not require international protection.[10]

Identification procedures, legitimized under the objective of searching for people in need of protection, also select those who—in the framework of mixed flows—are not eligible for international protection, or for the migratory route to regularization of entry and stay, and are therefore subject to voluntary return or deportation. In other words, protection-control operates as a filter in both directions: the protection of the asylum system is used as a basis for exclusion measures from access to protection, and in the illegalization of certain migrant presences, which highlights the institutional and nationalist prevalence of this relationship. The UNHCR (2011) has stated: "It is not possible to respond positively to the aspirations of all individuals. From a protection point of view, the ability to identify specific needs and direct people who do not seek international protection to alternative mechanisms can contribute to reaching more effective and efficient asylum procedures" (165).

The obligatory nature of non-refoulement as a jus cogens principle brings with it a commitment by states not to expel asylum seekers and persons recognized as refugees. However, criteria have been established that limit its application to any case that represents a threat or danger to national security.[11] In this sense, although the principle of non-refoulement is considered a cornerstone of the protection of refugees, even for situations that result in complementary protection, its compliance is subject to the interpretations and qualifications of different officials throughout the bureaucratic process (including border agents, eligibility officers, and representatives of international organizations and their partner agencies). At the various levels, officials verify not only those whose fears merit protection but also those whose presence does not pose a threat.

Protection and Asylum on Parallel Tracks:
The ETPV and the Didactics of Control

A third moment is framed in the recent context characterized by the increase and centrality of migrations of Venezuelan origin in the region and by the transformations that these displacements have brought to the regulation of migration. In particular, the process of implementing the Temporary Protection Statute for Venezuelan Migrants shows other modalities adopted by the protection-control relationship and changes in representations of the refugee figure, based on three issues: (1) From the emergence of international cooperation bodies and co-responsibility mechanisms has come a proliferation of measures aimed at dealing with Venezuelan migration, measures that highlight different rationalities in the political use of the notion of protection. (2) In the reconfiguration of the migration and border regime, the notion of protection refers to increasingly circumstantial and provisional measures where the application for asylum and the granting of refugee status have become scarce—even elusive—institutional resources, subjecting populations to constant supervision and approval of their presence. (3) In the transformations of the protection-control relationship, it is possible to identify what I call here the *didactics of control*. This notion refers to a set of techniques, methods, and resources—virtual and physical—by means of which the implementation of control procedures labeled as protection are disseminated, instructed, and conducted.

For the development of this section, I focus on the adoption and implementation of the ETPV (2021) to illustrate the paths and stages of control that operate in the implementation of these new mechanisms for regulating migrant presence raised as forms of protection. Thus, far from understanding the ETPV as an isolated measure, I think of it as an instrument made within the web of actors, practices, categories, and relations—asymmetrical and in constant dispute—produced within the framework of the migration and border regime in the South American space (Domenech and Dias 2020).

Migration of Venezuelan people to Colombia and vice versa has been occurring for a long time; however, since 2015, a greater volume of cross-border movements on foot has been observed.[12] *Migration on foot* impacted the visibility of displacement and the changes adopted to regulate it, including creation of the Regional Interagency Coordination Platform for Refugees and Migrants from Venezuela (R4V) in 2018, led by IOM and UNHCR, and the adoption of the ETPV in 2021. One of the objectives of this platform is "operational coordination" of the different national and local governments in the implementation of the Regional Response Plan for Refugees and Migrants (RMRP) (Platform R4V n.d.). In Colombia, the Interagency Group on Mixed Migration Flows (GIFMM) is the "national expression" of this regional platform (GIFMM 2021).

With the support of the GIFMM, the Colombian government adopted a Temporary Protection Statute for Venezuelan Migrants in March 2021 (through Decree 216 and Resolution 0971).[13] Through the ETPV,[14] the government's main objective is to "give the Venezuelan migrant population the opportunity to regularize their migratory status and integrate into the country's productive apparatus" (Decree 216 [2021]). Through the ETPV, a migrant can apply for a Temporary Protection Permit (PPT), which involves the fulfilment of a series of prior registration and identification procedures. This qualification "implies that the decision to authorize the collection of these data is not voluntary but obligatory and that refusing to do so is equivalent to being excluded from the Statute" (Pelacani et al. 2021, 35). The initiation and follow-up of the application are carried out virtually. To submit the application, one must also submit a Single Registry of Venezuelan Migrants (RUMV), a Characterization Survey, and a biometric data collection. All PPT applicants must complete the RUMV; however, "the fulfilment of the requirements does not imply the granting of the permit, which is at the discretion of the migration authority" (Migration Colombia, Ministry of Foreign Affairs 2021).

Likewise, the implementation of the ETPV reveals interlinkages between various institutions and the administrative unit Migration Colombia, the main state agency in charge of carrying out the use of this instrument. The proliferation of interinstitutional links was expressed both in the multiple forms that support tasks took and in the coverage of the national territory. The organizations that are part of the GIFMM in the fixed or mobile spaces have deployed in different cities and on various routes of the country, enabling the performance of tasks such as assisted pre-registration, training, service routes, internet access services, and transport to the biometric registration points called "Visible Points" (GIFMM 2021). The GIFMM Support Plan for the implementation of the ETPV evidences the coupling of this statute with the objectives of the Regional Response Plan. At this point, governmental bodies can also be thought of as implementing partners of regional and global guidelines on the regulation of migrant populations.

Regarding the asylum system and the concept of refugee, migrations of Venezuelan origin have gained visibility due to political interpretations of them as forced displacements. And they have been linked with the idea of *crisis*, a notion under which "various border conflicts derived from the emergence of new movements and border crossings associated with 'irregularity'" (Domenech and Dias 2020, 6) have been addressed. These mechanisms show other modalities of the protection-control relationship, which go beyond the asylum system, are detached from the refugee figure, and are associated with other temporalities and attributes.

In different countries in the region there is evidence of the construction of categories associated with humanitarian narratives, parallel to the recognition of refugee status. In the Colombian case, the institutional categorization linked to the protection of the Venezuelan migrant population addresses migrants and refugees together under the category "population in need." This category prioritizes classification according to the times and itineraries of movements (Platform R4V n.d.). Based on these categories, different ways of regulating entry, stay, and access to rights and services are established, separating protection from asylum, which is even considered incompatible with the Temporary Protection Permit. This, in turn, generates new connotations to the notion of protection and other representations of the needs of migrant populations. Thus, the ambiguity of eligibility, in which those who are classified under the category of "population in need" find themselves, is a terrain in which ambivalence (Moulin and Magalhães 2020) and discretionality are permanently re-created. Classification operations are biased by governmental expectations as part of the responses to migrants' demands for protection.

The differentiation between the ETPV and refugee recognition status is based on the notion of mixed flows and the limitations of the asylum system. The ETPV is defined as a "complementary mechanism to the international refugee protection regime, which fills the existing gaps in this regime, based on the reality of mixed population movements" (GIFMM 2021). The statute establishes that applicants for refugee status recognition are obliged to register in the Single Registry of Venezuelan Migrants and carry out the biometric data registration. However, "they must voluntarily choose to continue with the refugee status recognition process or to avail themselves of the Temporary Protection Status for Venezuelan Migrants"; if they opt for the ETPV, they must withdraw the refugee application process (Migration Colombia, Ministry of Foreign Affairs 2021).

Although all the documents insist that the choice between the asylum application and the ETPV should be voluntary, some statements and institutional materials discourage—implicitly—the continuation of the asylum application. As Gracy Pelacani and colleagues (2021) point out, "There is unequal treatment between asylum seekers holding a safe-conduct of stay and those who access the PPT, insofar as the safe-conduct is a very limited document for access to rights in Colombia" (44).

Another point in the institutional discourse concerns the ability to go to and return from Venezuela. As the director of Migration Colombia notes, "Technically, the vast majority of cases are not refugees, because they are not escaping persecution, but rather expulsion from their country due to poverty, misery, and hunger . . . this is not a refugee status, which is why they can go to and return from Venezuela" (Espinosa 2021). Finally, the massiveness of Venezuelan migration is also mentioned as one of the limitations to the proper functioning of the asylum system. "In terms of weakening refugee status," the same official adds, "I believe that rather than weakening it, it strengthens it, because what is needed is for the refugee status to be reviewed person by person . . . to provide them with special protection, and this is difficult when there are massive applications" (Espinosa 2021).

The third issue in this section refers to the *didactics of control*, a governmental strategy implemented through a set of techniques, tools, products, and resources for the implementation of the ETPV. The didactics of control facilitates the installation and appropriation of control practices based on the political use of the idea of protection, reconfiguring its scope. The deployment of this didactics facilitates the activation and involvement of migrants in control practices in a *self-managed manner*, without leading to the dissolution of the asymmetrical power relations between protectors and protected, or the state and the migrant population.

Through this didactics of control, other representations of those deserving protection are projected, and new forms of interaction between migrants and governmental bodies are facilitated, which also "prefigures" the horizons and capacity of migrants to act as political subjects (Moulin and Magalhães 2020). The didactics of control paves the way for instruction in a kind way and conveys proximity, institutional openness, and trust in and agility of procedures. Through didactics, the role of migrant populations as managers in the access to protection is proposed, along with that of institutions—in this case, those that make up the GIFMM—as *allies* and *facilitators*, which apparently shifts the emphasis to the criteria of selectivity and the search for control and management of the migrant trajectory and presence.

In the implementation stages of the ETPV, the didactics of control is evident in different ways. One is through the production and dissemination of a variety of materials, with detailed information presented in different ways, reproducing the institutional discourse on why and how to apply for the ETPV and request the PPT. This heterogeneous set of resources—in some cases using marketing techniques—is framed in the campaign "Visibles," a slogan used in all governmental materials, both virtual and physical, referring to the promotion of the ETPV. All these graphic and audiovisual resources facilitate the transmission of messages through empathetic communication that predisposes attention and memorization of the instructions. The didactics of control is also deployed in face-to-face instances, through the service points where different organizations that are part of the GIFMM come together. For example, the Referral and Orientation Points are multifunctional spaces where assistance practices are combined with ETPV promotion and monitoring tasks. The definitions of the guarantees offered by protection are interwoven with the counterperformances demanded of the protected, including a biographical scan through different instances of data collection. In short, the didactics contributes to migrants themselves activating control mechanisms and giving access to the information that the state seeks to collect.

Final Considerations

This chapter develops an analysis of the transformations of policies and the figure of the refugee in South America based on the relationship between protection and control latent in the production of categories in the framework of international protection policies. In this sense, I propose the *protection-control relationship* as a way of understanding the way in which protection and control measures are mutually constituted—as a unit—in the management of so-called forced displacements, understood here as *preservation migrations*. The inquiry focuses on the transformations of protection-control as a relationship that is part of the regional migration and border regime. It allows us to reveal the exercises of recategorization, the resonance between the definitions and practices adopted at different historical moments, and the ways in which the rationalities and scope of international protection policies have been reconfigured.

To highlight these transformations and illustrate how the protection-control relationship has operated, I look at three moments. First, the consolidation of the United Nations system, specifically the UNHCR as the lead agency in the management of asylum in the region, with the Cartagena Declaration and the broadening of the formal definition of the refugee category in the 1980s. This system associates refuge with mass movements that must be addressed under the umbrella of cooperation and shared responsibility. Second, the category of mixed flows was adopted in the first decade of the twenty-first century, in the context of the consolidation of the migration governance approach as a perspective suited to dealing with migration on a global, regional, and national scale. And, third, new mechanisms were developed for regulating migrant populations, in particular the ETPV, adopted in Colombia in 2021, defined as a temporary protection measure in a context marked by the increase in the number and centrality of migrations of Venezuelan origin.

A look through different historical moments allows us to identify the path of the protection-control relationship associated with different categories of intervention that have been redefined and used to legitimize the adoption of various governmental instruments in the framework of protection policies. In other words, it is possible to recognize the resonance in the discourses and practices of protection-control based on the recurrence of different categories, among which the following stand out: mass influx, mixed flows, temporary protection, cooperation, and co-responsibility.

First, the category of mass influx, used as an argument for the extension of the definition of refugee status, has been put forward as an inherent characteristic of migrations classified as forced. In the 1980s, it was used to justify the adoption of other mechanisms for accessing refugee status such as prima facie recognition—based on national origin—and the establishment of refugee camps. In subsequent decades, this category also came into play to characterize mixed flows and legitimize the imperatives of selection and the use of the refugee figure in the fight against so-called irregular migration. And in recent years, the construct has been taken up again as a basis for the adoption of protection-control mechanisms that discourage asylum and anchor protection to temporary forms of regularization.

Second, the category of mixed flows as a way of characterizing *irregularized* migration renewed the emphasis on the classification and selection of the displacement under dichotomous categories such as voluntary versus forced, founded versus unfounded, desired versus undesired. The adoption of the category of mixed flows—also conceived of as massive—produces new representations of the figure of refuge associated with irregular, or irregularized, migration as a characteristic of displacement classified as forced, and this association operates as an argument for the strengthening and implementation of control and selection mechanisms in the name of identifying those "deserving" of international protection. Categorization calls into question not only access to asylum but also displacement itself, given the institutional demand on people to fit into one of the categories that justify their movement. Although the processes of classifying mobility reveal singular transformations in different contexts, it is possible to argue that in the assignment of a particular category, the exercise of nomination based on the preservation of national order prevails.

Third, the category of temporary protection present in instruments such as the ETPV highlights the dissociation between protection and the asylum system. Protection appears to be linked to other categories and practices of institutional control and management of the population on the move, centered on interagency bodies associated with the categories of cooperation and co-responsibility, based on which harmonization is promoted in the forms of intervention at different scales. At the same time, these control mechanisms are based on *self-managed* practices for the identification, monitoring, characterization, and productive insertion adjusted to governmental expectations. In the framework of recent transformations in the regulation of migration, what I call the *didactics of control* emerges—a notion that alludes to a set of techniques and resources deployed in the implementation of measures such as the ETPV. The didactics facilitates the installation of new meanings that protection acquires, and the learning of what migrant populations are expected to do.

The analysis of the protection-control relationship reveals new mechanisms for the identification, selection, and projection of people's life trajectories in preservation migration. A look at the transformations of the protection-control relationship in the three periods analyzed allows us to identify some contrasts in the ways in which displacement is managed on a regional scale. There was an initial expansion of the refugee concept, followed by a progressive contraction with the rise of migratory governance and the emphasis on regularization as the heart of protection. The mechanisms for classifying and regulating the entry and stay of migrants under temporary regularization schemes are defined as responses to the protection needs of the displaced population. This problematization highlights reconfigurations of the notion of protection, which in principle referred to international protection—and the principle of non-refoulement—and which is now increasingly associated with humanitarianism as a predominant rationalization in the regional management of mobility. Thus, under the category of "population in need," humanitarian protection is blurred, acquiring new meanings associated with in situ practices whose scope is increasingly circumstantial. With the promise of protection, migrants sustain forms of control and monitoring as part of strategies to preserve their mobility and legitimize their presence.

NOTES

I am grateful to Eduardo Domenech for his generous support in the construction of this text. His sharp comments and the spaces for discussion shared over the years have been fundamental in the search for a critical reflection on refugee and protection policies.

1. The Cartagena Declaration has been taken up again in regional instruments such as the Declaration of San José (1994), the Mexico Declaration and Plan of Action (2004), the Brazil Declaration and Plan of Action (2014), and declarations in the Common Market of the South (Mercado Común del Sur, or MERCOSUR).

2. Multiannual Research Project 2021–2023 (PIP), directed by Eduardo Domenech, accredited and funded by CONICET.

3. This term is a structuring element of the formal definition of refugee status established by the 1951 Convention Relating to the Status of Refugees and its 1967 Protocol, a definition adopted in the guiding instruments in the region. The 1951 Convention makes explicit that the term *refugee* refers to a person who, "owing to a well-founded fear of being persecuted for reasons of race, religion, nationality, membership of a particular social group or political opinion, is outside the country of his nationality and is unable or, owing to such fear, is unwilling to avail himself of the protection of that country; or who, not having a nationality and being outside the country of his former habitual residence as a result of such events, is unable or, owing to such fear, is unwilling to return to it" (UNHCR 1951).

4. Other instruments were the Convention on Asylum, signed in Havana in 1928, and the Treaty on Asylum and Political Refuge of Montevideo (1939).

5. With reference to Conclusion N.22, Protection of asylum seekers in situations of large-scale influx (UNHCR 1982).

6. Salvadoran refugee camps in Honduras (Colomoncagua, Mesa Grande, and La Virtud), in Mexico along the border with Guatemala in the state of Chiapas, from the Montebello lakes to the bottom of the Lacandona jungle; camps in the Honduran Moskita and in Costa Rica, though in the latter country they were not on the border" (Franco and Santiesteban 2011, 128).

7. This global approach, "which emerged in the 1990s, emphasizes the idea of 'orderly' migration as an 'input' and 'contribution,' and the need to address migration through bi- and multilateral consensus" (Domenech 2007, 5). "From the perspective of migration governance, migration flows are classified as desirable and undesirable according to their orderly/disorderly, voluntary/forced and reduced/massive character" (Domenech 2013, 126).

8. It is argued that "mixed movements often involve different countries along a particular migratory route, which usually cannot be addressed by a single state" (UNHCR 2011, 24).

9. For example, in Argentina the "Special Regime for the Regularization of Foreigners of Senegalese Nationality" (Disposition 2 [2013]) and a temporary residence in the category of "Humanitarian Reasons" for Haitian nationals (Disposition 1143-E [2017]), prior to the establishment of a tourist visa for migrants of the same nationality.

10. The institutional documents clarify that "IOM's role with respect to persons intercepted by States is focused on facilitating voluntary return. . . . IOM's role is to support States in the implementation of their orderly migration practices, including return migration" (IOM 2001: 5).

11. The Convention stipulates that "no Contracting State shall expel or return a refugee in any manner whatsoever to the frontiers of territories where his life or freedom would be threatened. . . . However, the benefits of the present provision may not be claimed by a refugee who is regarded on serious grounds as a *danger to the security of the country in which he is*" (UNHCR 1951, Art. 33; emphasis added).

12. According to figures from the GIFMM-R4V platform, in August 2021 there were an estimated 1,842,390 Venezuelan nationals in Colombia (Platform R4V n.d.).

13. The ETPV is modeled on the Temporary Protection Statute adopted in Turkey in 2014 for the treatment of displaced persons from Syria.

14. Also characterized as "a humanitarian protection response that diminishes the motivation for irregular migration" (Ministry of Foreign Affairs and Migration Colombia 2021).

REFERENCES

Bigo, Didier. 2006. "Protection: Security, Territory and Population." In *The Politics of Protection: Sites of Insecurity and Political Agency*, edited by Jef Huysmans, Andrew Dobson, and Raia Prokhovnik, 84–100. New York: Routledge.

Butler, Judith. 2006. *Vida precaria: El poder del duelo y la violencia*. Buenos Aires: Paidós.

Clavijo, Janneth. 2018. "El proceso de elegibilidad en Argentina: Rituales y ambivalencias en el reconocimiento de los refugiados." *Revista Interdisciplinar da Mobilidade Humana* 26 (54): 171–88.

Clavijo, Janneth, Marcela Ceballos, and Adriana González. 2022. "Negación del sujeto migrante, itinerancias forzadas y preservación de la existencia: Migraciones en y desde Colombia." In *Movilidades, derecho a migrar y control fronterizo en América Latina y el Caribe*, edited by Eduardo Domenech, Gioconda Herrera, and Liliana Rivera Sánchez, 177–204. Buenos Aires: Consejo Latinoamericano de Ciencias Sociales–Siglo XXI.

De Genova, Nicholas. 2002. "Migrant 'Illegality' and Deportability in Everyday Life." *Annual Review of Anthropology* 31:419–47.

De Genova, Nicholas. 2021. "Forced Migration, the Antinomies of Mobility, and the Autonomy of Asylum." Seminar Series on Forced Migration, University of Vienna (video). April 20. Posted to YouTube by IWMVienna. https://www.youtube.com/watch?v=_kLguEhR3fs&ab_channel=IWMVienna.

Domenech, Eduardo. 2007. "La agenda política sobre migraciones en América del sur: El caso de la Argentina." *Revue européenne des migrations internationales* 23 (1): 1–23.

Domenech, Eduardo. 2011. "Crónica de una 'amenaza' anunciada: Inmigración e 'ilegalidad'; visiones de Estado en la Argentina contemporánea." In *La construcción social
del sujeto migrante en América Latina: Prácticas, representaciones y categorías*, edited
by Bela Feldman-Bianco, Liliana Rivera Sánchez, Carolina Stefoni, and Marta Inés
Villa Martínez, 31–77. Quito: Facultad Latinoamericana de Ciencias Sociales, Consejo
Latinoamericano de Ciencias Sociales, and Universidad Alberto Hurtado.

Domenech, Eduardo. 2013. "Las migraciones son como el agua: Hacia la instauración de
políticas de control con rostro humano." *Polis* 35. http://polis.revues.org/9280.

Domenech, Eduardo. 2019. "Espacios de la movilidad en disputa: El régimen sudamericano
de migración y fronteras." Paper presented to First International Workshop on "Contested Territories: How Do We Conceptualise and Research Contested Territories in
Latin America?" School of Geography, University of Leeds, Leeds, UK, May 20–21.

Domenech, Eduardo. 2021. "Régimen de migración y fronteras." In *Migración*, edited by
Iréri Ceja, Soledad Álvarez Velasco, and Ulla Berg, 69–78. Buenos Aires: CLACSO.

Domenech, Eduardo, and Gustavo Dias. 2020. "Regimes de fronteira e 'ilegalidade'
migrante na América Latina e Caribe." *Sociologias* 22 (55): 40–73.

Espinosa, Juan Francisco. 2021. "Migración Colombia en directo." March 25. Uploaded
to YouTube by Migración Colombia. https://youtu.be/jdVDfRljjLk?list=PLrDU
7ef42ZIMFAOxcVPjwCdi_iNm-ohha.

Fassin, Didier. 2010. "El irresistible ascenso del derecho a la vida: Razón humanitaria
y justicia social." *Revista de Antropología Social* 19: 191–204. https://revistas.ucm.es
/index.php/RASO/article/view/RASO1010110191A.

Fassin, Didier. 2016. *La razón Humanitaria: Una Historia Moral del Tiempo Presente*.
Buenos Aires: Prometeo.

Franco, Leonardo, and Jorge Santiesteban. 2011. "La Contribución del Proceso de Cartagena al Desarrollo del Derecho Internacional de Refugiados en América Latina." In *La
Protección internacional de refugiados en las Américas*, edited by Alto Comisionado de
las Naciones Unidas para los Refugiados, 89–172.

Federico, Verónica, and Sabine Hess. 2021. "Protection Regimes—a Critical Analysis."
Global Migration: Consequences and Responses. Working Paper No. 2021/78.
Zenodo, March 26. https://doi.org/10.5281/zenodo.4638793.

GIFMM. 2021. "Plan de apoyo del GIFMM a la implementación del Estatuto Temporal
de Protección para venezolanos." R4V. December 20. https://www.r4v.info/es
/document/gifmm-colombia-plan-de-apoyo-del-gifmm-la-implementacion-del
-estatuto-temporal-de.

Gómez, Carmen. 2021. "Refugiadxs." In *Migración*, edited by Iréri Ceja, Soledad Álvarez
Velasco, and Ulla Berg, 89–98. Buenos Aires: Consejo Latinoamericano de Ciencias
Sociales.

González Gil, Adriana. 2015. "Del desplazamiento forzado interno en Colombia a la
migración transfronteriza hacia Ecuador." *Estudios Políticos* (47), 177–97.

Hess, Sabine. 2012. "De-Naturalising Transit Migration: Theory and Methods of an
Ethnographic Regime Analysis." *Population, Space, and Place* 18: 428–40.

Hess, Sabine, and Bernd Kasparek. 2017. "Under Control? Or, Border (as) Conflict:
Reflections on the European Border Regime." *Social Inclusion* 5 (3): 58–68.

Huysmans, Jef. 2006. "Agency and the Politics of Protection: Implications for Security Studies." In *The Politics of Protection: Sites of Insecurity and Political Agency*, edited by Jef Huysmans, Andrew Dobson, and Raia Prokhovnik, 1–18. New York: Routledge.

Malkki, Liisa. 1995. "Refugees and Exile: From 'Refugee Studies' to the National Order of Things." *Annual Review of Anthropology* 24: 495–523.

Migration Colombia, Ministry of Foreign Affairs. 2021. "Concepto sobre la figura de refugio frente al estatuto temporal de protección para migrantes venezolanos."

Moulin, Carolina, and Bruno Magalhães. 2020. "Operation Shelter as Humanitarian Infrastructure: Material and Normative Renderings of Venezuelan Migration in Brazil." *Citizenship Studies* 24 (5): 642–62.

Naranjo Giraldo, Gloria. 2015. "El nexo migración-desplazamiento-asilo en el orden fronterizo de las cosas: Una propuesta analítica." *Estudios Políticos* 47:265–84.

Pelacani, Gracy, Carolina Moreno, Laura Dib-Ayesta, and Mairene Tobón Ospino. 2021. "Estatuto temporal de protección para migrantes venezolanos: Reflexiones de una política de regularización migratoria." *Informes CEM*, Informe 3. Bogotá: Centro de Estudios en Migración (CEM).

Picozza, Fiorenza. 2017. "Dublin on the Move: Transit and Mobility Across Europe's Geographies of Asylum." *Movements: Journal für kritische Migrations- und Grenzregimeforschung* 3 (1): 71–88.

Platform R4V (Plataforma de Coordinación Interagencial para Refugiados y Migrantes de Venezuela). n.d. "La Plataforma." Accessed April 2022. https://www.r4v.info/es/laplataforma.

Riaño, Pilar. 2008. "Introducción." In *Poniendo Tierra de por Medio: Migración forzada de colombianos en Colombia, Ecuador y Canadá*, edited by Pilar Riaño and Marta Villa, 8–34. Medellín: Corporación Región and University of British Columbia.

San Juan, César. 2004. "El asilo y la protección internacional de los refugiados en América Latina: Análisis crítico del dualismo—asilo-refugio—a la luz del Derecho Internacional de los Derechos Humanos." In *El Asilo y la protección internacional de los refugiados en América Latina*, 31–72. San José: Alto Comisionado de las Naciones Unidas para los Refugiados EDITORAMA.

Sharma, Aradhana, and Akhil Gupta, eds. 2006. *The Anthropology of the State: A Reader*. Malden, MA: Wiley-Blackwell.

Scheel, Stephan, Glenda Garelli, and Martina Tazzioli. 2015. "Politics of Protection." In "New Keywords: Migration and Borders," edited by Nicholas De Genova, Sandro Mezzadra, and John Pickles, 16–19. Special issue, *Cultural Studies* 29 (1).

Scheel, Stephan, and Philipp Ratfisch. 2013. "Refugee Protection Meets Migration Management: UNHCR as a Global Police of Populations." *Journal of Ethnic and Migration Studies* 40 (6): 924–41. https://doi.org/10.1080/1369183X.2013.855074.

Scheel, Stephan, and Vicky Squire. 2014. "Forced Migrants as Illegal Migrants." In *The Oxford Handbook of Refugee and Forced Migration Studies*, edited by Elena Fiddian-Qasmiyeh, Gil Loescher, Katy Long, and Nando Sigona, 188–99. Oxford: Oxford University Press.

Sciortino, Giorgio. 2004. "Between Phantoms and Necessary Evils: Some Critical Points in the Study of Irregular Migrations to Western Europe." *IMIS-Beiträge* 24:17–43.

Tazzioli, Martina, and Glenda Garelli. 2019. "Counter-Mapping Refugees and Asylum Borders." In *Handbook of Critical Geographies of Migration*, edited by Katharyne Mitchell, Reece Jones, and Jennifer L. Fluri, 397–409. Cheltenham, UK: Edward Elgar.

Ticktin, Miriam. 2015. "Los problemas de las fronteras humanitarias." *Disparidades. Revista de Antropología* 70 (2): 291–297.

UNHCR (United Nations High Commissioner for Refugees). 1950. *Estatuto de la Oficina del Alto Comisionado de las Naciones Unidas para los Refugiados 1950*. Online. http:// www.solidaritat.ub.edu/observatori/general/docugral/acnur.htm.

UNHCR (United Nations High Commissioner for Refugees). 1951. "Convention Relating to the Status of Refugees." http://www.acnur.org/t3/fileadmin/scripts/doc.php?file =biblioteca/pdf/0005.

UNHCR. 1982. Conclusión N⁰.22: Protección de las personas que buscan asilo en situaciones de afluencia en gran escala. https://www.acnur.org/fileadmin/Documentos /BDL/2002/0533.pdf.

UNHCR (United Nations High Commissioner for Refugees). 1984. "Declaración de Cartagena sobre refugiados," adopted at the "Coloquio Sobre la Protección Internacional de los Refugiados en América Central, México y Panamá: Problemas Jurídicos y Humanitarios," Cartagena, Colombia, November 19–22, 1984. http://www.acnur .org/t3/fileadmin/scripts/doc.php?file=t3/fileadmin/Documentos/BDL/2001 /0008.

UNHCR (United Nations High Commissioner for Refugees). 2002. Programa de protección, https://www.acnur.org/fileadmin/Documentos/BDL/2002/1586.pdf.

UNHCR (United Nations High Commissioner for Refugees). 2004. Declaración y plan de acción de México para fortalecer la protección internacional de los refugiados en América Latina. http://www.acnur.org/biblioteca/pdf/2973.pdf?view=1.

UNHCR (United Nations High Commissioner for Refugees). 2007. *Presentación del ACNUR: Programa interamericano para la promoción y protección de los derechos humanos de los migrantes*. Washington, DC, February 13. https://www.refworld.org.es /pdfid/57f76ce2a.pdf.

UNHCR (United Nations High Commissioner for Refugees). 2008. *La protección internacional de los refugiados en las Américas. Nuevos desarrollos*. https://www.acnur.org /fileadmin/Documentos/Publicaciones/2012/8340.pdf.

UNHCR (United Nations High Commissioner for Refugees). 2011. *La protección de los refugiados y la migración mixta: El plan de los 10 puntos del ACNUR*. https://www.acnur .org/5c40c7374.pdf.

UNHCR (United Nations High Commissioner for Refugees). 2014. *50 Años de presencia del ACNUR en el sur de América Latina (1965–2015)*. https://www.acnur.org/50-sur-de -america-latina/historia.html.

UNHCR (United Nations High Commissioner for Refugees). 2022. Protección. https:// www.acnur.org/proteccion.html.

UNHCR (United Nations High Commissioner for Refugees) and IOM (International Organization for Migration). 2001. "La protección de los refugiados y el control migratorio: Perspectivas del ACNUR y de la OIM." https://www.acnur.org/fileadmin /Documentos/BDL/2008/6016.pdf.

Varela, Amarela. 2020. "Caravanas de migrantes y refugiados centroamericanos: Un feminismo para abrazar las fugas de quienes buscan preservar la vida." *Revista de Antropología Social* 29 (2): 245–55.

Vidal, Roberto. 2005. *Derecho global y desplazamiento interno: La creación, uso y desaparición del desplazamiento forzado por la violencia en Colombia.* Bogotá: Pontificia Universidad Javeriana.

Zetter, Roger. 2007. "More Labels, Fewer Refugees: Remaking the Refugee Label in an Era of Globalization." *Journal of Refugee Studies* 20 (2): 172–92.

Zolberg, Aristide R. 1983. "The Formation of New States as a Refugee-Generating Process." *Annals of the American Academy of Political and Social Science* 467: 24–38.

10

Logistical Lives, Humanitarian Borders

MANAGING POPULATIONS IN
SOUTH–SOUTH CIRCULATIONS

Carolina Moulin

A strong logistics is power for combat.—Operation Welcome, presentation conclusions, 2018

Since 2015, South American countries have faced a growing influx of Venezuelans, reflecting the ongoing economic, social, and political crisis in the
country. As of March 2023, the International Organization for Migration
(IOM) and the United Nations High Commissioner for Refugees (UNHCR)
estimate that roughly 7.2 million Venezuelans had left the country (approximately 30 percent of the total population), the vast majority residing or en
route across the continent. Colombia has taken the largest influx with over
2.5 million Venezuelans, followed by Peru with 1.5 million, and Brazil with
more than 400,000. Brazil had, by the end of 2022, a quarter of all Venezuelans recognized as refugees globally (roughly 50,000 out of 200,000 globally),
and roughly 100,000 Venezuelans are waiting for their cases to be processed.[1]

On average, 300 people arrived daily on the northern border from 2017 to 2019. From March 2020, COVID dramatically impacted such trends, with the closure of border entries, specifically targeted at people crossing by land from Venezuela (Zapata and Moulin 2022). There was a massive decrease in the number of residency and asylum requests, partially reverted since June 2021 when the Brazilian-Venezuelan border reopened. Data from the third quarter of 2021 point to a threefold increase in asylum requests compared to the second quarter of the same year, with people of Venezuelan origin representing over 80 percent of the total number of asylum seekers (de Oliveira, Simões, and Cavalcanti 2021).

Such numbers point to the massive scale of the (mostly regional) humanitarian tragedy brought forth by the protracted socioeconomic crisis in Venezuela, amplified by the effects of global pandemics and the shutdown of borders. It is expected that the ongoing arrival of families and individuals in conditions of extreme poverty, famine, and malnutrition and enduring, in most cases, persecution will continue to require concerted regional and international efforts on the part of receiving countries and societies in the coming years. Food shortages and massive inflation rates (estimates now run to close to 1 million percent per year) have made it practically impossible to eat and buy ordinary medication (such as aspirin) in the country. Lack of food and healthcare is, in many cases, a consequence of constrained access to Venezuelan public services. Testimonies of Venezuelan migrants convey that, for instance, access to basic services (food, gas, medication, pensions, and health services) came to depend on enrollment of beneficiaries in the "Carnet de la Patria" (homeland card), a government-issued card with information about its holders, including data on "civic participation" (voting, for example). Some have said that refusal to enroll and provide personal information has made it nearly impossible to have any access to rights and that government officials use the "card" as a mechanism of political control and persecution.[2]

It is against this conjunctural backdrop that this chapter analyses the Brazilian response to Venezuelan migration. Rather than describing a specific and uniquely regional approach to humanitarian coordination, it proposes to narrate the Brazilian response as a part of ongoing "global modes" of mobility management. It investigates how governance structures and protection grammars inform statist responses to South–South circulations in this context and how global logistical planning and strategies—or forms of logistical thinking (Cowen et al. 2018, 218)—have structured the regulation and management of (human) circulations. Such logistical thinking has provided an increasingly transnational grammar for the government of mobile populations, encompassing such diverse realities as those of South America and Europe, converting the lives of the displaced into forms of logistical life (Reid 2006). Among the most perceptible effects of such trends are the way they connect a particular infrastructure with the spatial ordering of displacement and how they enact specific subjective formations for migrants and refugees, increasingly articulated in relation to controlling expectations, desires, and life possibilities in the host society.

This chapter is based on fieldwork conducted in 2018 and 2019 as part of a larger interdisciplinary project on mobile lives in the context of Venezuelan migration.[3] The project involved interviews with asylum seekers and migrants, international organizations and NGO workers, and government officials and military personnel, as well as visits, on two different occasions, to all shelters in Boa Vista and Pacaraima, Roraima. The team also visited reception, triage, and data-processing centers and followed some persons of Venezuelan origin through the application process of asylum and residence. In March 2020, the global SARS-COV-2 pandemic dramatically impacted (among many other things) the arrival, circulation, and reception of people of Venezuelan origin in Brazilian territory. Ongoing research has tracked normative changes (Zapata and Moulin 2022), the impact on policies (Zapata and Wenderoth 2022), and, more recently, the effects on integration and emergency protection (Silva 2022). Nevertheless, the humanitarian infrastructure and logistical rationale that have constituted the backbone of the Brazilian response since 2018 not only remained unchallenged but was, one might argue, reinforced as a standard of practice nationally and increasingly regionally. As such, (im)mobility in COVID times invites a continued conversation about the modes of production of borders and, this chapter argues, along with many others, the centrality of logistical thinking as a global grammar for governing people's circulations.

I start with a review of recent work on the historical evolution of logistics as a science of circulation and its linkages with humanitarianism in global politics. I then turn to the Brazilian case to articulate sets of spatial practices that have transformed the border into a logistical hub and the national territory into a grid of controlled displacements, reflecting, along the way, on their constitutive relation to protection efforts, particularly within the framework of migration and asylum as legal and sociological categories. We understand humanitarian infrastructure as a set of ideational and material practices and *things* necessary for the sustained efforts of providing protection and assistance to people in need, for connecting peoples and processes, and for allowing their circulation within controlled parameters. In the case of Venezuelans arriving in Brazil, such infrastructure is composed of, among other things, cables (necessary for internet connection), computational grids (with biometric collection equipment, data-processing centers, cameras, etc.), shelters, military outposts, offices for humanitarian personnel, reception and triage centers, improvised health facilities, and roads and trails that connect these disparate and often distant places and their peoples. For circulations to take place, critical infrastructures must be available. Therefore, we understand the relationship between humanitarian infrastructures and logistics as co-constitutive. And it is to the rise of this logic that this chapter now turns.

Logistics as a Science of Circulations

According to Brett Neilson (2012), "Logistics is the art and science of managing the mobility of people and things to achieve economic, communication, and transport efficiencies. It involves planning and implementing the acquisition and use of the resources necessary to sustain the operation of a system." Historically, logistics emerged as an eminently military affair. Warfare required strategy and tactics, but also the ability to circulate the means for combat. This capability required thinking about how to provide for troops' physical sustenance and military equipment, as well as reducing the need to plunder conquered spaces and populations. In her groundbreaking study on the "deadly life of logistics," Deborah Cowen (2014, 26) asserts that the Napoleonic Wars marked a turning point in military logistics. How to get men and material to the front signaled the "key role of supply lines for war." As transformations in modern warfare reached new heights in World War II, dependence on fuel, mechanized warcraft, and new systems of weapons turned logistics from a means to engage in warfare to its condition of possibility. As Cowen asserts, "While logistics had long been critical to warfare—with the rise of industrial war, military logistics has come to lead strategy and tactics: it has gone from being the practical afterthought to the calculative practice that defines thought" (Cowen 2014, 30).

If born as a military art, the "revolution in logistics" took place in civilian quarters in the 1960s. Incentivized by the learning curve of modern warfare logistics, business firms turned to logistics as a central element in the circuits of economic production and distribution. Helped by incremental leaps in software and computing technologies, business managers and gurus, as well as government officials, propelled a new understanding of the relationship between production and distribution as a "total system." Getting materials to factories and assembly lines and distributing final products to customers were no longer seen as discrete aspects of intrafirm businesses but as part of the total process—and cost of—production. Logistics became central to increasing profitability and, therefore, "was transformed from a least-cost analysis of discrete segments of distribution into a science of value added through circulatory systems" (Cowen 2014, 40).

Two breakthroughs are deemed important for the globalization of logistics in the 1970s through the 1990s: the invention of the container (and its subsequent standardization through multilateral forums) and the deregulation of the transport sector, initially in the United States and then affecting large swaths of the world, including the trucking, railroad, airline, and, later, telecommunications industries. As Cowen (2014) suggests, these two processes permitted the rise of intermodalism (the organization of transportation across more than one mode) and the rapid growth of intermediaries in the logistics industry. Such developments prompted investments in the critical infrastructure—or infrastructural networks—necessary for the creation of "seamless" circuits of production and the reduction of costs and bureaucracies necessary for such circulations, thus enabling a system "based not simply on connectivity but the speed of connectivity" (78).

In this sense, logistics can be best understood as a "science of circulation involved in planning and managing flows," encompassing in its thinking both a calculative logic and a spatiotemporal practice of circulation, intrinsically connected to the historical reorganization of capitalism and war (Cowen et al. 2018). The civilianization of logistics has given rise to an understanding of logistics as a value-generating practice for firms and, increasingly, for nations as the emergence of new logistical spaces—and their attendant security concerns and graduated sovereignty practices (Ong 2006) attests. (An example of such political spaces of logistics is the zone—free zones, export-processing zones, special economic zones, among others—defined as "meta infrastructures administered by public and private cohorts generating de facto, undeclared forms of polity" [Easterling 2012, 1].)

Recently, logistical thinking has traveled to new spaces and sectors, enlarging its reach into "the governance of populations, the regulation of bodies, and the reconfiguration of mobilities" (Cowen et al. 2018, 622). In the terrain of humanitarian aid provision and "humanitarian logistics," several books, manuals, and academic journals (including the *Journal of Humanitarian Logistics and Supply Chain Management*, founded in 2011) have been published in the past two decades. Humanitarian logistics is defined as "the process of planning, implementing and controlling the efficient, cost-effective flow and storage of goods and materials, as well as related information, from point of origin to point of consumption for the purpose of meeting the end beneficiary's requirements" (Thomas and Mizushima 2005, 60).

The field of migration and refugee studies has spawned important academic contributions reflecting on how logistical thinking is reshaping conventional practices of containment, circulation, and integration of displaced populations, particularly in the context of contemporary South–North migrations. Martina Tazzioli and Maurice Stierl (2021), for instance, investigate how a particular logistical grammar of hotspots, checkpoints, and circuits of dispersal and contention have structured responses, governmental and nongovernmental, to the recent influx of refugees and migrants in Greece and Italy. Moritz Altenried and colleagues (2018) have shown how the connections between migration, war, and capitalism are played out in Germany in reconfigurations of integration programs aimed at using refugee and migrant labor, sponsored by private corporations and NGOs. The authors use the concept of logistical borderscapes to highlight the increasing logistification of migratory regimes. Looking at the European migration regime through a "logistical gaze," the authors highlight "the widespread use of logistical terminology—hotspots, hubs, platforms, corridors—to establish a new geography and, in a way, a new rationality of migration management. The channeling of turbulent, unpredictable, and autonomous movements of mass migration through 'spaces of exception' and governmentalized routes is meant to enable a process of filtering and selection" (Altenried et al. 2018, 294). As Cowen and colleagues (2018) argue:

> Logistics is not only a form of calculative reasoning: it is also an essentially spatial and material practice, rooted in the expansion and reconfiguration of physical networks of production and distribution. As a set of techniques, discourses, instruments, strategies, and technologies aimed at optimizing circulation, business and military logistics seeks to affect the spatial disposition of bodies, information, and infrastructures in ways that promote the construction and operation of global supply—and we would add, human mobility—networks. (622)

I turn now to how this logistical approach has reshaped, sometimes in detrimental ways, the logic of governing displaced populations' circulations in the context of South–South migration.

Borders as Logistical Hubs

Roraima is the least populated and arguably the most isolated province of Brazil. Initially a territory, Roraima was only made a province, with an elected and autonomous government, after the Constitution of 1988. With over two thousand kilometers of borders with Venezuela, Roraima was until 2017 relatively unknown to the public in the rich and densely populated areas of southern Brazil. It made headlines occasionally as a focus of tensions between farmers (basically rice producers) and Indigenous populations, whose reserves occupy approximately 70 percent of the province's territory. As a border area, distant and largely disconnected from other parts of Brazil, Roraimenses (as the province's residents are called) had a long historical tie with Venezuela, both for access to basic products of high quality and for tourism. The closest Brazilian city is Manaus, accessible only through an arduous, twelve-hour journey on poorly kept roads that traverse Indigenous reserves. Cars cannot pass over the roads at night, due to restrictions of circulation imposed by Indigenous leaders. As a public official, a middle-class lawyer who manages affairs in the provincial government, stated, "We used to go to Santa Elena to buy clothes, drinks, and duty-free goods. Some people would go to buy groceries, for everything was of great quality, imported from the US, Mexico . . ." (fieldwork interview, 2018). The first sign of a change in the economic tide was observed by Brazilians traveling to Venezuela and not finding products in supermarkets.

The first arrivals of Venezuelans in Roraima, back in 2015 and 2016, were of middle-class families, small-business owners, civil servants, judges. From 2017 to 2018, a group of Indigenous Venezuelans, of Warao origin, as well as low-income and impoverished families began to change the profile and pose important dilemmas for assistance. Roraima has one hospital for the population of approximately 300,000 people. High unemployment rates combined with growing demands from the newcomers have created a scaling-up of hostilities between Venezuelans and the hosting society. Violent acts against migrants have been systematically reported,[4] and, in mid-2018, xenophobia became a central problem for the humanitarian response, with families and individuals being expelled from improvised street shelters, having their belongings burnt, enduring physical beatings, all while being filmed with pride by residents, the videos rapidly spreading in informal channels of communication and traditional media outlets.

The setting up of an institutional response to the "Venezuelan crisis at the border" was largely infused by political disputes between governmental levels in the context of profound institutional instability in Brazil. In 2018, running for reelection (and belonging to a party in opposition to the central government), then Provincial Governor Sueli Campos made "Venezuelan migration" the dominant theme of her campaign. She requested extra financial help from the federal government (around R$180 million, approximately US$45 million as of this writing) and asked the Supreme Court for an authorization to close the border to new arrivals. The federal government, pressured for a response but resisting any assistance to the provincial candidate, decided to set up a task force involving several ministries; border agencies, especially the Federal Police; international multilateral agencies; international, national, and local NGOs; and the military in order to respond to the "emergency." As of June 2019, over

R$280 million (about $US70 million) were allocated to Operation Welcome (Operação Acolhida) to provide for three priority areas: border control, reception (processing and providing shelter and food), and territorial dispersal (known as interiorization).

The operation, which began in July 2018, was structured around a humanitarian-logistical task force, with different actors responsible for specific aspects of the program. In the control arm, the army would be responsible for infrastructure, supply, and security; the Federal Police (assisted by IOM and UNHCR) was assigned migratory control and documentation; and the Brazilian Health Regulatory Agency (Agência Nacional de Vigilância Sanitária, or ANVISA) and the Health Ministry would oversee sanitary control. In the management arm, Receita Federal (Special Department of Federal Revenue) was responsible for issuing each migrant a CPF (an ID number required for fiscal and work-related processes),[5] the Labor Ministry (alongside the provincial secretary of social assistance) would issue work permits, and UNHCR and IOM would help process and assist asylum seekers and temporary residents, respectively. Vulnerable groups (unaccompanied minors, women with children, LGBT people, elderly people, people with disabilities, and the sick, especially HIV infected) would receive special attention from the Ministry of Social Development, UNICEF, and the United Nations Population Fund (UNFPA). Originally designed as a coordinated effort organized along functional lines, in less than four months, the operation became basically a militarized logistical experiment, centrally coordinated by the army, with most of the funding devoted to the development of infrastructural support and shelter and food provision (all largely under the responsibility and control of army personnel). Media narratives regarding the operation were highly controlled by communications and press officers of the military arm, who produced videos of activities and tasks and interviews for TV, radio, and newspapers. One of the first impressions we had from our fieldwork was precisely the tight control of the narrative and access to migrant spaces, requiring constant escort by one or two military officers. At times, as one colleague aptly remarked, visiting the shelters and spaces of reception resembled a choreographed tour, including, ironically, the opportunity at the end to buy products handcrafted by Venezuelans in the shelters, all neatly arranged in an improvised table for display.[6]

The militarization of assistance and of the implementation of the "migratory regime" for Venezuelans has, of course, been responsible for the central importance attributed to logistical thinking in the processes of reception, control, and dispersal. As Brett Neilson (2012) has argued:

This shift in the fields of generation and application of logistical knowledge appears as an instance of the militarization of society. Practices of measurement, standardization, and calculation devised in the military sphere are adapted for civilian purposes that revolutionize business and management practices (as well as migratory regimes). Such practices have, nonetheless, created a condition "in which logistics has actively formed a new terrain of politics on which struggles are and will continue to be played out." (324)

I highlight here two instances that, I hope, illustrate the logistification of humanitarian protection in this particular case (understood here as a set of practices devised to regularize, i.e., provide for the means of legal permanence in the host country, and minimize the suffering of asylum seekers and migrants) and the effect that military and civil hierarchical power relations have had in reducing protection to a calculative practice related to the management of mobilities and the goal of smooth, frictionless, and efficient circulation of Venezuelan bodies and subjectivities.

Mobility and Triage

One of the first initiatives of the task force, back in 2018, was to build the necessary critical infrastructure to order the border. This has involved the construction of two large structures for reception and processing of Venezuelans arriving in the border town of Pacaraima. On one side of the road that crosses the little town is the Post for Reception and Identification (PRI) and, on the other, the Post for Triage (PTRig). The military signed a contract with local firms whereby the latter provided the tents and wood and aluminum structures that constituted the basis for the project. The outposts were built in the vicinity of the Border Battalion, by then a small center with three buildings for lodging, eating, and athletic activities for stationed military personnel.

The PRI was the first encounter Venezuelans had with specific forms of border control. They were asked whether they intended to stay or just pass through Brazilian territory. In the first case, they were informed of the two modalities of regularization—the residency process (established by an executive directive allowing Venezuelans to reside and work legally in Brazil for two years) and the asylum process. They passed through a room with a nurse who checked their vaccination certificates and immunized those who volunteered to update their vaccinations. In the second case (a common occurrence as many traversed Brazil to reach Argentina or Uruguay), their travel document was stamped, and they entered the

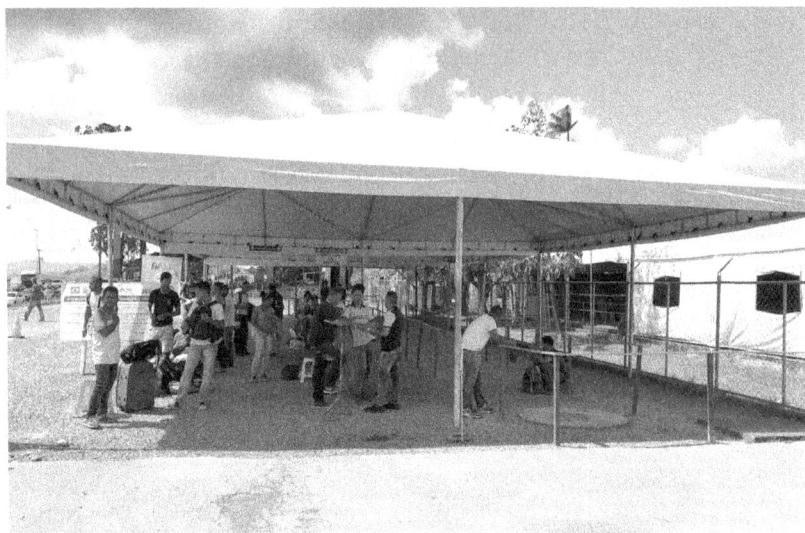

FIGURE 10.1. Entrance of the Post for Reception and Identification, Pacaraima, 2018. Photo by Carolina Moulin.

country. By the exit was a small table with mobile phones, provided by a French NGO, with which Venezuelans could make short phone calls to relatives or friends back home.

Those wishing to stay, after exiting the PRI, had to cross the street to enter the PTRig. There, they chose between two colored lines, ordering the flow: blue for refugees and red for residents. They received a paper bracelet, with empty cells that would be filled out as they traveled through numbered rooms, respectively in blue and red. The numbered rooms (from 1 to 7) encompassed the biometric screening by the Federal Police; the UNHCR and IOM offices, where forms, questionnaires, pictures, and data were taken and assessed; and rooms for medical and vulnerability assessment. Once processed, they received protocol numbers and provisional cards, allowing for their entry and stay in Brazilian territory. Medical emergencies were directed to the Advanced Medical Center, managed by the military with six beds and a stockpile of medications (Pacaraima did not have a hospital, but only one center for basic health assistance, understaffed and lacking in medical supplies). Late arrivals usually remained in Pacaraima and could sleep over at the BV-8, a transit shelter installed at the back of the PTRig compound, with dozens of bunk beds and separate areas reserved for families, men, and women.

FIGURE 10.2. Post for Triage Boa Vista, 2018. Photo by Carolina Moulin.

Some arrived in the capital without going through the regularization process on entry in Pacaraima. They had to present themselves at the Federal Police headquarters, where a similar regimen coordinated the work. During our visit, one of the officials remarked that in the early days of the response, a large, disorganized mass of people often occupied the entire entrance and vicinity of the building. A certain number of individuals could be processed each day, and many people would sleep there in order to receive the almost one hundred numbers given for Venezuelans each day. Migrants quickly figured out the numbered tickets (*senhas*) and mechanisms of control, and a small informal economy flourished in the neighborhood, with Venezuelans selling services such as printing documents, filling out forms, taking pictures, and selling numbered tickets for the Federal Police appointments.

As one of the interviewees stated, that was a logistical, managerial problem, not a humanitarian one. In response, Federal Police officials implemented the "line system": adhesive tape on the floor indicated the procedural flow, leading migrants and refugees to specific rooms where biometric data were collected, forms were delivered and signed, information processed via administrative systems connected to Brasilia, and resident cards issued and distributed. Numbered tickets were offered on presentation of documents and bore the person's name along with a specific date and time for their appointment.

Residency permits were processed through computational systems, with data directly submitted online. But asylum requests were all manual, with Venezuelans filling out the twelve-page questionnaire that had to be later digitized and sent to the National Committee for Refugees (CONARE) in Brasilia (responsible for deciding on the cases). A large pile of forms and documents mounted in the "refugee" backlog room, where one contracted employee and two UNHCR interns manually scanned each page of the individual asylum requests to be later emailed to CONARE. The hard copies were sent whenever possible by government mail.[7]

Efficiency and management of demand are central elements of the reception process just described. Paramount in the perspective of interviewees were concerns about time, cost efficiency, and minimization of the impact of migrant flows on other processes conducted by the Federal Police (such as passport issuance, control, and surveillance of illegal activities such as contraband and drug trafficking—seen by many as the backbone of the Federal Police's operations and mandate).

Anecdotally, one solution devised was to include military staff to assist in Federal Police (FP) responsibilities regarding regularization processes. Around fifteen young recruits were assigned to the computer room, where Venezuelans provided data, directly registering them in the online migration system. When asked why they were outsourcing the responsibility, the FP officer was quick to associate more personnel with higher numbers of cases processed and more efficient administrative procedures. It took one full day just to acquaint the military trainees with the intricacies of the software. Some seemed uncomfortable with the keyboard. By the end of the visit, I asked the FP officer whether he knew that those military men were leaving Roraima in the coming weeks and, therefore, he would have to request new personnel and provide continuous training. He was obviously profoundly disturbed by the news.

The messy mass occupying the main avenue where the FP headquarters was located prompted the replication of the Pacaraima experiment in the provincial capital, Boa Vista. Inaugurated in October 2018, the capital PTRig followed the same logic developed by its twin brother at the border: established flows, ordered through color codes, numbered rooms allocated to specific functions and agencies, a luggage area for migrants' belongings, and an area for distribution of donated clothes and basic hygiene kits. The main difference lay in the fact that, at PTRig Boa Vista (BV), military and UNHCR personnel also distributed the vacant spots in the (by then) twelve shelters that hosted Venezuelan migrants and refugees in several neighborhoods of the town. Not surprisingly, in the first weeks of operation, the number of individuals passing through PTRig BV had surpassed three hundred people per day, mainly because many Venezuelans who could not afford to leave Roraima on their own also could not afford to rent housing and thus were sleeping on the streets and in the vicinity of several shelters. The bus station had also become a central hub for homeless Venezuelans, so a booth was set up by the UNHCR and the military to assist them and provide information.

The process described here illustrate the articulation of logistical thinking in two interrelated fronts. First, it sets up the mobility apparatus as a calculative machine, aimed at enabling a measurable, quantifiable process and at improving efficiency and providing for a smooth network of circulations required for managing migration flows that "optimize the entire circuit of production and distribution of mobility demands" (Cowen 2018). The calculative machine enables a reductive logic in which stories, particularities, and diversity are subsumed in quantifiable categories such as number of attendees, number of regularized individuals, and time-efficiency in processing and shelter allocation. A major consequence of such logistical mentality has been a reduction of the protective dimension of refugee and residency status to an issue of bureaucratic regularization. The imposition of the mechanism of triage—of sorting migrant bodies in order to maximize the efficiency of document provision through established rational flows, with specific capacities and functions—has vacated discussion about the different nature and scope of juridical institutions and of their capacity for enforcing rights and duties in relation to displaced groups.

The decision to go either "blue" or "red," though UNHCR, IOM, and military personnel attest that it is informed and presented clearly to Venezuelans, is largely decided on the basis of whether applicants can present the required documents or not and thus will not disrupt the flow inscribed for each of these categories. For example, children under nine years old did not have an official Venezuelan document stating the name of their father or mother, and so determining parenthood becomes a matter of individual credibility assessment. Requisites for residency status demand the presentation of such proof, whereas for asylum applications, such demands are not present. Most—if not all—families with children under nine end up applying for refugee status, even though they might consider temporary residency a more appropriate venue for their migratory projects and even if the reasons for granting asylum remain, in some cases, largely absent (increasing chances of denial by CONARE).[8] The calculative machine thus "contributes to the material conditions through which the security and well-being of human and nonhuman lives are rendered subordinate to the imperative of smooth, efficient circulation" (Cowen et al. 2018, 622).

Second, the process shows the way "logistical rationalities are enacted through the production of vast infrastructural assemblages that inscribe calculative modes of spatial reasoning into the built environment" (Cowen et al. 2018, 622). A massive infrastructure of logistical hubs (the reception and triage posts), gateways and corridors, even though marked by chokepoints and disruptions (of staff, of energy, and often times of connectivity), has not only attributed specific meanings and subjective formations to Venezuelan bodies but has also constituted a political space organized around a transnationally operated network of circulations and bureaucracies, a "pipeline" of social relations underpinned by logistical processes. Such infrastructural assemblages involve spatial practices of circulation devoted both to control and to the will to care. Alongside reception posts and triage centers, shelters have become a central node in modulating mobile subjects' desires and converting the enlarging "operational fantasies" of logistical thinking to other parts of the country through the circulation of Venezuelan migrants and their families.

Roraima Province had fourteen shelters for displaced Venezuelans—two in Pacaraima and twelve in Boa Vista in late 2019.[9] Three of the oldest shelters in Boa Vista were originally public sports facilities and convention centers, adapted into temporary dormitories for the first wave of arrivals, back in 2016. Most of the shelters, however, were reformed or transformed after June 2018 under the umbrella of the task force, and half of the six thousand places available were built on empty terrains in more distant neighborhoods. Shelters were distributed in several parts of town and organized by specific profiles of displaced groups: LGBT groups have their own shelter, as do Indigenous populations, families with children, single men, single women, and groups selected for dispersal (the transit shelter). Usually, shelters were operated in partnership among UNHCR officials, contracted NGOs, and military personnel. The military provided logistical support (controlling entry, securing the perimeter, checking documents, and delivering supplies, especially food), whereas the UNHCR and NGOs coordinated activities inside the shelter and assisted with basic needs (for example, problems with access to school, social assistance, information on resettlement, and job placement).

The explosion of shelters across Boa Vista's landscape, composing the infrastructural assemblage of spatial practices of circulation, was a way of articulating the logistical reception process with the need to simultaneously locate and contain migrants' physical presence in the urban space while enabling the smooth operation of the circulation program designed by the operation. Growing tensions have arisen because of the massive presence of Venezuelans—many of whom remained homeless—and violent responses by locals, including the fencing off of public spaces and occasional beatings and killings. These instances of violence intensified the "urgency" of building up a protective infrastructure for the concomitant spatial control of the population and the operational demands of the circulation pipeline. Such circulation was premised on the need to remove migrants and refugees from Roraima, relocating them to other cities in Brazil, where "integration" could be more successful. Through labor intermediaries and the voluntary adherence in 2018 of roughly fifty municipalities, interiorization became the final goal of the production and distribution line of Venezuelan mobility in Brazil. The logistical rationale involved creating a steady flow among different nodes of the circulation pipeline: if, for example, three hundred migrants were processed per week at PTRig, the task force needed a similar number of shelter vacancies and, consequently, a similar number of people leaving under the interiorization program.

The first step was, then, to increase the number of vacancies in shelters: it nearly doubled in less than a year (from June 2018 to April 2019) with the construction of three massive shelters, with a capacity of 600 to 1,000 people. The second task was to impose a more forceful approach to interiorization, the greatest chokepoint in the pipeline. Most municipalities were not interested in receiving Venezuelans. Faced with a severe economic and unemployment crisis in most cases, cities resisted federal government proposals of dispersal. Early acceptances involved mainly NGOs, sponsored by UNHCR and IOM, working in no more than ten cities that had already set up infrastructure to receive small numbers of displaced. By the end of 2018, two dozen more cities, again largely convinced by local NGOs and by short-term projects and sponsorship by UNHCR, entered the program. As of February 2019, seventeen provinces and more than fifty cities participated in the interiorization process, and close to five thousand Venezuelans had left Roraima under its banner. The sponsored interiorization was led by the military and IOM; usually the air force and local army battalions were responsible for transportation and the IOM AND UNHCR provided information and logistical-financial support to participant cities and NGOs. The Casa Civil (Civilian House) of the Presidency was the official coordinator of the dispersal initiative, but difficulties in the relationship between federal and local governments have ended up, once again, prompting the already outsized role of army officials and international public servants in the process. As such, it seems fair to say that the subsumption of the humanitarian aspect by the logistical dimension of the task force has been accompanied by the increasing control of military staff in all phases of this network of circulation, from reception to production to delivery.[10]

Originally designed as temporary living spaces, shelters were transformed in the logistical hub of the humanitarian operation. A distinct element in the network, the shelters progressively became an integral and necessary part of the established flow expected of migrants and refugees. To be sent to another province, Venezuelans had first to be allotted a spot in one of the shelters, according to availability. Once in the shelters, they were enrolled for potential interiorization opportunities according to their profile and demand in receiving cities. Quotas for interiorization were established by the receiving node along race, gender, age and background education parameters.

The operation's official website states that interiorization is voluntary and that details about destination cities are explained in advance. Participants agree to a term of "voluntary participation" with the IOM. In practice, this is a much more complicated process, marked by highly unequal power relations and by the effects of logistical *dispositifs* in the making of displaced groups' desires and

FIGURE 10.3. Rondon Shelter, 2019. Photo by Carolina Moulin.

subjectivities. Earlier research indicated that many Venezuelans wanted to remain close to the border and in Roraima in order to provide for relatives and send them supplies, configuring what was termed as a circular migration flow. The logistical rendering of circulations, coupled with a context of deterioration of the crisis both in Venezuela and in Roraima (rising xenophobia, high living costs, and lack of opportunities), arguably promoted a *habitus*, an intensification of the disposition of displaced Venezuelans to keep moving through the pipeline set up by the task force. New arrivals were rapidly socialized in the shelter-in-and-flight-out routine of the program, and the desire to move, once relatively understated, became a recurrent trait of migrants' narratives. Many of those still on the streets and sleeping in the vicinity of the shelters hoped they would be picked up in one of the many night operations for enrollment and removal of street dwellers orchestrated by the UNHCR and the army.

Once migrants were in the shelters, expectations grew as to when a flight opportunity would materialize. In our interviews and participant observation, we encountered several occasions when lists of displaced people willing to leave were made on the fly and people were selected on the spot, just in time. One group of young men, for example, was holding a map of Brazil and asking where Rio Grande do Sul was (the most southern province of Brazil). They had learned a few minutes earlier that the next flight would go to Canoas, a city six thousand kilometers away from Boa Vista. The map was truncated, though, three provinces above Rio Grande do Sul. Some of men were called and had to present the next day for removal. They had no idea about Canoas, an eminently white town with cold weather and with a very different set of social rules and expectations from those they experienced in Boa Vista. Nor were they able to pinpoint spatially how far they would have to go.

The ways logistical thinking (calculative reasoning and spatial strategies) informed the shelter-in-and-flight-out routine created confusion and frustration among staff and the displaced. For staff, just-in-time decisions had to be made as to who could go and who fulfilled the criteria (who had taken all the required vaccines, who had a work permit, and so on). Not infrequently, names had to be eliminated from the lists—at great stress and cost for humanitarian workers—as other stakeholders imposed later restrictions on the process for selected individuals. For example, we witnessed the selection of a group of individuals and families for interiorization that had been removed to the transit shelter; some had quit their jobs in Boa Vista and sold their few belongings, like mattresses and kitchen apparel. On the same day, when they were about to enter the procedural routine for "flight out," they were informed by health professionals of the federal sanitary agency that there was one case of chickenpox and therefore the entire group would have to be quarantined. The spots assigned them earlier would be reallocated, and the group would have to reenter the waiting line for a vacancy in the dispersal program (probably another city, another province—after at least a forty-day wait).

Increasing frustrations with the government-led program have also prompted private initiatives of relocation, especially through NGOs and labor recruitment firms. The Jesuit Service, for example, built a database of résumés and potential employees, intermediating them with companies and services willing to hire them in other provinces. The Church of Jesus Christ of Latter-day Saints, also participating in the local effort of assistance, had secured an agreement with a private airline company guaranteeing a certain number of free tickets from Boa Vista to several destinations in Brazil. In response to our questions about the "privatization" and steady rise of intermediaries in the process of Venezuelan circulation, a task force agent responded: "The important thing is to get them out of here, get them to the final result . . . if they can do this by other means, even better for the Brazilian taxpayer."[11] Concern with securing the flow and speed of connectivity (i.e., a steady balance between entry and removal) informs such a reading of interiorization initiatives. Needless to say, very little has been said about what is going on with Venezuelans once they arrive and whether their needs, rights, and guarantees are being observed. The logistical gaze stops where the distribution line ends and, with it, the concerns over the humanitarian response to the Venezuelan "migration crisis."

Conclusions

These examples highlight the intricacies of military-civilian relations in realizing a prominent logistical rationale in the humanitarian response to Venezuelan displaced populations in Brazil. Logistics provides a means of calculating and managing effectively the network of circulations, of ordering borders and producing and distributing migrants' bodies and subjectivities. The grammar of logistics has infused the humanitarian landscape in recent years and, increasingly, informed the governance of globally displaced populations. As a technique of power, logistics not only spatially distributes functions along the network of circulations but also produces expectations about who the displaced are, what they can become, and how they will get there. Reception, containment, and dispersal have turned into central nodes for the smooth operation of the mobility pipeline. Such operations, nonetheless, are marked by chokepoints and bottlenecks, by appropriations on the part of the displaced, and by the need of constantly reevaluating the material and symbolic infrastructure required to successfully convert a spontaneous and largely uncontrolled movement of people and desires into an organized and rationalized flow of identifiable populations. Much complex learning and adapting are involved in the making up of logistical borderscapes and in the entwined parts and processes of its constitutive agents.

The deleterious impact of logistical thinking, despite its capacity to care and provide for the basic needs of migrants and asylum seekers, lies in the long-term effects it produces and in the fact that it ends up condensing, in its gaze and procedures, the whole condition of possibility and legibility of population circulations in such contexts. On one hand, it reduces the space and grammar of protection central to, for example, a proper discussion of the right to asylum. On the other, it pervades the potential sociability enacted in circulations with rationalized scripts and expectations, thus reducing the possibility of creative interventions. This is not to say that "counterlogistics" are not present but to emphasize that the reduction of displaced populations to a "logistical life" has profound consequences for the understanding of mobility as a freedom experiment.

The COVID-19 pandemic accelerated and exacerbated such trends. The humanitarian infrastructure galvanized its centrality in the protracted emergency response, and efficiency pressures have prompted the digitization of services, including regularization processes. Under the argument of administrative resolve, prima facie recognition of delayed asylum processes started coming out in late 2020. Residency permits have been renewed, and regularization have taken a front seat in discussions of assistance and protection in a context of growing labor informality, poverty and unemployment, and rising xenophobia. Having documents, as important as they are, does not translate into better integration and protection of rights, especially in structurally unequal societies like those of Latin America. Subsuming protection qua regularization has been an important development of the growing logistical approach to migration governance, particularly in the context of South–South circulations. Shelters have been closed, yet the number of spots has expanded in ever-large tracts that resemble, in logic and design, semiurban refugee camps. Controlled circulations are now enabled by a vast spatial network that connects, even if poorly, all provinces. Interiorization has been followed closely by other partners, and other countries in the region are adapting the strategy to their own national demands.

It is important to highlight, once again, that such logistical rationality applied to forced circulations has become increasingly global, thus permitting the expansion of techniques of government to disrupting the location of borders—as the European case powerfully attests—and widening the range of actors and stakeholders now included in power relations produced through mobility. Far from a situated experience, logistical lives and humanitarian borders have become ubiquitous and form an integral part of the landscape of global cooperation between migration regimes in rich and poorer areas of the globe. The rebordering of the world (Tazzioli and Aradau 2020) is under way, and Latin American countries have been fast learners and eager participants.

NOTES

1. Up-to-date data on Venezuelan migration can be accessed at the Regional Interagency Coordination Platform for Refugees and Migrants from Venezuela (R4V Platform), https://www.r4v.info/.

2. The *carnet de la patria*, implemented in 2017, serves as an identity card with a QR code. It is used to collect information on Venezuelan citizens and allow them access to financial and social assistance provided by the government. Some have argued that the registration system, using Chinese technology, serves as a social control mechanism; the government defends it as a tool for improving efficiency and access to public programs. See, for example, "Qué es y cómo funciona el carnet de la patria que permitirá seguir comprando gasolina a precio subsidiado en Venezuela," *BBC News Mundo*, August 14, 2018, https://www.bbc.com/mundo/noticias-america-latina-45182511.

3. Project "Asylum and Its Margins: Venezuelan Displacement in Brazil," 2018, approved by the Research Ethics Committee, PUC-Rio, under n.38/2018.

4. Reports of beatings, burning down tents, and threats against Venezuelans are a recurrent feature on local news and videos of violent episodes have circulated widely on social media. Some instances have made national and international news as the attempt to expel Venezuelans camping on the streets of Pacaraima in August 2018. See "'Bota

fogo!': O ataque de brasileiros a imigrantes venezuelanos em Pacaraima," BBC *News Brasil*, August 20, 2018, https://www.bbc.com/portuguese/brasil-45245644.

5. Shelters are spaces designed for living; they include in some cases individual tents, rooms, beds, bathrooms, and cooking-and-eating areas. Reception centers are spaces designed to process, triage, and refer Venezuelans, including sending those eligible to shelter areas.

6. As of April 2022, Operation Welcome remained the central cornerstone of the Brazilian response, hailed by international organizations and regional partners as an example of good practice in migration governance. The operation has gained in institutional complexity with several subcommittees designed to oversee specific aspects of the coordinated response, numerous local actors (both governmental and nongovernmental), increasing visibility and media attention, and an expanded territorial network, encompassing the border hub and more than seven hundred cities throughout the vast Brazilian territory. With greater complexity and reach, old and new problems have arisen. For some insight on the institutional overview of current trends in the operation, see Silva 2022.

7. One of the results of these developments (combined with an increased backlog caused by suspension of in-site requirements during the pandemic) was an acceleration of the digitization of migration systems and processes. Since mid-2021, asylum requests have been submitted electronically through a national system called SISCONARE.

8. After increasing pressure from Defensoria Publica da Uniao, the National Committee for Refugees issued a directive facilitating the regularization of undocumented minors.

9. As of April 2022, there were seven shelters in Boa Vista. Since 2021, there has been a trend toward a concentration of spaces in fewer yet bigger shelters. Again, the largest shelters were built after the infrastructural approach to the emergency response was adopted, using vast tracts of land on the city's outskirts (rather than downtown) to set up new, temporary housing units and facilitate assistance and provision. The largest shelter, Rondon 1, can house up to 2,000 people. There are roughly 10,000 spots available in that shelters, all mostly running at full capacity. See full data at "Perfil dos abrigos em Romaima," updated March 18, 2025, https://app.powerbi.com/view?r=eyJrIjoiZTRhOWVlOTgtYTk2M-SooYmY3LWEyY2YtMGM1Y2MzODFjMmVjIiwidCI6ImU1YzM3OTgxLTY2NjQtN-DEzNC04YTBjLTY1NDNkMmFmODBiZSIsImMiOjh9.

10. As of April 2022, more than seven hundred cities have received 72,000 people of Venezuelan origin under the interiorization program. Many have left border areas on their own and have been included in official data under the category of social reunion. The pandemic hit the interiorization strategy hard, with numbers crashing especially in 2020. The resumption of economic activity and the reduction of circulation restrictions prompted a renewed increase by mid-2021. Data can be found at http://aplicacoes.mds .gov.br/snas/painel-interiorizacao/ (last accessed May 2022).

11. Over the years, this has certainly been the experience for most migrants originating in Venezuela. Almost half of those who have been interiorized have done so under the rubric of social reunion, whereby individuals reunite with friends or acquaintances in the destination. In these situations, it is likely that many rely on their own networks for most of the integration demands and resort to local NGOs and services—when they exist

in situ—in case of urgent need. By comparison, only 18 percent have been relocated in a shelter-to-shelter strategy, in which they receive temporary housing and assistance by local partners in the destination.

REFERENCES

Altenried, Moritz, Manuela Bojadžijev, Leif Höfler, Sandro Mezzadra, and Mira Wallis. 2018. "Logistical Borderscapes: Politics and Mediation of Mobile Labor in Germany After the 'Summer of Migration.'" *South Atlantic Quarterly* 117 (2): 291–312. https://doi.org/10.1215/00382876-4374845.

Aradau, Claudia, and Martina Tazzioli. 2020. "Biopolitics Multiple: Migration, Extraction, Subtraction." *Millennium* 48(2): 198–220. https://doi.org/10.1177/0305829819889139.

Cowen, Deborah. 2014. *The Deadly Life of Logistics: Mapping Violence in Global Trade.* Minneapolis: University of Minnesota Press.

Cowen, Deborah, Charmaine Chua, Martin Danyluk, and Laleh Khalili. 2018. "Introduction: Turbulent Circulation—Building a Critical Engagement with Logistics." *Environment and Planning D: Society and Space* 36 (4): 617–29. https://doi.org/10.1177/0263775818783101.

de Oliveira, Antônio Tadeu R., Gustavo da Frota Simões, and Leonardo Cavalcanti. 2021. "La inmigración venezolana en Brasil: Perfil sociodemográfico e inserción en el mercado de trabajo formal." In *Inserción Laboral de la inmigración venezolana en Latinoamérica*, edited by José Koechlin, Joaquin Eguren Rodríguez, and Guerda Cecilia Estrada Villaseñor. Madrid: OBMID.

Easterling, Keller. 2012. "Zone: The Spatial Softwares of Extrastatecraft." *Places Journal.* https://doi.org/10.22269/120610.

Neilson, Brett. 2012. "Five Theses on Understanding Logistics as Power." *Distinktion: Journal of Social Theory* 13 (3): 322–39. https://doi.org/10.1080/1600910X.2012.728533.

Ong, Aihwa. 2006. *Neoliberalism as Exception: Mutations in Citizenship and Sovereignty.* Durham, NC: Duke University Press.

Reid, Julian. 2006. *The Biopolitics of the War on Terror: Life Struggles, Liberal Modernity and the Defence of Logistical Societies.* Manchester, UK: Manchester University Press.

Silva, João Carlos Jarochinski. 2022. *O ACNUR antes e depois da Operação Acolhida: Uma análise à luz da resposta humanitária brasileira.* Brazil: ACNUR (Alto Comissariado das Nações Unidas para Refugiados).

Tazzioli, Martina. 2018. "Containment Through Mobility: Migrants' Spatial Disobediences and the Reshaping of Control Through the Hotspot System." *Journal of Ethnic and Migration Studies* 44 (16): 2764–79. https://doi.org/10.1080/1369183X.2017.1401514.

Tazzioli, Martina, and Maurice Stierl. 2021. "'We Closed the Ports to Protect Refugees.' Hygienic Borders and Deterrence Humanitarianism During Covid-19." *International Political Sociology* 15 (4): 539–58. https://doi.org/10.1093/ips/olab023.

Thomas, Anisya, and Mitsuko Mizushima. 2005. "Logistics Training: Necessity or Luxury?" *Forced Migration Review* 22: 60–61.

Zapata, Gisela P., and Carolina Moulin. 2022. "(Des)continuidades pandêmicas no Brasil e no mundo: Fronteiras, migrações internacionais e a Covid-19." In *Crise, pandemia e alternativas*, edited by Eduardo Albuquerque, Frederico Jayme Jr., and Gustavo Britto. Belo Horizonte: FACE; UFMG.

Zapata, Gisela P., and Vicente Tapia Wenderoth. 2022. "Progressive Legislation but Lukewarm Policies: The Brazilian Response to Venezuelan Displacement." *International Migration* 60 (1): 132–51.

11

"Europe" in "Latin America"

ILLEGALIZED MOBILITIES, DEPORTABLE BODIES,
AND CONTESTED SOVEREIGNTIES IN THE
FRENCH-BRAZILIAN BORDERLAND

Fabio Santos

In August 2021, there was yet another episode in a deadly migration drama that keeps repeating itself between the waters of the Oyapock River, meandering through the Amazon rainforest, and the Atlantic Ocean. After leaving Brazil's northernmost city of Oiapoque downstream to the river's mouth, a small boat carrying Brazilian nationals entered the stormy Atlantic Ocean, heading north toward coastal French Guiana, an overseas department of France and an outermost region—that is, a full-fledged part—of the European Union. The boat, locally known as a *pirogue* or *catraia*, sank with twenty-five people on board. Only five survived.

The origins and consequences of hostile immigration and asylum law enforcement—often silenced or downplayed in mainstream academia, media, and politics—have been addressed by an increasingly rich and critical literature on migrant illegality with a focus on borderlands in Eurafrica and the Americas (Andersson 2014; De Genova 2004, 2017; De León 2015; Domenech and Dias

2020). Less well known even to scholars with an explicitly global approach to migrations and inequalities, however, are the unequal mobilities and deportabilities in spaces escaping and challenging the universality and normativity of the nation-state (Bonilla 2017; Boatcă and Santos 2023). One such space is French Guiana / Guyane[1] and its borderland with the Brazilian state of Amapá. In the second half of the twentieth century, with the transition from penal colony to French overseas department taking place in 1946, Guyane's entangled history of migration took yet another twist, as the territory became the destination for increasing numbers of people from the Caribbean, Europe, the Middle East, and Asia (Mam Lam Fouck 2015). This lasting yet increasingly controlled immigration has had an unparalleled demographic effect: Today, there are more people living in French Guiana who were born outside the department (including other parts of France) than people born within its borders (Wood 2019, 10). Haitians constitute the main immigrant group, followed by people of Surinamese and Brazilian nationality.

Forgetting about Guyane and its entwined histories of migration—also termed the "coloniality of memory" in sociological research on the topic (Boatcă 2018)—is common in societies conventionally grouped under the term *Global North*, where many people are unaware of the global dynamics beyond their own front yard. Forgetting is no option for those daily confronted with abundant inequalities, those whose front yard *is* the border: Many people living in or moving through the French-Brazilian borderland are keenly aware of the fact that they are navigating a microcosm of globally entangled inequalities (Santos 2022a). These are most visible in people's life expectancy, that is, the possibilities of sheer survival in an unequal world, determined by the arbitrary yet powerful institution of citizenship mostly acquired via bloodline or place of birth (Shachar 2009). At the same time, it is known that citizenship and its denial have, historically and up to the present, interacted with several axes of stratification reproducing inequalities (Boatcă 2015; Boatcă and Roth 2016; Jelin, Motta, and Costa 2018; Santos 2025). This speaks to the premises of this book and related works (De Genova 2017) in that racialized bodies deemed to be deviating from the self-proclaimed European whiteness permeate border politics just as much as formal citizenship. A perverse effect of migration regimes is that in trying to challenge them by cross-border mobility, people on the move risk having their lives shortened rather than extended (Cuttitta and Last 2019; De León 2015; Holmes 2013; Lo Presti 2019; McMahon and Sigona 2021; Rygiel 2016; Schindel 2019; Squire 2020). As emphasized in the introductory scene and further detailed on the following pages, the borderland shared by France and Brazil at the crossroads of Amazonia, the Atlantic, and the Greater Caribbean is no exception to this deadly rule of global inequality.

This chapter starts with a terminological and spatial (re)orientation, drawing attention to the social constructions and momentous consequences of shorthand and shortsighted notions such as "Europe" and "Latin America." What follows is a historical contextualization, as I do not want to be complicit in the naturalization of *the* border and its assumed need of control against illegalized migrants. The arguments in this chapter are grounded in the understanding that unequal mobilities in the case at hand must be analyzed through the lens of colonial conquest, racialization, enslavement, and forced migration that shaped the borderland as part of the Atlantic world and global Blackness (Beaman and Clerge 2024; Gilroy 1993). By reconnecting neglected and nationally segmented histories of mobilities across the *longue durée*, multiple exclusions become visible—from exclusion from rights to physical exclusion in the form of deportation. As I demonstrate in the section following the delineation of these interwoven histories, the more recent mobilities, as well as the set of measures aiming at preventing them, provide evidence of Guyane's function as a laboratory of legal exceptionalisms facilitating the illegality, deportability, and deterrence of migrants. Fast-track asylum processing and deporting, legally facilitated identity checks marked by racial profiling, and the deliberate shortage of accommodation and financial support for asylum seekers are among the anti-immigration policies enacted in recent years. Although relatively new, these developments are not disconnected from, or contradictory to, the historical entanglements in the region. The pinnacle of infrastructurally facilitated "illegality" is the Oyapock River Bridge: opened in 2017, the first bridge (de)linking Brazil and France has effectively become a one-way street, reinforcing unequal mobilities in a borderland that defies the neat geopolitical categories to which many social scientists have grown accustomed (Santos 2022b).

The case at hand differs from most other border constellations discussed in this volume, as French Guiana has never achieved independence and therefore has never autonomously "imported" migration policies from the center. It is more accurate to describe French Guiana as subject to a permanent state of exception, with sovereignty resting in the metropole, which has historically imposed various border policies on its "ultraperiphery." These include the forced migration of enslaved people, the deportation and incarceration of metropolitan convicts, and the exclusion of French Guiana from the Schengen Area, as well as from the exemption from the visa reciprocity that exists between Brazil and the rest of France. As noted by Olivier Kramsch (2012, 135) and further elaborated in this chapter, the French-Brazilian border is not a border between modern states but rather a modern/colonial front, allowing for experiments in state governance that were later reincorporated into the administration of the European metropolitan state.

While prevailing academic discussions continue to be underpinned by Occidentalist cognitive maps, critical attempts to deconstruct seemingly neutral spatial and cultural referents were made as early as the 1990s.[2] Stuart Hall famously unmasked the economic, political, and epistemic power structures pervading these maps by asking the simple question "Where and what is the West?" (Hall 1992, 276ff.). As if anticipating Hall's question—and echoing the sentiments of many of those the West has othered—in 1990, Édouard Glissant pointed to a seeming paradox in writing, "The West is not in the West. It is a project, not a place" (Glissant 1990). For both Hall and Glissant, "the West" is therefore a historical rather than a geographical concept. The self-definition of the West as culturally, economically, and morally superior resulted in oversimplified antinomies such as "the West and the Rest." These arguments can be extended to the very notion of "Europe": any attempt to define "Europe" has to confront the controversial question of its external and internal borders, implicitly tied to its contested status as a continent (Balibar 2002, 2009). While its textbook classification as a full-fledged continent separate from Asia has been critiqued by geographers and world historians with limited success (Hodgson 1963; Lewis and Wigen 1997), its borders are "polysemic," a term used by Étienne Balibar (2002, 81–83) to point out the different meanings and decisive consequences borders and border policies have for differently positioned people—an important caution to keep in mind throughout this chapter.

These important caveats and related works touch on more than "just" the dimensions of discourse and representation. "Europe," and by extension "the West," would not have risen to the rank of global power without "the Rest," as has been shown with respect to Afro-Eurasian economic entanglements (Abu-Lughod 1989; Frank 1998). These dynamics took another momentous twist with the incorporation of the Americas into the emerging capitalist world economy after 1492 (Quijano and Wallerstein 1992; Wynter 1995). This incorporation through exploitation, coming at the cost of tens of millions of Black and Indigenous lives, also led to the category "European" gradually becoming a self-designation of whites, replacing local and regional allegiances and identities, thus translating the colonial enterprise overseas into a collective self-identification "at home," or colonization into "Europeanization" (see also Hall 1991). Just as "Europe" became a powerful idea notwithstanding, or perhaps even legitimating, all sorts of internal and external hierarchies (Boatcă 2010; De Genova 2016), "America" and "Latin America" were similarly revealed as inventions (Mignolo 2005).[3]

The key difference between "Europe" on one hand and "America" and "Latin America" on the other lies in who gets to invent and cement these ideas. While "Europe" has largely been a self-designation, "America" and "Latin America" are geopolitically charged referents imposed by self-proclaimed "Europeans," erasing the previous spatial designations used by Indigenous peoples who inhabited these lands before 1492. While the term "America" (referencing Italian "voyager" Amerigo Vespucci) emerged in the long sixteenth century—that is, with the beginning of European colonialism on the other side of the Atlantic—the idea of "Latin America" was forged by France in the aftermath of formal independence gained by most, though not all, colonies in the Americas: "The concept of 'Latinidad' was used in France by intellectuals and state officers to take the lead in Europe among the configuration of Latin countries involved in the Americas (Italy, Spain, Portugal, and France itself), and allowed it also to confront the United States' continuing expansion toward the South—its purchase of Louisiana from Napoleon and its appropriation of vast swaths of territory from Mexico" (Mignolo 2005, 58–59). Why did the term gain currency among Creole elites of European descent, and why has it become the dominant denomination since then? Walter Mignolo has argued that the adoption of the term by Creole elites is undergirded by racialization: in attempting to emulate "Europeanness" and thereby whiteness, "'Latin' American Creoles turned their backs on Indians and Blacks and their faces to France and England" (Mignolo 2005, 67). In addition to these critical insights stemming from decolonial scholarship, it has also been suggested that Creole elites in "Latin America" strategically adopted the concept in reaction to US expansionism (Gobat 2013).

This brief excursus into the history of ideas underscores the need for reflection when using pseudogeographical concepts. The borderland between France and Brazil exemplifies how these political, economic, and epistemic power struggles manifest in a specific context, even adding a new dimension to the discussion: Why does a border still exist between the country (France) that originally coined the term "Latin America" and the largest independent nation-state in the region (Brazil)? And how has this impacted migration patterns over time and space?

Cross-Border Entanglements in the *Longue Durée*

The above-mentioned suppression of Indigenous peoples and their knowledges is part of a wider pattern of historical silencing. Prevailing historical narratives of spatial re-(b)orderings around the Oyapock River—today's official borderline between France and Brazil—usually begin with European "explorations" across the coastal Guianas from the early sixteenth century onward. However, such narratives overlook the fact that the region was home to a dense and complex network of Indigenous peoples prior to this watershed period. As historian Silvia Espelt-Bombin (2018) has shown, the region between the Amazon and Maroni Rivers was an "Amerindian space" not only prior to European colonization but also in the early phases of trading, military, and missionary "expeditions." From 1600 to 1730, Espelt-Bombin shows, these lands, rivers, lakes, and coasts were inhabited by multilingual and multiethnic groups that maintained exchange networks based on trade, rituals, alliances, and wars—networks that fueled processes of ethnogenesis. Such connections made this an Amerindian space because what gave unity and centrality to the space were the interactions between Indigenous peoples, their occupation and use of lands and waters, their patterns of use, and their frequent migration within this space. These migrations and networks predated the arrival of the Europeans and, while European colonization changed regional power relations, some Indigenous people maintained their autonomy within this space, which was neither defined by the physical limits of European expansion nor a refuge from European violence. Instead, it incorporated European settlements such as Belém, Cayenne, and surrounding missions, without being restricted by European-imposed borders like the Oyapock River (Espelt-Bombin 2018, 612).

Espelt-Bombin's research reveals that border struggles between the Portuguese and French empires, which led to the signing of a provisional treaty in 1700, cannot be understood without the acknowledgment of Indigenous agency. Accordingly, the French takeover of Portuguese forts south of the Oyapock River (Parú and Macapá) in 1697 was possible only because of the collective and strategic support of the French by Indigenous groups. This resembles the pro-French stance taken by the Indigenous Pa'ikwené (or Palikur), who sought to evade and prevent Portuguese raids and deportations of enslaved people (Passes 2009, 136).

These colonial struggles for control of land resulted in a provisional treaty that defined the border between the Portuguese and French territories as a river called Vicente Pinção (or Vincent Pinçon). In 1713, this pact was ratified via the Treaty of Utrecht, confirming agreement to establish the border between the French and Portuguese colonies at the Pinção/Pinçon River (Granger 2011). However, rather than resolving the border conflict, this designation introduced new ambiguities, as there was no consensus on which river was meant by that name. The Portuguese (from 1822 onward, Brazilian) view consistently favored the Oyapock River as the borderline, while French claims shifted progressively southward over time. Imprecise labeling, the lack of clear legal borders, and—consequently—ongoing disputes over the course of borders was a relatively common but particularly distinctive feature of the Guyanas in northern Amazonia (Baud 2000, 47). Both Portugal and France had a vital interest in securing access to the Amazon River, which would enable fast links to distant regions. But for two centuries—from the provisional agreement of 1700 to the final demarcation in 1900—the borderland remained contested, witnessing several territorial shifts and instances of "marginal migrations," a term coined by Shalini Puri (2003) to highlight Caribbean mobilities that are perhaps better understood as marginal*ized* migrations within seemingly "peripheral" regions (Santos 2020a).

In the French-Brazilian case, these migrations need to be situated within the histories of enslavement and racial subordination as well as Black and Indigenous agency (Beaman and Clerge 2024). The resistance of enslaved people and the formation of Maroon communities, known as *quilombos*, across the blurry border offer a poignant example. Flávio Gomes (2003) has explained:

> Escapes by slaves from colonial dominions in particular were an important cause for concern in the border regions. These borders were not fixed because they were the subject of constant disputes, particularly in the second half of the eighteenth century. The Amapá region—which bordered on French Guiana—was the greatest source of apprehension. With the help of settlers, merchants, and indigenous groups, black slaves were continually migrating and establishing mocambos. (256)

In other words, those who escaped the horrors of enslavement sought to establish their own autonomous spaces across borders, creating havens of freedom that stood both in opposition to and in interdependence with the spatial arrangements of other actors: "They looked to the other side of the border and saw French settlers and peasants and Amerindian settlements and other groups of fugitives and deserters who, although not good friends, became occasional trading partners" (259–60). Despite frequent interactions, border crossing was fraught with risk, as the capture of runaway enslaved persons was a regular occurrence in the region and it is documented that "canoes sailed down the Oyapock river carrying French officers hunting fugitives" (256). Likewise, "Portuguese troops occupied both banks of the Oyapock River, while patrol boats policed the waterway" (Spieler 2011, 267) after the temporary abolition of slavery in French Guiana (1794–1802), which triggered an influx of enslaved social actors from Brazil. While the enslavement of human beings was finally abolished in French Guiana in 1848, it persisted until 1888 in Brazil, even though in decline in the second half of the nineteenth century. After 1848 Guyane therefore became a prime destination for escaped enslaved persons from Brazil even though the French and

Portuguese authorities "signed a treaty [in 1732] by which each would send back the other's fugitives" (Gomes 2003, 254). Except for a short phase of exemption during the first abolition in Guyane, both parties tried to adhere to the agreement well into the nineteenth century, that is, even after Brazil's independence in 1822. However, the abolition of enslavement on the French side resulted in a significant change vis-à-vis reciprocal "restitution": "The escapes to Cayenne continued, but the restitution of fugitives became legally complicated. The provincial authorities in Grão-Pará argued that the governor of French Guiana had sent a letter clarifying that 'by virtue of the decree of the French Republic, which abolished slavery in its colonies and possessions, slaves from Brazil could no longer be returned'" (Gomes and De Queiroz 2002, 40).

The transatlantic trade in enslaved people with all its lasting consequences, including racialized unequal mobilities today, is by definition a transregional history of violence that cannot be understood within the confines of national, imperial, or regional borders (Gilroy 1993). This applies equally for revolts and revolutions in the Black diaspora, most impressively illustrated by the "unthinkable" and largely forgotten Haitian Revolution (Trouillot 1995). The Haitian Revolution's radical act of self-liberation and its implementation of equality and freedom beyond racial hierarchies sent shockwaves across the region, inspiring not only hope among the enslaved but also fear and repression among colonial powers (Scott 2018). As historical research has demonstrated, the Haitian Revolution also reverberated in the French-Brazilian borderland, sparking uprisings and other forms of subversion among the enslaved while prompting colonial authorities to impose tighter control of enslaved populations (Gomes 2003, 274). These dynamics of resistance and repression—sparsely documented in archives (Santos 2023)—highlight the far-reaching impact of the abolitionist struggles, even in seemingly remote and disputed territories.

Particularly striking is the fact that, after France "lost" its most profitable sugar-producing colony, Saint-Domingue, in the wake of the Haitian Revolution, French colonial administrators sought to emulate the monocrop sugar economy in the country's relatively sparsely populated and agriculturally little-used continental colony French Guiana (Yarrington 2018). However, this plan utterly failed, and French Guiana was instead destined to become a penal colony after the abolition of enslavement in 1848. Over the course of almost a century, until its formal closure in 1946, more than seventy thousand convicts, mostly dissidents and criminalized people from the French metropole, forcibly migrated to French Guiana, where they were incarcerated in several prisons and labor camps. Thus, "Guyane came to be seen as a less feasible space for agriculture and more feasible for the shipment, storage and punishment—forced agricultural labour, even—of people no longer in possession of French citizenship and undesirable to the mainland" (Yarrington 2018, 92). How the coloniality of citizenship has long been linked to multiple exclusions—from the exclusion from rights to physical exclusion in the form of deportation from the very territory from which those rights originated—becomes particularly apparent in this case (see also Boatcă and Santos 2023). The brutal conditions in these camps were lethal, leading to the death of half the deported convicts before they could complete their sentences (Redfield 2005, 57). The first such establishments on mainland Guyane were the facilities built on the shores of the Oyapock River, specifically chosen due to its confinement. "Yet the actual occupation of the area," as Peter Redfield (2000, 68) has shown, "was to prove disastrous: few preparations were made, the hygienic conditions quickly deteriorated, disease set in, and the death rate grew." As historian Miranda Spieler has noted, the disease-ridden camps of Montagne d'Argent and nearby Saint-Georges represented the only facilities in all of French Guiana where the original plan was to turn the colony into a "circum-Atlantic depository for black convicts" (Spieler 2012, 165).

However, this racial segregation was weakened slightly over time, and Guyane's colonial elite began to conceive of the penal facilities in Saint-Georges and Montagne d'Argent as installations for both white convicts and formerly enslaved people of African descent. Described as "an overgrown coffee plantation at the mouth of the Oyapock River," the Montagne d'Argent site became a place where the French "intended black convicts to prepare the ground for Europeans who had yet to move from the islands to the shore" (Spieler 2012, 164). Similar plans were made for what came to be Saint-Georges. In postemancipation French Guiana, before the official "use" of Guyane as a place for mostly white European convicts, "planters and local officials had hoped to gather European prisoners, immigrants, and former slaves in mixed facilities. Saint-Georges was a monument to that early ambition" (Spieler 2012, 166). In this "hybrid facility" next to the Oyapock River, captive people of color and a few whites forcibly worked under harsh conditions in a timber mill and on a sugar plantation. Notably, most resettled convicts of Saint-Georges were "marginal migrants": people of color from the Caribbean islands of Martinique and Guadeloupe, as well as from French Guiana. In addition, a number of white soldiers and guards worked in Saint-Georges, which became notorious for its extreme mortality rates and stark racial disparities. "Of the 248 prisoners who made their way to this site," Stephen Toth (2006) found, "on which a sugar and coffee plantation was to be put into operation in April 1863, only 147 were still alive by March of the following year" (15). As death rates peaked, partly due to malaria, the majority of white soldiers and guards were evacuated, while the convicts of color were abandoned to their fate. With emigration and death besetting Saint-Georges, the penal farm came to an end ten years after its founding.[4]

Despite death and decline, the foundations of Saint-Georges had been laid. A number of former convicts survived the time of their sentence and continued to live in the area, as Saint-Georges became the main village of the region within a few years and remained the principal trading point along the Oyapock River (Collomb 2013). Importantly, then, after its first construction as a precursor of the official penal colony, Saint-Georges and its surroundings were rebuilt by survivors and new inhabitants, including heterogeneous groups of people from south of the Oyapock River. These "marginal migrations" occurred at a time when the area south of the Oyapock River was a neutralized territory (1841–1900) over which neither France nor Brazil could exert full jurisdiction, a status brokered by British mediation to resolve escalating territorial disputes between France and Brazil in the 1830s (Granger 2011, 160ff.). However, this was only a postponement of the conflict, which reemerged when large amounts of gold were discovered in the late nineteenth century and around twenty thousand marginal migrants came there in search of gold (Mam Lam Fouck 2013, 23; Romani 2010, 87). Besides Brazilians, these included migrants from the Greater Caribbean, especially formerly enslaved people (and their descendants) from the overpopulated French Caribbean islands who could not or did not want to be absorbed by the one-sided plantation economic system (Romani 2013, 141). These migrants often resisted the exploitive plantation system controlled by the *békés* (French Caribbean planters), who effectively continued enslavement through starvation wages and brutal working conditions (Romani 2013, 141). The gold rush, which dominated the economy of Guyane until after the First World War (Marshall 2009, 224), triggered a revival of the border dispute between France and Brazil. It culminated in deadly confrontations, the most prominent of which was the so-called massacre of Amapá (1885), which ended with the death of between forty and sixty people (Romani 2010). As a result, the governments of Brazil and France convened a binational committee that agreed to allow a Swiss arbitration court led by Swiss president Walter Hauser to settle the border conflict (Romani 2013, 111–23). Consequently, in 1900, the court ruled in favor of the Brazilian claims, thus turning the Oyapock River into the national-imperial border that it remains until today.

What the seemingly unrelated histories highlighted in this section show is that mobilities in the French-Brazilian borderland have always, in one way or another, been inextricably related to the exploitability and deportability of racially subordinated or politically unwanted bodies since the beginning of colonialism. These mobilities took various forms: deportations (e.g., convicts deported to penal facilities), movements that were a consequence of prior forced deportations (e.g., fugitive enslaved persons crossing the border to escape enslavement, having been forcibly transported across the Atlantic), or movements that resulted in further deportations (e.g., recaptured fugitives from slavery being returned across the border). These largely forgotten histories, briefly revisited and reconnected here, make clear that the right to mobility has been unequally distributed from the moment "Europeans" began exerting control over large parts of "Latin America," even in a borderland all too often framed as particularly "remote" or "peripheral." These colonial power structures shaped the movement and containment of racially subjugated bodies in ways that endure in present-day mobility regimes.

Centering the (Inter)Dependent "(Ultra)Periphery"

The "peripheral" position of French Guiana becomes apparent when examining its official status within the politico-administrative structure of the European Union: it is designated as an "outermost region" (OMR; in French, *région ultrapériphérique*)—a designation ambivalently connoting that it is both in and out of "Europe." Like eight other OMRs in the Caribbean (Guadeloupe, Martinique, Saint Martin), the Atlantic Ocean (Azores, Canaries), and the Indian Ocean (Mayotte, Réunion), Guyane is a full-fledged EU member and, as such, is subject to EU legislation. Moreover, there are thirteen "overseas countries and territories" (OCTs) with different degrees of sovereignty.[5] These Danish (Greenland), Dutch (e.g., Aruba), and French (e.g., New Caledonia) colonies are not part of the single market, but their nationals are EU citizens.[6]

The preceding section of this chapter ended with the border demarcation of 1900, without addressing why the southern border between "Europe" and "Latin America" continued to exist. Why did French Guiana not achieve independence in the nineteenth century (like Brazil in 1822) or after World War II (like its other neighbor, Suriname, in 1975)? The reasons for this ever-closer dependence (often termed "integration") lie in more than three centuries of French colonial assimilationist policies culminating in the *loi de la départementalisation* (law of departmentalization), passed in 1946. In that year, Guyane and the other "old colonies" (Martinique, Guadeloupe, and Réunion) became legally integrated parts of the French Republic. At one stroke, their inhabitants—from Saint-Georges in the Amazon rainforest to Saint-Denis in the Indian Ocean—became full citizens of France. These were indeed "old colonies," given that "the islands of Guadeloupe and Martinique were colonized as early as 1635, and French Guiana in 1642. Paradoxically, then, these territories became French earlier, and have been French longer, than some areas of the hexagon, like Nice and Alsace-Lorraine, which are considered to be 'natural' elements of French territory" (Murdoch 2008, 16).

This formal transition, even if supported by many colonized people across the "old colonies" in their hope to achieve equality vis-à-vis the "metropole" under the French flag, should not be mistaken for an emancipatory decolonial move, as feminist political scientist Françoise Vergès (1999) argued: "1946 was *not* a decolonization. In the second half of our century, decolonization has signified rupture with the *metropole*, construction of a nation-state, access to sovereignty. There was no rupture, no construction of a nation-state, no access to sovereignty in the Old Colonies" (74; italics in original). Accordingly, the term *overseas* (*outre-mer*) not only locates these territories "elsewhere" and render them invisible but also masks the appropriate term: *colonial* (Vergès 2017, 166; see also Santos and Boatcă 2023). The arguments made by Vergès (2017) with regard to the ongoing yet reframed colonial relations in the French overseas departments "are to be found today in fragile economies, weak industry and high rates of unemployment, as well as rampant inequality" (165). French Guiana's GDP per capita, for example, was only 46 percent of the EU average as of 2022—only trumped by Mayotte's 32 percent (Gouardères 2025). Notwithstanding this structural inequality in relation to the metropole, French Guiana provides a quality and expectancy of life currently out of reach for countries from which most people migrate—an important aspect further elaborated in the next section.

The Borderland as Laboratory of Legal Exceptionalisms

The OMR and OCT status of spaces across the world comes with tremendous effects for migration routes and policies. Of all remaining colonies under the control of "Europe," the two Spanish "autonomous cities" Ceuta and Melilla have become the epitome of Europe's deadly border regime (Kobelinsky 2017, 2020). Tellingly not counted as "outermost regions," even though located in northern Africa and claimed by the Moroccan government to this day, Ceuta and Melilla have witnessed border "securitization" policies since Spain's accession to the EU in 1986. The razor-wire fencing and police brutality of Ceuta and Melilla, in turn, led to a detour of migration routes to the Canary Islands, where the first joint EU sea patrol mission was established under the aegis of Frontex: "The Atlantic waters lapping against the Canary Islands would soon become the laboratory for a 'migration management' model to be exported across Europe's southern borders" (Andersson 2014, 69). Migration research, including the critical scholarship on illegality and deportability, has hitherto located these southern borders in the

Mediterranean and thus failed to address the borders of "Europe" lying even far-ther to the south.

As shown in the opening lines of this chapter, dangerous journeys across waters also characterize migration toward Guyane. Over the past several decades, thousands of migrants from the northern, poverty-stricken states of Brazil have reached the coast of French Guiana on small, overcrowded *pirogues*. Instead of crossing the Oyapock River, the majority of migrants have left the tumultuous river mouth to reach Cayenne via the Atlantic Ocean. This dangerous crossing usually starts from the border village of Oiapoque, located opposite the French municipality of Saint-Georges-de-l'Oyapock. In the early 1990s, even the *New York Times* (Brooke 1992) reported that "without life jackets and packed into precarious wooden canoes, hundreds embark every week from here [Oiapo-que] for the perilous, seven-hour journey to Cayenne, the capital of the French department." During my fieldwork I encountered several people who had em-barked on this journey. João, a man who was around fifty years old and origi-nally came from Pará, for example, told me that he would never forget making this journey as a young man in the 1990s. As I talked to him on the porch of a pub in Vila Vitória, a neighborhood of Oiapoque, he said that more than forty people were crammed onto a boat made for twenty and that he had been afraid he would fall overboard.[7] Today he lives in Cayenne with a legal residence per-mit (*carte de séjour*) and works as a singer. Caroline, a Brazilian woman in her thirties who also lives in Cayenne, took the Atlantic route in the 2000s after be-coming pregnant. Like João, she remembers the dangerous boat ride, especially the high waves. Still, she described her experience—shared in a friend's home in Saint-Georges—as relatively unproblematic compared to others, who experi-enced serious accidents. Almost all of her Brazilian friends and acquaintances in Cayenne, she told me, came via this route, and some of them experienced distress at sea and survived only by clinging to plastic canisters.

In addition to this dangerous sea passage, other routes have become established. At 730 kilometers, the French-Brazilian border is France's longest external border. Although the Police aux Frontières have enhanced border controls, especially in the French border towns of Saint-Georges and Camopi, it is almost impossible to fully monitor this vast Amazonian border. For long stretches, the border is literally fluid and easy to cross by boat. Such river crossings in less policed areas, however, leave migrants in remote parts of the rain forest, far from any village, with no trails, and at the mercy of wild animals. This *rota pelo mato* (jungle route) is often used by people seeking work in the clandestine small-scale gold-mining industry, but Car-oline, for instance, also used it in the late 2000s after she had to return to Brazil for private matters. After a long trek through the rain forest, the route is continued by automobile. However, this continuation is possible only beyond the police check-point, which operates day and night, on the only road leading to Cayenne. This checkpoint is located in the village of Regina, about eighty kilometers north of Saint-Georges.

These dangerous crossings over water or land, or both, seem especially strik-ing in light of the Oyapock River Bridge, inaugurated between Saint-Georges and Oyapock in 2017 (figure 11.1). Hailed as a symbol of friendship and future cooperation by many politicians, the first bridge between the Brazilian state of Amapá and French Guiana has, in practice, turned out to be a one-way street, reinforcing mobility inequalities based on citizenship and entwined with other factors. To date, there is no visa reciprocity between Brazil and Guyane: While French and EU citizens can easily cross the river and get their visa stamps for ninety days in Oiapoque, Brazilians and most other non-EU citizens are required to manage the complicated, costly, and usually unsuccessful endeavor of visa application months before setting foot on "European" soil in "Latin America." It is important to note that Brazil's North is home to a largely impoverished population that simply cannot afford the costs involved in "legal" cross-border mobility: In addition to the application fees, there is the cost of a passport; and the application must also be accompanied by proof of salary and health and re-patriation insurance with a minimum coverage of €30,000. The introduction of the so-called transborder card (*carte de transfrontalier* or *carteira transfrontei-riça*), which grants French and Brazilian citizens with official residence in Saint-Georges and Oiapoque a seventy-two-hour stay in the respective other border town, has not significantly alleviated the inequalities in and between the two towns: all French citizens have visa-free access to all of Brazil for ninety days and are thus not necessarily in need of a transborder card, whereas only Brazilian citizens who are officially registered in Oiapoque can legally enter a small part of Guyane (Saint-Georges). The consequences of these unequal handlings are self-explanatory: of the average two thousand cars crossing the bridge per month in 2019 (the year prior to the temporary closure of the bridge due to the COVID-19 pandemic), only five had a Brazilian registration number (*Seles Nafes* 2019). A one-way street favoring white, relatively well-off French and EU citizens, the bridge is also marked by its rupture with traditional forms of border crossings. Many Indigenous communities and Maroons, for example, have never used the bridge and do not intend to do so, even if they were allowed to.

While Brazilians are often sent back to the Brazilian riverbank if they cannot present the necessary documents in Saint-Georges (a *carte de séjour* or *carte de transfrontalier*), asylum seekers cannot be officially turned away in this part of "Europe" in "Latin America." Any person who applies for asylum has the right to

FIGURE 11.1. Oyapock River Bridge. Photo by Fabio Santos.

stay on "European" soil, even at its "ultraperipheral" Amazonian edge. Over the past few years, many people have exercised this right and contributed to new migration patterns, thereby calling for the pending decentering of the "European Refugee Crisis" from an "ultraperipheral" perspective.[8]

Week after week, before the COVID-19 pandemic unsettled lives and mobilities across the world, asylum seekers from countries such as Haiti, Syria, and Afghanistan came to the Saint-Georges police station. After explaining their concerns, they were taken to the capital city of Cayenne, two to three hours away, where asylum applications were officially filed. Among these migrants was Mohammed, a Syrian man, aged twenty-seven, from Homs who reached French Guiana via Beirut and Brazil: "The cost of flight to Brazil is nearly the same price as the illegal journey across the Mediterranean. The trip cost him about $3,000, including airfare and travel costs from Brazil to French Guiana. Mohammed has urged his younger brother, 23, to make the same journey" (Alhamwi 2016).

Statistical data make clear that Mohammed is part of a larger structural change that has taken place in recent years. According to the Office français de protection des réfugiés et apatrides (OFPRA 2016), Guyane recorded by far the highest percentage increase in asylum seekers in all of France in 2015, the year of the "European Refugee Crisis." A total of 2,511 first-time asylum applications were filed in Guyane, roughly equivalent to 1 percent of the population there in 2015 (259,865). Taking all French departments together, the proportion of all first-time asylum seekers

(70,570) to the French population (66,992,699) in 2015 is about 0.1 percent. In other words, although the number of asylum seekers in French Guiana may seem marginal in absolute terms and at first glance, the proportion relative to the local population is ten times higher than in the rest of France.

Where did the people who sought asylum in Guyane in 2015 come from? Four out of five (79.8 percent) came from Haiti, 10 percent from the Dominican Republic, 2.2 percent from Peru, 1.4 percent from Colombia, and 6.6 percent from "other countries." Other countries included war-torn and geographically distant countries such as Syria. It was not until 2018 that French Guiana saw a significant decrease in asylum applications, similar to the general trend in the EU. Compared to the previous year, the number of asylum seekers in Guyane halved (to 2,383, a 52 percent drop), while the distribution of nationality remained relatively stable: 74.5 percent held Haitian nationality, 14.6 percent Dominican, and 2.2 percent Syrian. In light of these numbers, Mohammed, the young Syrian mentioned above, was only one of several hundred Syrian refugees in French Guiana.

Yet, given the fact that Haitians are the largest immigrant group—and the most structurally silenced while facing extraordinarily high levels of illegality and deportability in the Greater Caribbean (Belton 2011; Joseph 2015; Kahn 2019; Laëthier 2011; Santos 2025)—it is of crucial importance to focus on the racialized bodies deemed most "illegal" and "deportable" in Guyane. Unlike the migration of Syrians, the movement of Haitian nationals to Guyane is by no means a new pattern. In fact, Haitian immigration has been relatively stable since the 1960s, gaining intensity in the 1980s and leading to the establishment of a large Haitian diaspora in French Guiana. During the 1980s, France imposed stricter visa requirements for Haitians, making legal entry more difficult and fueling the growth of clandestine networks and illegal migration routes through Suriname and Brazil. Today, Haitians constitute about 30 percent of the immigrant population in French Guiana. However, applying for asylum is a relatively new—and often unsuccessful—procedure that has emerged in recent years as Haiti has faced overlapping environmental, political, and economic crises. Unlike the newly arrived Syrians, Haitian asylum seekers can often rely on established networks of family members and acquaintances who have previously migrated to French Guiana. Yet these networks do not protect against exclusion from French Guiana's society, riddled with racism and inequalities. The migrant hierarchies identified by sociologist Marie-José Jolivet as early as 1990 have remained largely intact: "Saint Lucians, for example, continued to be little or hardly accepted; Martinicans continued to be contested, in a way that remained ambivalent; as for the Haitians, who have arrived in greater numbers in the last ten years, they have been victims of a strong rejection" (Jolivet 1990, 25; my translation). Despite their long presence, Haitians remain marginalized, with their *creole-ness*, in French Guianese terms, remaining highly contested. Many perceive them as only temporarily welcome, tolerated primarily because they perform poorly paid, difficult labor in the forestry and agricultural sectors—jobs few others are willing to do.

The refusal to grant official residence to Haitians in French Guiana—whether as recognized refugees or as workers contributing to the department's fragile economy—contrasts with the self-perceptions and argumentative strategies of some Haitians who turn the "shared" French colonial history into a claim for having a historically and culturally more justified right to legal residence in Guyane than other racialized groups have, whose status is contested. This includes Maroons, born in Suriname or in "remote" regions of French Guiana, where no administrative facilities exist to document their place of birth (Benoît 2020). As Maud Laëthier (2015, 248) explains, Haitians "often feel that they have greater rights to French residency papers than Maroons because Haiti has historical ties with France and also because French is one of the official languages of Haiti. By contrast, Suriname, the imagined home of Maroons, only shares physical or geographical proximity with France, making Maroons 'less French' than Haitians." Such differentiations between people deemed "more" or "less" deserving of residence, refuge, or citizenship status attest to the ways the people in question themselves can adopt state-centered strategies that pit different communities against one another. In the case of Haitians in French Guiana, such hierarchizations have not led to a structural improvement in their own position. Instead, they have contributed to the further stigmatization of Maroons, a group with whom Haitians "share" the historical legacy of enslavement and forced mobility, and who today also experience illegality and deportability.

In French Guiana, the identity checks carried out primarily by white police officers exhibit clear practices of racial profiling, which is even legally facilitated in some areas of the overseas department. In precisely demarcated areas—particularly along seashores, riverbanks, and main traffic routes—police officers are exempt from the metropolitan requirement to have a written request from the prosecutor's office, which allows them to take full advantage of this legal flexibility. In the sleepy border town of Saint-Georges, barely ten minutes pass without encountering a police car patrolling slowly through the streets. I, as a white man without a French passport, was not checked once in six months. However, nonwhite individuals, both with and without French passports, have told me they are regularly stopped—sometimes several times a week. Migration thus cannot be delinked from the racialization of certain bodies and citizenships in

border-crossing processes. White privilege often enables smoother border crossings, even when not fully compliant with legal frameworks, whereas nonwhite
individuals are more likely to be stopped and required to present their "papers."
Their nationality (in this case, French) or residence status may be questioned,
even when they can provide proper documentation (see also Benoît 2020).

Besides racialized controls, a number of legal exceptions deviating from the
status quo of the metropole have been set up in the "(ultra)periphery." One of
the most significant changes is encapsulated by the Décret 2018-385, a decree
with the telling descriptor "Experimenting with certain procedures for processing asylum applications in French Guiana." Since the introduction of this
decree in 2018, asylum law has witnessed a drastic change in terms of temporality: Its main goal has been the reduction of time spent on asylum applications,
and thus the time spent by asylum seekers on "French" soil in "Latin America." In
metropolitan France, asylum seekers are given twenty-one days to submit their
asylum application, but in French Guiana, this window is shortened to just seven
days. In cases where the OFPRA requests additional information before making
a decision, the asylum seekers have only three days to submit the required documents in person (as opposed to the eight days in the metropole, where these
documents can also be provided by post). Overall, the time frame within which
the OFPRA examines asylum applications in French Guiana has been reduced to
fifteen days. The "experimental" character of these measures—also highlighted
by journalists Cécile Massin and Maïa Courtois (2020)—are apparent once we
take into consideration that they were also applied in the French overseas departments of Guadeloupe and Martinique in 2020, on "positive" review of impacts
on migrant deterrence and deportability. Activists and experts have pointed out
that France's remaining colonies are often used as testing grounds for restrictive
immigration policies that may later be implemented in metropolitan France:
The overseas territories, says Lucie Curet (quoted in Massin and Courtois 2020),
who represented the NGO La Cimade, "are used by the French government as
experimental laboratories that will then eventually be implemented in metropolitan France." The latest example of these legal exceptions and partial inclusions
is that the French government, in 2024, ended automatic *jus soli*—the right to
citizenship by birth—for children born in Mayotte.

In addition to overturning timelines and procedures for asylum applications,
financial and infrastructural policies are being used to deter migrants in French
Guiana. Despite the higher cost of living compared to mainland France—with
public officials earning 40 percent more than in the metropole—the *allocation pour demandeur d'asile* (asylum seeker's allowance) is significantly reduced
in French Guiana. While asylum seekers in mainland France receive up to

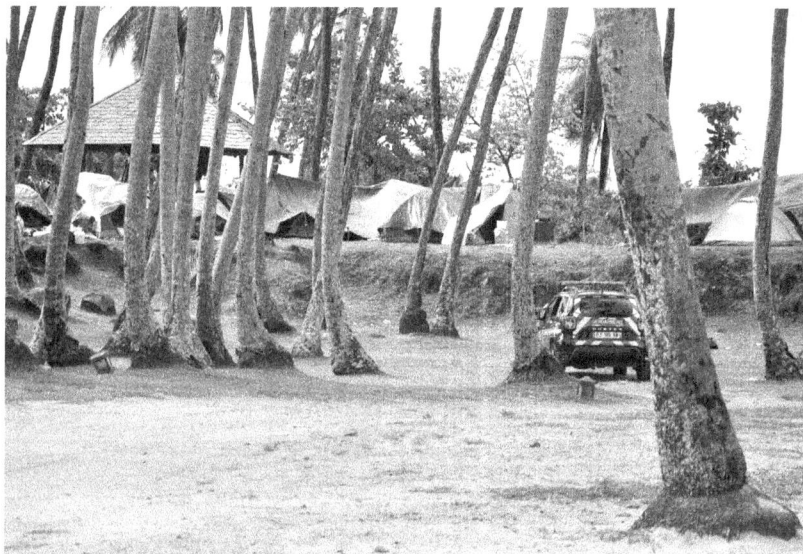

FIGURE 11.2. Impromptu tent housing at Pointe Buzaré, facing the Atlantic coast near the city center of Cayenne. Photo: Dana Alboz / InfoMigrants.

€6.80 per day, those in French Guiana are given only €3.80, which exacerbates the already challenging conditions for migrants in the region.

Moreover, despite decades of migration flows into French Guiana, the French government has not established a single accommodation center for asylum seekers. This systemic failure to provide adequate housing worsens an already precarious situation. Scarce housing options are primarily managed by the Red Cross, and only in exceptional circumstances does the prefecture rent hotel rooms or apartments for temporary shelter. The shortage of proper housing has led to visible consequences in the capital city of Cayenne. The blatant results can be seen not only on the city's outskirts but also in its center, where neighborhoods full of tents have sprung up in the past few years (figure 11.2).

Concluding Remarks and COVID Postscript

Strongly hit by the coronavirus, with infection rates higher than the French and Brazilian national averages, the borderland shared by Guyane and Amapá has proven once more to be a microcosm making visible today's unequal mobilities and existential inequalities in the otherwise invisibilized "(ultra)periphery." On confirmation of the first cases in Oiapoque and Saint-Georges, the borderland witnessed an unprecedented state of emergency, and both sides announced closing and strongly controlling their borders beginning March 19, 2020. The bridge, already a one-way street prior to the pandemic, became completely closed, while police patrols, which were already frequent in the streets but less so on the river, have been carried out regularly on the Oyapock ever since. Still, at no point did border crossings come to a complete standstill, as people learned to take a *pirogue* to the other side when there was no police boat in sight. Despite these illegalized crossings in both directions, the situation in the borderland has been precarious since the outbreak of the pandemic. Isolated from and neglected by their respective regional and national centers, the residents of the borderland waited for weeks and months to have access not only to protective equipment such as face masks and hand sanitizers but also to testing facilities and appropriate healthcare. Rather than seeing this worrying situation, as well as the deadly scene depicted at this chapter's outset, in temporal and spatial isolation, we should place them within long-term processes of uneven power relations in the French-Brazilian borderland and in the Greater Caribbean more generally (see also Di Stefano, Boatcă, and Santos 2023).

Starting from the observation that French Guiana and other remaining colonies of European states—this in itself unmasking myths of sovereignties and continents—have not been sufficiently acknowledged to date, I have focused here on border crossings, as well as the countermeasures taken to increase the illegality and deportability of persons deemed undesirable in this beacon of "Europe" in "Latin America." I have done so in the very long term in order to reconnect the ties often cut in migration research between past and present (im)mobilities (Boatcă and Santos 2023; Wyss and Dahinden 2022). A historically informed look at present inequalities reveals both continuations and ruptures at this polysemic border. Measures such as blocking and redirecting cross-border mobility by a bridge, fast-track asylum processing and deporting, legally facilitated identity checks marked by racial profiling, and the deliberate shortage of housing and financial support for asylum seekers, all are recent manifestations of control. Yet they are extensions of a much older history of exploitability and deportability in the region, dating back to the beginning of colonial history. French Guiana has long been a place where racialized and politically unwanted bodies are subjected to exclusionary practices, exemplified by the deportation of metropolitan and Caribbean convicts and those fleeing enslavement from Brazil. Once reconnected, these forgotten histories underscore that today's legal exceptionalisms concerning unequal mobilities in the French-Brazilian borderland are not anomalies; they are consistent with how "Europeans" have historically (ab)used their colonies in "Latin America." These exceptions are thus only exceptions in relation to the metropole, for there is no such thing as systematic exceptions. The entangled inequalities established, reproduced, and contested in French Guiana and its borderland with Brazil are not isolated, "peripheral" phenomena. Rather, they alert us to the exclusionary patterns systematically reproduced by the ongoing non-sovereignty and coloniality shaping our world. As Ann Laura Stoler (2016, 177) points out, "temporary exclusions, partial inclusions and legal exemptions are not occasional and ad hoc strategies of rule but the racialized modus operandi of imperial states." This observation critically underscores the systemic nature of such practices, which are neither anomalies nor isolated incidents, but rather inherent features of how imperial and colonial powers have historically governed. The present-day use of colonies like French Guiana as "laboratories" for experimenting with exclusionary measures against migrants exemplifies this enduring legacy. Understanding the *longue durée* of colonial rule in "Latin America" thus requires a remapping of the world, inverting the typical Eurocentric perspective: By placing the "(ultra)periphery" at the center, we can more effectively unravel and tackle the entwined roots of coloniality, illegality, and deportability that continue to shape our world.

NOTES

1. *French Guiana* and *Guyane* are used synonymously in this chapter.

2. Together with Manuela Boatcă, I have engaged in a more detailed discussion of the problematic (mis)understandings of "Europe" and "Europeanization" in two publications (Santos and Boatcă 2022, 2023). The following two paragraphs draw on these works.

3. Arguments along similar lines were made in relation to "Africa" (Mudimbe 1988) and "Asia" (Ge 2000).

4. The Brazilian side of the Oyapock River was transformed into a deadly penal settlement (1924–27) for approximately one thousand dissident young Brazilian soldiers on the eve of the Brazilian Revolution of 1930, strikingly echoing the histories of expulsion and surveillance made on the opposite riverbank. As the focus of this chapter rests on the histories of the present "European" migration regime in "Latin America," I can only refer to another text in which I juxtaposed the French and Brazilian penal systems in the borderland (Santos 2020b).

5. In trying to capture the paradoxical logic behind the functioning of state structures in the nonindependent world, especially in the Caribbean, scholars have begun to denounce "the myth of sovereignty" (Lewis 2013) and instead make use of concepts such as "extended statehood" (De Jong and Kruijt 2005), "postcolonial sovereignty games" (Adler-Nissen and Gad 2013), and "non-sovereign futures" (Bonilla 2015). In a similar vein, the interrelated concepts "overseas Europe" (Santos 2017), "forgotten Europes" (Boatcă 2019), and "European elsewheres" (Boatcă and Santos 2023) attempt to provide spatial referents and visibility to political and administrative entanglements that continue to be structurally silenced.

6. With the withdrawal of the United Kingdom from the EU in 2020, known as Brexit, thirteen British overseas territories are no longer OCTs. Overall, the United Kingdom currently administers fourteen overseas territories, but only thirteen of them were previously counted as OCTs within the EU framework, excluding continental Gibraltar.

7. All names mentioned in this chapter are pseudonyms.

8. As numerous scholars have highlighted, the discourse around the "refugee crisis" is charged with hostile meanings toward non-"European" others who have allegedly sparked a "crisis" when, in fact, the non-"European" others seeking refuge are the ones experiencing a crisis (e.g., Bojadžijev and Mezzadra 2015; De Genova 2016, 2018; Georgi 2019).

REFERENCES

Abu-Lughod, Janet L. 1989. *Before European Hegemony: The World System A.D. 1250–1350*. Oxford: Oxford University Press.

Adler-Nissen, Rebecca, and Ulrik Pram Gad, eds. 2013. *European Integration and Postcolonial Sovereignty Games: The EU Overseas Countries and Territories*. London: Routledge.

Alhamwi, Mohamad Khair. 2016 "Syrian Refugees Find Brazilian Backdoor to Europe." *Newsweek*, April 13. https://www.newsweek.com/syrian-refugees-find-brazilian-backdoor-europe-446994.

Andersson, Ruben. 2014. *Illegality, Inc.: Clandestine Migration and the Business of Bordering Europe*. Berkeley: University of California Press.

Balibar, Étienne. 2002. "What Is a Border?" In *Politics and the Other Scene*, 75–86. London: Verso.

Balibar, Etienne. 2009. "Europe as Borderland." *Environment and Planning D: Society and Space* 27 (2): 190–215. https://doi.org/10.1068/d13008.

Baud, Michiel. 2000. "State-Building and Borderlands." In *Fronteras: Towards a Borderless Latin America*, edited by Arij Ouweneel, Pitou van Dijck, and Annelies Zoomers, 41–79. Amsterdam: CEDLA (Center for Latin American Research and Documentation).

Beaman, Jean, and Orly Clerge. 2024. "Ain't I a Migrant?: Global Blackness and the Future of Migration Studies." *International Migration Review* 58 (4). https://doi.org/10.1177/01979183241271685.

Belton, Kristy A. 2011. "Dry Land Drowning or Rip Current Survival? Haitians Without Status in the Bahamas." *Ethnic and Racial Studies* 34 (6): 948–66. https://doi.org/10.1080/01419870.2010.526236.

Benoît, Catherine. 2020. "Fortress Europe's Far-Flung Borderlands: 'Illegality' and the 'Deportation Regime' in France's Caribbean and Indian Ocean Territories." *Mobilities* 15 (2): 220–40. https://doi.org/10.1080/17450101.2019.1678909.

Boatcă, Manuela. 2010. "Multiple Europes and the Politics of Difference Within." In *The Study of Europe*, edited by Hauke Brunkhorst and Gerd Grözinger, 51–66. Baden-Baden, Germany: Nomos. https://doi.org/10.5771/9783845225487-51.

Boatcă, Manuela. 2015. *Global Inequalities Beyond Occidentalism*. Farnham, UK: Ashgate.

Boatcă, Manuela. 2018. "Caribbean Europe: Out of Sight, Out of Mind?" In *Constructing the Pluriverse: The Geopolitics of Knowledge*, edited by Bernd Reiter, 197–218. Durham, NC: Duke University Press.

Boatcă, Manuela. 2019. "Forgotten Europes: Rethinking Regional Entanglements from the Caribbean." In *Critical Geopolitics and Regional (Re)Configurations: Interregionalism and Transnationalism Between Latin America and Europe*, edited by Breno Bringel and Heriberto Cairo, 96–116. London: Routledge.

Boatcă, Manuela, and Julia Roth. 2016. "Unequal and Gendered: Notes on the Coloniality of Citizenship." *Current Sociology* 64 (2): 191–212. https://doi.org/10.1177 /0011392115614781.

Boatcă, Manuela, and Fabio Santos. 2023. "Of Rags and Riches in the Caribbean: Creolizing Migration Studies." *Journal of Immigrant and Refugee Studies* 21 (2): 132–45. https://doi.org/10.1080/15562948.2022.2129896.

Bojadžijev, Manuela, and Sandro Mezzadra. 2015. "'Refugee Crisis' or Crisis of European Migration Policies." *Focaalblog*, updated November 12. https://www.focaalblog.com /2015/11/12/manuela-bojadzijev-and-sandro-mezzadra-refugee-crisis-or-crisis-of -european-migration-policies/.

Bonilla, Yarimar. 2015. *Non-Sovereign Futures: French Caribbean Politics in the Wake of Disenchantment*. Chicago: University of Chicago Press.

Bonilla, Yarimar. 2017. "Unsettling Sovereignty." *Cultural Anthropology* 32 (3): 330–39. https://doi.org/10.14506/ca32.3.02.

Brooke, James. 1992. "Perilous Jungle Passage Leads Poor to 'France.'" *New York Times*, July 4. https://www.nytimes.com/1992/07/04/world/oiapoque-journal-perilous -jungle-passage-leads-poor-to-france.html.

Collomb, Gérard. 2013. "'Indiens' ou 'Brésiliens'? Mobilités karipuna vers Cayenne (Guyane française)." *Revue européenne des migrations internationales* 29 (1): 113–31. https://doi.org/10.4000/remi.6312.

Cuttitta, Paolo, and Tamara Last, eds. 2019. *Border Deaths: Causes, Dynamics, and Consequences of Migration-Related Mortality*. Amsterdam: Amsterdam University Press.

De Genova, Nicholas. 2004. "The Legal Production of Mexican/Migrant 'Illegality.'" *Latino Studies* 2 (2): 160–85. https://doi.org/10.1057/palgrave.lst.8600085.

De Genova, Nicholas. 2016. "The European Question: Migration, Race, and Postcoloniality in Europe." *Social Text* 34 (3 [128]): 75–102. https://doi.org/10.1215/01642472 -3607588.

De Genova, Nicholas, ed. 2017. *The Borders of "Europe": Autonomy of Migration, Tactics of Bordering*. Durham, NC: Duke University Press.

De Genova, Nicholas. 2018. "The 'Migrant Crisis' as Racial Crisis: Do Black Lives Matter in Europe?" *Ethnic and Racial Studies* 41 (10): 1765–82. https://doi.org/10.1080 /01419870.2017.1361543.

De Jong, Lammert, and Dirk Kruijt, eds. 2005. *Extended Statehood in the Caribbean: Paradoxes of Quasi-Colonialism, Local Autonomy, and Extended Statehood in the USA, French, Dutch, and British Caribbean*. Amsterdam: Rozenberg.

De León, Jason. 2015. *The Land of Open Graves: Living and Dying on the Migrant Trail*. Berkeley: University of California Press.

Di Stefano, Corinna A., Fabio Santos, and Manuela Boatcă. 2023. "Marginalized Bodies in Caribbean Europe." In *Creating Europe from the Margins*, edited by Kristín Loftsdóttir, Brigitte Hipfl, and Sandra Ponzanesi, 125–39. London: Routledge. https://doi .org/10.4324/9781003269748-8.

Domenech, Eduardo, and Gustavo Dias. 2020. "Regimes de fronteira e 'ilegalidade' migrante na América Latina e no Caribe." *Sociologias* 22 (55): 40–73. https://doi.org /10.1590/15174522-108928.

Espelt-Bombin, Silvia. 2018. "Makers and Keepers of Networks: Amerindian Spaces, Migrations, and Exchanges in the Brazilian Amazon and French Guiana, 1600–1730." *Ethnohistory* 65 (4): 597–620. https://doi.org/10.1215/00141801-6991253.

Frank, Andre Gunder. 1998. *ReOrient: Global Economy in the Asian Age*. Berkeley: University of California Press.

Ge, Sun. 2000. "How Does Asia Mean? (Part I)." *Inter-Asia Cultural Studies* 1 (1): 13–47. https://doi.org/10.1080/146493700360980.

Georgi, Fabian. 2019. "The Role of Racism in the European 'Migration Crisis': A Historical Materialist Perspective." In *Racism After Apartheid: Challenges for Marxism and Anti-Racism*, edited by Vishwas Satgar, 96–117. Johannesburg: Wits University Press.

Gilroy, Paul. 1993. *The Black Atlantic: Modernity and Double Consciousness*. Cambridge, MA: Harvard University Press.

Glissant, Édouard. 1990. *Poétique de la relation*. Poétique 3. Paris: Gallimard.

Gobat, Michel. 2013. "The Invention of Latin America: A Transnational History of Anti-Imperialism, Democracy, and Race." *American Historical Review* 118 (5): 1345–75. https://doi.org/10.1093/ahr/118.5.1345.

Gomes, Flávio. 2003. "Other Black Atlantic Borders: Escape Routes, 'Mocambos,' and Fears of Sedition in Brazil and French Guiana (Eighteenth to Nineteenth Centuries)." *New West Indian Guide / Nieuwe West-Indische Gids* 77 (3–4): 253–87. https://doi.org /10.1163/13822373-90002524.

Gomes, Flávio, and Jonas De Queiroz. 2002. "Amazônia, Fronteiras e Identidades: Reconfigurações Coloniais e Pós-Coloniais (Guianas -Séculos XVIII–XIX)." *Lusotopie* 9 (1): 25–49.

Gouardères, Frédéric. 2025. "Outermost Regions (ORs)." Fact Sheet, European Union. https://www.europarl.europa.eu/factsheets/en/sheet/100/outermost-regions-ors-.

Granger, Stéphane. 2011. "Le Contesté franco-brésilien: Enjeux et conséquences d'un conflit oublié entre la France et le Brésil." *Outre-mers* 98 (372): 157–77. https://doi.org /10.3406/outre.2011.4577.

Hall, Stuart. 1991. "Europe's Other Self." *Marxism Today* (August): 18–19.

Hall, Stuart. 1992. "The West and the Rest: Discourse and Power." In *Formations of Modernity*, edited by Stuart Hall and Bram Gieben, 275–332. Cambridge: Polity Press.

Hodgson, Marshall G. S. 1963. "The Interrelations of Societies in History." *Comparative Studies in Society and History* 5 (2): 227–50.

Holmes, Seth M. 2013. "'Is It Worth Risking Your Life?': Ethnography, Risk and Death on the U.S.-Mexico Border." *Social Science and Medicine* 99 (December):153–61. https://doi.org/10.1016/j.socscimed.2013.05.029.

Jolivet, Marie-José. 1990. "Entre autochtones et immigrants: Diversité et logique de positions créoles guyanaises." *Études Créoles* 13 (2), 11–32.

Joseph, Handerson. 2015. *Diaspora: As dinâmicas da mobilidade haitiana no Brasil, no Suriname e na Guiana Francesa*. Universidade Federal do Rio de Janeiro/Museu Nacional.

Jelin, Elizabeth, Renata C. Motta, and Sérgio Costa, eds. 2018. *Global Entangled Inequalities: Conceptual Debates and Evidence from Latin America*. London: Routledge.

Kahn, Jeffrey S. 2019. *Islands of Sovereignty: Haitian Migration and the Borders of Empire*. Chicago: University of Chicago Press.

Kobelinsky, Carolina. 2017. "Exister au risque de disparaître: Récits sur la mort pendant la traversée vers l'Europe." *Revue Européenne des Migrations Internationales* 33 (2–3): 115–31. https://doi.org/10.4000/remi.8745.

Kobelinsky, Carolina. 2020. "Border Beings: Present Absences Among Migrants in the Spanish Enclave of Melilla." *Death Studies* 44 (11): 709–17. https://doi.org/10.1080/07481187.2020.1771849.

Kramsch, Olivier Thomas. 2012. "'Re-conociendo la frontera UE-MERCOSUR: Espacio, visión e imaginación 'dreyfusard' sobre el puente del río Oyapock.'" In *Espacios urbanos y sociedades transfronterizas en la Amazonia*, edited by Carlos Gilberto Zárate Botía and Jean-Pierre Goulard, 127–53. Leticia: Universidad Nacional de Colombia.

Laëthier, Maud. 2011. *Être migrant et haïtien en Guyane*. Paris: Comité des travaux historiques et scientifiques.

Laëthier, Maud. 2015. "The Role of Suriname in Haitian Migration to French Guiana: Identities on the Move and Border Crossing." In *In and Out of Suriname: Language, Mobility, and Identity*, edited by Eithne Carlin, Isabelle Léglise, Bettina Migge, and Paul Brendan Tjon Sie Fat, 229–51. Leiden: Brill.

Lewis, Linden, ed. 2013. *Caribbean Sovereignty, Development, and Democracy in an Age of Globalization*. New York: Routledge.

Lewis, Martin W., and Kären Wigen. 1997. *The Myth of Continents: A Critique of Metageography*. Berkeley: University of California Press.

Lo Presti, Laura. 2019. "Terraqueous Necropolitics." *ACME: An International Journal for Critical Geographies* 18 (6): 1347–67. https://doi.org/10.14288/ACME.V18I6.1829.

Mam Lam Fouck, Serge. 2013. *Nouvelle histoire de la Guyane française: Des souverainetés amérindiennes aux mutations de la société contemporaine*. Matoury: Ibis Rouge Éditions.

Mam Lam Fouck, Serge. 2015. *La société guyanaise à l'épreuve des migrations du dernier demi-siècle, 1965–2015*. Matoury: Ibis Rouge Éditions.

Marshall, Bill. 2009. *The French Atlantic: Travels in Culture and History*. Liverpool: Liverpool University Press.

Massin, Cécile, and Maïa Courtois. 2020. "Guyane française: Des demandeur.euse.s d'asile de seconde classe?" *Guitinews*, updated October 16. https://guitinews.fr/ici-et-la-bas/2020/10/16/guyane-francaise-des-demandeur-euse-s-dasile-de-seconde-classe/.

McMahon, Simon, and Nando Sigona. 2021. "Death and Migration: Migrant Journeys and the Governance of Migration During Europe's 'Migration Crisis.'" *International Migration Review* 55 (2): 605–28. https://doi.org/10.1177/0197918320958615.

Mignolo, Walter. 2005. *The Idea of Latin America*. Malden, MA: Blackwell.

Mudimbe, Valentin-Yves. 1988. *The Invention of Africa: Gnosis, Philosophy, and the Order of Knowledge*. Bloomington: Indiana University Press.

Murdoch, Adlai. 2008. "Introduction: Departmentalization's Continuing Conundrum—Locating the DOM-ROM Between Home and Away." *International Journal of Francophone Studies* 11 (1): 15–32. https://doi.org/10.1386/ijfs.11.1and2.15_2.

OFPRA (Office français de protection des réfugiés et apatrides). 2016. "Rapport d'activité 2015." https://ofpra.gouv.fr/sites/default/files/atoms/files/rapport_dactivite_ofpra _2015_hd.pdf.

Passes, Alan. 2009. "Tongues in Space: Pa'ikwené (Palikur) Language(s), Relatedness, Identity." In *Anthropologies of Guayana: Cultural Spaces in Northeastern Amazonia*, edited by Neil L. Whitehead and Stephanie W. Alemán, 135–44. Tucson: University of Arizona Press.

Puri, Shalini, ed. 2003. *Marginal Migrations: The Circulation of Cultures Within the Caribbean*. London: Macmillan Caribbean.

Quijano, Aníbal, and Immanuel Wallerstein. 1992. "Americanity as a Concept, or the Americas in the Modern World-System." *International Journal of Social Sciences* (134): 549–57.

Redfield, Peter. 2000. *Space in the Tropics: From Convicts to Rockets in French Guiana*. Berkeley: University of California Press.

Redfield, Peter. 2005. "Foucault in the Tropics: Displacing the Panopticon." In *Anthropologies of Modernity: Foucault, Governmentality, and Life Politics*, edited by Jonathan Xavier Inda, 50–79. Malden, MA: Blackwell.

Romani, Carlo. 2010. "O 'Massacre de Amapá': A guerra imperialista que não houve." *Caravelle* 95: 85–118.

Romani, Carlo. 2013. *Aqui começa o Brasil!: histórias das gentes e dos poderes na fronteira do Oiapoque*. Rio de Janeiro: Multifoco.

Rygiel, Kim. 2016. "Dying to Live: Migrant Deaths and Citizenship Politics Along European Borders: Transgressions, Disruptions, and Mobilizations." *Citizenship Studies* 20 (5): 545–60. https://doi.org/10.1080/13621025.2016.1182682.

Santos, Fabio. 2017. "Re-Mapping Europe. Field Notes from the French-Brazilian Borderland." *InterDisciplines: Journal of History and Sociology* 8: 173–201. https://doi.org/10 .4119/unibi/indi-v8-i2-181.

Santos, Fabio. 2020a. "From French Guiana to Brazil: Entanglements, Migrations, and Demarcations of the Kaliña." *Espace Populations Sociétés* (1–2). https://doi.org/10 .4000/eps.9727.

Santos, Fabio. 2020b. "Crisscrossing the Oyapock River: Entangled Histories and Fluid Identities in the French-Brazilian Borderland." In *Migrants, Refugees, and Asylum Seekers in Latin America*, edited by Raanan Rein, Stefan Rinke, and David Sheinin, 217–41. Leiden: Brill. https://doi.org/10.1163/9789004432246_011.

Santos, Fabio. 2022a. *Bridging Fluid Borders. Entanglements in the French-Brazilian Borderland*. London: Routledge. https://doi.org/10.4324/9781003193555.

Santos, Fabio. 2022b. "The Oyapock River Bridge as a One-Way Street: (Un)Bridgeable Inequalities in Saint-Georges (French Guiana) and Oiapoque (Brazil)." In *Twin Cities Across Five Continents: Interactions and Tensions on Urban Borders*, edited by Ekaterina Mikhailova and John Garrard, 223–34. London: Routledge.

Santos, Fabio. 2023. "Mind the Archival Gap: Critical Fabulation as Decolonial Method." *Historical Social Research* 48: 330–53. https://doi.org/10.12759/HSR.48.2023.50.

Santos, Fabio. 2025. "The Necropolitics of Statelessness: Coloniality, Citizenship, and Disposable Lives." *Citizenship Studies* 29 (1–2): 17–40. https://doi.org/10.1080/13621025.2025.2467270.

Santos, Fabio, and Manuela Boatcă. 2022. "Europeanization as Global Entanglement." In *Sociology of Europeanization*, edited by Sebastian Büttner, Monika Eigmüller, and Susann Worschech, 105–32. Berlin: De Gruyter. https://doi.org/10.1515/9783110673630–005.

Santos, Fabio, and Manuela Boatcă. 2023. "European Elsewheres: Global Sociologies of Space and Europe." In *Considering Space: A Critical Concept for the Social Sciences*, edited by Dominik Bartmanski, Henning Füller, Johanna Hoerning, and Gunter Weidenhaus, 136–58. Abingdon, UK: Routledge. https://doi.org/10.4324/9781003361152-10.

Schindel, Estela. 2019. "Death by 'Nature': The European Border Regime and the Spatial Production of Slow Violence." *Environment and Planning C: Politics and Space* 40 (2): 428–46. https://doi.org/10.1177/2399654419884948.

Scott, Julius S. 2018. *The Common Wind: Afro-American Currents in the Age of the Haitian Revolution*. London: Verso.

Seles Nafes. 2019. "Por mês, 2 mil carros cruzam a Ponte Binacional e apenas 5 são Brasileiros." March. https://selesnafes.com/2019/03/por-mes-2-mil-carros-cruzam-a-ponte-binacional-e-apenas-5-sao-brasileiros/.

Shachar, Ayelet. 2009. *The Birthright Lottery: Citizenship and Global Inequality*. Cambridge, MA: Harvard University Press.

Spieler, Miranda Frances. 2011. "The Destruction of Liberty in French Guiana: Law, Identity and the Meaning of Legal Space, 1794–1830." *Social History* 36 (3): 260–79. https://doi.org/10.1080/03071022.2011.601104.

Spieler, Miranda Frances. 2012. *Empire and Underworld: Captivity in French Guiana*. Cambridge, MA: Harvard University Press.

Squire, Vicki. 2020. *Europe's Migration Crisis: Border Deaths and Human Dignity*. Cambridge: Cambridge University Press.

Stoler, Ann Laura. 2016. *Duress: Imperial Durabilities in Our Times*. Durham, NC: Duke University Press.

Toth, Stephen A. 2006. *Beyond Papillon: The French Overseas Penal Colonies, 1854–1952*. Lincoln: University of Nebraska Press.

Trouillot, Michel-Rolph. 1995. *Silencing the Past: Power and the Production of History*. Boston: Beacon Press.

Vergès, Françoise. 1999. *Monsters and Revolutionaries: Colonial Family Romance and Métissage*. Durham, NC: Duke University Press.

Vergès, Françoise. 2017. "Overseas France: A Vestige of the Republican Colonial Utopia?" In *The Colonial Legacy in France: Fracture, Rupture, and Apartheid*, edited by Nicolas Bancel, Pascal Blanchard, and Dominic Thomas, 165–71. Bloomington: Indiana University Press.

Wood, Sarah L. 2019. "How Empires Make Peripheries: 'Overseas France' in Contemporary History." *Contemporary European History* 28 (3): 434–45. https://doi.org/10.1017/S0960777318000917.

Wynter, Sylvia. 1995. "1492: A New World View." In *Race, Discourse, and the Americas: A New World View*, edited by Vera Lawrence and Rex Nettleford, 5–57. Washington, DC: Smithsonian Institution Press.

Wyss, Anna, and Janine Dahinden. 2022. "Disentangling Entangled Mobilities: Reflections on Forms of Knowledge Production Within Migration Studies." *Comparative Migration Studies* 10 (33): 1–17. https://doi.org/10.1186/s40878-022-00309-w.

Yarrington, Jonna. 2018. "Producing the Periphery." In *Locating Guyane*, edited by Sarah Wood and Catriona MacLeod, 91–104. Liverpool: Liverpool University Press.

12

The Trans-American Border Regime

TOWARD A GENEALOGY

Nicholas De Genova, Soledad Álvarez Velasco,
Eduardo Domenech, and Gustavo Dias

To shed a sharper light on some of the decisive features of the borders of (our) America—and the emergence, consolidation, and ongoing reconfiguration of a trans-American border regime across Latin America and the Caribbean—it remains for us to supply a somewhat more extended historical contextualization in the effort to trace a history of our present. In other words, without pretending to provide any semblance of an exhaustive history as such, we seek in this concluding chapter to construct an instructive genealogy of the formation and continuing entrenchment of this border regime across the Americas, signaling a variety of pertinent historical antecedents that are indispensable for adequately comprehending the transformations that are taking place before our eyes.

Colonialism and Postcoloniality in the Americas

In the genesis of the trans-American border regime, as with *any* border regime, there is a constitutive and unresolved tension between mobility and control. These are indeed tensions that have shaped the Americas since colonial times. As Michel-Rolph Trouillot (2003) reminds us: "The twentieth century did not invent mass migration. Since the seventeenth century human beings travelled en masse to faraway lands for much the same reasons as they do today. Except for the early gold rush of the sixteenth century, the major migrations of the Atlantic moment, voluntary or coerced, were generated by the global distribution of labor in the capitalist world system" (30). As part of brutal colonization schemes, Europeans—British, Spanish, Portuguese, French, Dutch, and Danish—traversed the Atlantic Ocean, invaded, and violently conquered the lands of the Indigenous Americans; millions of Africans were kidnapped and forcibly trafficked into permanent enslavement; and millions of Indigenous people were subjected to genocidal extermination, violent dispossession, and dislocation, as well as enslaved or subjected to other forms of coerced labor, often including forced intraregional mass movements (Wolf [1982] 2010; Quijano 2000). European projects of settler colonialism eventually but inevitably also entailed the mass recruitment of millions of other Europeans—variously, as the military and administrative personnel of expanding projects of conquest and colonization; as overseers of the forced labor of those enslaved on plantations, mines, and sugar mills; as settlers seeking opportunities for independent small-scale farm ownership in frontier lands; as indentured servants; or as "free" labor migrants. By the late nineteenth century, similarly, at least a million Asians coming primarily from China and the Indian subcontinent, but also from Japan, Java, and Sri Lanka, were transported to the Americas, mainly as indentured migrant labor, with enduring legacies across the hemisphere (Meagher 2008; Hu-DeHart and López 2008; McKeown 2008; Mongia 2018). These monumental intercontinental and intraregional mobilities are the veritable source of what by now we understand to be Our America.

These global mobilities have resulted in a remarkable hybridity of racialized identities, languages, religions, and cultures that have long been recognized to be a defining and enduring characteristic of the Americas (Trouillot 2003). Indeed, these legacies of global mobility and intermixing have long been officially celebrated by postcolonial nationalisms across Spanish- and Portuguese-speaking Latin America through ideologies of racial mixture (*mestizaje* and *mestiçagem*) that uphold such hybridity as the veritable foundation of each country's putatively distinctive "national" identity. Here, it is noteworthy that dominant Latin American ideologies of race operate according to a strikingly opposite rationality from the segregationist logic of racial "purity" that has historically undergirded the particular sociopolitical order of white supremacy in the United States or Canada. The Caribbean, as the region with the longest and most complex colonial history—encompassing France, Spain, England, Denmark, and the Netherlands—has, in turn, conceptualized the sociocultural practices and emotional attachments that emerged in the context of the mobilities to the plantation societies under the term *creolization*, a process deeply shaped by hierarchy and inequalities (Hall 2015). Yet, even that critical concept has been misinterpreted and euphemistically framed as a process of harmonious coexistence, thereby obscuring the persistent patterns of racialized social stratification in the Caribbean (Boatcă and Santos 2023). This contrast in racial ideologies between the Anglophone nation-states originating from British projects of settler colonialism in North America and those across the rest of the hemisphere with origins in Spanish, Portuguese, French, Dutch, Danish, and British colonialism in Latin America and the Caribbean, however, only underscores the extent to which *all* these racial logics have served to constitute *all* of these "New World" sociopolitical orders as regimes of white supremacy, their peculiar differences and discrepancies notwithstanding, and to reinstitute their respective postcolonial but invariably Eurocentric political projects as varieties of white nationalism. Of course, the specific manifestations of racism have consequently assumed somewhat divergent forms in these disparate contexts. Nevertheless, the racial subjugation of Indigenous peoples subjected to protracted projects of genocide and violent dispossession and the enslavement and unrelenting exploitation and repressive marginalization of Africans and their American descendants have been remarkably constant and indubitably remain paramount.

Overwhelmingly, during the colonial era and beyond, enslaved or otherwise coerced Indigenous and African–African American labor was employed on plantations or in sugar mills and mines, producing cash crops, raw materials, and finished commodities for export to European metropoles. The freedom of movement of those workers was subordinated by a variety of labor regimes, including slavery, peonage, serfdom, and wage labor, which coexisted as disparate features of the expansion of the modern capitalist world system (Cohen 2006; Wallerstein [1978] 2011). What may be recognized to have originally been extraordinarily mobile labor-power, then, commonly came to be temporarily or permanently immobilized, "fixed" in place to their workplaces, violently subjugated by their "lords" and "masters," often stripped of their most elementary human personhood and dignity, and systematically deprived of their freedoms (Holloway 1994; Moulier-Boutang 2006; Trouillot 2015). In these respects, class inequalities across the hemisphere have always been deeply racialized, just as racialized differences have always tended to be deeply coded according to hierarchies of class and social status. For our purposes here of positing a critique of the contemporary trans-American border regime, therefore, it is necessary to highlight how a centuries-long constellation of global human mobilities has not only generated the characteristic heterogeneity and hybridity of the Americas, historically, but also has been the catalyst instigating the development and continuous deployment of ferocious mechanisms to control and contain those mobilities.

The colonial contours of what would become the geopolitical borders of post-colonial Latin America and the Caribbean remain as an enduring legacy of these racial divisions and the attendant dynamics of domination and marginalization. Those colonial geopolitical lines arbitrarily instituted and enforced ongoing separations between spaces, histories, communities, and peoples. However, as Fabio Santos (this volume, ch. 11) notes in his analysis of the border between Brazil and French Guiana, cross-border mobilities have challenged, resisted, and subverted those geopolitical boundaries for more than five hundred years. Indeed, this sort of resistance has been extensive across the Americas. Nonetheless, that colonial outline, intrinsically plagued by racism, has territorially demarcated not only the geography of the countries of the Americas but also their political matrix. In the complex genealogies of the contemporary trans-American border regime, racism, selectivity, and differential inclusion have left an indelible imprint. In the genesis of the tension between mobility and control, racism has always figured as a salient constituent element that has served to justify the vicious division of labor and the unequal mobility of migrant workers, securing the emergence, expansion, and stabilization of capital accumulation for centuries. Colonial racism was the historical foundation of the repressive mechanisms for subjugating populations, suppressing their prospects for desertion and escape, and thus also for controlling migrants' mobilities.

With the eventual demise of colonialism, the emerging independent nation-states of Latin America sought to attract foreigners to populate their lands and invigorate the incipient capitalist economic expansion of these nascent states' "national" economies (Acosta 2018; Olaya 2018). Yet not everyone was welcomed with open borders. Defined by Florestan Fernandes (1965, 1975) as a project of "conservative modernization" (with specific reference to the example of Brazil following the abolition of slavery), people of color across the region continued to be systematically marginalized. "White"-identified elites widely implemented explicit policies aimed at "whitening" their "nations" (in Portuguese, *branquea-mento*; in Spanish, *blanqueamiento*) and "improving the race" (*mejorando la raza*) through the recruitment and facilitation of migration from Europe that deliberately sought to retroactively engineer (white, or at least whiter) "national bloodlines."

Beginning in the late nineteenth century and continuing into the early twentieth century, the first immigration laws across the region deliberately sought to "encourage" or "promote" immigration by those who were deemed the most "desirable," "suitable," and "capable" (Olaya 2018). In a classic example of what Aníbal Quijano (2000) has called the "coloniality of power," whereby the newly independent "post"-colonial nationalist projects remained deeply compromised by the colonized mentalities of European-identified elites who arrogated to themselves the task of rule, those first immigration laws explicitly favored the migration of Europeans and North Americans who would presumably "whiten" and supposedly "improve" the national racial stock to the detriment of the local populations of people of color (Acosta 2018; Gómez 2022). The ensuing era of mass European migrations—above all, in the countries of the Southern Cone (Argentina, Uruguay, Chile, and Brazil)—notably coincided with the mass migrations from Europe to the United States and Canada. In South America, the entrenchment of policies promoting immigration transpired in concert with the institutionalization and fortification of administrative-bureaucratic agencies. The first immigration and colonization laws in the late nineteenth century commonly established the state bodies responsible for promoting and selecting immigration. The official definitions in these laws contributed to generally constructing the desirable "immigrant" as a working-age male manual laborer from Europe who could provide evidence of the desired skills or competencies and who would affirm the will to remain in the host country.

With the exceptions of Argentina and Brazil, however, the efforts of most Latin American states to encourage transatlantic (mainly European) migration did not result in a massive influx of new migrants. The policies for promoting immigration during this era nonetheless did gradually establish regulatory state apparatuses dedicated to the normative scheme of attracting and recruiting "good immigrants" while also preventing and rejecting "undesirable" migration. The duties and powers of Argentina's General Department of Immigration, created in 1876, evinced this dual intention: "To protect immigration that was honorable and laborious and to advise measures to contain the flow of which was vicious or useless."[1] This objective was repeatedly replicated in various national contexts. For example, in Ecuador, the first Ley de Extranjería of 1886, the second in 1892, and the Constitution of 1897 explicitly stated that Europeans and North Americans were welcome in preference to other foreigners (Terán Najas 2020; Eguiguren 2019; Ramírez 2013). Similarly, in Colombia in the early 1920s, immigration legislation promoted a selectivity that defined the "desirable" immigrant as an agent of "civilization and progress" while disparaging migration that would purportedly disturb the social order or make it difficult to achieve the "economic and intellectual development of the country" and the "improvement of ethnic conditions, both physical and moral."[2] This same criterion of "desirability" was evident in other countries, such as Chile (see Quinteros, Ramos, and Dufraix-Tapia, this volume, ch. 7).

Categorizing migrants as "desirable" (of European origin) and "undesirable" (people not racialized as white) has been a common feature of immigration policies across the Americas. The Chinese Exclusion Act of 1882 in the United States, which was in fact the country's first significant law regulating migration, and then Canada's Chinese Immigration Act of 1885, were indeed mirrored—and in some cases, anticipated—in numerous Latin American countries, which during the same epoch imposed their own anti-Asian immigration measures (Carrillo 2012; Gao 2021; Meagher 2008; Hu-DeHart and López 2008; Lee 2002; McKeown 2008). Countries such as Peru, Colombia, and Ecuador explicitly enacted the rejection of migrants from Asia, particularly China. Ruling elites did not consider Asian migration as "advantageous" or "convenient," because it did not correspond to the image of the immigrant imagined as an agent of "civilization" and "progress." In Peru, already by the mid-nineteenth century, although Asian migration, mainly Chinese, was included in policies promoting migration, it soon was rebranded as "undesirable." In 1853, the Immigration and Colonization Law that had initially provided for a cash award to those who successfully recruited "settlers from China" was repealed on the grounds that Chinese migration had "not corresponded to the wishes of the Nation."[3] Later, a decree of 1856 declared that Asian migration was "not convenient for the country," on the grounds that Asians were deemed to be "a degraded race," and prohibited the recruitment of contract labor. Toward the end of the century, in the context of the more robust development of policies to expressly promote European migration, the Immigration and Colonization Act of 1893 offered a definition of "immigrant" that exclusively counted foreigners of the "white race." In the late nineteenth century, the other South American states on the Pacific coast that had previously welcomed Chinese immigration also decreed its prohibition. In Colombia, the large presence of Chinese workers recruited for the construction of the Panama Canal was met with racist anxieties and invocations of a "Chinese peril." In 1887, a law decreed the prohibition of "the importation of Chinese for any work in Colombian territory,"[4] but after five years, the rule was repealed, and the entry and settlement of Chinese migrants were reauthorized with the racist justification that they were an industrious workforce particularly adapted to withstanding adverse climatic conditions. In Ecuador, a decree in 1889 prohibited "the entry of Chinese" and formulated the prospect of their "expulsion." As in North America, Latin American and Caribbean scholars have not only analyzed the phenomenon of Chinese exclusion as an iconic example of the global emergence of immigration lawmaking, but also underscored how the region's legal architecture governing migration and borders has, since its inception, been founded on explicitly exclusionary and racist rationales.[5]

Beginning in the 1920s, states made substantial changes in how they classified and sought to select migrants. In this era, notably in the aftermath of the Russian Revolution of 1917, with the further development of policies ostensibly designed to promote immigration, new rules nonetheless implicitly contained various formulas of exclusion: foreigners were welcome but with important "exceptions." Thus, various South American states began to redefine entry requirements and establish categories of individuals or groups that would not be admitted to the national territory (Domenech and Pereira 2022). Revising the official definitions of "immigrant" desirability instituted in legislation of the latter nineteenth century, states relegated those who did not fit the image of the "good immigrant" to an expanded and more heterogeneous universe of the "undesirable." "Undesirable" migrants continued to be those who did not fit the hegemonic (white supremacist) parameters of nation and race, but now also included those deemed "subversives," "deviants," or "threats" who were imagined to corrode national identity, the health of the population, public and moral order, or the security of the state. The contributors to this book not only extend this line of historical inquiry into the contemporary moment but also demonstrate that even in a period when an ideological and political shift apparently turned toward "progressive" laws enacted by "leftist" governments, as transpired during the first decade of the twenty-first century, exclusionary selectivity and racism in immigration policies have endured and been reactivated as an indelible historical hallmark shaping the complex dynamics of the heterogeneous trans-American border regime.

The Americas During and After the "American" Century

The unresolved tension between mobility and control in the Americas has also been defined by the incommensurable asymmetry between the ascendancy of the global hegemonic power of the United States and the rest of the Americas. In 1823, at the dawn of Latin American independence and the inauguration of the postcolonial era, US President James Monroe launched the so-called Monroe Doctrine, arrogating to the United States a self-assigned role of de facto imperial superintendent to monitor and "protect" the putative sovereignty of the newly independent states of the Americas against any attempt by the European powers to reestablish colonies or renew their imperial presence in the Americas. The Monroe Doctrine declared that all of the newly independent nation-states of the Western Hemisphere would thenceforth be presumptively considered by the United States to compose its own exclusive sphere of influence and interest, such that any intervention by the European colonial powers in the Americas would be taken as "an unfriendly disposition," not toward the sovereignty and self-determination of those Latin American peoples but toward the United States and its own "rights," "peace," "happiness," "safety," and "defense" (De Genova 2017a, 33). The doctrine became the centerpiece of US justifications for its military interventions and other policies of political and economic interference in the hemisphere for the greater part of the following two centuries (Grandin 2007, 4–5).

With the Roosevelt Corollary (1905) to the Monroe Doctrine, enunciated at the dawn of the twentieth century, when the United States had just acquired Puerto Rico as a colony and Cuba as a military protectorate as spoils of the Spanish-American War (1898), the United States promulgated an expansive vision of its own prerogative to exercise an "international police power" to preserve political stability and social order and protect private property interests across the hemisphere. Soon thereafter, there ensued US invasions and protracted military occupations of Nicaragua (1912–33), Haiti (1915–34), and the Dominican Republic (1916–24), as well as military expeditions into Mexico (1916–17) during the Mexican Revolution. Particularly in the post–World War II context of decolonization and the Cold War, and continuing into the twenty-first century, the United States meddled in national affairs across the region whenever it considered the self-determination of the Latin American and Caribbean peoples as jeopardizing its political and economic projects of global hegemony. The United States orchestrated military coups to overthrow democratically elected governments in Guatemala (1954), Brazil (1964), Chile (1973), and Honduras (2009), as well as the failed Bay of Pigs invasion in 1961, perpetrated against the Cuban Revolution of 1959. Against the Nicaraguan Revolution of 1979, the United States commandeered a counterinsurgency proxy war throughout the 1980s. Direct US military interventions in the second half of the twentieth century included the invasion and occupation of the Dominican Republic (1965), the invasion of Grenada (1983), and the invasion of Panama (1989). More generally, across the twentieth century, US interventionism took the more banal form of installing, funding, militarily training, and sustaining ruthless dictatorships aligned with the United States politically and committed to enforcing a reign of terror in order to protect US business interests. Among the long list of cruel dictators in this rogue's gallery, distinguished for rule by torture, state and paramilitary death squads, assassinations, and disappearances, we may note only the most no-torious: Rafael Trujillo in the Dominican Republic (1930–61); Fulgencio Batista in Cuba (1952–59); François "Papa Doc" Duvalier in Haiti (1957–71), immediately succeeded in power by his son Jean-Claude "Baby Doc" Duvalier (1971–86); Anastasio Somoza in Nicaragua (1967–72; 1974–79), Efraín Ríos Montt in Guatemala (1974–77; 1982–83), and Augusto Pinochet in Chile (1973–90). In South America, the US-backed military dictatorships in Ecuador, Peru, Chile, Argentina, Uruguay, Paraguay, Bolivia, and Brazil throughout the 1960s and 1970s were part of a campaign of state repression, eventually coordinated under Operación Cóndor (formally initiated in 1975). As part of this continental counterinsurgency campaign during the extended aftermath of the Cuban Revolution, the United States trained Latin American military, police, and other state officials in torture techniques and other tactics of state terror at the School of the Americas (located in Panama from its founding in 1946, and then relocated in 1984 to Fort Benning in the US state of Georgia). Indeed, over the course of the twentieth century, there is not a single country in Latin America or the Caribbean where the United States did not exert its imperial political and economic power to uphold "order" in its proverbial "backyard."

This extensive and often direct US intervention into the exercise of state power in the Americas supplies the indispensable background context for understanding the externalization of border policing that is central to the consolidation of the trans-American border regime. During the 1970s and early 1980s, for instance, the South American military dictatorships reformed their laws governing immigration and foreigners, adopting Cold War anticommunist "national security" policy frameworks that reinforced and systematized the already selective and racist historical biases and punitive and repressive features of their immigration laws. In Argentina, by introducing criminalizing discourses about migration and police power over foreigners to the national immigration control agency through the so-called Videla Law (1981), the dictatorship carried out multiple campaigns aimed at identifying internal and external "enemies," which encompassed both "subversives" and "illegal" or "clandestine" foreigners. Furthermore, within the framework of a "policy to promote immigration," the Argentine state promulgated a principle of selectivity based on racialized national-origin criteria, reinforcing the historical division between "desirable" and "undesirable" migrants. The immigration laws created under South American military governments reinforced arbitrary, discriminatory, and openly criminalizing criteria against migrants that have persisted into the twenty-first century (Álvarez Velasco; Domenech, this volume, chs. 6 and 8).

US imperial interventionism has been both a geopolitical and a fundamentally geo-economic project. Along with military and political domination, US-based corporations have long dominated key areas of economic extraction, production, and exchange in the Americas, culminating in recent decades in radical experiments with neoliberal policies. "The first experiment with neoliberal state formation," notes David Harvey (2005), "occurred in Chile after Pinochet's coup" (7). The historically dependent, peripheral, and extractive character of Latin American and Caribbean economies (Gunder Frank 2018; Svampa 2019) has gone hand in hand with their confinement to external indebtedness. Since the 1970s, amid the global turn to neoliberalism, in the desperate effort to supposedly achieve the long-deferred and never reachable condition of "development," Latin American and Caribbean countries were induced to become still more dependent on loans from the World Bank and the International Monetary Fund (IMF) (Furtado 1981, 1982; Harvey 2005; Maciel 2008). Such loans were proffered with perverse conditions attached, such as the obligation to adopt policies that resulted in the privatization of public assets and government services, reducing social investment and shrinking the state's capacity to provide social protection for its population (Escobar 2014; Gudynas and Acosta 2011). The neoliberal formula expanded Latin American and Caribbean countries' public debt and their dependency on the United States while accelerating the hyperprecaritization of human lives across the hemisphere. While the United States has long enjoyed the status of the world's largest economy, Latin America and the Caribbean constitute the most unequal regions on the planet, where poverty afflicts approximately a third of their people, rising to nearly half of the population in rural areas (ECLAC 2022).

In the wake of neoliberalism and a convulsion of civil wars during the 1970s and 1980s, the region as a whole plunged into a deep and protracted economic and political crisis, which was intensified in the ensuing decades through the promotion and adoption of the standardized package of neoliberal economic policy recommendations that came to be known as the "Washington Consensus," prescribed since 1989 by both the US government and global financial institutions such as the IMF and the World Bank. In the case of Brazil, for instance, the economic crisis that arose after the end of the military dictatorship (1964–85) became the pretext for the implementation (for the first time) in the 1990s of measures aimed at reducing state intervention in the economy. Neoliberal doctrine promoted this retreat of the state from supporting social welfare and economic protections as a type of necessary "modernization" that would allow Brazil to better adapt to the requirements of the global economy. Since then, the country has witnessed a succession of large-scale emigrations. Recurrent crises, job insecurity, chronic unemployment, and widening precarity have been central features distinguishing these migrations (Dias 2016; Dias and Martins 2018).

While augmenting inequality, poverty, and hyperprecaritization, US political, military, and economic interventionism has also multiplied and exacerbated internal conflicts, often culminating in merciless civil wars. The unceasing exodus of both migrants and refugees to the United States—and, by extension, to Canada (see Landolt and Goldring, this volume, ch. 1)—is in fact one of the most visible and predictable effects of the protracted history of US intervention in the region. As Laura Gómez (2022) contends, US neocolonialism and migration are part of the same continuum (56). Indeed, in Juan González's (2000) memorable phrase, the arrival of millions from Latin America and the Caribbean to the United States can only be understood as a "harvest of empire." Particularly since the late 1970s, ever greater numbers of people from across the region have continuously been compelled to desert or flee from their countries of origin—economically devastated, disfigured by political malfeasance, corruption, or authoritarianism, and in many cases also physically ruined by the carnage of civil war, punitive counterinsurgency campaigns, or state terror. Whether as "migrants," "asylum seekers," or "refugees," traversing both regularized and irregularized (illegalized) migratory pathways, those who have pursued such strategies of exit through projects of cross-border mobility have also nevertheless answered the insatiable demand of capital for "cheap" migrant labor power to fuel the US economy. Consequently, the hemisphere is crisscrossed by an ever-multiplying proliferation of land, sea, and air routes, by now already used by multiple successive generations of migrants to reach the United States.

Combating Global "Threats": The Consolidation of the Trans-American Border Regime

Only in the late twentieth century did the trans-American border regime begin to assume its current form. With the fall of the Berlin Wall in 1989, followed soon thereafter by the dissolution of the Soviet Union and thus the abrupt end of the bipolar geopolitics of the Cold War era, the United States was left as the lone "superpower" in what some commentators depicted, without irony, as a "unipolar" condition. The preceding decades of "anticommunist" counterinsurgency campaigns and right-wing dictatorships across Latin America and the Caribbean likewise were brought to a close, and the region ushered in a new era distinguished by a return to electoralism and parliamentary democracy (Hobsbawm 2008; Svampa 2017). As a result, US interventionist policies in the region shifted from a protracted campaign of militarized combat against the putative menace of left-wing subversion to a new quest to combat so-called "clandestine trans-national actors" (Andreas 2003). Under that vacuous umbrella category, US interventionism adopted as its new targets an eclectic array of multifarious "security threats": drug cartels, smugglers, traffickers, criminal gangs, and finally, "terrorists." This shift in the ideological rationale and rhetorical justification for US intervention was already evident in the 1989 invasion of Panama, where the United States sought to depose Manuel Norriega, a dictator whom it had long supported but now deemed an inconvenient and obstreperous liability, rebranding him as a "narco-terrorist." In the ensuing years, there arose what Elana Zilberg (2011) has identified as "the gang–crime–terrorism continuum" (17) in her study of El Salvador's transition from the Cold War to the "War on Terror." As a kind of revised formulation of the notorious School of the Americas (itself notably renamed officially in 2001 as the Western Hemisphere Institute for Security Cooperation), the International Law Enforcement Academy (ILEA) in El Salvador has operated since 2005 as a regional hub for training Latin America and Caribbean law enforcement agents, "to provide them with modern tools and techniques, to combat transnational crime."[6]

Perhaps predictably, even irregularized migrants and refugees seeking asylum came to be figured as "threats" to be targeted with new measures of border "security" (De Genova 2007, 2009; Miller 2019; Zilberg 2011). Alison Mountz (2020, 41–42) argues that this reconfiguration of a new global scenario of "risk" has widely served to deny the recognition and admission of refugees and to foreclose states' obligations to provide asylum. The pretext of protecting the "victims" of migrant smugglers was invoked during the 1990s to justify the expansion of the US migrant detention system into the Caribbean Sea to interdict and deter Haitian and Cuban boat migrants (Loyd and Mountz 2018). Since then, the enforcement of the US maritime border has expanded through security cooperation agreements with Caribbean states to enhance surveillance and control (Haughton 2009; Loyd and Mountz 2018). It was during this same period that the full extent of Mexico's territory was transformed into the externalized preliminary border of the United States with a shift in emphasis to the reinforced policing of Mexico's southern border. The complex dynamics that have shaped both Mexico's northern and southern borders are incomprehensible without understating the effects of US border externalization (Velasco Ortiz; Basok and Rojas Wiesner, this volume, chs. 2 and 3). The constant reinforcement of the US-Mexico border thus instigated a mirroring dynamic along the Mexico-Guatemala border as the two borders were aligned to impose new controls against illegalized migrations originating mainly from Central America. The proliferation of legal reforms, transformations of border infrastructures, and the multiplication of humanitarian actors operating in Mexico over recent decades, notably, have been accompanied by a concomitant escalation in human rights abuses, state and extrastate violence, and generalized predation against migrants and refugees.

The discourse of security, particularly as formalized in 2000 with the signing of the Palermo Protocol,[7] has served to authorize campaigns against human trafficking and migrant smuggling, purportedly in the name of the humanitarian duty of protecting their "victims," and has been deployed globally as the ostensibly unquestionable justification for legitimating and partly disguising new forms of border enforcement against migrants and refugees, particularly those traveling from impoverished or war-torn countries and generally racialized as nonwhite. The Palermo Protocol is a binding international criminal law agreement that obliges signatory states to adopt similar legal frameworks, create specialized police units, and conduct operations to dismantle migrant-smuggling and human-trafficking networks (UNODC 2000). Indirectly, these states are thereby authorized to deploy new tactics and techniques for more generally policing irregularized migration. By the early 2000s, the thirty-three member states of the Group of Latin America and Caribbean Countries (GRULAC) of the United Nations Regional Groups had signed and ratified the Palermo Protocol.[8] They proceeded to revise their legal and border-policing strategies with an emphasis not on securing "human rights" but on securing borders and criminalizing autonomous migratory movements (Mansur Dias 2015).

This securitarian rationale has likewise served the United States in the externalization of its border control mechanisms to an ever larger number of so-called third countries, in a new form of indirect interventionism that subcontracts "security" to junior partners (Huysmans 2000; Miller 2019; Mountz 2020; Zilberg 2011). It is precisely this sort of "burden sharing" among multiple nation-states that characterizes the increasing harmonization and coordination of the heterogeneous border regime across the Americas. Under bilateral cooperation agreements, via the US Department of State, its ambassadorial personnel, and the US Agency for International Development (USAID), the United States has increasingly intervened directly in the design and implementation of security policies across the region, including antitrafficking programs and more general campaigns against "illegal" migration, militarized operations and raids purportedly targeting migrant smugglers and traffickers, and providing direct assistance in the reinforcement and renovation of border surveillance technologies (García Hernández 2018; Menjívar 2014; Miller 2019; Rodríguez Rejas 2018; Zilberg 2011).

The signing of the Palermo Protocol was an important moment, signaling the advent in the American context of what scholars, such as William Walters (2011), have identified as the "humanitarian border" (Andersson 2014, 2017; Garelli and Tazzioli 2017, 2018; Heller and Pezzani 2017; Pallister-Wilkins 2015; Pezzani 2015; Tazzioli 2015a, 2015b; Ticktin 2016; Williams 2015, 2016). The language of (criminal) "villains" and (trafficked) "victims" contributed to the continuous reworking of a mass-mediated "border spectacle," as Nicholas De Genova (2002, 2013b) has described it, in which a spotlight is constantly focused on "the border" as a scene of transgression where "irregular" (illegalized) migration is staged as an intractable "problem" demanding urgent measures. Such border spectacles systematically disregard the structural causes that produce those mobilities. Likewise, these spectacles of "illegal" migration divert our attention from how states are responsible for "the legal production of migrant 'illegality'"(De Genova 2002, 2004, 2005, ch. 6), as well as obfuscating the direct role of intensified border enforcement in compelling migrants to increasingly depend on a proliferation of smuggling and trafficking networks in order to successfully navigate the most perilous and violent border-crossing routes. The accompanying rhetoric justifying increased border enforcement, securitization, and militarization is notably enhanced by the recourse to a humanitarian discourse of border policing as the putative "protection" or "rescue" of migrant "victims" subjected to the predations of criminalized smugglers and traffickers, against whom hardened border security measures are made to appear to be a moral imperative. Thus, humanitarianism's discourses of "compassion" and "protection" serve to reinforce sharp partitions between "innocents" and "criminal" culprits, and thereby intensify the means for governing irregularized migrants and refugees. Border crossers are thus deemed worthy of compassion and protection only if they can be reduced to perfectly passive objects, first as victims of exploitive traffickers and then as the objects of states' measures to "rescue" and "protect" them, but in both instances stripped of all subjectivity and autonomy. The smugglers who facilitate migrants' and refugees' illegalized border crossings, on the other hand, are criminalized and demonized, thereby obfuscating the larger structural violence of the border regime itself that creates the conditions of possibility for migrants' dependency on smuggling (Keshavarz and Khosravi 2022).

Not long after the signing of the Palermo Protocol, in the aftermath of the events of September 11, 2001, and the promulgation of the "global war on terrorism," the fight against migrant smuggling and human trafficking came to be still further subsumed under the rubric of "security" (Dias 2016; Miller 2019). The permeability of the US-Mexico border was newly problematized as a security risk, and "illegal" migrants, especially those hailing from Middle Eastern, African, and Asian countries where the United States pursued campaigns of military intervention, were branded as potential terrorists (Andreas 2003; De Genova 2007). If we assess their real effects, however, these purportedly antiterrorist measures systematically targeted noncitizens in general, and migrants in particular, for heightened surveillance and unprecedented punitive repercussions (De Genova 2009, 2011). Under the mandate of these securitarian pretexts, new restrictions and penalties targeting migrants were adopted by US partners around the world, including across Latin American and the Caribbean (Mountz 2020). Mexico in particular reinforced its incipient role as the primary buffer zone in the region by implementing new restrictive visa schemes targeting "suspect" categories of migrants, further militarizing its borders, introducing criminalizing policies, and coordinating programs and practices of detention and expulsion with the United States (París Pombo 2016, 2022; Villafuerte Solís and García Aguilar 2017; Márquez Covarrubias 2015; Izcara Palacios 2016; Vogt 2017; Glockner 2020; Varela Huerta and McLean 2021). Over the ensuing years, these measures would be further externalized to Central American countries, particularly Guatemala (Miller 2019). The militarized tactics of containment deployed against the migrant population in Central America have increasingly resembled state practices during armed conflicts where the weight of US interventionism was pronounced and decisive (Núñez Chaim, Varela Huerta, and Glockner Fagetti, this volume, ch. 4; see also Zilberg 2011).

Across the region, security cooperation has also been promoted for combating drug trafficking. Undoubtedly, the most iconic case has been the Plan Colombia, an initiative aimed at combating both drug cartels and left-wing insurgent groups in Colombia, for which the United States dedicated a multibillion-dollar package of foreign aid, including an expansive program of support for the military. Between 2000 and 2015, when the Plan was implemented in its original form, Colombia was the top recipient of US military aid in the Western Hemisphere and its main ally in its so-called War on Terror, particularly in the Andean region (Guevara Latorre 2015; Scahill 2021; Tokatlian 2001). Although the Plan's objective was the "eradication, interdiction, and alternative development" of coca fields used to produce cocaine, with the express aim of offering social and economic assistance to rural areas that had been controlled for half a century by the Fuerzas Armadas Revolucionarias de Colombia (Revolutionary Armed Forces of Colombia; FARC), in reality it served primarily as a revised strategy of US military interventionism in the region that utterly failed to reverse any of the structural causes underlying the complex transnational political economy of cocaine (Moreno Romero and Silva Serna 2009; Tokatlian 2001).

Meanwhile, Colombian state security forces, fortified by the massive infusion of US aid and trained to protect oil pipelines belonging to US companies, have continued to maintain intimate relationships with long-standing right-wing death squads, organize new paramilitary forces, and directly perpetrate rampant abuses and massacres (Amnesty International 2000; Scahill 2021). Thus, such "security" measures have proven to intensify militarization and exacerbate the conditions driving migration, including the continuous dislocation of internally displaced people and an exodus of Colombian asylum seekers across the region (CODHES 2019).

The installation and entrenchment of the trans-American border regime has been uneven and heterogeneous, however. Depending on various geopolitical and geo-economic circumstances and the diverse cooperation histories between the United States and various "third countries," the forms of US intervention, border externalization, and outsourced border control have included "harder" and "softer" versions. In all cases, nonetheless, these experiments and improvisations have required what in the European context has been called a "neighborhood policy" (Casas-Cortes, Cobarrubias, and Pickles 2015), where bilateral agreements, usually signed under dramatically unequal conditions, are pivotal for its operation (Faist 2019). The undisputed global geopolitical weight of the United States, coupled with the geo-economic fact that it is ordinarily the largest market for Latin American exports, has meant that the countries which have been converted into buffer zones have almost no negotiating leverage in security and immigration control agreements since their economies depend almost entirely on access to the US market (Miller 2019). As the chapters in this volume demonstrate, the unfailing justification of combating "irregular" (illegalized) migration across the Americas, especially through the criminalization of migrant smuggling, has consistently authorized the adoption of policies that have served to contain or interrupt autonomous migrant and refugee mobilities directed toward the United States, and have been highly effective in reinforcing and augmenting states' military and police powers. Notably, this has been the case even for ostensibly "progressive" or putatively "leftist" governments.

The heterogeneous character of this border regime's disparate and diffuse control mechanisms should thus be recognized as also reflecting various particularities from one nation-state to the next, and from one local context of bordering to the next. State actors engaged in border control at multiple levels are never simply passive recipients of political dictates but rather are active participants, often with competing interests and imperatives (Andersson 2016; see also Mezzadra and Nielson 2013). Border control tactics and technologies are locally adopted and adapted, corroborating the active role that buffer states play and the often equivocal ways they exert power over human mobilities (Missbach and Philips 2020; Stock et al. 2019). Indeed, the junior-partner states operating as buffer zones in a larger transnational border regime can often be found to serve not only as de facto border guards enforcing the outer perimeters of an extended space of externalized control but also, simultaneously, as occasional facilitators, cynically complicit with the autonomy of migration, sometimes enabling migrants' onward transits toward the next border (De Genova 2017b; Kasparek 2016; Kasparek and Speer 2015; Mezzadra and Neilson 2013). The empirical research in each chapter of this volume supplies ample evidence of these tensions, frictions, and incoherences operating across this heterogenous regime of often-competing bids for sovereign power.

An exceptional but particularly revealing case is presented by the magnitude and spread across the region of Venezuelan migration, which, as of March 2023, exceeded 7 million people. This contemporary exodus, codified as a migration "crisis"—almost never explained as an effect of the US economic sanctions imposed on Venezuela, together with its internal collapse—gave rise to a "regional response" that has involved the US government through state agencies such as USAID and the Bureau of Population, Refugees, and Migration (PRM) of the US State Department. The Interagency Coordination Platform for Refugees and Migrants from Venezuela, better known as Platform R4V ("Response for Venezuelans"), created in 2018 and led by the International Organization for Migration (IOM) and the United Nations High Commissioner for Refugees (UNHCR), manifests what can be characterized as the "soft" mode of US border externalization policy. Officially, the objective of this region-wide platform is to address the "protection," "assistance," and "integration" needs of Venezuelan refugees and migrants in the affected Latin American and Caribbean states, according to the principles established in the New York Declaration for Refugees and Migrants (2016). Nonetheless, the institutional rationale, guidelines for action, composition, donors, service sectors, and practices deployed through Platform R4V in the name of "deterrence" effectuate a strategy of containment aimed at channeling Venezuelan "transit migration" by means of a "humanitarian response" funded primarily by the US government but carried out by multiple nonstate actors. As of 2023, Platform R4V involved more than two hundred organizations in developing the Regional Response Plan for Refugees and Migrants (RMRP) from Venezuela in seventeen countries across Latin America and the Caribbean.

The consolidation and reinforcement of what we have defined as the trans-American border regime would thus be inexplicable without attending to the complex, contradictory, and ambiguous coexistence of the securitization and criminalization of human mobility, on one hand, that have been enacted as responses within a larger reaction formation that confronts the primacy and incorrigibility of the upsurge in intraregional, transcontinental, cross-border migratory movements, on the other. These contending forces of mobility and control are further complicated, moreover, by the operations of humanitarian actors and institutions. These contradictory dynamics that together shape the contours of the trans-American border regime must be further understood in light of a larger global shift toward migration "management" and "governance."

The Neoliberal Quest for Migration "Governance" Across the Americas

The term *governance* came to enjoy widespread currency in the implementation of neoliberal measures in the 1980s and 1990s. The term arose as the expression of a new and more expansive notion of government beyond the state, exercised by private sector or other nongovernmental authorities, and signaled the adoption of a more pronouncedly managerial discourse that explicitly favored market logics. *Governance* therefore tended to imply the creation or facilitation of nonstate networks and partnerships to ensure the provision of services that had customarily been within the exclusive purview of the exercise of state power. With the notion of governance, then, came the neoliberal sensibility that states increasingly must depend on markets, the private sector, international organizations, or nongovernmental organizations (NGOs) to execute policies and exercise rule. As systemic contradictions in the capitalist world economy have deepened, producing and exacerbating endemic socioeconomic, environmental, and political crises, and as cross-border regional interconnections and dynamics have multiplied, regional suprastate forms of "governance" have become a prominent scheme of rule.

Border regimes—involving regional externalizations of the policing of human mobility, efforts at harmonizing multiple nation-states' immigration and asylum policies, and other forms of integration, however uneven and contradictory—are an important manifestation of the entrenchment of neoliberal governance strategies on a global scale. Global organizations, beginning with the United Nations and its subsidiary bodies, such as the UNHCR and the IOM, have become pivotal in this type of governance (Andrijasevic and Walters 2010). While presenting themselves as somehow neutral or even "apolitical," purportedly motivated by "humanitarian" imperatives, these international agencies of global governance nonetheless remain deeply implicated in international geopolitics. Consequently, the political weight of particular nation-states, such as the United States, or supranational (quasi-)state formations such as the European Union, have come to rely heavily on these apparently more diffuse forms of global governance while yet sustaining and perpetuating the (post)colonial historical asymmetries of power and prestige that remain decisive in shaping how this neoliberal form of rule operates. With an upsurge of migrants' and refugees' mobilities worldwide, the conceit of transregional border governance and the neoliberal quest for global "migration management" have nonetheless been recurrently confronted by the autonomy of migration, which can be met only with a compulsive recourse to invocations of border "crisis" and appeals for "emergency" measures (De Genova 2016, 2017b, 2018; New Keywords Collective 2016).

The mantra of "safe, orderly, and regular" migration is the consecration of a technocratic formula for governing human mobility on a global scale. While its origins date back to the post–World War II period, its resurgence occurred in the context of reconfiguring the world order and the expansion of neoliberal globalization in the 1990s. In this context, governance proponents questioned the effectiveness of traditional forms of immigration and border control and recommended that states revise their policies and enforcement tactics. As states in different parts of the world began to consider migration among the most critical issues for international policy making to address, positing "irregular migration" as a global "security" concern, there emerged an explicit interest in evaluating the technical and political desirability of an international migration regime.[9]

In the early 1990s, within the universe of such governance discourse, "experts" increasingly suggested that "migratory pressures" should be "managed" so that sudden mass border-crossing movements and humanitarian emergencies could be prevented. They promoted the panacea that forced migrations arising from life-threatening disruptions, both political and economic, could be eliminated only if migration "flows," which in any event should be considered "unavoidable," could be regulated and channeled through specific mechanisms (Meissner 1992). Others contended that international migration was a "valuable resource" that should be "carefully managed" but also that, through various mechanisms of "cooperation," uncontrolled "migration pressures" could be alleviated by "keeping migrants at home" (Rogers 1992, 40–44). At the same time, others warned of the risks to international security and stability that increased population movements could entail, and invoked the specter of a "global migration crisis" (Weiner 1992, 1995, 1996). Thus, during the 1990s, several proposals for the construction of an international migration regime emerged. One of the best known was the project called the New International Regime for the Orderly Movement of People, which served as the basis for the IOM's strategy and was initially supported by the United Nations Population Fund and various European governments. It was inspired by the guidelines of a proposal presented in 1993 to the Commission on Global Governance by Bimal Ghosh, a consultant to various multilateral and intergovernmental agencies (including the IOM) (Ghosh 2012). The foundations were thus laid for establishing an "orderly" migration model based on the principle of regulated openness and the adoption of multilateral mechanisms, the model promoted as "migration management." At the same time, the creation of specialized consultative spaces on migration issues (linked to regional integration processes), such as the Budapest Group in 1993 and the Puebla Process in 1996, where different institutional actors converged, further evidenced the crystallization of new ways of regulating international migration. Following the International Conference on Population and Development held in Cairo in 1994, which marked a turning point in the global agenda on international migration, there were numerous initiatives aimed at consolidating specific ways of thinking and acting on migration and instituting international accords. By the beginning of the twenty-first century, the creation of expert committees, such as the Global Commission on International Migration and the Global Migration Group, gave rise to numerous policy proposals and recommendations for the construction of an international migration regime.

During these years, the IOM consistently devoted its *World Migration Report*s to the ascendant theme of "migration management" (IOM 2003) and published a handbook for technicians and policy makers on the fundamental elements of this approach (IOM 2004). Within a few years, IOM publications began to emphasize the issue of "migration governance." The IOM began to energetically disseminate its governance framework to facilitate "an orderly, safe, regular and responsible migration and mobility of people through planned and well-managed migration policies" (IOM 2015). Remarkably, the rise of this cheerful neoliberal discourse regarding the "management" of migration as a "resource" coincided with the concomitant rise of global antiterrorist "security" imperatives and newly securitarian forms of border policing (De Genova 2013a).

The IOM has had a long-standing influence across the Americas. In the IOM's history, Latin America, particularly South America, was remarkably prominent in the implementation of experimental intergovernmental agreements for the "orderly" reception and settlement of migrants and in the training of border and immigration personnel during the 1950s and 1960s (Damilakou and Venturas 2015). Between the 1980s and early 2000s, the IOM sponsored and developed "capacity-building" programs for government officials and disseminated policy strategics aimed at "good governance." Through this lens, the effects of changes in international migration patterns across the region in the 1990s, the difficulties Latin American states had in responding, and the increase in irregularized

migration, human trafficking, and migrant smuggling all came to be folded together under the notions of migration "ungovernability" and border "crisis."

Overcoming such "crises" was accordingly understood to require transregional partnerships and security measures favoring the "orderly" control of
human mobilities, including visa programs, reinforcements of border policing,
and joint operations to combat irregularized migration, human trafficking, and
migrant smuggling (Domenech 2018, 116–18). In 2016, the IOM became a UN
agency. The same year, all 193 UN member states signed the New York Declaration on Refugees and Migrants, which triggered the 2018 Global Compact
for Safe, Orderly, and Regular Migration and the Global Compact on Refugees. These compacts are the first intergovernmentally negotiated nonbinding
agreements that expressly insist that "governability" in refugee and migration
matters can be achieved only through international partnership. Hence, member states, NGOs, civil society organizations, and private sector entities such as
banks and corporations—including MasterCard, IKEA, INDITEX, Uniqlo, and
SONY, among others—participate together as partners (UNHCR 2022). As in
any multilateral initiative, however, certain states and certain suprastate bodies
inevitably have more weight than the rest: As of December 31, 2021, the United
States, the EU, and Germany were the top donors (IOM 2021). In other words,
these initiatives are predictably dominated by the wealthiest and most powerful
state powers, which have long outsourced their border policing to third countries, contributing to the formation of extended migratory corridors across multiple countries that have predictably become spaces of predation, violence, and
death for migrants. The IOM has thus subtly been converted into an appendage
of these states' efforts at remote border control (Andrijasevic and Walters 2010;
Ashutosh and Mountz 2011; Pécoud 2010). The role that the UNHCR and IOM
play in the management of the refugee "crisis" in South America presents a clear
case for understanding how humanitarianism coexists with and fuels the securitization of migration as part of the complex and uneven dynamics of the trans-
American border regime (Clavijo, this volume, ch. 9).

This quest for migration governance has gained traction among national
immigration agencies across the Americas, particularly in intergovernmental spaces such as the aforementioned Puebla Process (1996) and the South
American Conference on Migration (2000). These regional consultative processes (RCPs), based on the technocratic model of "global governance," are part
of the new architecture for controlling migration and must be recognized as a
nodal element when analyzing the heterogenous trans-American border regime.
Their development is related to the neoliberal formation of regional blocs
for economic integration and trade liberalization. One of the first RCPs in the

world—the Regional Conference on Migration (RCM), better known as the Puebla Process—emerged shortly after the North American Free Trade Agreement (NAFTA) took effect in 1994. Since its inception, this intergovernmental framework has explicitly adhered to the basic postulates of migration management. This regional regime has likewise played a central role in reframing migration as a matter of public "security" (Kron 2012).

The hegemony of the governance model has been further consolidated through the regional reaction against the massive Venezuelan exodus. With the support of the IOM, among other UN and multilateral organizations, the Quito Process was launched in 2018 as a nonbinding initiative seeking "safe, orderly, and regular" Venezuelan migration across the region. This process emerged from the so-called Lima Group, endorsed by the United States, the European Union, and the Organization of American States (OAS). In the context of the return to power of right-wing governments across the region, the first Trump administration promoted the Lima Group after various states within the OAS were considered to have not responded adequately to what the US government deemed a violation of democratic process in Venezuela. Through the Declaration of Quito, the collaborating governments advocated "strengthening policies for the reception of Venezuelan migrants" and "coordinating efforts through international organizations" in the face of the "crisis." Moreover, the Quito Process highlighted the necessary role of UN agencies and international cooperation in achieving the explicit goal of an emphatically regional-scale governance of the Venezuelan exodus. Infrastructures of humanitarianism and reinforced border control have operated in tandem to supply "orderly assistance" to the Venezuelan exodus, as Carolina Moulin demonstrates for Brazil (this volume, ch. 10). Another example: confronting the rise in irregularized global migrations across the Americas with the United States as their destination, frequently over land through the treacherous and deadly Darién Gap at the border of Colombia and Panama (Ordóñez and Echeverri Zuluaga, this volume, ch. 5), a high-level ministerial meeting of multiple states was convened in April 2022 by Panama with IOM support to reinforce a multilateral transcontinental fight against irregularized migration and smuggling networks.

Amid the proliferation of new border and migration "crises" across Latin America and the Caribbean, notably, the IOM has recently expanded its geographical reach in the Americas, operating now with two regional offices: the Regional Office for South America (based in Argentina) and the Office for Central America, North America, and the Caribbean (located in Costa Rica). These IOM offices delineated two Regional Strategies (2020–24), corresponding to their respective geographic focal areas, articulating an agenda reinforcing the commitment to global migration governance. In these endeavors, the United States remains prominent as "a vital partner for IOM in the region" (IOM 2020, 7). Thus, in the guise of multilateral migration governance, we discern the long shadow of US interventionism across the hemisphere, now frequently embellished with a "humanitarian" face. As the contributors to this volume demonstrate, humanitarianism and control, far from being antagonists in polar opposition, in fact, nourish each other as interrelated features of a heterogeneous trans-American border regime dedicated to governing ungovernable mobile subjects.

The Hemisphere as the New "Region" of Mobility Control

In an era of global expansion of neoliberal narratives and schemes of migration and border governance, the production of "regional solutions" has evidenced the primacy of regionalization in contemporary geopolitics: the "region" is created in various ways through migration management (Mountz and Loyd 2014). Seeing the operation of political and economic forces in the larger sociopolitical production of space reminds us that the Western Hemisphere is not merely a given "natural" fact of physical geography: the Americas, and consequently what we are calling the borders of America, have been and continue to be actively *produced* as a global region with its own internal dynamics and contradictions as well as its distinct articulations with the rest of the world. The trans-American border regime should be critically examined in light of such regionalizing solutions, for which the externalization of the US border has been of central significance. Thus, the entire hemisphere has increasingly become a "region" of mobility control, primarily for managing the autonomous movements of "irregular migrants" heading north.

In addition to a territorial designation, *region* has become a generic term for nonbinding intergovernmental and interagency forums on diverse core topics with a "Western Hemisphere" focus. The North American Free Trade Agreement (1994) exemplifies this evolution. This international agreement, signed by Canada, the United States, and Mexico, established a trilateral trade bloc in North America. It also included border security agreements and created unequal privileges for freedom of movement, allowing US and Canadian citizens greater mobility while imposing visa requirements on Mexicans entering both countries (see Landolt and Goldring, this volume, ch. 1). Other regional spaces include the Central American Northern Triangle and the Common Market of the South (MERCOSUR).

Since the 1990s, a consensus has formed around the need for a "regional approach" to address the migratory question across the Americas. Such an approach requires nation-states to cooperate in dealing with migration, particularly when controlling the mass movements of "irregular" migrants, since each state, acting alone, would be unable to solve the "problems" those mobilities entail. In Latin America and the Caribbean, as some authors have shown, it is possible to recognize the formation of a North and Central American migration and border regime (Kron 2012), as well as a South American migration and border regime (Domenech 2019; Domenech and Dias 2020), each emerging as an effect of regionalization processes and strategies in the field of migration and border control. These regional geopolitical spaces, that during the first years of the twenty-first century were established as border zones with relative independence, were gradually conjoined as a result of transformations in autonomous migration movements and in the policies and strategies of mobility control, especially from various practices of externalization of the US border in the Central and North American context. Indeed, "extraregional" or "extracontinental" migration has been central to the articulation of these unstable regional migration and border regimes and the consolidation of the larger heterogeneous and contradictory trans-American border regime.

In this process, different regional migration forums inspired by technocratic and neoliberal migration governance schemes and assisted by the IOM have been crucial. Notably, as already noted, the Regional Conference on Migration, or Puebla Process, and the South American Conference on Migration (SAC) were established between the mid-1990s and early 2000s. Although officially a Mexican initiative, the Puebla Process responded to the interests of the US government in reducing "irregular migration." This regional process was created when concerns intensified about "irregular migration" (IOM 2001), not only of Central American migrants but of people from South America, Africa, Asia, and Eastern Europe en route to the United States. As evidenced by the personal account of a Mexican government official who participated in the creation of the RCM, so-called extraregional migration was "one of the most contentious issues on the regional migration agenda" (Mohar 2001).

The emergence of the notion of "region" through migration management thus gave rise to the production of an official discourse of otherness: "extraregional" or "extracontinental" migration. In other words, regional boundaries and extraregional differences were established through the regionalization process. *Extraregional* may sometimes refer to the movements of migrants not part of the North and Central American region. At other times, it may operate as a synonym for *extracontinental*, designating people on the move from the Eastern Hemisphere, mainly originating in Africa, Asia, or Eastern Europe.

In the framework of regional spaces such as the RCM, "extraregional" migration has been represented as a special target of control, for it is assumed that these movements are "flows of irregular migrants," customarily associated with the demonized figures of migrant "smuggling" or "trafficking." As early as the first RCM, held in Puebla, Mexico, in 1996, regional states highlighted the need to "control the flow of irregular extra-regional migrants." Within the plan of action approved at the following RCM meeting in Panama, regional states requested that the IOM prepare a proposal that would include activities and possible solutions to "extraregional" migration and migrant smuggling. The first measures formulated as a "solution" were under the figure of an "assisted-return program," signaling that the "extraregional" could be taken only to be the figure of an exteriority, a racialized otherness, which could not be tolerated as having a proper place in the American region and would have to be subject to more or less coercive "return": it was necessary to restore an (inter)national and hemispheric order altered by that type of migration.

This program was approved at the 2004 RCM annual meeting. It targeted "extraregional" migrants who had entered the territory as undocumented migrants and were not subject to special protections, as well as those who were intercepted in international waters. Before the implementation of this program, the United States had already been promoting and funding through various federal agencies the return of "extraregional migrants," particularly from China and India. Their repatriations were executed with funds from the US Immigration and Naturalization Service (INS), through its office in Mexico, the State Department's Bureau of International Narcotics and Law Enforcement Affairs, and logistical support from the IOM. The INS office in Mexico City was also involved in negotiations with various embassies for the delivery of travel documents to "extraregional" migrants captured in countries of transit and awaiting their de facto deportations (euphemized as "assisted" and "voluntary").

From the 1990s until the early 2000s, the presence of "extraregional" migrants was an issue of political relevance only in Central and North America. By the second decade of the twenty-first century, however, "extraregional" migration acquired a fully hemispheric scope and played a fundamental role in reconfiguring the South American border regime, whose relative stability was based on multilateral consensus and regulations linked to "intraregional" cross-border migration. The historically unprecedented visa exemption measure in Ecuador between 2008 and 2010 had a transcendent impact in that it enabled the arrival of numerous "undesirable" migrants from different parts of the global periphery. New migrations from African and Asian countries as well as the Caribbean (especially from Haiti, the Dominican Republic, and Cuba) disrupted the institutional arrangements of regional migration and border re-gimes (See Álvarez Velasco, this volume, ch. 6). By disrupting the regional bor-der order, the cross-border mobility practices of these "extraregional" migrants provoked various reactions at the continental level.

The growth and expansion of these ungovernable movements of illegalized subjects, largely racialized as Black or "Asian," caused national and international bureaucracies to convene to confront the uncertainties and anxieties provoked by the increase and expansion of "extraregional" or "extracontinental" migrants in transit across the hemisphere. In 2010, the OAS organized a workshop it called "Extracontinental Migration in the Americas" at its headquarters in Wash-ington, DC, which brought together government officials and international organizations. The arrival of these migrant movements was widely considered at the time to be an altogether new migratory phenomenon in the region (OAS 2010).

The emergence of multiple border conflicts referred to as "migration crises" unveiled the defining role that *transit migration* has had in the Americas, both as a framework for apprehending and naming new migratory formations and thus giving rise to a new target of intervention, and therefore also as a new ob-ject of regional migration governance based on the *containment* of movement.

Among the multiple "migration crises" raised by the continuous border clo-sures in Central America during 2015, the trapping of Cubans in transit in La Cruz—a small town on the northern border of Costa Rica—highlighted essen-tial changes in the relationship between mobility and control in the region. The intensification of Cuban emigration responded primarily to speculation about the consequences of the reestablishment of diplomatic relations between the United States and Cuba in 2015, caused, in part, by the exponential growth in the arrival of Cuban migrants at the southern border of the United States since Cuba's immigration reform in early 2013.[10] Among the island's inhabitants, it was presumed that the reestablishment of diplomatic relations could mean the end of the "wet feet, dry feet" policy, established in 1995 after the so-called Balsero (raf-ter) Crisis of the preceding year, when thousands of Cubans fled to the United States by sea. At the same time, Ecuador began to offer greater opportunities as a gateway to the extended migratory routes traversing the hemisphere through its national territory, displacing other customary routes. Notably, in 2014, the Ecuadorian migration authorities stopped requesting letters of invitation as a requirement for granting visas to Cuban citizens. Tensions and claims arising from the immobility caused by the successive border closures in Nicaragua, Costa Rica, and Panama were initially dissipated through the application of hu-manitarian visas (or "safe conducts") and air bridges for the transfer of stranded migrants to Mexico, carried out with the assistance of the IOM, in addition to the holding of special intergovernmental meetings. Thus, the official production of a "humanitarian corridor" facilitated some mobilities, while subjecting them nonetheless to transit permits and diplomatic agreements established between states and the involvement of international organizations.

The persistence of the autonomous movement of Cuban migrants was confronted with new bilateral negotiations and punitive measures. After Mexico and Cuba agreed to stop giving Cuban migrants safe conducts, the Mexican state began to execute deportations of "undocumented" Cubans. The international conflicts created by the border closures in several Central American countries and the deprivation of movement of thousands of Cuban, Haitian, African, and Asian migrants led to diplomatic negotiations that resulted in the Ecuadorian government reinstating visas for Cuban citizens and thereby also the deportation of Cuban migrants (see Álvarez Velasco, this volume, ch. 6). Border conflicts also led the governments of Colombia and Ecuador to sign a protocol of deportation a few months later, through which they sought agreement on a procedure for determining the inadmissibility and deportation of foreigners from third countries under the rubric of the fight against migrant smuggling. The Cuban "crisis" was followed by "the Haitian crisis," which led to the closure of the border between Colombia and Ecuador and the imposition of an ad hoc visa or tourist registration for Haitian citizens attempting to enter Ecuador.

The various migratory "crises" placed "extraregional" or "extracontinental" migration among the main concerns of states being brought to regional intergovernmental forums. In 2016, for instance, the Permanent Council of the OAS welcomed the request for an "urgent study of the migration situation in the region" made by Costa Rica's representatives to the organization's General Secretariat. This request was in response to the "recent increase in the flow of migrants in irregular migratory situations" from African, Asian, and Caribbean countries, particularly Cuba and Haiti. A regional report was prepared based on an agreement with the IOM (OAS and IOM 2016).

The so-called Venezuelan migration crisis, for its part, which has disrupted the hemisphere's mobility and control dynamics, also entailed a "regional response" of broad scope. In this regard, as part of its border externalization strategy, the US government actively worked to construct a "response" involving numerous Latin American and Caribbean countries. First, the Lima Group, created in 2017 (made up of Argentina, Brazil, Canada, Chile, Colombia, Costa Rica, Guatemala, Honduras, Panama, Paraguay, Peru and Venezuela), articulated the regional position on migration and refuge of the new-right governments that promoted the so-called Quito Process. As discussed earlier, the Interagency Coordination

Platform for Refugees and Migrants from Venezuela, launched in 2018 and implemented from 2019 through the leadership of IOM and UNHCR, became the primary tool in the hemisphere for the containment, deterrence, and channeling of the "disorderly" movements of "transit migration," especially of Venezuelans, through multiple actors and varied practices of humanitarian intervention (Biondini et al. 2023).

The persistent movement of migrants of various national origins across the Americas and the successive "migration crises" that their mobilities instigated, especially in the context of the COVID-19 pandemic, both across Latin America and at the southern border of the United States, resulted in revisions to the tactics of managing and controlling irregularized transit migration. In this sense, the trapping of thousands of Haitians along with other migrants in 2021 in Necoclí, on the Colombia-Panama border, updated specific "responses" based on bilateral and multilateral cooperation schemes previously used in the Central American context to govern this type of migration (see Ordóñez and Echeverri Zuluaga, this volume, ch. 5). It is no longer just a matter of governing Mexican and Central American irregularized migrations, but also those incessant massive movements of irregularized migrants traveling from South America to the United States via the Darién Gap. Particularly between the disruption of the pandemic and the restabilization efforts of the postpandemic years, USAID—a central player in US interventionism in Latin America and the Caribbean and US border externalization policies—sought to explicitly promote a renewed "hemispheric approach" to "irregular migration" and "forced displacement."

The rationale for this new approach would lie precisely in the changes in regional "migration patterns," and the Los Angeles Declaration on Migration and Protection is a clear case in point. It emerged in the framework of the ninth Summit of the Americas in 2022 as one of the United States' recent diplomatic achievements in adopting and promoting a hemispheric approach under the principles of "orderly, safe, humane and regular migration," the IOM's global mantra. In addition to the United States and Canada, twenty Latin American and Caribbean states endorsed the declaration. Predictably, the declaration subscribed to the vision embodied in the Global Compact for Safe, Orderly, and Regular Migration and the Global Compact on Refugees. It also recognized the relevance of the Regional Conference on Migration and the South American Conference on Migration in implementing the declaration. At the same time, it highlights the work of the Quito Process and Platform R4V. In this process, the IOM has been positioned as an architect and strategic partner in US foreign policy on migration issues, and it welcomed this hemispheric-scope agreement.

Many other political actors, including US-based NGOs and think tanks, also supported the regional approach adopted by the declaration.

Finally, in the current context of unceasing south–north transit migrations heading to the United States, at the end of April 2023, the US Department of State and the Department of Homeland Security announced new measures "to further reduce unlawful migration across the Western Hemisphere, significantly expand lawful pathways for protection, and facilitate the safe, orderly, and humane processing of migrants."[11] Under the Los Angeles Declaration on Migration and Protection, the United States, with the support of the participating states, promoted the opening of "regional processing centers." These centers, later renamed "safe mobility offices" (SMOs), are "key locations throughout the Western Hemisphere to reduce irregular migration and facilitate safe, orderly, humane, and lawful pathways from the Americas." Such processing facilities have been established in Colombia, Guatemala, Costa Rica, and Ecuador and are managed by UNHCR and IOM. The program is highly selective and exclusionary in that only people of specific nationalities can apply, and only according to the country where they resided until June 2023 (October in the case of Ecuador): in Colombia, only Cubans, Haitians and Venezuelans; in Guatemala, only Guatemalans; in Costa Rica, only Nicaraguans and Venezuelans; in Ecuador, only Cubans, Haitians, Nicaraguans, Venezuelans, and Colombians. Eligible persons may be transferred to the United States, Canada, or Spain, depending on how their profiles fit the established parameters. Under the official rationale of protection, this "safe mobility" program would help migrants avoid the risks associated with "irregular" migration generally and, more specifically, circumvent their dependency on "smugglers" for realizing their migratory projects by placing these centers closer to the home countries from which they depart. Proximity to home, however, occludes and conceals a strategy of enforced remoteness from the next border and the succession of borders that together encompass the hemispheric border regime. This new hemispheric approach to mobility control is suggestive of a veritable renovation of US border externalization policy and, thus, may signal a new moment in the larger history of consolidating the trans-American border regime.

Conclusion

At the end of the first quarter of the twenty-first century, the Americas have been profoundly reconfigured by the fundamentally ungovernable mobilities of migrants and refugees from across the globe. This phenomenon shows no signs of relenting; instead it is multiplying as the effects of profound systemic contradictions, including deepening misery, ecological devastation, wars, civil conflicts (including political, religious, and ethnic persecution), and gender violence, as well as racist anti-immigrant campaigns of violence that are themselves effects of border and immigration regimes. Due to their instability, unpredictability, volatility, and contested nature—above all, identified with their illegalization and criminalization—these massive global migrant mobilities unsettle fixed notions of borders, nation-states, home, community, membership, social movements, social justice, and struggles over the right to the city. These migratory projects therefore compel us to rethink such categories in relation to the permanent fact of migration as a cross-border social movement undertaken to sustain human lives and livelihoods and to remake social life itself.

These migrant mobilities are spatially transforming the Americas and cultivating new sociopolitical connections across the hemisphere and, indeed, across the globe. Many Latin American border towns—such as Necoclí (in Colombia), Metetí (in Panama), Tapachula (in southern Mexico), and Tijuana and Ciudad Juárez (at Mexico's northern border with the United States), among so many others—serve as pivotal sites along the migratory corridors traversing the Americas and have been converted into connecting nodes for the circulation of capital, commodities, and labor-power in local, regional, and global economies. Complex dynamics of waiting and transit shape those locations as a result of the contradictory ways the trans-American border regime cuts across the hemisphere, expanding both licit and illicit economic enterprises and generating multimillion-dollar profits in the otherwise impoverished border economies that thrive around facilitating this type of migration.

This genealogy of the trans-American border regime has shown how the Americas have been profoundly shaped by the transformative force of global migrations. Beginning with the brutalities of European conquest, particularly Indigenous genocide and transcontinental African enslavement, followed by the long and ongoing history of global migrations, including a contemporary escalation in migrant disappearances and deaths as an effect of border enforcement and externalization, migrant and refugee mobilities continuously instigate border struggles and provoke often brutal reaction formations perpetrated by various regimes of border enforcement violence. Consequently, this complex, contradictory, and profoundly unequal hemispheric region becomes increasingly apprehensible as a fraught intersection of heterogeneous tactics and strategies of mobility control that respond to the primacy of those human mobility projects. Thus, there has emerged a trans-American border regime that is something greater than the mere sum of its disparate parts. Indeed, as the preceding chapters demonstrate, this hemispheric border regime has also been the product of a deliberate and increasingly calculated project. Nonetheless, this has never been simply a story of the efficacy of the border regime's violence and tactics of control. Our America is being remade by these human mobilities and the subjective force of these autonomous movements to remake life. Analyzing the convulsive dynamics of this larger hemispheric regime of border making and policing, revealing the fissures where potential or incipient forms of migrant resistance disrupt and sometimes subvert the machinations of the border regime's power, and accompanying and supporting migrant struggles across the Americas, all remain fundamental and urgent imperatives for critical research, now more than ever.

NOTES

1. Law No. 817, on immigration and colonization, October 19, 1876, Argentina.

2. Law No. 114, on immigration and agricultural colonies, December 30, 1922, Colombia.

3. Law of November 19, 1853, Peru.

4. Law No. 62, 1887, Colombia.

5. For some of the most renowned case studies, see those of Argentina (Cook-Martín 2006, 2008; Devoto 1999, 2001; Di Liscia and Fernández Marrón 2009; Domenech 2011; Quinteros 2008; Sánchez Alonso 2004, 2007); Brazil (Seyferth 1997, 2002; Cook-Martín and FitzGerald 2015); the Caribbean (Tate and Law 2015); Chile (Tijoux 2016; Téllez 2016); Colombia (Olaya 2018); Ecuador (Ramírez 2012; Pagnotta 2011; Terán Najas, 2020); and Mexico (Alanís Enciso 1996; Yankelevich, 2015, 2020).

6. ILEA (International Law Enforcement Academy), "Welcome to ILEA San Salvador," https://sansalvador.ilea.state.gov.

7. The Protocol to Prevent, Suppress, and Punish Trafficking in Persons Especially Women and Children (Palermo Protocol), supplementing the UN Convention Against Transnational Organized Crime, was adopted by the UN General Assembly in November 2000 (UNODC 2000).

8. The member states of GRULAC include: Antigua and Barbuda, Argentina, the Bahamas, Barbados, Belize, Bolivia, Brazil, Chile, Colombia, Costa Rica, Cuba, Dominica, the Dominican Republic, Ecuador, El Salvador, Grenada, Guatemala, Guyana, Haiti, Honduras, Jamaica, Mexico, Nicaragua, Panama, Paraguay, Peru, Saint Lucia, Saint Kitts and Nevis, Saint Vincent and the Grenadines, Suriname, Trinidad and Tobago, Uruguay, and the Bolivarian Republic of Venezuela (https://www.ipu.org/about-ipu/members /geopolitical-groups/grulac-group-latin-america-and-caribbean).

9. In such technocratic usages, notably, the notion of *regime* corresponds to the hegemonic statist perspective of the discipline of international relations, not the more expansive and heterogeneous formulation that we have adopted in this volume.

10. Through this reform, the Cuban government eliminated the requirement for an exit permit and extended the permissible time of stay outside the island.

11. US State Department and Department of Homeland Security, "Fact Sheet: U.S. Government Announces Sweeping New Actions to Manage Regional Migration," April 27, 2023, https://www.dhs.gov/archive/news/2023/04/27/fact-sheet-us -government-announces-sweeping-new-actions-manage-regional-migration.

Acosta, Diego. 2018. *The National Versus the Foreigner in South America*. New York: Cambridge University Press.

Alanís Enciso, Fernando S. 1996. "Los extranjeros en México, la inmigración y el gobierno: ¿Tolerancia o intolerancia religiosa?, 1821–1830." *Historia Mexicana* 45 (3): 539–66.

Amnesty International. 2000. "Colombia: Amnesty International's Position on Plan Colombia." https://www.amnesty.org/en/documents/amr23/049/2000/en/.

Andersson, Ruben. 2014. *Illegality, Inc.: Clandestine Migration and the Business of Bordering Europe*. Berkeley: University of California Press.

Andersson, Ruben. 2016. "Europe's Failed 'Fight' Against Irregular Migration: Ethnographic Notes on a Counterproductive Industry." *Journal of Ethnic and Migration Studies* 42 (7): 1055–75.

Andersson, Ruben. 2017. "Rescued and Caught: The Humanitarian-Security Nexus at Europe's Borders." In *The Borders of "Europe": Autonomy of Migration, Tactics of Bordering*, edited by Nicholas De Genova, 64–94. Durham, NC: Duke University Press.

Andreas, Peter. 2003. "Redrawing the Line: Borders and Security in the Twenty-First Century." *International Security* 28 (2): 78–111.

Andrijasevic, Rutvica, and William Walters. 2010. "The International Organization for Migration and the International Government of Borders." *Environment and Planning D: Society and Space* 28 (6): 977–99.

Ashutosh, Ishan, and Alison Mountz. 2011. "Migration Management for the Benefit of Whom? Interrogating the Work of the International Organization for Migration." *Citizenship Studies* 15 (1): 21–38.

Biondini, Valentina, Eduardo Domenech, Alfonso Hinojosa, and Ruby Espinosa. 2023. "Movimientos de migración y políticas de movilidad en el espacio sudamericano: La producción de Bolivia como zona precaria de tránsito." In *Migrar en el siglo XXI: Conflictos, políticas y derechos*, 185–248. Buenos Aires: Consejo Latinoamericano de Ciencias Sociales.

Boatcă, Manuela, and Fabio Santos. 2023. "Of Rags and Riches in the Caribbean: Creolizing Migration Studies." *Journal of Immigrant & Refugee Studies* 21 (2): 132–45.

Carrillo, Ana. 2012. "Comerciantes de fantasías: El Estado ecuatoriano ante la inmigración china." In *Ciudad-Estado, inmigrantes y políticas: Ecuador 1950 (1890)*, edited by Jacques Ramirez, 169–233. Quito: Instituto de Altos Estudios Nacionales.

Casas-Cortes, Maribel, Sebastian Cobarrubias, and John Pickles. 2015. "Riding Routes and Itinerant Borders: Autonomy of Migration and Border Externalization." *Antipode* 47 (4): 894–914.

CODHES (Consultoría para los Derechos Humanos y el Desplazamiento). 2019. "Informes de Desplazamiento en Colombia llegan a la Comisión de la Verdad." December 6. https://codhes.wordpress.com/2019/12/06/informes-de-desplazamiento-en-colombia-llegan-a-la-comision-de-la-verdad/.

Cohen, Robin. 2006. *Migration and Its Enemies: Global Capital Migrant Labour and the Nation-State*. Aldershot, UK: Ashgate.

Cook-Martín, David. 2006. "Soldiers and Wayward Women: Gendered Citizenship and Migration Policy in Argentina, Italy, and Spain Since 1850." *Citizenship Studies* 10 (5): 571–90.

Cook-Martín, David. 2008. "Rules, Red Tape, and Paperwork: The Archeology of State Control over Migrants, 1850–1930." *Journal of Historical Sociology* 21 (1): 82–119.

Cook-Martín, David, and David FitzGerald. 2015. "Vender el mito de la democracia racial: Selección étnica en las políticas migratorias de Brasil desde la República hasta el presente." In *Migraciones trans-atlánticas: Desplazamientos, etnicidad y políticas*, coordinated by Elda González Martínez, and Ricardo González Leandri, 29–53. Madrid: Catarata.

Damilakou, Maria, and Lina Venturas. 2015. "Discourses on Latin America: The Migration-Development Nexus." In *International "Migration Management" in the Early Cold War: The Intergovernmental Committee for European Migration*, edited by Lina Venturas. Corinth: University of the Peloponnese.

De Genova, Nicholas. 2002. "Migrant 'Illegality' and Deportability in Everyday Life." *Annual Review of Anthropology* 31 (1): 419–47.

De Genova, Nicholas. 2004. "The Legal Production of Mexican/Migrant 'Illegality.'" *Latino Studies* 2 (1): 160–85.

De Genova, Nicholas. 2005. *Working the Boundaries: Race, Space, and "Illegality" in Mexican Chicago*. Durham, NC: Duke University Press.

De Genova, Nicholas. 2007. "The Production of Culprits: From Deportability to Detainability in the Aftermath of 'Homeland Security.'" *Citizenship Studies* 11 (5): 421–48.

De Genova, Nicholas. 2009. "Conflicts of Mobility and the Mobility of Conflict: Rightlessness, Presence, Subjectivity, Freedom." *Subjectivity* 29:445–66.

De Genova, Nicholas. 2011. "Alien Powers: Deportable Labour and the Spectacle of Security." In *The Contested Politics of Mobility: Borderzones and Irregularity*, edited by Vicki Squire, 91–115. London: Routledge.

De Genova, Nicholas. 2013a. "The Perplexities of Mobility." In *Critical Mobilities*, edited by Ola Söderström, Shalini Randeria, Didier Ruedin, Gianni D'Amato, and Francesco Panese, 101–22. London: Routledge; Lausanne: Presses Polytechniques et Universitaires Romandes.

De Genova, Nicholas. 2013b. "Spectacles of Migrant 'Illegality': The Scene of Exclusion, the Obscene of Inclusion." *Ethnic and Racial Studies* 36 (7): 1180–98.

De Genova, Nicholas. 2016. "The 'Crisis' of the European Border Regime: Towards a Marxist Theory of Borders." *International Socialism* 150:33–56. http://isj.org.uk/the-crisis-of-the-european-border-regime-towards-a-marxist-theory-of-borders/.

De Genova, Nicholas. 2017a. "The Incorrigible Subject: Mobilizing a Critical Geography of (Latin) America Through the Autonomy of Migration." *Journal of Latin American Geography* 16 (1): 17–42.

De Genova, Nicholas. 2017b. "Introduction: The Borders of 'Europe' . . . and the 'European' Question." In *The Borders of "Europe": Autonomy of Migration, Tactics of Bordering*, edited by Nichols De Genova, 1–36. Durham, NC: Duke University Press.

De Genova, Nicholas. 2018. "The 'Migrant Crisis' as Racial Crisis: Do Black Lives Matter in Europe?" *Ethnic and Racial Studies* 41 (10): 1765–82.

Devoto, Fernando 2001. "El revés de la trama: Políticas migratorias y prácticas administrativas en la Argentina (1919–1949)." *Desarrollo Económico* 41 (162): 281–303.

Devoto, Fernando. 1999. "Ideas, políticas y prácticas migratorias argentinas en una perspectiva de largo plazo (1852–1950)." *Exils et migrations ibériques au XXe siècle* 2 (7): 29–60.

Di Liscia, María Silvia, and Melisa Fernández Marrón. 2009. "Sin puerto para el sueño americano: Políticas de exclusión, inmigración y tracoma en Argentina (1908–1930)." *Nuevo Mundo Mundos Nuevos.* http://nuevomundo.revues.org/57786.

Dias, Gustavo. 2016. "Brazilian Migration into London: Mobility and Contemporary Borders." PhD diss., Goldsmiths College, University of London.

Dias, Gustavo, and Eduardo Domenech. 2020. "Sociologia e fronteiras: A produção da ilegalidade migrante na América Latina e no Caribe." *Sociologias* 22 (55): 24–38.

Dias, Gustavo, and Angelo Martins Jr. 2018. "The Second Brazilian Migration Wave: The Impact of Brazil's Economic and Social Changes on Current Migration to the UK." *Século XXI: Revista de Ciências Sociais* 8 (1): 112–43.

Domenech, Eduardo. 2011. "Crónica de una 'amenaza' anunciada: Inmigración e 'ilegalidad'; visiones de Estado en la Argentina contemporánea." In *La construcción social del sujeto migrante en América Latina: Prácticas, representaciones y categorías*, 31–77. Buenos Aires: Consejo Latinoamericano de Ciencias Sociales, Facultad Latinoamericana de Ciencias Sociales–Ecuador, Universidad Alberto Hurtado.

Domenech, Eduardo. 2018. "Gobernabilidad migratoria: Producción y circulación de una categoría de intervención política." *Temas de Antropología y Migración* 10:110–18.

Domenech, Eduardo. 2019. "Contested Spaces of Mobility: The South American Migration and Border Regime." Paper presented at First International Workshop on Contested Territories, University of Leeds, Leeds, May 20–21.

Domenech, Eduardo, and Gustavo Dias. 2020. "Regimes de fronteira e 'ilegalidade' migrante na América Latina e Caribe." *Sociologias* 22 (55): 40–73.

Domenech, Eduardo, and Andrés Pereira. 2022. "Migration and Border Control Policies in South America (1900–1945): Non-Admission, Identification, and Deportation." In *Social, Political, and Religious Movements in the Modern Americas*, edited by Pablo Baisotti, 169–98. New York: Routledge.

ECLAC (Economic Commission for Latin America and the Caribbean). 2022. "Las tasas de pobreza en América Latina se mantienen en 2022 por encima de los niveles prepandemia, alerta la CEPAL." https://www.cepal.org/es/comunicados /tasas-pobreza-america-latina-se-mantienen-2022-encima-niveles-prepandemia -alerta-la.

Eguiguren, Mercedes. 2019. *Movilidades y poder en el sur del Ecuador, 1950–1990.* Quito: Facultad Latinoamericana de Ciencias Sociales–Ecuador.

Escobar, Arturo. 2014. *La invención del desarrollo.* Popayán, Colombia: Editorial Universidad del Cauca.

Faist, Thomas. 2019. "Contested Externalisation: Responses to Global Inequalities." *Comparative Migration Studies* 7 (1): 1–8.

Fernandes, Florestan. 1965. *A integração do negro na sociedade de classes*. São Paulo: Dôminus Editora.

Fernandes, Florestan. 1975. *A revolução burguesa no Brasil: Ensaio de interpretação sociológica*. Rio de Janeiro: Zahar.

Furtado, Celso. 1981. *O Brasil pós-"milagre."* São Paulo: Paz e Terra.

Furtado, Celso. 1982. *A nova dependência: Dívida externa e monetarismo*. São Paulo: Paz e Terra.

Gao, Jian. 2021. "Chinese Migration to Latin America: From Colonial to Contemporary Era." *History Compass* 19 (9): 1–13.

García Hernández, César C. 2018. "Deconstructing Crimmigration." *UC Davis Law Review* 52:197.

Garelli, Glenda, and Martina Tazzioli. 2017. "Choucha Beyond the Camp: Challenging the Border of Migration Studies." In *The Borders of "Europe": Autonomy of Migration, Tactics of Bordering*, edited by Nicholas de Genova. 165–84. Durham, NC: Duke University Press.

Garelli, Glenda, and Martina Tazzioli. 2018. "The EU Humanitarian War Against Migrant Smugglers at Sea." *Antipode* 50 (3): 685–703.

Ghosh, Bimal. 2012. "A Snapshot of Reflections on Migration Management: Is Migration Management a Dirty Word?" In *The New Politics of International Mobility: Migration Management and Its Discontents*. Osnabrück: IMIS-Beiträge.

Glockner, Valentina. 2020. "Régimen de frontera y la política de separación de familias: Racialización y castigo de la migración forzada a través de los cuerpos infantiles." In *#Jóvenesymigración: El reto de converger; agendas de investigación, políticas y participación*, edited by Mónica Valdez González and Juan Carlos Narváez Guiérrez, 47–69. Mexico City: Universidad Nacional Autónoma de México.

Gómez, Laura E. 2022. *Inventing Latinos: A New Story of American Racism*. New York: New Press.

González, Juan. 2000. *Harvest of Empire: A History of Latinos in America*. New York: Viking Penguin.

Grandin, Greg. 2007. *Empire's Workshop: Latin America, the United States, and the Rise of the New Imperialism*. New York: Metropolitan Books.

Gudynas, Eduardo, and Alberto Acosta. 2011. "La renovación de la crítica al desarrollo y el buen vivir como alternativa." *Utopía y praxis latinoamericana* 16 (53): 71–83.

Guevara Latorre, Juan Pablo. 2015. "El Plan Colombia o el desarrollo como seguridad." *Revista Colombiana de Sociología* 38 (1): 63–82.

Gunder Frank, Andre. 2018. "The Development of Underdevelopment." In *Promise of Development*, edited by Peter F. Klaren, 111–23. New York: Routledge.

Hall, Stuart. 2015. "Créolité and the Process of Creolization." In *Creolizing Europe: Legacies and Transformations*, edited by Encarnación Gutiérrez Rodríguez and Shirley Anne Tate, 12–25. Liverpool: Liverpool University Press.

Harvey, David. 2005. *A Brief History of Neoliberalism*. Oxford: Oxford University Press.

Haughton, Suzette A. 2009. "The US-Caribbean Border: An Important Security Border in the 21st Century." *Journal of Borderlands Studies* 24 (3): 1–17.

Heller, Charles, and Lorenzo Pezzani. 2017. "Liquid Traces: Investigating the Deaths of Migrants at the EU's Maritime Frontier." In *The Borders of "Europe": Autonomy of Migration, Tactics of Bordering*, edited by Nicholas De Genova, 95–119. Durham, NC: Duke University Press.

Hobsbawm, Eric. 2008. "War, Peace, and Hegemony at the Beginning of the Twenty-First Century." In *War, Peace, and Hegemony in a Globalized World*, edited by Chandra Chari, 33–42. London: Routledge.

Holloway, John. 1994. "Global Capital and the National State." *Capital and Class* 18 (1): 23–49.

Hu-DeHart, Evelyn, and Kathleen López. 2008. "Asian Diasporas in Latin America and the Caribbean: An Historical Overview." *Afro-Hispanic Review* 27 (1): 9–21.

Huysmans, Jef. 2000. "The European Union and the Securitization of Migration." *JCMS: Journal of Common Market Studies* 38 (5): 751–77.

IOM (International Organization for Migration). 2001. *The Role of Regional Consultative Process in Managing International Migration*. IOM Migration Research Series 3. Geneva.

IOM (International Organization for Migration). 2003. *World Migration Report 2003: Managing Migration*. Geneva.

IOM (International Organization for Migration). 2004. *Essentials of Migration Management: A Guide for Policy Makers and Practitioners*. Managing Migration 3. Geneva.

IOM (International Organization for Migration). 2015. "Facilitation of Safe, Regular, and Orderly Migration." Global Compact Thematic Paper. https://www.iom.int/sites/g /files/tmzbdl486/files/our_work/ODG/GCM/IOM-Thematic-Paper-Facilitation-of -Safe-Orderly-and-Regular-Migration.pdf.

IOM (International Organization for Migration). 2020. *Centroamérica, Norteamérica y el Caribe: Estrategia Regional 2020–2024*. San José.

IOM (International Organization for Migration). 2021. *World Migration Report 2022*. Geneva.

Izcara Palacios, Simón P. 2016. "Violencia postestructural: Migrantes centroamericanos y cárteles de la droga en México." *Revista de Estudios Sociales* 56;12–25.

Kasparek, Bernd. 2016. "Routes, Corridors, and Spaces of Exception: Governing Migration and Europe." *Near Futures Online* 1 (1). http://nearfuturesonline.org/routes -corridors-and-spaces-of-exception-govern-ing-migration-and-europe/.

Kasparek, Bernd, and Marc Speer. 2015. "Of Hope: Hungary and the Long Summer of Migration." Bordermonitoring.eu, September 9. http://bordermonitoring.eu/ungarn /2015/09/of-hope-en/.

Keshavarz, Mahmoud, and Shahram Khosravi, eds. 2022. *Seeing Like a Smuggler: Borders from Below*. London: Pluto.

Kron, Stefanie. 2012. "¿Legitimidad política por despolitización de la migración? Una reflexión crítica del arreglo institucional de un nuevo régimen regional de migración en Norte y Centroamérica." In *Democracia y reconfiguraciones contemporáneas del derecho en América Latina*, edited by Stefanie Kron, Sérgio Costa, and Marianne Braig, 387–404. Madrid: Iberoamericana Vervuert.

Lee, Erika. 2002. "Enforcing the Borders: Chinese Exclusion Along the US Borders with Canada and Mexico, 1882–1924." *Journal of American History* 89 (1): 54–86.

Loyd, Jenna. M., and Mountz, A. 2018. *Boats, Borders, and Bases: Race, the Cold War, and the Rise of Migration Detention in the United States*. Berkeley: University of California Press.

Maciel, David. 2008. "De Sarney a Collor: Reformas políticas, democratização e crise (1985–1990)." PhD diss., Federal University of Goiás.

Mansur Dias, Guilherme. 2015. "Notas sobre as negociações da 'Convenção do Crime' e dos Protocolos Adicionais sobre Tráfico de Pessoas e Contrabando de Migrantes." *REMHU: Revista Interdisciplinar da Mobilidade Humana* 23:215–34.

Márquez Covarrubias, Humberto. 2015. "No vale nada la vida: Éxodo y criminalización de migrantes centroamericanos en México." *Migración y desarrollo* 13 (25): 151–73.

Meagher, Arnold. 2008. *The Coolie Trade: The Traffic in Chinese Laborers to Latin America, 1847–1874*. Bloomington, IN: Xlibris.

McKeown, Adam. 2008. *Melancholy Order: Asian Migration and the Globalization of Borders*. New York: Columbia University Press.

Meissner, Doris. 1992. "Managing Migrations." *Foreign Policy* 86:66–83.

Menjívar, Cecilia. 2014. "Immigration Law Beyond Borders: Externalizing and Internalizing Border Controls in an Era of Securitization." *Annual Review of Law and Social Science* 10:353–69.

Mezzadra, Sandro, and Brett Neilson. 2013. *Border as Method; or, The Multiplication of Labor*. Durham, NC: Duke University Press.

Miller, Todd. 2019. *Empire of Borders: The Expansion of the US Border Around the World*. London: Verso Books.

Missbach, Antje, and Melissa Phillips. 2020. "Introduction: Reconceptualizing Transit States in an Era of Outsourcing, Offshoring, and Obfuscation." *Migration and Society* 3 (1): 19–33.

Mohar, Gustavo. 2001. "Reflexiones sobre el grupo de Puebla en busca de un diálogo pendiente." *Notas de Población* 28 (73): 253–72.

Mongia, Radhika. 2018. *Indian Migration and Empire: A Colonial Genealogy of the Modern State*. Durham, NC: Duke University Press.

Moreno Romero, María Fernanda, and Juan Sebastián Silva Serna. 2009. "Erradicación de cultivos de uso ilícito: Fracaso del Plan Colombia y éxito del efecto globo." *Criterios* 2 (1): 235–53.

Moulier-Boutang, Yann. 2006. *De la esclavitud al trabajo asalariado*. Madrid: Akal.

Mountz, Alison. 2020. *The Death of Asylum: Hidden Geographies of the Enforcement Archipelago*. Minneapolis: University of Minnesota Press.

Mountz, Alison, and Jenna M. Loyd. 2014. "Constructing the Mediterranean Region: Obscuring Violence in the Bordering of Europe's Migration 'Crises.'" *ACME: An International Journal for Critical Geographies* 13 (2): 173–95.

New Keywords Collective. 2016. "Europe/Crisis: New Keywords of 'the Crisis' in and of 'Europe.'" Edited by Nicholas De Genova and Martina Tazzioli. *Near Futures Online* 1:1–16. http://nearfuturesonline.org/europecrisis-new-keywords-of-crisis-in-and-of -europe/.

OAS (Organization of American States). 2010. "Migración extracontinental en las Américas." Washington, DC.

OAS (Organization of American States) and IOM (International Organization for Migration). 2016. "Flujos de migrantes en situación migratoria irregular provenientes de África, Asia y el Caribe en las Américas." Washington, DC.

Olaya, Iván. 2018. "La selección del inmigrante "apto": Leyes migratorias de inclusión y exclusión en Colombia (1920–1937)." *Nuevo Mundo Mundos Nuevos*, 1–14.

Pagnotta, Chiara. 2011. "Italian Immigration to Ecuador in the 1930s and 1940s." *Diasporas: Circulations, migrations, histoire* 19:72–81.

Pallister-Wilkins, Polly. 2015. "The Humanitarian Politics of European Border Policing: Frontex and Border Police in Evros." *International Political Sociology* 9:53–69.

París Pombo, Dolores. 2016. "Trayectos peligrosos: Inseguridad y movilidad humana en México." *Papeles de Población* 22 (90): 145–72.

París Pombo, Dolores. 2022. "Externalización de las fronteras y bloqueo de los solicitantes de asilo en el norte de México." *REMHU: Revista Interdisciplinar da Mobilidade Humana* 30:101–16.

Pécoud, Antoine. 2010. "Informing Migrants to Manage Migration? An Analysis of IOM's Information Campaigns." In *The Politics of International Migration Management*, edited by Martin Geiger and Antoine Pécoud, 184–201. Basingstoke, UK: Palgrave.

Pezzani, Lorenzo. 2015. "Liquid Traces: Spatial Practices, Aesthetics, and Humanitarian Dilemmas at the Maritime Borders of the EU." PhD diss., Goldsmiths College, University of London.

Quijano, Aníbal. 2000. "Coloniality of Power and Eurocentrism in Latin America." *International Sociology* 15 (2): 215–32.

Quinteros, Marcela. 2008. *Os olhos da nação: As imagens construídas sobre o estrangeiro nas políticas imigratórias argentinas (1930–1955)*. Curitiba: Instituto Memória.

Ramírez, Jacques. 2012. *Ciudad-Estado, inmigración y políticas: Ecuador 1890–1950*. Quito: Instituto de Altos Estudios Nacionales.

Ramírez, Jacques. 2013. *La política migratoria del Estado ecuatoriano: Rupturas, tensiones, continuidades y desafíos*. Quito: Instituto de Altos Estudios Nacionales.

Rodríguez Rejas, María José. 2018. *La norteamericanización de la seguridad en América Latina*. Madrid: Akal.

Rogers, Rosemarie. 1992. "The Politics of Migration in Contemporary World." *International Migration* 30 (1): 33–55.

Sánchez Alonso, Blanca. 2004. "Algunas reflexiones sobre las políticas de inmigración en América Latina en la época de las migraciones de masas." *Estudios Migratorios Latinoamericanos* 53:155–76.

Sánchez Alonso, Blanca. 2007. "La racionalidad de las políticas migratorias en la primera globalización: El caso argentino." *Revista de Instituciones, Ideas y Mercados* 46:233–64.

Scahill, Jeremy. 2021. "1999–2000: Plan Colombia." *The Intercept*. https://legacy .theintercept.com/empire-politician/biden-plan-colombia/.

Seyferth, Giralda. 1997. "Questões eugênicas no Brasil: Eugenia, racismo e o problema da imigração no Brasil." In *Anais do VI Seminário Nacional de História da Ciência e da Tecnologia*, 248–52. Rio de Janeiro: Sociedade Brasileira de história da Ciência, 1997.

Seyferth, Giralda. 2002. "Colonização, imigração e a questão racial no Brasil." *Revista USP* 53:117–49.

Stock, Inka, Aysen Üstübici, and Susanne Schultz. 2019. "Externalization at Work: Responses to Migration Policies from the Global South." *Comparative Migration Studies* 7 (1): 1–9.

Svampa, Maristella. 2017. "Cuatro claves para leer América Latina." *Nueva Sociedad* 268.

Svampa, Maristella. 2019. "Las fronteras del neoextractivismo en América Latina: Conflictos socioambientales, giro ecoterritorial y nuevas dependencias." Bielefeld, Germany: Bielefeld University Press.

Tate, Shirley A., and Ian Law. 2015. *Caribbean Racisms: Connections and Complexities in the Racialization of the Caribbean Region*. London: Palgrave Macmillan.

Tazzioli, Martina. 2015a. "The Desultory Politics of Mobility and the Humanitarian-Military Border in the Mediterranean: Mare Nostrum Beyond the Sea." REMHU: *Revista Interdisciplinar da Mobilidade Humana* 23 (44): 61–82.

Tazzioli, Martina. 2015b. "The Politics of Counting and the Scene of Rescue: Border Deaths in the Mediterranean." *Radical Philosophy* 192:2–6.

Téllez, Josefina. 2016. "La inmigración como 'problema' o el resurgir de la raza: Racismo general, racismo cotidiano y su papel en la conformación de la nación." In *Racismo en Chile: La piel como marca de la inmigración*, edited by María Emilia Tijoux, 35–45. Santiago de Chile: Editorial Universitaria.

Terán Najas, Rosmary. 2020. "'En mi condición de apátrida . . .': La inmigración sirio-libanesa en Ecuador durante la primera mitad del siglo XX." *Revista Complutense de Historia de América* 46, 65–84.

Ticktin, Miriam. 2016. "Thinking Beyond Humanitarian Borders." *Social Research* 83 (2): 255–71.

Tijoux, María Emilia, ed.. 2016. *Racismo en Chile: La piel como marca de la inmigración*. Santiago de Chile: Editorial Universitaria.

Tokatlian, Juan G. 2001. "Colombia, el Plan Colombia y la región andina." *Nueva Sociedad* 173:126–43.

Trouillot, Michel-Rolph. 2003. "North Atlantic Fictions: Global Transformations, 1492–1945." In *Global Transformations: Anthropology and the Modern World*, by Michel-Rolph Trouillot, 29–46. London: Palgrave Macmillan.

Trouillot, Michel-Rolph. 2015. *Silencing the Past: Power and the Production of History*. Boston: Beacon Press.

UNODC (United Nations Office on Drugs and Crime). 2000. "Protocol to Prevent, Suppress, and Punish Trafficking in Persons, Especially Women and Children." New York.

UNHCR (United Nations High Commissioner for Refugees). 2022. "Refugee Data Finder." https://www.unhcr.org/refugee-statistics/.

Varela Huerta, Amarela, and Lisa McLean. 2021. "From Vulnerable Victims to Insurgent *Caravaneros*: The Genesis and Consolidation of a New Form of Migrant Self-Defence in America." In *Migration and the Contested Politics of Justice*, edited by Giorgio Grappi, 184–99. London: Routledge.

Villafuerte Solís, Daniel, and María del Carmen García Aguilar. 2017. "La política antimigrante de Barack Obama y el programa Frontera Sur: Consecuencias para la migración centroamericana." *Migración y Desarrollo* 15 (28): 39–64.

Vogt, Wendy. 2017. "The Arterial Border: Negotiating Economies of Risk and Violence in Mexico's Security Regime." *International Journal of Migration and Border Studies* 3 (2–3): 192–204.

Wallerstein, Immanuel. (1978) 2011. *The Modern World-System I: Capitalist Agriculture and the Origins of the European World-Economy in the Sixteenth Century*, Volume 1. Berkeley: University of California Press.

Walters, William. 2011. "Foucault and Frontiers: Notes on the Birth of the Humanitarian Border." In *Governmentality: Current Issues and Future Challenges*, 138–64. London: Routledge.

Weiner, Myron. 1992. "Security, Stability, and International Migration." *International Security* 17 (3): 91–126.

Weiner, Myron. 1995. *The Global Migration Crisis: Challenge to States and to Human Rights*. New York: HarperCollins.

Weiner, Myron. 1996. "A Security Perspective on International Migration." *Fletcher Forum of World Affairs* 20 (2): 17–34.

Williams, Jill M. 2015. "From Humanitarian Exceptionalism to Contingent Care: Care and Enforcement at the Humanitarian Border." *Political Geography* 47:11–20.

Williams, Jill M. 2016. "The Safety/Security Nexus and the Humanitarianisation of Border Enforcement." *Geographical Journal* 182 (1): 27–37.

Wolf, Eric. (1982) 2010. *Europe and the People Without History*. Berkeley: University of California Press.

Yankelevich, Pablo. 2015. *Inmigración y racismo: Contribuciones a la historia de los extranjeros en México*. Mexico City: El Colegio de México.

Yankelevich, Pablo. 2020. *Los otros: Raza, normas y corrupción en la gestión de la extranjería en México 1900–1950*. Mexico City: El Colegio de México.

Zilberg, Elana. 2011. *Space of Detention: The Making of a Transnational Gang Crisis Between Los Angeles and San Salvador*. Durham, NC: Duke University Press.

Contributors

SOLEDAD ÁLVAREZ VELASCO is assistant professor in the Latin American and Latino Studies Program and the Department of Anthropology at the University of Illinois Chicago. She is a social anthropologist and human geographer whose research analyzes the interrelationship between mobility, control, and spatial transformations across the Americas. She investigates the intersection between irregularized Global South–North and Global South–South transit migration, border regimes, the formation of migratory corridors across the Americas, and the migrant struggle across these transnational spaces, including that of migrant children. She is the author of *Frontera sur chiapaneca: El muro humano de la violencia* (2016), and coeditor (with Ulla D. Berg and Iréri Ceja) of *Migraciones: Colección Palabras Clave* (2021). She has also published articles in numerous journals, including *Geopolitics, Antipode: A Radical Journal of Geography, Journal of Latin American Geography, Migration and Society, Annals of the American Academy of Political and Social Science, Anales de Antropología, Sociologias, Revista Estudios Sociológicos, Revista EntreDiversidades,* and *Íconos: Revista de Ciencias Sociales.* She founded and co-coordinated the transnational digital project (Im)Mobilities in the Americas and COVID-19. She holds a BA in sociology from the Universidad San Francisco de Quito (Ecuador), an MA in social anthropology from the Universidad Iberoamericana de México, and a PhD in geography from King's College London.

TANYA BASOK is professor in the Department of Sociology and Criminology at the University of Windsor, Ontario, Canada. Her research focuses on migrant rights and pro-migrant advocacy, including labor rights and social integration of Mexican farmworkers in Canada, the role of labor organizations and other activists in advancing the rights of temporary migrants in Canada and female migrants in South and Central America, Mexico, and the Caribbean; and Central American refugees and labor migrants in Mexico. She is the author of *Tortillas and Tomatoes: Transmigrant Mexican Harvesters in Canada* (2003), coauthor (with D. Bélanger, M. Rojas Wiesner, and G. Candiz) of *Rethinking Transit Migration: Precarity, Mobility, and Self-Making in Mexico* (2015), and coauthor (with L. Vosko and C. Spring) of *Transnational Employment Strain in a Global Health*

Pandemic: Migrant Farmworkers in Canada (2023), as well as numerous journal articles and book chapters on migrants from and in Latin America.

JANNETH CLAVIJO is a political scientist at the National University of Córdoba. She works as an assistant researcher at the National Council for Scientific and Technical Research (CONICET) at the Provincial University of Córdoba. She is currently participating in the group project "Borders in Dispute: Control Policies, Containment Practices and Experiences, and Strategies of Mobility in the South American Space" (CONICET). She is a member of the "South-South Migrations" working group of the Latin American Council of Social Sciences. Her main interests and research focus on the configuration of international migration, refugee and asylum policies, and the transformation of eligibility processes and practices for access to international and humanitarian protection, particularly in South America. She holds a master's degree in international relations from the Centre for Advanced Studies and a PhD in political science from the National University of Córdoba–Argentina.

NICHOLAS DE GENOVA is professor in the Department of Comparative Cultural Studies at the University of Houston, where he was also department chair for six years. He previously held academic appointments in anthropology at Stanford, Columbia, and Goldsmiths / University of London, and in geography at King's College London, and held visiting researcher positions at the Universities of Warwick, Bern, and Amsterdam. He is the author of more than one hundred articles and book chapters, and author or editor of several books, including *Working the Boundaries: Race, Space, and "Illegality" in Mexican Chicago* (2005); *The Deportation Regime: Sovereignty, Space, and the Freedom of Movement* (2010); and *The Borders of "Europe": Autonomy of Migration, Tactics of Bordering* (2017).

GUSTAVO DIAS is professor and researcher with the Graduate Program in History and with the Graduate Program in Society, Environment, and Territory at the State University of Montes Claros, Brazil, and also coordinator of the Odyssey: Abdelmalek Sayad Research Group, registered at the National Council for Scientific and Technological Development. He completed his PhD in sociology at Goldsmiths / University of London, United Kingdom. His research is concerned with Brazilian international migration, border regimes, and Abdelmalek Sayad's critical perspectives on migration.

EDUARDO DOMENECH is a researcher at the National Scientific and Technical Research Council (CONICET) in Argentina. He has served as a member and coordinator of the working group on "Migration, Culture, and Policies" of the Latin American Council of Social Sciences (CLACSO). Most recently, he was a senior fellow at the Maria Sibylla Merian Center for Advanced Latin American Studies (CALAS), based at the Latin American Faculty of Social Sciences (FLACSO) in Ecuador. His research focuses on the transformation of migration and border control policies and practices in South America, approached from a critical, historical, and multiscalar perspective. He is coeditor (with Gioconda Herrera and Liliana Rivera Sánchez) of *Movilidades, control fronterizo y luchas migrantes* (2022) and author of *Fronteras en disputa: Migración y crisis* (2025).

ROBERTO DUFRAIX-TAPIA is assistant professor of Criminal Law at the University of Tarapacá in Iquique, Chile. He has coordinated and participated in national and international research projects on migration control, human trafficking, and smuggling. He holds a PhD in law from the University of the Basque Country, Spain.

JONATHAN ECHEVERRI ZULUAGA is assistant professor at the Universidad de Antioquia, in Medellín, Colombia. His main topic of interest is human movement. In his research trajectory, he has developed the concept of *errance* as an alternative to understanding the travel stories of Africans who look for better horizons beyond the African continent. His most recent project, located in the northwest tip of Colombia, is entitled "Following the Thread of *Errance*: Itineraries of South–South Travelers Through Uraba." The main ethnographic site for this project is Necoclí, a port in the Gulf of Urabá, where the journeys of people from Africa, Asia, the Caribbean, and Latin America periodically get suspended. Other research interests are economic anthropology and audiovisual technology as a powerful tool for creating with the testimony that comes from ethnography. He earned a PhD in anthropology from the University of California, Davis.

LUIN GOLDRING is professor of sociology at York University in Toronto. She is interested in how social inequalities are dynamically assembled and negotiated within and across borders by a range of social and institutional actors, with attention to precarious legal status dynamics. She is coeditor (with Patricia Landolt) of *Producing and Negotiating Non-Citizen Precarious Legal Status in Canada* and (with Sailaja Krishnamurti) *Organizing the Transnational*. Earlier research addressed Latin American community organizing in Toronto; transnational families; and migrant-state-society relations in the context of Mexico-US migration.

VALENTINA GLOCKNER FAGETTI (1981–2023) was a Mexican anthropologist whose latest appointment was in the Departamento de Investigaciones Educativas at the Centro de Investigación y de Estudios Avanzados del Instituto Politécnico Nacional de México. Her work focused on the many dimensions of child mobility and child labor, childhood studies, forced displacement, the anthropology of the state, and humanitarianism in Mexico, the United States, and India. Her research also explored reflexive and participatory methodologies and ethnographic self-representation through art, ethnography, and visual media. She was the director or codirector of multiple research projects funded by the National Science Foundation (USA), the National Council for Science and Technology (Mexico), and the National Geographic Society. She was a fellow at the Institute for Advanced Studies at Princeton, the Matias Romero Program at the Teresa Lozano Long Institute of Latin American Studies at the University of Texas at Austin, and an Edmundo O'Gorman Scholar at the Institute of Latin American Studies at Columbia University.

PATRICIA LANDOLT is professor of sociology at the University of Toronto. Her research examines the relationship between global migration and social inequality. Her specific areas of research and teaching include transnational migration, precarious legal status and precarious work, the politics of citizenship and noncitizenship and community-engaged methods.

CAROLINA MOULIN is professor of international relations at the Center for Regional Planning and Development at the Federal University of Minas Gerais (UFMG), Brazil. Her latest project, in partnership with the UN High Commissioner for Refugees (UNHCR) and UN Women delves into the intersection of gender and migration in South America. She coordinates UNHCR's Sergio Vieira de Mello Chair on Refugee Protection and Rights Promotion at UFMG. She was an associate editor for the *Review of International Studies* (2020–24) and has published journal articles and book chapters on refugee issues and critical border studies. She holds a PhD in political science from McMaster University, Canada.

MARGARITA NÚÑEZ CHAIM is a human rights defender. She coordinates the Migration Affairs Program at the Universidad Iberoamericana, Mexico City. She has worked with migrants in Mexico, specializing in working with Central American migrant women from a feminist gender approach. She holds a PhD in anthropology from the Centro de Investigaciones y Estudios Superiores en Antropología Social, Mexico City. To carry out her fieldwork, she was awarded a Young Researcher Fellowship at the Consortium for Comparative Research on Regional Integration and Social Cohesion.

JUAN THOMAS ORDÓÑEZ is associate professor in the anthropology program at the School of Human Sciences, Universidad del Rosario in Bogotá, Colombia. He has published on asylum seekers and day labor in the United States, as well as on transnational indigenous migrations from Ecuador and Colombia. He currently works on the Colombian borderlands and studies Venezuelan migration and, with Jonathan Echeverri Zuluaga, the transit of Caribbean, African, and Asian migrants trying to reach North America through the Colombia-Panama border. He holds a PhD in medical anthropology from the University of California, Berkeley.

DANIEL QUINTEROS is an academic researcher and a politician. He is the Presidential Delegate for Tarapacá, Government of Chile, and a PhD candidate in social and behavioral sciences, Universidade da Coruña, Spain. He holds a bachelor's degree in sociology from Diego Portales University, Chile, and a master of research degree in criminology from the University of Manchester.

ROMINA RAMOS is associate professor of social work and researcher at the University of Tarapacá in Iquique, Chile. She has coordinated and participated in several research projects on borders, migrations, and human trafficking and smuggling. She holds a PhD in social sciences from the University of the Basque Country, Spain.

MARTHA LUZ ROJAS WIESNER is researcher at El Colegio de la Frontera Sur in San Cristóbal de Las Casas, Mexico, as a member of the Academic Group for Studies in Migration and Transborder Processes of the Department of Society and Culture. Her research focuses on border and cross-border mobility, with an emphasis on the participation of women; vulnerabilities and social exclusion of migrants in border contexts; living and working conditions in migratory processes; and the right to mobility and migration. She holds a PhD in social science with a specialty in sociology from El Colegio de México.

FABIO SANTOS is assistant professor at the Centre for Advanced Migration Studies at the University of Copenhagen. He holds a BA in anthropology and in cultural history and theory from Humboldt-Universität zu Berlin, an MA in sociology from Freie Universität Berlin, and a PhD in sociology from the German-Mexican graduate school Entre Espacios, awarded by Freie Universität Berlin. He previously held academic appointments at Freie Universität Berlin, the University of Vienna, Aarhus University, and the University of California, Berkeley. He is the author of *Bridging Fluid Borders: Entanglements in the French-Brazilian Borderland* (2022) and is currently writing his second monograph, excavating the US offshoring of Haitian refugees from Florida to Puerto Rico in the early 1980s. The recurring themes of his teaching and writing—migration, inequality, and colonialism—are explored through ethnographic and archival methods.

AMARELA VARELA HUERTA is professor at the Universidad Autónoma de la Ciudad de México. She holds a PhD in sociology from the Universidad Autónoma de Barcelona, a specialization in migration from the Universidad Pontificia de Comillas de Madrid, and a degree in journalism and communication sciences from the Universidad Nacional Autónoma de México. She works on migration and migratory social movements. She is a member of the Seminar Narrando Fronteras desde los Feminismos and participates in networks and collectives that study, defend, and negotiate processes of migrant insurgency.

LAURA VELASCO ORTIZ is a sociologist, researcher, and professor in the Department of Cultural Studies at El Colegio de la Frontera Norte, Tijuana (Mexico). Her research focuses on Indigenous migrations in Mexico and clandestine migrations in the Mexico–United States region. Her recent publications include *Caravanas migrantes y desplazamientos colectivos en la frontera México–Estados Unidos* (coedited with Camilo Contreras and María Dolores Paris; 2021); "Migration, Borders, and Identity," in *The Oxford Handbook of Sociology of Latin America*, edited by Xóchitl Bada and Liliana Rivera Sánchez (2020); and "Indigenous Migration in Latin America," in *The Routledge History of Modern Latin American Migration*, edited by Andreas E. Feldmann, Xóchitl Bada, Jorge Durand, and Stephanie Schütze (2022).

Index

family reunification programs, migration statistics and, 69
family separation policies, US imposition of, 124–26
Fassin, Didier, 70
Federal Police (Argentina), 229–30
Federal Police (Brazil), border regime and, 285–90
Federal Rights (Ley Federal de Derechos, Mexico), 101
Feierstein, Daniel, 173
femicide, Mexican refugeeship and, 45
Fernandes, Florestan, 332
Fernández de Kirchner, Cristina, 225
Fifty-Day Caravan, 126–35, 138n18
flu pandemic of 1918, Chilean border control and, 195–97
forced migration, classification of, 253–56
Forma Migratoria de Visitante Agrícola (FMVA) (Mexico), 98
Forma Migratoria de Visitante Local (FMVL) (Mexico), 98
Foucault, Michel, 169, 184
France: Brazilian visa reciprocity with, 303; French Guiana migration policies and, 302–21; Latin American colonization by, 306–7; Latinidad ideology in, 305; migration policies in former colonies of, 314–19
Franko, Katja, 193, 195
Fraser, Nancy, 21–22
Frei, Eduardo, 196
French Guiana: Brazilian border corridor with, 301–21; colonialism in, 306–11; EU status of, 311–13; Indigenous culture in, 305–6; migrant policies in, 238, 312–19; peripheral status in Europe of, 311–12
Fuerzas Armadas Revolucionarias de Colombia (Revolutionary Armed Forces of Colombia; FARC), 343–44

Galaz, Caterine, 199
gangs: border policies linked to, 340; migrant reliance on, 14; migrant risks from, 76–77
Garibó, Georgina, 132
gatekeeping institutions, regularization of migrants and, 95–96
General Population Law (Ley General de Población) (Mexico), 90, 97
Germany: European migration regime and, 282; trans-American migration governance and, 349
Ghosh, Bimal, 348

Glick Schiller, Nina, 63
Glissant, Édouard, 304
Global Commission on International Migration, 348
Global Compact for Safe, Orderly, and Regular Migration (UPMRIP, 2020), 102–3, 198, 349, 356
Global Compact on Refugees, 356
globalization of border control: caravans and, 128–29; colonialism and postcoloniality and, 330–35; cross-border regime consolidation and, 340–46; French Guiana–Brazilian border corridor and, 301–21; human mobility regime and, 62–66; inter-American asylum transition to UN system, 256–59; international migration governance and, 347–51; labor subordination to, 7–9, 72–77; logistics and, 280–85; migration patterns and, 9–11; national migration policies and, 233–36
Global Migration Group, 348
Global South countries, soft migration control in, 8–9
Glockner Fagetti, Valentina, 117–35
Gokee, Cameron, 128
gold mining, in Brazil and French Guiana, 310–11
Goldring, Luin, 33–54
Gomes, Flávio, 307
Gómez, Laura, 339
Gómez Cueva, Vanessa, 233–35, 244n14
Góngora-Mera, Manuel, 177
González, Juan, 339
governance and governmentality: caravans as response to, 119–20, 127–28, 131–35, 136nn2–3; logistics and, 281–85; migration and, 169; mixed migration flows in Latin America and framework of, 259–63; mobility regime and, 63–66; trans-American migration governance and, 346–51
Grenada, US invasion of, 336
Group of Latin America and Caribbean Countries of the United Nations Regional Groups (GRULAC), 341, 359n8
Guadeloupe, colonialism in, 309–10, 311–19
Guatemala: cross-border regime consolidation and, 340, 343; international border control systems and, 256–59; migrants in Mexico from, 11, 91–92, 97–99, 103–6; migration data for, 11; US deportations to, 8; US intervention in, 336–37
guerrillas, migrant reliance on, 14
guest worker programs, 74–75

330–35; Europeanization and, 301–5; Mexican migration and distancing of, 90

informalized economies: in Ecuador, migrant participation in, 179–81; Mexican migrant restrictions for, 103–6; migrant formation of, 16–17

in-land refugee claims (RC) (Canada), 36, 49–50

instrumentalization of legality, crimmigration and, 194–95

Interagency Coordination Platform for Refugees and Migrants from Venezuela (Platform R4V), 252, 264–67, 345–46, 355–56

Interagency Group on Mixed Migratory Flows (GIFMM), 252, 264–67

inter-American asylum system, UN displacement of regional systems, 256–59

Inter-American Commission on Human Rights (IACHR), 233–34

"Inter-American Programme for the Promotion and Protection of the Human Rights of Migrants" (UNHCR 2007), 260

Interchurch Committee on Human Rights in Latin America (ICCHRLA), 40–42

interior immigration policing, 7–9

internal bordering practices, illegality creation and, 90–92

internal migration, US-Mexico mobility control regime and, 66

International Conference on Central American Refugees (CIREFCA, 1989), 258–59

International Conference on Population and Development (1994), 348

International Convention on the Protection of the Rights of all Migrant Workers and Their Families, 196

International Law Enforcement Academy (ILEA), 175, 185n9, 340

International Monetary Fund (IMF), 338

International Organization for Migration (IOM), 79, 119, 238, 259–60, 264, 271n10, 277, 286–90, 292, 345–51, 354–55; hemispheric framework for border control and, 352–59

intraregional migration: agreements involving, 3, 23n2, 249–52; Latin American border zones and, 251–52

Jarochinski Silva, João Carlos, 149

Jesuit Migrant Service (Servicio Jesuita a Migrantes), 201, 294

Jolivet, Marie-José, 316–17

Karakayali, Serhart, 4

Khosravi, Shahram, 234–35

Könönen, Jukka, 93

Kramsch, Oliver, 303

labor: colonialism and postcolonial demand for, 331–35; cross-border mobility of, 72–73; global subordination of, 7–9; Mexican transborder agricultural workers, 98; Mexican work visas for, 99–100, 103–6; national origin diversity and, 74–77; neoliberalization of, 118–20, 136n1; undocumented workers, 73–77

Landolt, Patricia, 33–54

Lasso, Guillermo, 183

late refugee claims (LRCs) (Canada), 36

Latin America: Asian migrant restrictions in, 334–35; border regimes in, 16–17, 122, 165–84, 238; colonialism and postcoloniality in, 330–35; crimmigration effects on migration in, 194–95; dam system for migration containment in, 73–74; dictatorships in, 339–46; differential inclusion and refugeeships in, 49–51; European influence in, 301–5; extraregional migration in, 238–41; global migrant population in, 9–11; hemispheric framework for border control in, 352; independence movements and migration to, 332–35; inter-American asylum transition to UN system in, 256–59; IOM influence in, 348–49; migration in, 13–14, 66–68, 144–48; military dictatorships in, 336–37; mixed migration flows in, 259–63; pandemic-era border restrictions in, 18–19; Pink Tide in, 12–13; politics of refugeeship in, 37–51; population management in, 277–96; protection-control relationship in border regimes of, 249–70; refugees in Canada from, 33–54; South-South influxes in, 182–83; US Cold War activities in, 137; US hegemony and intervention in, 335–39; Venezuelan migratory flow in, 194–95

Law 3446 (Chile), 195–97

law of departmentalization (*loi de la départementalisation*), former French colonies and, 312–13

Law of Interculturality, Attention to Migrants, and Human Mobility in the Federal District, 133

Law of Transparency (Chile), 199

legality: clandestine practices for creation of, 91–92; crimmigration and, 194–95; cross-border mobility and, 92–96; Ecuadorian "illegal legality" and, 168–70; "illegal legality" and, 21–23, 106–7, 109n1, 261; international litigation on migrants and, 233–326; legal exceptionalism in French Guiana border policies and, 312–19; regularization program and, 14–15; violence and, 105–6

Legislative Decree 1094 (1975, Chile), 195

Ley de Extranjería (Immigration Law, 1886) (Ecuador), 174

Lima Group, 350, 355

Lipsky, Michael, 109n4

logistics, Brazilian border mobility and, 280–85, 288–96

Loma de la Muerte (Hill of Death), 181

López Obrador, Andrés Manuel, 120–21, 125, 130

Los Angeles Declaration on Migration and Protection, 356–57

Macri, Mauricio, 225, 235

Marcus, George, 170

Margheritis, Ana, 176

Maroon communities, 307, 314, 317

Martí, José, 1–2

Martinique, colonialism in, 309–19

masking practices, clandestine cross-border mobility and, 73

Masoumi, Azar, 48

Massin, Cécile, 318

McLean, Lisa, 76

media coverage: Brazilian migration controls and, 284–85, 295n4; Canadian refugee policies and, 43; Chilean border policies and, 209–11; of Colombian migrant crisis, 153–57; Colombia-Panama border crossings, 149; cross-border regime consolidation and, 342; Mexican refugeeship in Canada and, 46

Menjívar, Cecilia, 105, 175

MERCOSUR (Common Market of the South), 165, 260, 351–52; visa provisions, legalization of migrants and, 96

mestizo communities, in Colombia-Panama border region, 149

metering policy, US adoption of, 124

Mexican Revolution (1916–17), 336

Mexico: administrative bordering in, 92–96; alternative border town regularization in, 103–6; asylum seekers' mobility in, 75–77;

Canada and refugees from, 33, 37, 44–52; caravans and border control regime in, 117–35; Central American migrant caravans in, 13–14, 69–70, 79, 108–9; Colombian migrants in, 159–60; cross-border mobilities and clandestine practices in, 70–72; cross-border regime consolidation and, 340–41, 343; Cuban migrants and, 175–76; decline in migrants from, 67–70, 81n4; documentation of illegalized migrants in, 97–103; drug trafficking industry in, 78–79; externalization of US border control in, 7–9, 68–70, 89–92; Fifty-Day Caravan in, 126–35; illegal illegality in border control policies of, 89–109; internal displacement in, 81n3; migrant death rates at US border with, 73–74; migration policies in, 12–15; politics of refugeeship in, 34; Salvadoran refugees in, 41; Southern border detention centers in, 97–98, 126; transit migration through, 148–49, 354–55; Ukrainian migrants in, 136n8; undocumented labor workers and asylum seekers, US border crossings and, 73–77; US occupation of, 336; US politics and migration in, 148

Mexico-Canada border concept, Canadian refugee policies and, 45, 51, 53–54

Mexico Declaration and Plan of Action (PAM), 252, 260

Mezzadra, Sandro, 5, 63, 66, 183

Middle Eastern migrants: cross-border regime consolidation and, 434; in French Guiana, 313–19

Mignolo, Walter, 305

Migración Colombia, 145, 147, 152, 154–55, 157, 159–60, 264–66

migrante irregular (official Colombian label), 149, 151, 160n1

Migrant Protection Protocol (MPP) (Remain in Mexico), 69, 77, 124–26, 131

Migration Law (1971) (Ecuador), 168, 173–78

Migration Law (2011) (Mexico), 90, 98–99, 137n11

Migration law No. 25.871 (Argentina), 226–27, 231–32, 234–36

migration processes: in Canada, 35–36; in Chile, 195–211; colonialism and postcoloniality and, 330–35; current scholarship on, 19–23; forced vs. economic classifications of, 253–56; hemispheric framework for, 2–3; illegalization in US of, 10; intraregional

Programa Integral Frontera Sur (Southern Border Program) (Mexico), 97

Programa Temporal de Regularización Migratoria (PTRM-2015 and 2017), 99–102, 109n7

protection: asylum and refugee systems and role of, 250–56, 263–67; cross-border regime consolidation and, 342–46; intervention categories in, 253; mixed migration flows in Latin America and framework of, 259–63; United Nations framework for, 257–59

Protocol of 1967, 249, 256–59, 270n3

public safety discourse, Argentinian politics of hostility and, 227

Puebla Process (1996), 348–50, 352–59

Puerto Rico, US colonization of, 336

Puri, Shalini, 307

Quijano, Aníbal, 333

Quinteros, Daniel, 191–211

Quito Process (2018), 350, 355, 356

racism and racial nativism: Canadian refugee policies and, 43–44; colonialism and, 330–31; crimmigration effects and, 194–95; Ecuadorian migrant "illegal legality" and, 168–70, 174–75, 180–81; in French Guiana and Brazil, 307–11, 316–19; hemispheric framework for border control and migrants from, 354; legality-illegality for Mexican migrants and, 93–96; Mexican restrictions on migrants and, 90–92; Mexican status policies and, 100–101; rejection of migrants based on, 14

Ramírez, Jacques, 96, 176

Receita Federal (Special Department of Federal Revenue, Brazil), 284–85

Red Cross, Argentinian detention centers and, 229–30

Redfield, Peter, 309

Reeves, Madeleine, 105–6

Refugee Law 20.430 (Chile), 196

"Refugee Protection and Migration Control: UNHCR and IOM Perspectives" (UNHCR and IOM 2001), 260

refugees: Canadian policies concerning, 35–36; Chilean political activists as, 33; Colombian recognition status for, 265–67; expanded international definitions of, 257–59; Latin American policies concerning, 12–17, 37–51, 249–52, 255–56, 270n3; logistics and treatment of, 281–85; migration management

policy and, 35–36; migration patterns for, 11; militarization of border control and, 68–70; pandemic-era restrictions concerning, 18–19; politics of, 34, 251–52; protection vs. control in policies for, 251–56, 263–67

regime: protection and control in context of, 252–56; terminology and connotations linked to, 4–6

Regional Conference on Migration (RCM). See Puebla Process (1996)

regional consultative processes (RCPs), 349–50

regional integration agreements, intraregional dynamics and, 3, 23n2

regional processing centers, hemispheric framework of border mobility and, 357

regional protection policies: hemispheric framework of mobility control and, 351–59; in Latin America, 249–52

Regional Response Plan for Refugees and Migrants (RMRP), 264–67, 345

Regional Strategies (IOM), 350–51

Regional Visitor's Card (Tarjeta de Visitante Regional, TVR) (Mexico), 99, 103–6, 108

regularization programs for migrants, 14–15; in Brazil, 285–90; in Chile, 201–3; gate-keeping institutions, 95–96; in Mexico, 90–92, 95, 100–106

Reiffen, Franziska, 148

religion, transit migration and, 148

religious conflict, migration as escape from, 170–73

remote border control techniques, emergence of, 89–92

resettlement, Canadian refugee policies and role of, 35–36, 38–41, 49, 51–54

residency applications: Brazilian migrant programs and, 285–90; in Mexican Migration Law, 99–103

Réunion, colonialism in, 311–19

Ríos, Viridiana, 78

Ríos Montt, Efraín, 337

Roa Ortega, Pedro, 148

Rojas Wiesner, Martha Luz, 89–109

Roosevelt Corollary to Monroe Doctrine, 336

Roy, Ananya, 169–70

Rubilar, Gabriela, 199

Ruhs, Martin, 95

Ruiz, Olivia, 76–77

Rumford, Chris, 64